*Baedeker*

# Portugal

# Contents

# Contents

# Principal Sights of Tourist Interest

# Preface

This guide to Portugal is one of the new generation of Baedeker guides.

These guides, illustrated throughout in colour, are designed to meet the needs of the modern traveller. They are quick and easy to consult, with the principal places of interest described in alphabetical order, and the information is presented in a format that is both attractive and easy to follow.

The present guide covers the whole of mainland Portugal and the Mediterranean islands of the Azores and the Madeira archipelago. It also includes an outline of Macao, the territory on the south coast of China which is under Portuguese administration.

The guide is in three parts. The first part gives a general account of the country, its geography, climate, flora and fauna, population, education system, government and society, economy, communications, notable personalities, culture and art. After a small selection of quotations there follows a number of suggested routes for visitors which provide a lead-in to the second part, in which the places and features of tourist interest – cities and towns, regions and provinces, and islands – are described. The third part contains a variety of practical information. Both the sights and the practical information are listed in alphabetical order.

The new Baedeker guides are noted for their concentration on essentials and their convenience of use. They contain numerous specially drawn plans and colour illustrations; and at the end of the book is a large map making it easy to locate the various places described in the "A to Z" section of the guide with the help of the co-ordinates given at the head of each entry.

---

## How to use this book

Following the tradition established by Karl Baedeker in 1844, sights of particular interest and hotels and restaurants of particular quality are distinguished by either one ★ or two ★★ stars.

To make it easier to locate the various sights listed in the "A to Z" section of the Guide, their co-ordinates on the large country map are shown in red at the head of each entry, e.g. Lisbon (Lisboa) A6.

Only a selection of hotels and restaurants can be given; no reflection is implied, therefore, on establishments not included.

The symbol ⓘ on a town plan indicates the local tourist office from which further information can be obtained. The post-horn symbol indicates a post office.

In a time of rapid change it is difficult to ensure that all the information given is entirely accurate and up to date, and the possibility of error can never be completely eliminated. Although the publishers can accept no responsibility for inaccuracies and omissions, they are always grateful for corrections and suggestions for improvement.

# Facts and Figures

This relatively small country, which in earlier centuries was one of the European great powers and has lost its large overseas possessions only in quite recent times, offers a wide range of both scenic and cultural attractions which are still relatively little known.

The mainland has an 832km/520 mile Atlantic coastline, the finest parts of which are to be found at its climatically favoured southern end, in the Algarve, with its beautiful sandy beaches and rugged cliffs. The country's cosmopolitan capital, Lisbon, on the broad estuary of the Tagus, is one of the most strikingly situated cities in the world.

In the interior of the country, too, there are many culturally and historically interesting and attractive towns, villages and abbeys, as well as a wide range of varied and beautiful scenery – hills, valleys and plateaux – in every region of Portugal.

## General

The Portuguese mainland lies in the extreme south-west of Europe between latitude 42°9' and 36°58'N, and 6°11' and 9°30'W. Portugal has a common frontier of some 1300km/800 miles – more than half its total length of frontier – with Spain, its only neighbouring state, with the other half formed by the Atlantic Ocean.

Geographical Situation

Also included within the territory of Portugal are the "Ilhas adjacentes", the two Atlantic archipelagos of Madeira and the Azores, and the former colony of Macao on the southern coast of China, which is administered by Portugal but enjoys self-government in internal affairs.

The mainland of Portugal, with an area of 88,944 sq.km/34,332 sq.miles, occupies roughly a sixth of the Iberian peninsula, and is broadly rectangular in shape, measuring some 550km/340 miles from north to south and averaging some 150km/95 miles from west to east (greatest width 200km/125 miles). The archipelagos of Madeira and the Azores have a total area of 3041 sq.km/1173 sq.miles.

Area

Mainland Portugal has preserved its frontiers unchanged for almost eight centuries – a circumstance which can be attributed mainly to its geographic situation. As a frontier territory of the Old World, rather than an area of passage, the kingdom of Portugal remained after its foundation in the 12th c. a region of only marginal significance in the conflicts between European states. The country's military efforts were directed solely towards the consolidation of its frontiers, at first against the Moors, then being driven back during the Reconquest, and later against Spanish claims to sovereignty.

National Territory

Most of Portugal's common frontier with Spain follows the course of the three great Iberian rivers – the Minho (Spanish Miño) in the north, the Duoro (Spanish Duero) in the north-east, and the Guadiana in the south-east – or the rugged ranges of the hills in the north of the

◄ *View of Óbidos*

country. These sections of the frontier which are easily accessible and without natural barriers are nevertheless readily identifiable as frontier areas, since the maintenance of the same frontier for so many centuries and the building of castles and other fortifications during those centuries have led to a movement of population away from these areas. As almost half of Portugal's frontier is formed by the Atlantic Ocean it is not surprising that throughout its history the whole country, including the inland as well as the coastal regions, should have shown a marked orientation towards the sea and should – thanks also to its traditional hankering for national independence – have differentiated itself so strikingly from its Spanish neighbour.

**Former Overseas Provinces**

The large overseas provinces of the old Portuguese colonial empire have been given up only quite recently. Portuguese India was annexed by India in 1961; Portuguese Guinea became independent as Guinea-Bissau in 1974; and in 1975 Mozambique, the Cape Verde Islands (Cabo Verde), the islands of São Tomé and Príncipe, and finally Angola, one after the other, achieved independence. In 1975 Portuguese Timor was invaded by Indonesian troops, and in 1976 it was officially incorporated in Indonesia.

## Topography

**General**

Geologically Portugal is the south-western part of the Iberian land mass, a region of gneisses, granites, quartzites, greywackes, limestones and Palaeozoic schists subjected to ancient folding movements, making up the Iberian mesetas, averaging some 700m/2300ft in height. It slopes gradually down from the higher hills in the north and has been much reduced and levelled by erosion.

Many perennial rivers traverse this rump formation and they play a major part in determining the climatic pattern and plant life. In recent years they have acquired additional importance as sources of hydroelectric power. Only a few of the larger rivers, including the Minho, Douro, Tagus, Sado and Guadiana, are navigable in the lower parts of their courses, but there are no river ports of any size.

Two of Portugal's great rivers, the Douro and the Tagus, both with their source in Spain, effectively divide the country into three sections topographically.

**Northern Portugal**

Northern Portugal is the area between the Minho, which forms the northern frontier, and the Douro in the south. The rump formations in this part of the country are overlaid by a number of massifs of early volcanic origin, often of imposing size, rising to heights of almost 2000m/6560ft and forming part of the Spanish mountain system. The "Montanhas" hill and mountain scenery is particularly wild and rugged in the Serra do Soajo, Serra da Peneda and Serra do Gerês, making this a region of extraordinary natural beauty and tourist interest (Peneda-Gerês National Park).

The Douro valley is equally picturesque. On the terraced slopes of the valley, in this "Pais do Vinho" (land of wine), are grown the grapes used for making port, which is carried down to the "lodges" of Oporto and shipped from there to countries all over the world.

**Central Portugal**

South of the Douro rises the mighty ridge of the Serra da Estrêla (Malhão da Estrêla; 1991m/6532ft), the western spur of the Castilian dividing range, much broken up by erosion and battered by violent storms from the west – the highest mountain in mainland Portugal and the country's only major winter sports area. The Serra da Estrêla is continued to the south-west in the uplands of Estremadura, a region of pleasant climate and great fertility; its westernmost spurs reach down to the coast and form promontories such as the Cabo da Roca, the most westerly point in Europe.

**Major rivers, lakes and mountains in Portugal**
(mainland)

© Baedeker

*Vineyards in north Portugal*

Central Portugal is not all mountainous and here, as in the south, the Iberian rump formations are broken up by tectonic depressions. These are found particularly in the Ribatejo area and around the estuary of the Rio Sado, where the land is highly fertile as a result of the soil deposited by the river and the abundant water supply. These areas are still subject to earth tremors and contain numerous thermal springs.

Just before reaching the Atlantic the valley of the lower Tagus (Portuguese Tejo, Spanish Tajo) opens out into a kind of inland sea, forming a huge natural harbour for the country's capital, Lisbon (Lisboa).

Southern Portugal

To the south of the Tagus is Alentejo, a great expanse of rolling country and level plateaux with occasional small ranges of hills (Serra da Ossa, etc.) rising to 700m/2300ft. This vast and featureless tract of arable country interspersed with heathland extends south to the Serra de Monchique, a range rising to some 900m/2950ft, which forms a protective barrier against cold weather from the north and with its numerous streams provides an abundance of nourishment for the subtropical and tropical vegetation of the Algarve.

Coastal Topography

The rump formations of the Iberian land mass extend for some 15–20km/9–12 miles out to sea at a shallow depth and then plunge steeply down to 300m/1000ft. Along the whole coastline they are overlaid by a fringe of Mesozoic sedimentary rocks deposited by the sea, which then reached farther inland. In the course of geological time these rocks were thrust upwards, forming the famous and exceedingly picturesque cliffs and stacks which are seen at their finest in the "Rocky Algarve", interspersed with bays and coves containing broad sandy beaches which shelve gently into the sea. In the estuaries of the Douro and Tagus in northern Portugal and of the Guadiana in the "Sandy Algarve" the sedimentary rocks have been much eroded and ground down, forming a landscape of dunes and lagoons.

*Tejo near Santarém*

## Climate

General

Its position on the western edge of the Iberian peninsula means that mainland Portugal, together with Madeira and the Azores, enjoys a maritime version of the Mediterranean climate, which as a general rule is wet and fairly warm in winter, and hot and dry in summer. This seasonal variation is because the weather is governed by the sub-tropical dry high pressure area in summer and, in winter, the western cyclone area from the temperate latitudes, which shift during the year according to the position of the sun. Portugal's climate is maritime insofar as there is little temperature variation between day and night, or between summer and winter, and there is also the heavy rainfall that can occur in the north and along the coast in particular, even in summer.

Climatic Variations

Within Portugal the climate varies according to the part of the country. In the west, on the coast, the climate is very much maritime, but towards the east continental influences become stronger, with a steadily greater range of variation between summer and winter, and day and night, temperatures, and increasingly less rainfall. Towards the south temperatures increase and rainfall decreases (annual average temperatures of Oporto 14.4°C/58°F, Coimbra 15.9°C/60.6°F, Lisbon 16.6°C/62°F, and Praia da Rocha 16.9°C/62.4°F). The number of dry summer months increases along the same lines. The greater the altitude the lower the temperature and the higher the rainfall. This correlation between altitude and precipitation means that rainfall is high on the mountain ridges near the coast facing the westerly winds and the sea, but gets less towards the east in the lee of the mountains.

Climate Tables

The climate tables show the features of the climate in particular regions in terms of temperature and rainfall from January (J) to

# Climate in Portugal

**Typical regional climates on the mainland**

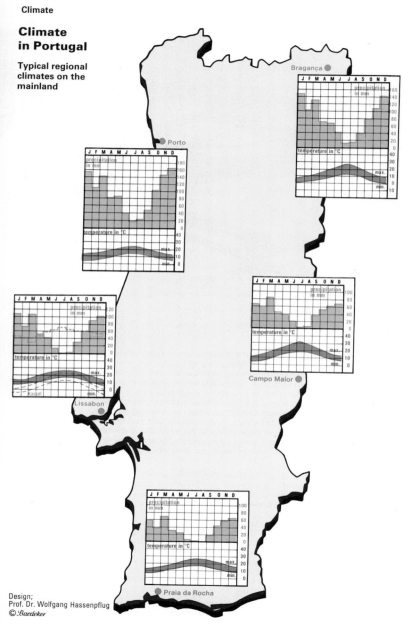

December (D). The blue columns show the monthly rainfall in milli-metres, and the orange curve shows the temperatures in centigrade, with the upper edge of the band representing average maximum daytime temperatures, and the lower edge average minimum night-time temperatures. These tables can also be used to estimate what the climate will be like for the parts of the country between these particular measuring points – Oporto represents the northern coastal area, Bran-gança the northern interior, Lisbon the central coastal area, Campo Maior the southern interior and Praia da Rocha the Algarve.

Rainfall in the coastal area of northern Portugal (around Oporto) is quite heavy and even in the summer months there are more than five to seven days of rain. Winds in summer are predominantly north-westerly, averaging 5m/197ft per second. These "nortadas", blowing from the area of high pressure over the Azores, are accompanied by northerly currents in the sea, resulting in relatively cold water temper-atures. In the height of summer these are only 17–18°C/62.5–64.5°F, some 6–7°C/42–45°F less than the Costa Brava on the Spanish east coast of the Iberian peninsula. Rainfall in Coimbra, 100km/62 miles south of Oporto and 40km/25 miles inland, is distinctly lower at 900mm/35in. Fogs along the coast in summer are relatively frequent.

*Northern Coastal Area*

The Atlantic has little effect on the climate in the northern interior measured at Bragança. The temperature variations as between day and night and winter and summer are markedly greater than in the lowland on the coast, and this is reflected in the steeper curve and broader band for temperature in the climate table. Much of the rain coming from the Atlantic falls in the mountains west of the city, so that despite the altitude annual rainfall is lower than on the coast. The drop in rainfall in summer is indicative of the Mediterranean climate. This area is bordered in the south by the mighty mountain ridge of the Serra da Estrêla, rising to almost 2000m/6560ft, and the annual rainfall at altitudes over 1400m/4595ft exceeds 2000mm/80in. a year, with snow-fall in winter in excess of 300mm/11in. a month, and correspondingly low temperatures.

*Northern Interior*

Portugal's central coastal area, around Lisbon, is sheltered on the north by the south-western continuation of the Serra da Estrêla, which wards off the northerly and north-easterly winds and the rain they carry with them. Temperatures are therefore perceptibly higher than in the north, as can be seen from comparison with the table for Oporto, and the summer months are markedly drier than in the north, with an annual rainfall of 708mm/28in. and only two days rain on average in July and August. Water temperatures, at around 18–19°C/64.5–66°F, are also several degrees higher than in the northern coastal area.

*Central Coastal Area*

This part of Portugal, around Campo Maior, has the most markedly continental climate in the country. The annual rainfall gets progres-sively less the further east you go until it can be under 500mm/19in.; the only exceptions being in the mountains with their greater precipitation.
  The variations in temperature between day and night and summer and winter are much greater than in Lisbon. During the year the varia-tions as between the hottest and the coldest months are between 11° and 17°C/51.8 and 64.5°F.

*Southern Interior*

The southward facing Atlantic coast (measuring point Praia da Rocha) has Portugal's mildest winters, tempered by the Atlantic and in the shelter of the ridge of the Alto Algarve to the north. The smallest annual range in temperature in the whole of the Iberian Peninsula is recorded at Cape St Vincent in the west (6.2°C/43°F). Minimum temperatures drop only briefly in winter, and even then they go little below 10°C/50°F.

*Algarve (south coast)*

In summer maximum temperatures stay well below 30°C/86°F but minimum temperatures also drop below 20°C/68°F so that it is often advisable to wear warmer clothing in the evening.

Summers are long and dry. There is likely to be less than a day's rainfall in July and August, and the hours of sunshine are correspondingly lengthy as well. With a total of 3162 hours a year, 387 of them in July, the Algarve gets more hours of sunshine than anywhere else in Portugal.

**Madeira**

The island of Madeira has a climate that is very maritime but warm as well, owing to its location in the lower latitudes. The weather is governed by low pressure areas from further north in the winter and north-easterly trade-winds in the summer. This makes for dramatic differences in climate between the windward side of the island in the north and the lee side in the south, where there are also distinct variations according to altitude. The northern side, where the trade-winds impact on the mountain slopes, gets heavy rainfall, mostly in winter (Santana: annual 1314mm/52in., July 27mm/1in., November 215mm/8½in.). Higher up the annual rainfall is over 2000mm/78in. (Encumeada pass at 950m/3115ft, 2675mm/105in.). On the southern side, where the annual rainfall stays under 600mm/23in., there are distinct zones: below 400m/1313ft a warm dry bottom zone that is hot and dry in summer, above that a more temperate, less dry zone, followed by a cloud zone, starting at 1000m/3282ft, below the condensation level, with rainfall all the year round, and, finally, from 1400–1500m/4595–4923ft, an upper dry zone above the cloud formed by the trade-winds, similar to the Canaries.

**The Azores**

The Azores high pressure area moves from north to south and back again with the sun, so that the islands lie on the frontier zone between polar and tropical air masses. Out in the Atlantic and constantly exposed to strong winds which in summer blow mainly from the north-east and in winter from the south-west, they have rainfall all the year round – at its sparsest in summer – and a more equable climate.

The variations in climate are considerable both during the year and as between one island and another, not to mention one side of an island and the other. The annual rainfall decreases from north-west (1447mm/57in.) to south-east (697mm/27½in.). In the mountains it can be as high as 3000mm/118in.

The Azores have distinctly fewer hours of sunshine than the Portuguese mainland. For Ponta Delgada these amount to 1626 hours per annum, with the most hours' sunshine in August (204, cf. Lisbon 357) and the least in January (80, cf. Lisbon 161).

# Flora and Fauna

**Flora**

**General**

The natural vegetation of Portugal originally consisted of sparse forest, but the country's forests have been decimated by centuries of over-felling and neglect and the original natural forests are now only to be found in the less accessible mountain regions. Reforestation is urgently necessary if the land is to be prevented from degenerating into a steppe-like waste. Accordingly in recent years there has been planned replanting in the dune and mountain areas. The trees now found mainly in the north of the country are deciduous species, with coniferous woodlands in the higher altitudes. In the south evergreens predominate, and the dunes along the coast are fringed with pines.

**Conifers**

The umbrella pine (*pinus pinea*), which owes its name to the shape of its crown, is an inescapable feature of the Portuguese landscape, and can be found growing singly, in groups or, very occasionally, in small

*Olive trees in the Alentejo*

stands. The seeds of the big round cones are edible and taste like hazelnuts.

Whereas the umbrella pine requires a relatively fertile site the clustered pine (*pinus pinaster*) can actually grow in dry infertile soil. This species of pine, which characteristically retains its dead branches, is very fast-growing in its early years, and is mainly used as a source of resin, obtained by tapping through small incisions in the bark.

Cypresses are also among the typical trees of Portugal. These "cupressus sempervirens", to use their Latin title, were known as "everlasting" because they can be up to 2000 years old. Their pillar shape, which cuts down the area exposed to the glaring light, makes them particularly suited to the climate.

As in the rest of the Mediterranean region the olive tree (*olea europea*) is widespread throughout Portugal. It enjoys ideal conditions in Alentejo, but grows in the north of the country as well. For the olives to ripen the trees need a long dry summer and relatively low temperatures in winter. They form inconspicuous pale yellow flowers in May/June and the harvest starts in November, carrying on until March. Whether the olives are green or black depends on how ripe they are.

Deciduous trees

Since Portugal has become the world's biggest cork producer (see Economy), large stands of cork-oaks (*quercus suber*) are very much in evidence in the southern and central parts of the country. Cork-oaks form a layer of cork from dead cells to counteract temperature fluctuations and prevent waterloss. When this layer is stripped from the tree the sap-bearing layer of bark must be left undamaged for the tree to survive. The stripped surface of the trunk appears pinkish-yellow at first, turning later to reddish-brown.

The *quercus occidentalis*, which is mainly found in northern Portugal, is a species of cork-oak with very little cork on its bark.

The Peneda Gerês National Park, in particular, has big stands of holm-oaks (*quercus ilex*), an evergreen species of oak with dark-green leathery leaves that have whitish felty undersides.

Another relatively common tree, especially in southern Portugal, is the eucalyptus (*eucalyptus globulus*). The leaves are round on the young trees but distinctly narrower on the older ones. To protect itself against too much light this tree species can position its leaves in a north/south direction so that the sunlight only hits the edges of the leaves. A noticeable feature of the eucalyptus is that it often casts long strips of its bark, revealing a smooth green gleaming trunk.

The vegetation of the north of the country, with its harsher climate, also includes plenty of sweet chestnut, lime, maple, poplar and beech trees.

Palms

Portugal's only native palm is the dwarf palm (*chamaerops humilis*), which occurs mostly in its trunkless, sprouting form.

Also, as throughout the Mediterranean, the Canary date-palm (*phoenix canariensis*) is a familiar sight in parks and gardens. Closely related to the north African-Arabic date palm, it has a stockier trunk and a more decorative, fuller crown with larger and lusher fronds. Its small fruits are woody and inedible.

Shrubs and herbs

In the undergrowth of the rainier regions of the north-west gorse and heather predominate; in the south and east large areas are covered with aromatic herbs and semi-shrubs, including broom, cistus, rosemary, thyme and lavender, with various colourful bulbous plants.

In spring and summer most parks and gardens are truly a magnificent display of blooms, awash in many places in a sea of oleander, camellia and hibiscus blossom.

Fauna

The wildlife of mainland Portugal is similar to that of Central Europe. In the wooded hills of northern Portugal are found not only species which occur north of the Alps, including roe-deer, chamois and foxes, but also wolves, lynx, wild horses, golden eagles and aurochs. In the Peneda Gerês National Park rare species enjoy full statutory protection. Nevertheless many of Portugal's animals are very much endangered species, and its population of wolves, for example, is thought to number only one to two hundred animals.

The coastal lagoons are the haunt of numerous waterfowl, including flamingo. Small game is abundant everywhere, and shooting is a popular sport. The many rivers, lakes, and reservoirs, are well stocked with trout, pike, salmon, carp and eel.

# Population

Density

Portugal's population of about 10.3 million is very unevenly distributed over the country (see map page 17). The average density of 110 inhabitants per sq. kilometre/284 per sq.mile is below the figure for other European countries. Some 35% of the population is concentrated in the large urban regions around Lisbon and Oporto, which have the very high densities of 770 and 697 per sq.km/1995 and 1806 per sq.mile. At the other extreme is Alentejo, with the very low density of 18 per sq.km/47 per sq.mile in the Beja district and 24 per sq.km/62 per sq.mile and 23 per sq.km/60 per sq.mile in the districts of Évora and Portalegre. In addition the drift of population from the rural areas to the rising industrial areas is still continuing.

Trends

The birth rate (12 per 1000) is relatively high but falling. The expected population increase is moderated by the traditionally high rate of emigration to the United States, Canada, France and South America (Brazil, Venezuela). During the last decade, however, large numbers of

# Population in Portugal's mainland districts

over 600

180–250

90–180

60–90

30–60

under 30

Inhabitants per sq. Kilometre

VIANA DO CASTELO

Viana do Castelo

BRAGA

Braga

Bragança

VILA REAL

BRAGANÇA

PORTO

Vila Real

Porto

AVEIRO

VISEU

Viseu

GUARDA

Guarda

Aveiro

Coimbra

COIMBRA

CASTELO BRANCO

LEIRIA

Leiria

Castelo Branco

Nazaré

Peniche

SANTARÉM

Portalegre

PORTALEGRE

Santarém

LISBOA

Cabo da Roca

LISBOA

Setúbal

Évora

ÉVORA

SETÚBAL

Sines

Beja

BEJA

FARO

Lagos

Faro

District boundary

© Baedeker

people have returned to Portugal from the country's former overseas possessions, so that overall the population growth has been quite reasonable, averaging 0.7% in the first half of the eighties and about 0.4% thereafter.

Structure

The earliest inhabitants of Portugal were the Lusitanians, a Celtiberian people. The native population, particularly in the coastal region, received an admixture of blood at an early stage from visiting seamen and traders – Phoenicians, Carthaginians, Greeks, Jews. The 600 years of Roman rule not only left their mark on the ethnic composition of the population but gave Portugal its language. Evidence of the relatively brief stays of the Suevi and the Visigoths can still be seen in the north of the country, where tall, fair-skinned types are occasionally encountered. Particularly marked, and in the south of the country quite unmistakable, are the traces left by the Moorish period, which influenced both the physical type and the way of life of the population. During the Middle Ages the Inquisition drove large numbers of Jews out of Spain into Portugal, where – still persecuted and harried by pogroms – they became converts to Christianity and were absorbed into the Portuguese people.

Thus in the course of millennia this mingling between the native population and successive incomers, combined with the country's isolation from Spain and the rest of Europe, gave rise to a population structure which was homogeneous and distinctively Portuguese, both ethnically and culturally.

The Portuguese are predominantly dark-haired, of small to medium height and of sturdy, almost stocky, build. In contrast to the lively Spaniards they tend to be quiet, gentle, thoughtful, warm-hearted and friendly, strongly attached to their home and their family – a characteristic reflected in the return of so many emigrants. The relatively peaceful course of the 1974 "Carnation Revolution" can also be ascribed to these qualities.

The small African minorities in the population are either descendants of former slaves or have come to Portugal from the country's former African possessions.

Settlement

Outside the large urban regions the predominant form of settlement is the densely built-up village which sometimes reaches the status of a small town. In the fertile valley basins scattered settlements predominate. Villages built along one main street are rare, being found mainly in newly developed agricultural areas on the coast.

Religion

More than 95% of the population are Roman Catholic. Of the remainder an estimated 38,000 are Protestants, 15,000 Muslims and 6000 Jews.

Constitutionally there is no established church and since no tithes are levied clerics have to be funded locally, with fees charged for marriages, christenings and funerals. Administratively Portugal is divided up into three Catholic ecclesiastical provinces – Lisbon (plus Madeira and the Azores), Braga and Évora.

Language

Portuguese (*português*), a Romance language, is spoken in mainland Portugal, the Portuguese Atlantic islands (the Azores and Madeira) and the territory of Macao in southern China. It is also still used in the former Portuguese colonies in Africa, India and Indonesia. Portuguese, in a locally modified form, is also the official language of the 115 million inhabitants of Brazil, while Galician, spoken in north-west Spain, is a dialect of Portuguese.

Altogether between 125 and 135 million people in the world speak Portuguese, giving it seventh place (after Chinese, English, Spanish, Hindi, Russian and Arabic) among the world's most widely spoken languages.

Portuguese is the direct descendant of the Lusitanian form of Vulgar Latin (the ordinary spoken Latin language). Among the Romance languages it is most closely related to Spanish, though it tends to be of more archaic form than Spanish. The differences between the various dialects of Portuguese are less marked than dialectal differences in other western Romance languages.

The vocabulary of Portuguese is overwhelmingly Romance (i.e. Latin). There are only trifling Basque and Germanic elements, the latter mainly of Visigothic origin. Since Portugal was reconquered from the Moors considerably earlier than Spain there are fewer traces of Arabic influence in Portuguese than in Castilian. The Portuguese spoken in Brazil includes a significant vocabulary of words taken over from the indigenous Indian population or from Africa.

The Portuguese literary language and the received pronunciation – mainly influenced by the language of educated people in Lisbon and Coimbra – assimilated French, Italian and Spanish elements from an early stage.

## State and Society

The 1933 Portuguese constitution was swept away by the almost bloodless "Carnation Revolution" of April 1974 and replaced by a new one, promulgated on April 25th 1976, making the Portuguese Republic (República Portuguesa) a parliamentary democracy. In November 1982 the original underlying socialism was watered down by amendment of the constitution.

**Constitution and Government**

The head of state is the President, who is elected for a five-year term. The current incumbent is Mário Soares, former Prime Minister and General Secretary of the Socialist Party (PS), who was voted into office at the Presidential Election in February 1986 by the left and right of centre electorate.

The Portuguese parliament, the Assembly of the Republic (Assembleia Nacional), is elected every four years and has 254 members, including four representatives of Portuguese citizens living abroad. Abiding by the verdict of the polls, the President appoints the Prime Minister, currently right wing businessman and former Chancellor of the Exchequer Anibal Cavaco Silva from the PSD – the Popular Democratic Party (Partido Popular Democratico), but also known as the Social Democratic Party (hence the acronym of its Portuguese initials).

Currently the strongest party, the PSD was founded in 1974 and is a party of the Centre that also tries to embrace groupings further to the Right, with an economic policy favouring the private sector and business interests. The party suffered a landslide loss of votes in October 1985 but was able to regain some ground in subsequent elections. The Democratic Renewa Party (Partido Renovador Democratico, PRD) was founded in 1985 by supporters of the former Prime Minister General Eanes with a left wing liberal manifesto. Although the PRD endorses EU and NATO membership it also wants to see Portugal less dependent on Europe. The PRD emerged the biggest loser from the 1987 elections, holding only 38 of the 55 seats it had won in 1985. The right of centre party is the Social Democratic Centre (Partido do Centro Democrático Social, CDS), standing for a planned free society. 1987 saw its vote drop from 17.3% to 4.5%. The Portuguese Communist Party (Partido Comunista Português) supported the 1974 revolution's economic aims regarding nationalisation of the banks, insurance and big business, and it too saw its vote go down in 1987 from 15.5% to 12.1%.

**Political Parties**

Portugal has national conscription, although conscientious objection is possible. Service in the Army is for 16 months, in the Navy and Air Force 21–24 months. The total armed forces currently number 73,000, the Supreme Commander being the President.

**Armed forces**

**State and Society**

International Organisations

Portugal is a member of the United Nations, NATO, OECD, EFTA, the European Union, and CERN (European Nuclear Research Centre).

Employment

Portugal currently has over 6 million in work, around 56% of them male. Wages are by far the lowest in the EU, with most people earning between £150 and £250 a month. They have a 36 to 45-hour working week, usually with four weeks paid holiday. Unemployment is down to 4.6%, although many jobs are only seasonal. Open-ended contracts of employment are the exception rather than the rule.

Standard of Living

According to the statistics almost every second Portuguese family lives below a "relative poverty line", and about 25% of the population probably has to survive on minimum subsistence, due to the low earnings and minimal social security. There is no social assistance and very little unemployment benefit, with about 75% of all unemployed getting no help whatsoever, and this is made worse by the fact that many employers do not pay their workers for months on end, or do not let them have the full amount. Many put up with these awful conditions for fear of losing their jobs, so innumerable families are left with no alternative but to keep themselves going by begging.

Housing Market

Housing in Portugal is in dire straits, with a national shortage of about 400,000 dwellings. For the poorest of the poor (about 36,000) there are only the miserable corrugated-iron shanty-towns, the "*bairros da lata*", such as those in Lisbon and Porto. This housing misery can partly be ascribed to a rent-freeze enacted in 1974, from which only the new rental agreements concluded after 1981 were excluded. Even some very well-off tenants paid ludicrously low rents, landlords had no interest in any kind of repairs, and the number of dwellings fell between 1970 and 1981 by 6%. Following a Rent Act in 1985 rents are gradually being phased upwards to bring them into line with the

*Évora: façades*

**Portugal**
**República**
**Portuguesa**
Administrative
districts (mainland)

P

© Baedeker

## Area and Population

| Administrative District | Area in sq.km/sq. miles | Population |
|---|---|---|
| Aveiro | 2808/1084 | 665,500 |
| Beja | 10,225/3947 | 177,700 |
| Braga | 2673/1032 | 771,400 |
| Bragança | 6608/2551 | 184,700 |
| Castelo Branco | 6675/2577 | 223,700 |
| Coimbra | 3947/1524 | 446,500 |
| Évora | 7393/2854 | 174,300 |
| Faro | 4960/1915 | 341,200 |
| Guarda | 5518/2130 | 196,200 |
| Leiria | 3515/1357 | 435,900 |
| Lisboa | 2761/1066 | 2,126,400 |
| Portalegre | 6065/2341 | 137,500 |
| Porto/Oporto | 2395/924 | 1,670,600 |
| Santarém | 6747/2604 | 460,600 |
| Setúbal | 5064/1955 | 779,600 |
| Viana do Castelo | 2255/870 | 266,400 |
| Vila Real | 4328/1671 | 262,900 |
| Viseu | 5007/1933 | 423,300 |
| Açores (Azores) | 2247/867 | 252,200 |
| Madeira (archipelago) | 794/306 | 252,800 |
| **Portugal** (mainland and islands) | **91,985/35,506** | **10,249,400** |

price of new housing, with housing benefit available for those who need it.

Administration    Portugal is divided into 22 administrative districts (*distritos*), of which 18 are in mainland Portugal and 4 in the Azores and Madeira. The districts are subdivided into urban and rural councils (*concelhos*), made up of *municipios* and *freguesias*. The eleven historical provinces (see map p.21) no longer have any political significance. Macao has a special status as an autonomous territory under Portuguese administration. Its return to China in 1999 was agreed in 1987.

Health care is only adequate in the bigger towns and cities — almost 75% of Portugal's specialists are in Lisbon and Oporto. Since many people have no medical insurance proper treatment is often beyond their reach, and although maternal and infant mortality may have fallen considerably Portugal's figures are still the highest in Europe.

In Portugal, as elsewhere, few people choose to have a traditional large family these days, but in the countryside the extended family of several generations under one roof still tends to be the rule. In northern Portugal in particular there are still more families with a number of children than there are in Lisbon, Oporto or southern Portugal, where the one or two child family is predominant.

The place of women in modern Portugal is distinctly historical by nature. Under the Salazar 1933 Constitution women were excluded from universal suffrage "because of their variable temperament and in the interests of the family". Women did not get the vote until 1968, and could not vote in local elections until 1974. Men and women are now equal under the 1976 constitution, although the traditional gender roles still tend to be commonplace. Generally speaking women are less well educated than men, and less professionally qualified, while in public life male dominance goes virtually unchallenged.

## Education

Since 1987 compulsory schooling in Portugal has been for nine years compared with four years until the mid-Sixties and then six years. These nine years are made up of four years primary school, two years middle school and three years secondary school, with the option of continuing for another three years at upper school, the final year being

*Coimba: the Old University*

orientated towards vocational or academic study. Schooling is free for the first nine years, but fees are charged for attendance thereafter.

An astonishing number of youngsters – as many as 34.7% in the first year of secondary school in 1982/1983 – fail to make enough progress to move up into the next class at the end of the school year. Even more disturbing is the fact that 20% of the children of school age do not attend school at all, or leave before they have been there six years; 45% leave before the end of their ninth year, and a further 22% go at the end of that year.

Universities

About 8–10% of school pupils go on to University. There is no general entrance qualification which means that they have to decide on what they want to study by the start of their final year in order to gain the relevant qualification.

There is also a "numerus clausus" for all subjects studied and every year each of Portugal's nine universities (in Lisbon, Porto, Coimbra, Évora and Braga) and its many colleges of further education stipulate anew the minimum marks required of school-leavers for entry to each subject.

# Economy

Economic Performance

Although Portugal has experienced a considerable economic upsurge, it still remains one of the poorest countries in the European Union. Its economic performance measured against population figures puts the country last but one, only Greece having worse figures.

Limitations

Besides its relatively undeveloped industrial sector and what is economically a rather inefficient farming sector, Portugal also has to contend with the impact on its economy and society of what has become outdated legislation. It has a State-owned sector of about 1000 enterprises, responsible for well over 14% of the gross national product, and 85% of it – breweries, for example – not subject to free competition. The fact that some prices are set without being subject to market forces runs counter to the principles of a free market economy and hence EU interests. For some time now privatisation of state industries has been proceeding with some success.

Economic crisis

Some years ago Portugal was in a state of severe economic crisis. A balance of payments deficit in excess of 3 billion dollars (13% of the gross domestic product) and foreign indebtedness of at least 13 billion brought it to the brink of insolvency, with 27% of its exports simply going on servicing the debt. In the end Portugal had to be helped out by a loan from the International Monetary Fund.

Effects of EC entry

Since it joined the European Community in 1986 Portugal's fortunes have taken a distinct turn for the better, and its economic growth has shown a yearly average of 4.6%. Year by year foreign investment has doubled. Unemployment has fallen to 4.6%, a figure which is bettered only by Luxembourg. Inflation is still about 8.5% (about 22% between 1980 and 1985).

Every sector of the Portuguese economy has since been concentrating its efforts on modernisation and diversification so that it could measure up to the advent of Europe's Single Market in 1992.

Since 1980 the negative side of the Portuguese "economic miracle" has become apparent: a growing deficit in the trading balance and increasing foreign debt.

Farming, Forestry and Fisheries

About 40% of the land area of Portugal is arable and 21% of this (over 630,000ha/1,556,730 acres) is irrigated. The most important agricultural area is between the Douro and the Tagus, where the river valleys, warmed by the summer sun, provide the country with its major wine-producing areas, as well as citrus fruits, peaches, figs and almonds. The arable land, dotted everywhere with olive-trees, is in the uplands, interspersed with Portugal's famous cork-oak forests. Crops grown include cereals, potatoes and pulses. Wheat, rye, oats, barley and rice are the major cereals and grown mostly in the south, with the cultivation of maize and potatoes concentrated in the north.

Fruit is still grown very largely for the home market. Olive production, which is relatively small-scale, also goes mainly for domestic consumption. However, exports of oranges, cherries, almonds, olives, new potatoes and onions are on the increase. Tomato production has long since been aimed at the export market, with most of it going abroad as tomato pulp.

Domestic Market/ Exports

Wine is produced throughout Portugal, but the most important vine-growing areas are in the northern part of the country. The best known Portuguese wine is, of course, port. Madeira, the sweet dessert wine grown on the island of the same name, goes almost exclusively for export. With an average annual output of 10 million hectolitres/2.2 million gallons Portugal ranks seventh among the wine-producing countries.

Wine

Stock-farming is particularly a feature of northern Portugal, where cattle predominate. The areas south of the Tagus, away from the coast, are given over mainly to sheep and pigs, grazing in the extensive cork-oak forests. In terms of numbers Portugal has 1.1 million cattle, 737,000 of them dairy-cows, 3.5 million pigs and 5.1 million sheep.

Stock-farming

Dairy-farming is also chiefly centred on northern Portugal, together with the fodder production that goes with it. There are also many intensive dairy units around Lisbon, although as a general rule dairy cattle are kept in small numbers. Very often farms only have a single cow, and only 3% actually have more than five.

The yields from Portuguese agriculture tend to be relatively small. This is due to poor soil quality, old-fashioned farming methods, unsuitable crop rotation and insufficient fertilisation, together with a failure to get to grips with pest infestation. Livestock farming is also often prone to suffer because of the spread of disease.

Productivity

The agricultural sector nevertheless still feeds nearly a quarter of the population, even though, given the poor productivity, this is largely at subsistence level.

In terms of size of holdings small farms predominate, with at the last count 44% of the 784,000 holdings less than 1ha/2½ acres, 53% between 1 and 20ha/49 acres and only 3% greater than 20 ha. In northern Portugal in particular fragmentation of ownership has left holdings that would not generally be considered viable in European terms, and the farms there are so small – and all the time getting smaller – that they operate on a subsistence basis. In the south of the country, on the other hand, farms tend to be the traditional larger holdings, and more than 45% of the cultivable area is farmed by holdings of over 100ha/247 acres. Here the concentration of large co-operatives after the land reforms, which had proved unproductive, has changed nothing so far as the earlier picture of very low productivity is concerned. In 1975 the former farmworkers were organised into 550 co-operatives, covering 1.1 million ha of agricultural land, but the land-tenure affected by this agricultural reform only encompassed 14% of the cultivable area. As part of the adjustment to the EU market the Government plans to dissolve the loss-making co-operatives. Only a few are left of the original 550 formed after the 1974 revolution. The considerable fragmentation of holdings in northern Portugal meant there was no need

Farm Structure

initially for agrarian reform. So far as European market harmonisation is concerned any restructuring in northern Portugal, where the average farm size is 4 ha, now appears particularly complicated.

**Forestry/Cork Production**

The main feature of Portugal's forestry is the fact that its 750,000ha/1,853,250 acres of cork-oak make it the world biggest producer of cork. Portuguese exports account for almost half the world consumption of cork bark.

Most of Portugal's 70 million cork-oaks grow in Ribatejo, Alentejo and the Algarve. The trees are 8–10m/26–33ft high and average a lifespan of 165 years. Cork cannot be taken from the trees until they are 25 years old, after which it is harvested every nine or ten years. Harvesting must be carried out in the summer months since the trees need to be full of sap. The freshly harvested cork is left to dry in the open for three months before being taken to plants for further processing.

**Fisheries**

Traditionally of considerable importance, Portugal's fisheries net an annual sea-catch of between 260,000 and 280,000 tonnes, with sardine and tuna coming mainly from Portuguese coastal waters, haddock from off the North American coast between Greenland and Newfoundland, and sperm-whale from around the Azores. The sardine fisheries are particularly important, accounting for a third of all landings. About 5% of landings are from Madeira and the Azores. Portugal's most productive fishing grounds are off its northern coast and these provide almost half the inshore catch. The country's 18,000 strong fishing fleet was deprived of almost half its traditional fishing grounds by the general extension of fishing zones to 200 miles in 1977. The European Union is to assist with the modernisation of the fleet and the associated training for its crews planned for the near future.

**Salt**

Salt-pans in the Vouga, Tagus and Sado estuaries and around Faro in the Algarve supply sea-salt for Portugal's canning industry.

*Sesimbra: the fishing harbour*

*Fish laid out to dry*

*Salt-pans near Aviero*

Its mining offers Portugal considerable opportunities to boost its economic development. It has, for example, become one of the world's most important producers of tungsten, and is already seventh in the world so far as uranium mining is concerned, with the second largest uranium deposits in Europe after France. It has substantial pyrites deposits in eastern Alentejo and its sources of iron ore in the north-east are the biggest on the Iberian peninsula. The mining of manganese, lead, copper, and tin is leading to the building of foundries and refineries.

Portugal's good quality marble and granite also make their particular sector ripe for development. Portugal's coal, petroleum and natural gas resources are, however, so far very meagre, and although off-shore exploration is well under way the prospects of finding oil and natural gas are rather slim.

Its as yet comparative lack of industrialisation has meant that Portugal has the lowest energy consumption per capita in the European Union. Half its electricity supply comes from hydro-electric plants in the north and centre of the country.

Oil is the second most important source of energy for the electricity supply. Coal provides the fuel for thermal power stations near Oporto and Sines, and there are also plans for four nuclear power stations.

Portugal's industrial production so far accounts for about 1% of EU production. Compared with the rest of Europe, and considering its poor productivity, its industrialisation is only just beginning.

Textiles traditionally play a crucial part in manufacturing, especially in terms of exports to which it contributed 31% of the total in 1986. Leather goods, and shoes in particular, are very much an up and coming industry compared with a few years ago. In 1980 shoe exports amounted to

**Mining and Energy Supply**

Raw Materials

Energy Supply

**Industry**

Textiles and Leather Goods

barely 4 million pairs but in 1987 they totalled 57 million and in 1989 rose to 80 million. Only 10% of output stays in Portugal. The rest finds its way to the EU market, especially France and Germany.

**Light and Heavy Engineering**

Engineering, including the manufacture of vehicles, machinery and electrical goods, accounts for close on 30% of industrial exports. Plant and machinery alone provide more than 16% of Portugal's total exports. This shows that it has long since ceased to be simply a buyer of equipment and other capital goods but also is quite a considerable exporter of such products in its own right, with growth in the electrical sector particularly vigorous. It is now even the case that Portugal annually exports some 200,000 tonnes of iron and steel products.

**Timber, Paper and Cork**

Large exports of cork and wood-pulp in particular make this sector a mainstay of Portuguese foreign trade. In terms of cork production Portugal has no equal. The Amorim Group from near Oporto, the world's biggest cork-maker, not only leads the field when it comes to selling winecorks but also markets 26 other cork products and is also engaged in research.

**Tourism**

Earlier balance of payments deficits are now being partly offset by earnings from tourism. Recent years have seen this growing in Portugal at such an extraordinary rate that all the available accommodation has been filled to overflowing, and hotels and holiday homes have sprung up everywhere. Its 16 million foreign visitors in 1988 meant that Portuguese tourism had experienced 500% growth within a decade. Since 1986 the tourist trade balance has shown a billion dollar surplus, bringing in almost as much foreign currency as that sent back by the Portuguese who work abroad.

The Spanish provide the majority of Portugal's foreign holidaymakers, followed by the British and Germans.

*Cork-oaks*

*Cork piled up to dry*

The most popular destinations are the Algarve and the Lisbon area, each of which accounts for a third of Portugal's tourist facilities, with the remaining third spread throughout the rest of the country. The colder and rougher weather in the north makes the development of international tourism there more difficult, and holidaymakers in search of bathing beaches are catered for in the resorts of the Algarve in the extreme south, the only part of Portugal to enjoy a truly Mediterranean climate. Consequently this has been where there has been the biggest upsurge in tourism, not only in terms of hotel accommodation but also in holiday flats and large visitor complexes. Higher-spending tourists are being lured into the country by new luxury hotels and exclusive leisure facilities. Around Lisbon, on the other hand, visitors tend to be more interested in sightseeing.

## Communications

Portugal's road network is full of contrasts, with the coastal regions in particular served by proper motorways, while some villages in the interior still cannot be reached by vehicles at all, or only in good weather. Another problem is the congestion on many roads, especially in northern Portugal and the Algarve coastal resorts, compared with sparsely settled Alentejo, where traffic can speed along. There are currently about 200km/125 miles of privately operated toll-paying motorways, and the motorway linking Lisbon and Oporto has been completed.

Road

Little importance is attached so far to east–west communications, and crossing into Spain is not without its problems. To effect an improvement a bridge has been built over the Guadiana at Ayamonte and another across the Minho is planned at Tuy.

*Mules are a popular form of rural transport*

## Communications

Of late car-ownership has risen dramatically in Portugal, and the number of cars has gone up by a third since entry into the European Union, although they still remain very much a luxury. Consequently very good care is taken of even the oldest models. Many vehicles are well over ten years old, and, not surprisingly since there is no MOT, their technical aspects may be rather unconventional. Donkeys, mules and horse and cart are also popular means of transport, especially in the rural areas.

**Rail**

The Portuguese railway network totalling some 3600km/2240 miles is rather limited, and the only stretch that is fully two-way and electrified is the line between Lisbon and Oporto, which takes about half the country's rail traffic. The lack of a rail bridge over the Tagus at Lisbon means there is still no direct rail link between the capital and the south of the country. Although adaptation of the existing bridge to take rail traffic has been planned for years, passengers still have to change from their trains to a ferry, and freight has to make a 100km/62-mile detour.

**Sea and River**

Portugal has a long seafaring tradition and although the importance of its shipping has been declining for some time much of its foreign trade still goes by sea, and there are also regular services between the mainland and Madeira and the Azores. Because of the nature of parts of the Atlantic coastline there is not much shipping in those coastal waters. Lisbon is Portugal's major port, but there are also important seaports for trade and fisheries at Oporto (Leixões), Setúbal, Sines and Aveiro.

Inland shipping is confined to the lower reaches of a few rivers, particularly the Tagus, and the Douro is also being made more navigable.

**Air**

Recent years have seen a speedy growth in air traffic. The international airports on the mainland are at Lisbon, Faro (charter flights for the Algarve) and Oporto.

TAP (Transportes Aéros Portugueses), Portugal's national airline, operates scheduled domestic flights to Bragança, Chaves, Coimbra and several other cities.

# History

## From Prehistory to Emergence of the Nation State

The coastal regions of present-day Portugal were already occupied by man in the Palaeolithic period. The nature of the indigenous population is not yet clearly established, but the Portuguese were probably a mixture of Ligurians in the south, Iberians in the middle of the country and Celts in the north. Only at a very late period, in the 12th c. A.D., were they able to establish their position as a separate country with a history of its own and to assert their independence of Spain.

| | |
|---|---|
| Evidence of Mesolithic occupation in large cemeteries (in one of which more than 200 skeletons were found). | 10,000–5000 B.C. |
| Megalithic culture – monumental cult structures erected in the Chalcolithic period (e.g the well-preserved Dolmen da Barrosa, north of Vila Praia de Ancora). | 2000–1600 |
| Iberians arrive in the peninsula, probably coming from North Africa. | From 2000 |
| Phoenicians probably trading in amber and copper on the Portuguese coast. | From 1000 |
| Celtic peoples settle in Portugal and in subsequent centuries mingle with the Iberians to become Celtiberians. Some 30 tribes of Lusitanians settle in southern Portugal (the larger part of the country), building strongly fortified hilltop settlements (castros, citânias), some of which – e.g. the Citânia de Briteiros and the Castro de Sabroso, near Braga – are still occupied in Roman times. | From 700 |
| Trading posts founded by Carthaginians and Greeks at a few places on the coast. | From 500 |
| During the Second Punic War the Romans fight mainly on Carthaginian territories in the Iberian peninsula and try to defend the frontiers against the Lusitanians in the west and the Celtiberians in the north. | 218–206 |
| After the bitterly contested Lusitanian War Lusitania is incorporated in the Roman province of Hispania Ulterior. | 197–179 |
| The Lusitanians rebel against the Romans under the leadership of Viriathus (later honoured in literature and art as a national hero). Their resistance collapses only after the murder of Viriathus near Viseu in 139. | 147–139 |
| During the Roman civil war the Lusitanians support Sertorius against Sulla. | 80–72 |
| After the death of Sertorius (72) Pompey quells the Lusitanian rising. Rapid Romanisation starts in the south and along the coastline. | 71 |
| Caesar finally subdues the province of Hispania Ulterior. | 61–54 |
| Under Augustus the peninsula is pacified (*pax romana*) and Roman authority consolidated by the extensive settlement of colonists. The province of Hispania Ulterior is divided into the two provinces of Baetica (Andalusia) and Lusitania. Lusitania, a province of only marginal importance within the Roman Empire, comprises the whole of | 27–15 B.C. |

Portugal south of the Douro, together with the Spanish region of Extramadura and province of Salamanca. The region north of the Douro falls within the Roman province of Gallaecia. Emerita Augusta (Spain's Mérida) becomes Lusitania's capital, and Bracara Augusta (Braga) is one of Gallaecia's main settlements. The Romans demolish the old Castros but encourage development of towns such as Bracara Augusta (Braga), Portus Cale (Oporto), Aeminium/Conimbriga (Coimbra), Felicitas Iulia/Olisipo (Lisbon), Pax Iulia (Beja) and Scallabis (Santarém).

From A.D. 200     The Christianisation of Lusitania is believed to have begun at a very early stage, and the establishment of the bishoprics of Braga and Évora are attested in the 3rd c.

From 410     During the Great Migrations of the Germanic peoples the Suevi press into northern Gallaecia, the Asdingian Vandals into southern Gallaecia and the Alans into Lusitania.

About 414–418     The Visigoths defeat the Alans and the Vandals, who withdraw to the south of Spain (and later to Africa).

585     The Suevic kingdom is conquered by the Visigoths under their king Leovigild (568–586), who unites it with the powerful Visigothic kingdom of Toledo.

589     King Reccared and the Visigoths adopt the Roman Catholic faith. Soon afterwards the persecution of the Jews begins.

711     After the victory of the Arabs (Moors) over the last Visigothic king, Roderick, they occupy the whole of the Iberian peninsula except the mountainous regions in the north (713–718). The territory of present-day Portugal becomes part of the Arab Emirate (later Caliphate) of Córdoba; although the only evidence of Moorish influence (e.g. in farming, buildings, words borrowed from Arabic, etc.) is in the southern part of the country (Algarve).

717     The Reconquista (the recovery of Arab-occupied territory) starts out from the Visigothic kingdom of Asturias.

From 722     Asturias recovers the territory between the Minho (Miño) and the Douro (Duero), with the stronghold of Portus Cale (Portucale, now Oporto).

1035–65     Under King Ferdinand I, the Great, of Castile and León the reconquest of the main part of Portugal begins. In 1064 he manages to recapture Coimbra.

1094     King Alfonso VI of León (from 1065) and Castile (from 1072), after repeatedly advancing to the Tagus, is thrown back by the Moors at Lisbon.

## From the emergence of Portugal as an independent state to the end of the Portuguese empire in the 16th c.

After establishing its independence as a state Portugal achieves territorial unity at a very early stage – the first European state to do so. In the 15th c. Prince Henry the Navigator initiates the Portuguese voyages of discovery in the Atlantic and along the African coast, and thus lays the foundations of the later Portuguese empire.

1095     Alfonso VI of León and Castile establishes the County of Portucalia (named after the town of Portus Cale, now Oporto), between the rivers

Douro and Mondego, and grants it as a fief to his son-in-law Count Henry of Burgundy (1095–1112), a Capetian.

After the death of Alfonso VI, Henry of Burgundy frees Portugal for a time from its feudal dependence on León-Castile. 1109

Henry of Burgundy's widow Teresa, illegitimate daughter of Alfonso VI of Castile, acting as regent on behalf of her son Afonso Henriques (1112–85), takes advantage of the turbulent situation in Castile to gain greater independence for Portucalia. From 1112

After a brilliant victory over the Moors at Ourique (Beja district) Afonso Henriques assumes the title of King as Afonso I and shakes off Castilian overlordship. 1139

Afonso I submits himself to the feudal superiority of the Pope. Alfonso VII of León-Castile recognises the independence of Portugal under the Burgundian dynasty. 1143

During the Second Crusade Afonso captures Lisbon from the Moors. His successors extend the kingdom by further conquests in the south. 1147

Pope Alexander III recognises Portugal as a kingdom. 1179

Rapid progress in the development of towns (Lisbon, Oporto, Braga, Coimbra, Lagos, etc.), craft industry and maritime trade (thanks to Portugal's favourable situation on the Atlantic coast). From 1200

With the help of the knightly order of Santiago Afonso III (1245–79) conquers the province of Algarve in southern Portugal. The Portuguese Reconquista is thus complete, and the frontier with Castile established on the Guadiana. *Circa* 1250
   Portugal as the first European state reaches the limits of its territorial expansion which remain unchanged to the present day.

The towns are represented in the Cortes (parliament). From 1254

Lisbon becomes capital, displacing Coimbra. 1256

New taxes to be levied only with the agreement of the Cortes. 1261

King Dinis, the "Farmer", promotes agriculture, afforestation, mining, trade and navigation. 1279–1325

Dinis concludes a concordat with Pope Nicolas IV to settle the disputes with the Church. 1289

The first Portuguese university is founded in Lisbon (later transferred in 1307 to Coimbra). 1290

The frontier between Portugal and Castile is definitively established. 1297

Treaty of friendship with England. 1308

Afonso IV (1325–57) sides with the Castilians in the Battle of Salado against the Sultan of Morocco whose invasion is rebuffed. 1340

The murder of Inês de Castro to whom Pedro, the heir to the throne, is secretly betrothed, leads to a war between Afonso IV and his son, who becomes king as Pedro I ("the Cruel", 1357–67). 1355

In order to prevent Portugal reverting to Castile after the extinction of the male line, the Cortes elect Pedro's illegitimate son as Regent and 1383 later king. As João I (1383/85–1433) he becomes the founder of the House of Avis.

| | |
|---|---|
| 1385 | João's decisive victory over Castile at Aljubarrota consolidates the independence of Portugal. His reign sees the beginnings of the colonial expansion in Africa and the voyages of discovery which prepare the way for Portugal's rise as the leading maritime and colonial power in western Europe.<br><br>With the rapid expansion of the merchant shipping fleet Lisbon develops into a major commercial city. |
| 1386 | The alliance with England is renewed in the Windsor Treaty. |
| 1415 | Capture of the trading post of Ceuta in Morocco. |
| From 1418 | João I's younger son Henry the Navigator (Henrique "O Navigador"; 1394–1460) promotes voyages of discovery along the West African coast and in the Atlantic. School of navigation founded at Sagres. |
| 1419–57 | Discovery and settlement of Madeira, the Azores and the Cape Verde Islands. Beginnings of the negro slave trade (abolished by law only in 1850). |
| *Circa* 1470 | Occupation of the coast of Guinea. |
| 1471 | Afonso V, the "African" (1438–81), takes Tangier and other coastal settlements. |
| 1476 | Afonso V, who is betrothed to a natural daughter of Henry IV of Castile and therefore lays claim to the Castilian throne, is defeated by Ferdinand of Aragon at Toro. |
| 1482 | The Portuguese reach the mouth of the Congo. |
| 1488 | Bartolomeu Dias rounds the southern tip of Africa, the Cape of Good Hope. |
| 1494 | In the Treaty of Tordesillas Portugal and Spain agree on a demarcation line between their colonial spheres of interest in Latin America. |
| 1495–1521 | Manuel I, the Fortunate, establishes Portugal's commercial power, with the foundation of trading posts in the East Indies, Eastern Asia, South Africa and Brazil. Lisbon becomes a focal point of world trade. |
| 1498 | Vasco da Gama discovers the sea route to India. |
| 1500 | Pedro Alvares Cabral reaches Brazil. |
| From 1510 | Franciso de Almeida and Afonso de Albuquerque, appointed viceroys in India, establish trading posts in India and south-east Asia (Goa 1510, Malacca 1511, Ormuz, Diu, etc., 1514) and for a time hold the monopoly of the world spice trade.<br><br>Thanks to its worldwide trade Portugal enjoys an upsurge of prosperity during the reign of Manuel I. The crown, nobility and merchants enjoy fabulous riches, but the unusual colonial expansion places such a strain on the Portuguese people that population figures drop rapidly from two to one million.<br><br>However, the contacts with foreign lands act as a powerful stimulus to art and literature. Portugal's greatest poet, Luis Vaz de Camões (1524–80), glorifies the great voyages and conquests in his "Lusiads", in which he describes Vasco da Gama's voyage to India. |
| 1518 | Capture of Ceylon. |

**The Great voyages of discovery of the Portuguese**

⟶ School of navigation founded at Sagres by Henry the Navigator (1394–1460); capture of Ceuta, 1415; Madeira, 1420; Azores, 1427; Gil Eanes at Cape Bojador, 1434.

- -⟶ Sea route to India:
Diogo Cão reaches the mouth of the Congo, 1482.
Bartolomeu Dias rounds the Cape of Good Hope, 1492.
(Columbus, sailing in the Spanish service, reaches the West Indies, 1492.)
Pedro Álvares Cabral reaches Brazil, 1500.
Vasco da Gama sails in 1497 from Belém, near Lisbon, rounds the Cape of Good Hope, calls in at Mozambique in SE Africa (1498) and reaches India. (The poet Luís de Camões describes the voyage in "The Lusiads".)

- -⟶ Gaspar Corte Real reaches Newfoundland, 1501.

- - -⟶ Fernão de Magalhães (Magellan) sails in the Spanish service from Sanlúcar de Barrameda, crosses the S Atlantic and continues through the Strait of Magellan, at the souther tip of S America, into the Pacific, and is killed in 1521 during a fight with natives on the island of Mactan in the Philippines. One of his ships returns to Europe in 1522 by way of the Indian Ocean and the S Atlantic, thus completing the first circumnavigation of the globe.

⟶ David Melgueiro sails from Japan in a Dutch ship which makes the passage along the N of Asia and Europe and so to Portugal.

| | |
|---|---|
| Under João III the colonial empire in the Far East disintegrates and economic prosperity starts to wane. | 1521–57 |
| Treaty of Saragossa (Zaragoza), a further agreement between Portugal and Spain on the demarcation of their colonial spheres of interest. Taking of the Moluccas. | 1529 |
| The establishment of the Inquisition in Portugal and the foundation of a Jesuit university at Évora (closed 1759) promote the success of the Counter Reformation. | 1536/58 |
| The Portuguese establish a trading post at Macao, the first European settlement in China. | 1557 |
| King Sebastião I (1557–78) undertakes a crusade against Morocco but is killed, along with many Spanish nobles, in the battle of Alcácer-Kibir. | 1578 |
| Death of King (and Cardinal) Henrique II (1578–80), the last ruler of the House of Avis. | 1580 |

# Rulers of Portugal

### House of Burgundy

| | |
|---|---|
| Henrique (Henry of Burgundy) Count of Portucalia | 1093–1112 |
| After Henry's death his widow Teresa acts as Regent during the minority of her son Afonso | |
| Afonso Henriques, the Conqueror King of Portugal | 1139–85 |
| Sancho I, the Populator | 1185–1211 |
| Afonso II, the Fat | 1211–23 |
| Sancho II (deposed 1245, d. 1248) | 1223–45 |
| Afonso III, the Restorer (brother of Snacho II) | 1245–79 |
| Dinis I, the Farmer | 1279–1325 |
| Afonso IV, the Brave | 1325–57 |
| Pedro I, the Cruel or the Inexorable | 1357–67 |
| Fernando | 1367–83 |

### House of Avis

| | |
|---|---|
| João I, Defender of the Kingdom (illegitimate son of Pedro I; Grand Master of the Order of Avis) Regent | 1383–85 |
| King of Portugal | 1385–1433 |
| Duarte | 1433–38 |
| His brothers are Pedro (Duke of Coimbra), Henrique (Henry the Navigator), Fernão (d. in Moorish captivity) and João (Grand Master of the Order of Santiago) | |
| Afonso V, the African | 1438–81 |
| João II, the Perfect Prince | 1481–95 |
| Manuel I, the Fortunate | 1495–1521 |
| João III, the Pious | 1521–57 |
| Sebastião (grandson of João III) | 1557–78 |
| Henrique II (brother of João III; Cardinal Archbishop of Lisbon) | 1578–80 |

### Spanish Kings of the House of Habsburg

| | |
|---|---|
| Filipe I (Philip II of Spain) King of Portugal | 1580–98 |
| Filipe II (Philip III of Spain) | 1598–1621 |
| Filipe III (Philip IV of Spain) | 1621–40 |

### House of Bragança

| | |
|---|---|
| João IV (Duke of Bragança) King of Portugal | 1640–56 |
| Afonso VI | 1656–67 |
| Pedro II (brother of Afonso VI) | Regent 1667–83 King 1683–1706 |
| João V, the Magnanimous | 1706–50 |
| José | 1750–77 |
| Maria I (wife of Pedro III, who d. 1786) | 1777–92 |
| João VI | Prince Regent 1792–1816 King 1816–26 |
| Pedro IV (Emperor Pedro I of Brazil) | 1826–28 |
| Miguel (brother of Pedro IV) | 1828–34 |
| Maria II (daughter of Pedro IV; m. Duke Ferdinand of Saxe-Coburg-Koháry 1836) Duke Ferdinand rules as Regent during the minority of his son Pedro | 1834–53 1853–55 |
| Pedro V | 1855–61 |
| Luís | 1861–89 |
| Carlos (assassinated in Lisbon in 1908 together with his heir Luís Filipe) | 1889–1908 |
| Manuel II (second son of Carlos I; leaves Portugal 1910, d. in exile 1932) | 1908–10 |

## From Spanish rule to the fall of the monarchy

Although Portugal succeeds, with British help, in winning its independence from Spain, it falls increasingly under British influence, politically and economically. Despite the huge influx of money from its colonial possessions the country grows poorer since it fails to establish a productive economy of its own. Portugal remains a backward agrarian country, wracked in the 19th c. by civil war, political and constitutional conflicts, and financial and economic crises that finally lead to the fall of the monarchy.

| | |
|---|---|
| Philip II of Spain, a grandson of Manuel I on his mother's side, occupies the whole of Portugal by force and expels the Portuguese claimant to the throne, António. | 1580 |
| Portugal is united with Spain through rule from the Spanish throne. | 1580–1640 |
| The Cortes recognise Philip II of Spain as King Filipe I of Portugal. The country is ruled by viceroys; the colonies have a separate administration of their own. | 1581 |
| During the period of Spanish rule Portugal loses part of its colonial empire. The Dutch take the Moluccas (1607), Ceylon (1638), Malacca (1641) and north-eastern Brazil (1630 onwards; recovered 1654). | 1607–30 |
| The heavy taxation imposed to finance Spanish wars, combined with much activity by French agents, leads to a successful rising in Lisbon. Its leader, the Duke of Bragança, descended from the old royal family through his grandmother, restores the independent kingdom of Portugal and is crowned king as João IV (1640–56). | 1640 |
| A treaty of friendship and commercial co-operation with Britain (ratified in 1656) ensures Portugal's independence of Spain but also guarantees British predominance in Portugal. | 1654 |
| Catherine of Braganza (Bragança), sister of King Afonso VI (1656–67), marries Charles II of England. | 1661 |
| Treaty of Lisbon: Spain recognises Portugal's independence. | 1668 |
| During the war of the Spanish Succession Pedro II (1683–1706) signs a treaty of alliance with France, but under British military pressure is forced to revoke it. | 1701 |
| Under pressure from Britain, Austria and Holland, Portugal is compelled to join the anti-French coalition.<br>The Methuen Treaty, a commercial treaty between Britain and Portugal, provides for the sale of Portuguese wine in exchange for British textiles. The Portuguese woollen industry is thus destroyed. | 1703 |
| Under its spendthrift King João V, who sides with Austria in the War of Spanish Succession, Portugal becomes totally impoverished despite its vast holdings of Brazilian gold and diamond mines, and grows financially dependent on Great Britain. | 1706–50 |
| The reign of King José I is the great age of enlightened absolutism. His chief minister, the Marquês de Pombal (1699–1782), carries through a series of reforms based on the principles of the Enlightenment and Mercantilism – the encouragement of manufacturing and trading companies, the reorganisation of the fiscal and financial systems and of the army, the promulgation of a new code of laws, the secularisation of education, etc. | 1750–77 |
| After the devastating Lisbon earthquake (November 1st), in which more than 30,000 people are killed, Pombal directs the rebuilding of the shattered capital. | 1755 |

# Historic Provinces of Portugal
(mainland)

© Baedeker

Boundary of Historic Provinces

Boundaries of Districts

| | |
|---|---|
| Expulsion of the Jesuits from Portugal and the Portuguese colonies and confiscation of their property. | 1759 |
| Portugal repulses Spain's invasion attempt in the Seven Years' War. | 1762 |
| Refoundation of Coimbra University. | 1772 |
| After the death of José I the authoritarian Pombal is compelled to go into exile. During the reign of Maria I, the Mad (1777–92/1816), there is a clerical reaction and the Jesuits return. Most of Pombal's reforms are reversed, and the ideas of the Enlightenment are combated with the help of the Inquisition. | 1777 |
| João VI becomes Regent in place of his mentally disordered mother. During the French Revolution Portugal allies itself with Britain as a member of the anti-French coalition. | 1792 |
| João VI refuses to take part in the Continental System or to fight alongside the French against Britain. | 1805 |
| Under the Treaty of Fontainebleau (October) between France and Spain Napoleon gains the right to march his troops through Spain. The French General Junot is thus able to occupy the whole of Portugal. The royal family flees to Brazil under the protection of the British fleet (November). | 1807 |
| War of National Liberation against rule by the French: General Arthur Wellesley (later Duke of Wellington) lands in Portugal in August 1808 with a British force and defeats Junot's French army. Under the Convention of Cintra (Sintra) on August 30th the French withdraw from Portugal. Napoleon himself, with 300,000 soldiers, now seeks to reconquer Spain and Portugal.<br><br>In 1810 Wellesley succeeds in repelling an attack on Lisbon by Marshal Masséna at Torres Vedras. | 1808–10 |
| After the complete liberation of Portugal, General William Carr Beresford remains in control of the country, the king being still in exile in Brazil. | 1811 |
| British forces quell a rising by Portuguese army officers. | 1817 |
| Liberal revolution, starting in Oporto. | 1820 |
| A new liberal constitution (modelled on the Spanish constitution of 1812) is proclaimed by the Cortes, confirming João as king on his return to Lisbon. | 1821 |
| With British help João VI defeats a conspiracy, directed against the new liberal measures, which is supported by his wife Carlotta (sister of Ferdinand VII of Spain) and their younger son Dom Miguel. Miguel is banished from Portugal. | 1824 |
| Since Pedro I of Brazil (Pedro IV of Portugal) is unable to unite his two kingdoms, he abdicates the Portuguese crown after his father's death in favour of his seven-year-old daughter Maria da Glória (Maria II), promulgating a moderate constitution and appointing Miguel as Regent. | 1826 |
| After a counter-revolution Miguel revokes the constitution and has himself elected king by the Cortes as Miguel I. | 1828 |
| Miguelist Wars. Pedro I of Brazil, having renounced the Brazilian throne in 1831 in favour of his son Pedro II, overthrows the reactionary regime of Miguel I, with British help. Miguel leaves Portugal. | 1832–34 |

## History

| | |
|---|---|
| Carlos is assassinated in Lisbon, along with the heir to the throne, Luis Filipe (February 1st). | 1908 |
| Carlos's younger son Manuel II is unable to save the monarchy, in spite of an amnesty and minor concessions. | 1908–10 |
| Revolution in Lisbon; Manuel is compelled to abdicate and flees to Britain. | 1910 |

## From the foundation of the Republic to the present day

After the abolition of the monarchy continuing party strife prevents the necessary radical reforms (particularly land reform) from being carried through, and the new form of government is accordingly unable to achieve stability. Although Salazar overcomes the financial crisis, his authoritarian Fascist regime and colonial policy lead after the Second World War to the isolation of Portugal in the United Nations and the Western world. After the fall of the dictatorship the development of a new pattern of government is hampered by political, economic and social problems resulting from the country's colonial wars. Conflicts between parties of the left and the right make it difficult to form a stable government. Entry into the European Community confirms democratic Portugal's stated intent to help create a united Europe.

| | |
|---|---|
| Proclamation of the Republic (October 5th). The interim President, Joaquim Teófilo Fernandes Braga, forms an anti-clerical government. | 1910 |
| Separation of State and Church (April 20th). Republic constitution comes into force (September 11th); Manuel d'Arriaga becomes President (1911–15). Reforms are carried through, but the urgently necessary land reform is not. Party strife among the Republicans, who are divided among themselves, together with revolutionary unrest, strikes, political corruption, the continuing financial crisis and other problems, prevent the formation of a stable government (between 1911 and 1926, under 8 Presidents, there are no fewer than 44 governments). | 1911 |
| The use of troops to repress disturbances in Évora leads to a general strike in Lisbon. | 1912 |
| During the First World War Portugal at first remains neutral then in 1915 is persuaded by Great Britain to come into the war on the side of the Allies. | 1914–18 |
| Social conflicts become more acute (frequent strikes). | 1919/20 |
| Foundation of the Portuguese Communist Party. | 1921 |
| After a military rising (May 28th) under General Manuel de Oliveira Gomes da Costa Parliament is dissolved and the constitution suspended. The Communist Party is banned. | 1926 |
| Gomes da Costa is displaced by General António Oscar de Fragosa Carmona, who represses uprisings in Oporto and Lisbon aimed at returning to a parliamentary regime. | 1927 |
| General Carmona is elected President (until 1951). He dissolves the Cortes and puts down several revolts against the military dictatorship. The economist António de Oliveira Salazar (1889–1970), finance minister in the new government, brings the national finances under control within a year and becomes the dominant political figure in Portugal. | 1928 |

## History

| | |
|---|---|
| 1930 | Salazar founds the National Union (União Nacional), the Fascist party of a one-party state. |
| 1931 | Suppression of riots on Madeira and in Lisbon. |
| 1932 | Salazar becomes prime minister. |
| 1933 | The new constitution is ratified by a national referendum (March 19th). The Estado Novo (New State) is an authoritarian corporative state on the Fascist model. Strikes are prohibited and the trade unions dissolved. |
| 1936–38 | During the Spanish Civil War Portugal is officially neutral but favours General Franco by indirect means. |
| 1939 | Iberian Pact, a treaty of friendship and non-aggression with Spain (continued for another ten years in 1948). Renewal of the alliance with Britain. Concordat with the Vatican. |
| 1939–45 | During the Second World War Portugal remains neutral. It breaks off diplomatic relations with Germany in May 1943, and gives Britain and the USA bases in the Azores in 1943 and 1944 respectively. |
| 1948 | Portugal receives Marshall Aid and joins the Organisation for European Economic Co-operation (OEEC). |
| 1949 | Portugal becomes one of the founder members of the North Atlantic Treaty Organisation (NATO). |
| 1951 | Agreement with the United States (later extended several times) allowing the Americans and other NATO countries to establish military bases in the Azores.<br>    Francisco Higino Craveiro Lopes becomes President on the death of President Carmona.<br>    The Portuguese colonies are declared to be part of Portugal (overseas provinces). |
| 1955 | Portugal becomes a member of the United Nations. Treaty with Brazil providing for mutual consultation. |
| 1958 | Admiral Américo de Deus Rodrigues Tomás is elected President. |
| 1960 | Portugal becomes a member of the Organisation for Economic Co-operation and Development (OECD) and the European Free Trade Area (EFTA). |
| 1961 | Seizure of the Portuguese liner "Santa Maria" in the Caribbean by opponents of Salazar (January).<br>    Annexation by India of the Portuguese enclaves of Goa, Damão and Diu (not recognised by Portugal until 1974). Increasing unrest in Angola and Mozambique. The United Nations repeatedly condemn Portuguese colonial policy. |
| 1962 | Officers fail in an attempt to overthrow the dictator in Beja. |
| 1963 | An agreement with West Germany allows German troops to be stationed at a NATO airbase in Beja. |
| 1964 | Portugal concludes an agreement with France allowing it a base in the Azores. |
| From 1967 | Inflationary trend in Portugal as a result of the country's colonial wars and its entry to EFTA. |

Salazar retires on health grounds and is succeeded by Marcelo José das Neves Alves Caetano, a lawyer who has long been associated with him in the government. He tries briefly to take a more liberal line but is frustrated by steadily increasing opposition, particularly in the army.

1968

PIDE, the notorious secret police organisation, is renamed the Directorate General of Security (DGS).

1969

The period of compulsory military service is extended from two to three (in case of emergency four) years (February 5th). The National Union becomes the National People's Action (Acção Nacional Popular: February 21st).
    Portugal fails to win its colonial war against Guinea.

1970

Treaty between the European Community and EFTA states not willing to join the Community providing for the reduction of duties on industrial products (July 22nd)

1972

Portuguese-Guinea declares its independence, recognised by Portugal in 1974. Earthquake in the Azores.

1973

The dictatorship is overthrown (April 25th) in the "Carnation Revolution", an almost bloodless coup d'état by the MFA (Movimento das Forças Armadas, Armed Forces Movement). Tomás and Caetano are removed from office, and General António Sebastião Ribeiro de Spínola (whose book "Portugal and its Future" prepared the ground for the military putsch) becomes President. He is succeeded on September 30th by General Franciso da Costa Gomes.
    The head of the left-wing democratic government is Adelino da Palma Carlos, a lawyer, who gives place on July 15th to Colonel Vasco dos Santos Gonçalves. A Council of State is established as an instrument of government, and a variety of parties are permitted. The government's domestic plans, which include the nationalisation of banks, insurance corporations and large companies and the expropriation of large estates as the first stage in land reform, give rise to violent political conflicts.
    The country's acute economic problems are aggravated by the influx of refugees from the newly independent colonies. The overseas provinces are granted the right of self-determination (August).

1974

Unsuccessful attempt at a putsch by right-wing elements under the leadership of General Spínola (March 11th); Spínola emigrates to Brazil. The Council of State is superseded by a Council of the Revolution, composed of military leaders, which initiates the nationalisation of the economy and land reform.
    The elections for a new legislative assembly show a strong body of opinion in favour of a pluralist democracy (April 25th). When the Council of the Revolution takes no account of this there are bitter conflicts between the MFA and members of the socialist and communist parties. The MFA sets up a "Triumvirate" of three military men (F. da Costa Gomes, V. dos Santos Gonçalves and Otelo Saraiva de Carvalho) as the highest political authority (end July). Vice-Admiral José Baptista Pinheiro de Azevado becomes prime minister (end August). Unsuccessful putsch by extreme left-wing paratroopers in which Carvalho plays an ambiguous role (end November); Carvalho is removed from office.
    The former colonies of Mozambique, the Cape Verde Islands, the islands of São Tomé and Príncipe, and Angola become independent during 1975.

1975

The effects of the worldwide energy crisis and economic recession aggravate Portugal's internal difficulties: increased inflation (35%),

Mid 1975 to mid 1976

high unemployment (over 15%), a growing stream of refugees from the former colonies (nearly half a million), anti-communist riots in northern Portugal, occupation of large estates in the south by peasants, strikes and unrest in industry, flight of capital. Economic and financial collapse is averted only by financial help from the European Community and credits from Germany and other countries.

**1976**

The Constitutional Assembly promulgates (although the Social Democratic Centre Party votes against it) the new socialist constitution establishing a democratic parliamentary Republic (April 2nd). The Socialists are victorious in an election on April 25th, but without an absolute majority.

After a rising in Portuguese Timor the territory becomes part of Indonesia (June 24th).

General António Ramalho Eanes is elected President (June 26th) and appoints the Socialist Mário Soares as head of a minority government.

Portugal becomes a full member of the Council of Europe (September 22nd).

Resumption of relations with Angola (September 30th).

**1977**

Foundation of a new party of the right, the Independent Movement for National Reconstruction (MIRN). Devaluation of the escudo (February) – the first devaluation since 1931. Extension of Portuguese territorial waters to 200 miles from the coast (March 11th). The government officially applies for membership of the European Community (March 28th).

Second law on land reform, providing on the one hand for the return of illegally occupied land to the owner and on the other for further collectivisation of large estates (August 11th); it gives rise to protests and unrest in the south. Government control of exchange rates is abandoned (August–September). Political and economic problems lead to the fall of the minority Socialist government (December 8th).

**1978**

Coalition government of the Socialists and Social Democratic Centre Party led by Mário Soares (February 12th).

Portugal receives a large credit from the International Monetary Fund, with conditions as to restriction of imports and consumption; further devaluation of the escudo (May). Ten-year treaty of friendship and co-operation with Spain (May 5th). Fascist organisations banned (June 16th).

After the dissolution of the coalition government President Eanes appoints the former minister of industry, Alfredo Nobre da Costa, head of a government of technocrats (August 28th). After only 17 days Nobre da Costa's non-party government is defeated by the Socialists and Centre Democrats (September 14th). The return to private ownership of nationalised land in the Alentejo wheat belt, which gives rise to protests, mainly from the Communists, leads to violent incidents in the agricultural areas (October). Mass demonstrations in Lisbon against the interim government formed by Nobre da Costa (November).

Carlos Mota Pinto, a non-party man with Social Democratic leanings, forms another government of technocrats, which takes the oath on November 22nd. The Council of the Revolution rejects the electoral laws passed by Parliament as unconstitutional (December 14). Wave of resignations by Socialists (December).

**1979**

Mota Pinto demands State aid for the private sector. Country-wide demonstrations and strikes against the amendment of the land reform laws. Foundation of the Socialist Trade Union in Oporto (January). The government's plans for putting the country's finances on to a proper footing meet violent opposition. Mass demonstrations by both the left and the right face the government with another crisis (March 17th).

Split in the Social Democratic Party over the premature demand for an election by the party leader, Francisco Sá Carneiro. New electoral law passed by Parliament (April).

After no-confidence motions by the Communists and Socialists the Mota Pinto government resigns (June 6th). The parties of the central right — Social Democratic Centre Party, Popular Monarchist Party, Social Democratic Party and breakaway Socialists — form a "Democratic Alliance" (July 5th).

President Eanes asks Maria de Lurdes Pintassilgo, Portuguese representative at UNESCO, to form an interim government (July 19th).

A special election on December 2nd (in which 87.5% of the electorate vote) gives the conservative Democratic Alliance a clear majority. A liberal Social Democrat, Francisco Sá Carneiro, becomes prime minister.

A severe earthquake in the Azores on New Year's Day takes a heavy toll in human lives and damage to property.　　　　　　　　　　　1980

The Conservative "Democratic Alliance" wins the normal elections (October 5th). Sá Carneiro again forms the government. A little later he is killed in an air crash (December 4th).

General Ramalho Eanes is once more elected as President (December 12th). Portugal's caretaker government under the acting Prime Minister Amaral resigns (December 8th).

The Social Democrat Francisco Pinto Balsemão (PSD) becomes prime　1981
minister (January 5th). Mário Soares is confirmed as General Secretary of the Socialist Party of Portugal (May 10th). After disagreements within the PSD Pinto Balsemão resigns (August 11th). Three weeks later he again forms a government (September 1st).

On the occasion of a pilgrimage to Fatíma Pope John Paul II escapes an　1982
attempt on his life (May 13th). Changes in the cabinet (June 5th).

As a result of the early elections on April 25th the Socialists with 36.3%　1983
of all votes emerge as the strongest party. Together with the Social Democrats (PSD) they form a coalition of the left centre led by Prime Minister Mário Soares.

Parliament accepts the abortion bill put forward by the Socialists, the　1984
Conservatives voting against (January).

The ruling coalition breaks up and the Soares government resigns　1985
(October). The Social Democrats (PSD) emerge as the largest party from the early general elections but the new prime minister, Anibal Cavaco Silva, has to govern with a minority cabinet.

On January 1st Portugal (and Spain) become full members of the EEC.　1986
Former prime minister Mário Soares is elected President in the second round of presidential elections.

Anibal Cavaco Silva's minority government is toppled by an opposi-　1987
tion vote of no confidence. President Mário Soares dissolves parliament and calls new elections for July 19th. Cavaco Silva's PSD scores a convincing victory and becomes the first party since the 1974 Revolution to achieve an absolute majority, winning 148 of the 250 parliamentary seats. As on-going prime minister Cavaco Silva's programme is uncompromisingly aimed at reducing state influence on the Portuguese economy and amending the constitution to water down or eliminate its basic Socialist principles.

The visit by US Secretary of Defence Frank Calucci in February occa-　1988
sions a Portuguese government statement that the Lajes base in the Azores will continue to be available to the American Air Force.

Cavaco Silva's measures meet with stubborn resistance from some of the population and March sees a wave of strikes protesting against planned new labour laws to facilitate dismissals and fixed-term working.

A fire on August 25th destroys much of Lisbon's inner city Chiado district.

1989    An American charter flight crashes on landing at Santa Maria in the Azores, killing all on board.

1991    In January Mário Soares is re-elected President with a large majority.

In October Cavaco Silva wins an absolute majority of parliamentary seats for the PSD.

# Famous People

The following famous people were all connected in some way or other with Portugal, whether as the place of their birth or death, or because they lived or worked there.

Afonso Henriques, later Afonso I, founded the Portuguese monarchy. Born in 1109 or 1110 (or even 1112, according to some sources), he was the son of Count Henry of Burgundy who had been invested with the fiefdom of Portugal by León-Castile but had succeeded in freeing it from its feudal dependence as early as 1109. When his father died in 1112 Afonso succeeded him, initially under the regency of his mother then, from 1128, in his own right.

Afonso I (1109/ 1110–85)

His brilliant victory over the Moors at Ourique in 1139 brought him such prestige he was able to assume the title of King of Portugal. In 1143, by submitting himself to the feudal authority of the Pope, he forced León-Castile to recognise his independence. Further military successes, including capturing Lisbon from the Moors in 1143, enabled him to keep on extending the boundaries of his kingdom.

Afonso probably did not actively take part in all the campaigns, but he masterminded the plan of action and also ensured that the newly conquered territory was properly defended and administered.

Little is known of the life of Afonso I apart from the famous conquests. In 1145 or 1146 he married Matilda (d. 1158 and the daughter of Count Amadeus of Moriana) and they had several children. Afonso's heir – subsequently Sancho I – was born in 1154.

Afonso received a wound during an assault on Badajoz in 1168 which made it impossible for him ever to ride again. From 1170 onwards he lived in Coimbra where he died on December 6th 1185 after a short illness. In accordance with his wishes he was buried in the church of the monastery of Santa Cruz.

The Portuguese nun Mariana Alcoforado figures in European literature as the author of the love letters addressed to Noël Bouton de Chamilly, Count of Saint-Léger, which form the so-called "Letters of a Portuguese Nun" (Lettres Portugaises) of 1669. It may well be that she was not, however, the author of these letters which, as well as being very full of feeling, are extremely well-expressed. They are as likely to have come from the pen of the French author G.-J. de Guilleragues who purports to have translated them. The "Letters" were translated into English for the first time as early as 1678 by Sir Roger l'Estrange. At the time when the Letters were first published the name of the presumed authoress was not known; it was not until the nineteenth century that it was discovered, and efforts were made to cast light on the nun's biography. Modern critics generally treat the Letters as nothing other than a work of fiction.

Mariana Alcoforado (1640–1723)

Mariana Alcoforado was born in 1640, the daughter of Francisco Alcoforado, an army officer, and of Leonor Menezes, a lady of wealth. She was still very young when she entered the convent of Nossa Senhora da Conceição in Beja. It was through the bars of the window of her convent cell that in 1665 she is supposed to have first set eyes on a young Frenchman, Noël de Bouton de Chamilly, who was serving in the same regiment as her brother (at the time France was supporting Portugal in the Spanish–Portuguese War). They struck up a friendship and, despite the convent walls, fell in love. 1667 spelt the end of their happiness when the count had to return home. Mariana Alcoforado sent him letters which at first were full of passion and then, as she came to realise that she had been no more than a passing fancy for the count,

47

## Famous People

*Afonso I*

*Luís Vaz de Camões*

*Vasco da Gama*

became expressions of her disappointment and her sense of distance. Her former lover is supposed to have felt nothing but amusement when he received her letters and to have enjoyed reading them out aloud to his friends.

In her last letter the nun hinted that she might put an end to her life, but she must have managed to overcome her grief, since she died in the convent at the ripe old age of 83. Her memorial, which survives to this day, records that for thirty years she subjected herself to the strictest penance.

**Diogo de Boytaca (c. 1470–1520)**

Although the exact dates of the life of the architect Diogo de Boytaca (or Boytac or Boitaca) are uncertain, it is known that he was active between about 1490 and 1520. His nationality is also unclear, and he may have been French, Italian or actually Portuguese – for which there are some grounds in that there is a village near Batalha with the similar-sounding name of Boutaca.

Boytaca is inseparably linked with the Manueline style of architecture. His buildings are almost without exception characterised by their exuberant decoration. His first major work was the Convent of Jesus in Setúbal, then after 1509 he headed the building of the abbey at Batalha and, after 1514, the Hieronymite convent in Belém. He also worked on the palace at Sintra, and in Galegã, Caldas da Rainha and Montemor-o-Velho, as well as being responsible for many fortifications in North Africa.

**Luís Vaz de Camões (1524/1525–80)**

Lisbon and Coimbra dispute the honour of being the birthplace of Luís Vaz de Camões, who is certainly Portugal's most important poet. There are doubts too about the date of his birth, which may be either 1524 or 1525. He came from a respected family, his father holding the King's command of one of his ships.

After studying in Coimbra, Camões went to Lisbon where he was received at court and commissioned to write plays and poems. He was, however, soon to be banished from court circles because of a love affair. In the hope of winning his way back into favour he volunteered to serve in North Africa where he lost his right eye in a skirmish. He had scarcely arrived back in Lisbon when he was imprisoned in 1552 for taking part in a duel. He was pardoned, but ordered to leave the kingdom. He was first sent to Goa, where he again fell out of favour, and had to go further afield, presumably to Macao. His post, which involved responsibility for those who were dead or missing in China, left him enough time for his poetry. There is a rocky cave which now bears his name in which he is supposed to have written his great epic "The Lusiads", (Os Lusíadeas, a reference to Lusus, the mythical ancestor of the Portuguese).

It was not until 1570 that Camões returned to Lisbon, where "The Lusiads" was first published two years later. Even then, however, fate was unkind to Camões, who nowadays is revered as the Portuguese national poet. He lived out his last years in abject poverty. In 1580, on June 10th – now celebrated as a national holiday – he died of the plague.

Besides "The Lusiads" Camões published numerous poems and several comedies.

Inês de Castro was born of a distinguished Castilian noble family and came to Portugal in the entourage of Constança, the wife of the Infante Dom Pedro. She and Pedro, the heir to the throne, soon fell passionately in love. This did not suit the reigning monarch, King Afonso IV, who had Inês sent back to Spain. Pedro had to accept his father's decision, but did not forget the woman he loved. When his wife died giving birth to a son, he had Inês brought back to Portugal. He lived with her quite openly and the couple had four children.

Inês de Castro  
(c. 1320–55)

Their happiness was, however, short-lived. The king feared the de Castros would become too influential and got the Privy Council to order the death of Inês. She was murdered in Coimbra in the "Jardim das Lágrimas", the "Garden of Tears", as it henceforth was known, and her body was interred in the convent of Santa Clara in Coimbra. Pedro dreamt of revenge but was obliged at first to bow to his father's will. When, however, his father died in 1357 and he succeeded to the throne he ordered those who had taken part in the murder of his beloved to be most cruelly tortured and executed. Not satisfied with that, he ordered the exhumation of the corpse of Inês which was then crowned queen in a macabre ceremony in Coimbra Cathedral and thereafter reinterred in Alcobaça Abbey.

This love story has been treated in more than 200 literary works, the first being the third canto of Camões' "Lusiads".

The seafarer Vasco da Gama came from Sines, the port in southern Portugal. The actual year of his birth is not known, but it is put at somewhere between 1460 and 1469. It was King Manuel I who ordered da Gama to find the sea route to India, though precisely why he was chosen remains uncertain. What is known is that he had already won something of a name for himself when serving in the fleet under João II. Opinions differ as to his temperament. In contemporary sources he is described as valiant, tough and proud, but also irascible and hot-tempered.

Vasco da Gama  
(1460?–1524)

Da Gama left the harbour of Restelo near Lisbon with four ships on July 8th 1497. The crews totalled 170 men (of whom a third would perish on the voyage), plus priests and some convicts who could escape execution by going on particularly dangerous enterprises. One week out the ships passed the Canaries, and on November 22nd they rounded the Cape of Good Hope to continue sailing up the east coast of Africa and finally, in May 1498, anchored off the west coast of India. Da Gama started the return voyage on October 8th 1498, arriving back in Lisbon on July 10th 1499. Although he had in fact returned almost empty-handed from his travels, he was envied and admired by the whole world of his day for the contacts he had forged with the spice lands. The King rewarded him richly, awarding him an annuity and granting him the title of "Dom".

In 1502/1503 da Gama set out on his second India voyage, this time at the head of an armada charged with setting up trading relations and compelling recognition of Portuguese dominion. On this voyage da Gama allowed his irascibility full rein "lapsing into near transports of cruelty". This time he returned to Portugal richly laden with treasure.

The seafarer embarked on his third and final voyage to India in 1524. The King had appointed him viceroy, and now it was a matter of assuming this office in India. Within four months of his arrival "ulcers were forming in his neck", and he died on December 24th 1524.

Vasco da Gama's deeds were glorified by Camões in "The Lusiads".

**Calouste Sarkis Gulbenkian (1869–1955)**

Virtually every visitor to Lisbon will come across the name Gulbenkian. The son of a well-to-do Armenian petroleum dealer, Calouste Sarkis Gulbenkian was born near Istanbul on March 1st 1869 and studied engineering in London. So great was his success that as early as 1891 he was appointed adviser to the Ottoman court on petroleum matters. In the years that followed he became one of the most important experts in this field, and in 1911 he founded the Iraq Petroleum Company, incorporating all the biggest oil companies of the day. Gulbenkian's 5% share of the profits won him the nickname "Mr Five Per Cent" and also a huge fortune: at times he was reckoned to be the richest man in the world.

For the most part Gulbenkian invested his wealth in Great Britain. He had in fact held British nationality since 1902, but at the start of the Second World War the British confiscated Gulbenkian's goods and chattels as "enemy property". His efforts to leave the country were not successful until he managed to get to neutral Portugal in 1942. He settled in Lisbon, living in a suite in the Aviz Hotel (on the site of the present Sheraton) and set about rebuilding his fortune.

Calouste Gulbenkians' great love, after the oil business, was art ("I'm head over heels in love with beauty and every form of artistic expression"). Before the war and during his stay in Lisbon he collected choice works of art, buying Egyptian statuary and French furniture, Chinese porcelain and Turkish faïence, as well as works by Rembrandt, Rubens, Van Dyck, Frans Hals, Degas and Monet. Over the years he purchased some 5000 works of art, making him owner of one of the most important private collections in the world.

Gulbenkian lived in Lisbon until his death in 1955, and bequeathed his whole estate said to be over 66 million dollars, and works of art worth at that time 15 million dollars, to the Fundação Calouste Gulbenkian.

This foundation built a large cultural centre with several theatres, concert halls and cinemas, a library and a museum that has become world-famous since its opening in 1969. A centre for modern art was added to the complex in 1984.

**Henry the Navigator (1394–1460)**

Henry (Henrique in Portuguese), born the third son of King Joāos I on March 4th 1394, has gone down in history as "Henry the Navigator" (o Navegador), though he himself never went on any long sea voyages.

The Prince distinguished himself at the conquest of Ceuta (1415), and as a result his fame soon spread throughout Europe. The King granted him the titles of Duke of Viseu and Lord of Covilhã, at the same time entrusting him with the defence and administration of Ceuta.

It was then, if not before, that the prince began to take an interest in seafaring, poring over charts and documents and seeking information from seafarers. Otherwise, according to Zurora, the court biographer, he lived a very secluded life, dressing extremely simply, a man of deep piety and asceticism.

Henry's appointment in 1418 as Grand Master of the Order of Christ (the successor to the the Order of Knights Templar in Portugal) brought him huge financial resources. This allowed him from then on to turn his seafaring dreams into reality. He had a home built in Sages, in the extreme south west of Portugal, with a school of seafaring attached to it. Here new techniques were tried out and passed on to young seafarers. In the shipyards a new type of vessel was built, the caravel, which was far superior to conventional sailing ships in terms of manoeuvrability and seaworthiness.

Since Sagres was not suitable as a port because it lacked a hinterland, the voyages of exploration that Henry financed and organised set

*Calouste Sarkis Gulbenkian*  *Henry the Navigator*  *Marquês de Pombal*

out from nearby Lagos, first discovering (or rediscovering) the islands of Madeira (colonised by 1423), then the Azores (1427). Later Henry the Navigator's ships pressed on further along the west coast of Africa, reaching Cape Verde, Gambia and finally Guinea. Henry's seafaring enterprises, which laid the foundation for Portugal's development as a colonial power, were motivated as much by the struggle against Islam as by the desire to set up trading networks, and the lure of gold, spices and slaves.

By the end of his life Henry had nearly exhausted the vast riches of the Order of Christ, since the expenditure on the voyages of discovery was offset by very little in the way of income.

Henry the Navigator died of fever in his palace at Sagres on November 13th 1460.

Manuel (or Emanuel) I is also known as Manuel "the Great" or "the Fortunate" because it was under him that Portugal experienced its golden age.

*Manuel I
(1469–1521)*

He was born in 1469, the youngest son of the Infante Fernando. When the heir to the throne, the Infante Afonso, died unexpectedly after a riding accident, Manuel was proclaimed King in Alcácer do Sal on October 27th 1495.

Manuel I used his marriage policy to establish close links with the Spanish royal house. His first marriage, in 1497, was to Isabella of Castile, the widow of the Infante Afonso. After her death he married her sister, Maria of Castile, who was to provide him with his heir, João III. His third and last wife was Leonor of Spain, who had, in fact, been promised to his son.

Manuel I's rule was aimed at strengthening royal power against the nobility. Administration was centralised, taxation and customs duties were standardised, and the "Fortunate King" was able to keep his country out of any wars, but above all Manuel's reign is associated with the voyages of discovery which he encouraged, primarily out of trading policy considerations. It was on his orders that Vasco da Gama found the sea route to India and Pedro Alvares Cabral sailed to Brazil. These seafaring feats made Lisbon Europe's paramount trading port, and riches poured into the country, leading to a great flowering in the arts and sciences and, above all, architecture. In their magnificent buildings Belém, Batalha and Tomar still bear impressive witness to the Manueline Style named after the king.

Portugal's "Golden Age" was, however, only short-lived, and had already passed its peak when Manuel died of a fever in Lisbon in 1521.

During his lifetime Fernando Pessoa – Fernando António Nogueira Pessoa, to give him his full name – who is considered to be Portugal's

*Fernando Pessoa
(1888–1935)*

51

greatest poet after Camões, published nothing but various articles in newspapers and journals and just the one book. Only after his death was the discovery made of two trunks full of manuscripts, primarily fragments.

Fernando Pessoa was born in Lisbon on June 13th 1888. His childhood was sadly clouded by the premature death of his father. On his mother's second marriage, to the Portuguese consul in Durban, the whole family moved to South Africa. Pessoa grew up to be bilingual, enjoyed a good education and composed his first poems in English; until his death he continued to write poetry and stories in both English and Portuguese. With the intention of studying at the University of Lisbon, Pessoa went back to Portugal when he was seventeen, but found it hard to settle down there. He soon abandoned his studies, and made poetic writing the most important thing in his life. He earned his living doing foreign language correspondence for various Lisbon firms, and, since this only afforded him a modest income, lived with relatives or in furnished rooms.

To stop himself being lonely Fernando Pessoa had already begun as a boy to create companions to talk to in his poetry, and as an adult he lived almost without any human ties, in total isolation. He got over the situation by using several different names as a poet, signing his work not only with his own name but also Albert Caeira, Alvaro de Campos and Ricardo Reis. For Pessoa each of these poets' names represented an independent poetic personality complete with his own biography, a particular style and a special choice of themes.

Pessoa's utter introspection meant that there is little of any note to report about his private life. Apart from his mother there was only one woman in his life, a colleague called Ophélia. It was, he himself records, out of consideration for his poetic work that he decided not to marry her.

Towards the end of his life Pessoa became increasingly addicted to alcohol, dying of liver failure on November 30th 1935.

Sebastião José de Carvalho e Mello Marquês de Pombal (1699–1782)

Marquês de Pombal made a decisive impact on the history of his country as the man who paved the way for enlightened despotism. Born into Lisbon's minor aristocracy, his first experiences of the diplomatic service were as envoy to London and Vienna, where he also dealt particularly with economic matters. José I appointed him Foreign Secretary in 1750 and Prime Minister in 1756.

Pombal proved skilful at carrying out the offices he held entirely to suit his own ideas, although he showed himself none too squeamish about the means he judged necessary to achieve his long-term ends. He saw his most important tasks as reorganising state finances, reforming education, promoting trade and industry so as to get free of Britain's economic hegemony, and the abolition of slavery.

The part he played in the reconstruction of Lisbon after the devastating earthquake of 1755 was outstanding. He fought passionately with the Jesuits and minor nobility whose inherited privilege stood in the way of his attempts at reform.

The Marquês lost favour after the death of José I and in 1781 the pressure from his many enemies brought about his banishment to Pombal where he died the following year.

António de Oliveira Salazar (1889–1970)

Verdicts differ widely on the politician António de Oliveira Salazar. Some see him as a repressor par excellence while others view him as the man who helped his country to regain respect and a degree of prosperity.

Salazar was born into a modest background on April 28th 1889 in a small village in the Dão valley, the son of an estate steward. He had a happy childhood imbued with the values of Catholicism. At eleven he entered the seminary at Viseu where he was to be educated by the Jesuits until he was twenty. In 1910 he went to Coimbra to study law and economics, earning his living by undertaking various teaching duties. His academic career progressed smoothly, and in 1916 he became professor of economics at Coimbra, quickly making a name for himself as a finance expert. In 1928 Carmona brought him into the government as Minister of Finance, and in 1932 he was promoted to Prime Minister, an office he held until 1968. The new constitution adopted in 1932 provided him with the basis for an elitist, authoritarian state (with only about 16% of the population permitted to vote), which he headed, backed by the União Nacional that he founded.

During his 40 years in government Salazar succeeded in reorganising the country's finances, improving the administration, taking a firmer stand on corruption and, last but not least, keeping Portugal out of the Second World War. However, Salazar implemented his policies using total censorship and a state security police (the PIDE) which did not hesitate to use terror and torture. The independence movements in Portugal's overseas territories were ruthlessly suppressed.

Privately Salazar lived extremely simply and in some seclusion, hating anything like a personality cult and was always reserved towards his friends, in so far as he could be said to have any. His closest confidante in his final years could be considered to have been his housekeeper, Dona Maria.

In September 1968 Salazar suffered a stroke, leaving him paralysed on his left side and unable to work. Marcello Caetano was appointed the new Prime Minister but Salazar still sometimes believed he was in charge right up until his death on July 27th 1970.

# Art and Culture

Until the 12th c. Portugal to a great extent shared the destinies of its neighbour Spain. With the emergence of a Portuguese national consciousness in the reign of King Afonso Henriques (1139–85) there began also the country's independent artistic development – though political circumstances often involved a close relationship with Spain. Throughout its history Portuguese art reflects a great variety of influences: the old pre-Christian and pagan heritage, the Christian civilisation of Asturias, itself strongly influenced by France, Moorish culture, vigorous folk elements and later echoes of the cultures of Portuguese colonial territories in India, Africa and South America.

Phoenicians, Greeks, Carthaginians

Although this old-established area of settlement, occupied by the stocky and dark-skinned Iberians, and later by the mixed race of Celtiberians, lay on the outermost edge of Europe, remote from the rest of the Western world, it was already being visited in antiquity by seafaring Mediterranean peoples. At the mouth of the Tagus the Phoenicians established a staging point on the route to Britain which they called *Alis Ubbo*, later known as Olisipo and now as Lisbon. Thereafter Greeks and Carthaginians also settled at Alis Ubbo.

Romans

Under the Romans – who took almost 200 years (until A.D. 19) to subdue the Iberians – the Romanisation of the province of Lusitania proceeded relatively slowly (prehistoric and Roman antiquities in the Archaeological and Ethnological Museum at Belém, near Lisbon). In Lisbon (*Felicitas Iulia*), which during the Roman period was apparently a place of no particular consequence compared with Mérida in Spain, few Roman remains have been preserved (Open-air Archaeological Museum in the church of the Carmo which was destroyed by the 1755 earthquake). On the highest point in the town of Évora, which seems to have been a flourishing place in Roman times (*Liberalitas Iulia*), are the impressive remains, with 14 Corinthian columns, of a temple of the 2nd or 3rd c. A.D., traditionally ascribed to Diana. The temple, of which the cella is missing, was converted into a fortress in the Middle Ages and restored only in 1870.

During the period of Roman rule numbers of *villae rusticae* – country houses – were built by Roman landowners, the forerunners of the *quintas* which are so characteristic of Portugal. Some of the finest of these are: the famous Quinta das Lágrimas ("House of Tears") near Coimbra (see A to Z), in the gardens of which Pedro I's tragic bride Inês de Castro was murdered in 1355; the Quinta da Penha Verde, near Sintra, built in the 16th c. by Dom João de Castro, fourth Viceroy of India, with a beautiful park (round chapel in Renaissance style, with 17th c. faïence, probably by Miguel de Arruda); and the Oriental-style Quinta de Monserrate, also near Sintra (see A to Z), built in 1856 for Sir Francis Cook, which likewise has beautiful gardens.

The site of Conimbriga (see A to Z Coimbra), a Roman town originally founded in the 2nd c. B.C. and destroyed by the Suevi in A.D. 468, has yielded remains of walls, an aqueduct, fountains and baths with magnificent mosaics (Museu Monográfic, near the excavations). In Coimbra, which took over the name of Conimbriga after its destruction, Roman remains can be seen in the Museu Machado de Castro, housed in the former Bishop's Palace in the Largo da Feira, a picturesque old building originally dating from the Romanesque period (restored 1529). There are also remains of Roman buildings at Beja (*Pax Iulia*; walls and an arched gateway) and at Milreu in the Algarve (*Ossonoba*, discovered 1876).

*Roman Temple at Évora*

*Mosaic from the Roman age*

## Art and Culture

**Migration, Visigoths**

The great migrations brought Germanic peoples into Portugal – the Vandals, the Suevi and the Visigoths, who originally settled in the Roman provinces as *foederati*. These were allies of Rome, who were granted land in return for the performance of certain services, but who established their own independent states after the fall of the Western Empire. Thus the Suevi established themselves in the north, with Braga as their capital and Oporto as their port, while the southern part of the country was incorporated in the Visigothic kingdom. Surviving buildings from the Visigoth period are the Byzantine-style chapel of São Frutuoso, near Braga, and the hall-church of São Pedro de Balsemão at Lamego.

**Moors**

After the battle of La Janda in 711 Portugal fell into the hands of the Moors, but was of relatively minor importance compared with the Spanish part of the Caliphate. Lisbon, now known as Al Oshbuna or Lashbuna, probably changed relatively little under Moorish rule; the castle, originally built by the Visigoths in the 5th c. (now the Castelo de São Jorge), became the Moorish king's residence. Moorish rule seems to have left a more obvious mark on the Algarve, and certain features (house types, chimneys) are often ascribed to Moorish influence – though it must be said that this has not been established beyond doubt. Buildings of the Moorish period – and indeed of the migration period – are few and far between in Portugal, but the churches at Mértola and Lourosa (10th c.) are based on Moorish models.

**Reconquista**

The Reconquista, the recovery of Christian territory from the Moors, left a distinctive imprint on Portugal. Starting from Asturias in the middle of the 8th c., it moved south stage by stage and was concluded by the occupation of the Algarve in 1249.

**Romanesque**

The art and architecture of the Romanesque period in Portugal were influenced both by the magnificent cathedral of Santiago de Compostela in north-west Spain and by the architecture of France (particularly Auvergne and Normandy). Evidence of these influences can be seen in the cathedrals (originally designed as defensive structures) of Lisbon, Coimbra, Évora, Oporto and Braga.

Lisbon Cathedral (the Sé: Latin *sedes*, the "seat" of the bishop; see A to Z Lisbon), the oldest church in the city, is said to have been built by Afonso Henriques in 1147 on the site of an earlier mosque. Over the centuries it was much altered and rebuilt, and its Romanesque lantern tower and Gothic choir were destroyed by the 1755 earthquake; but the Romanesque nave, triforium and aisles still survive. The fortress-like west front dates from 1380. The cloister contains a fine Romanesque wrought-iron screen. Oporto Cathedral (see A to Z), also built in the 12th c. on the site of a Suevic castle, was originally Gothic but was completely rebuilt in the 17th and 18th c. There are remains of a late Romanesque cloister and its Gothic successor of 1385. The interior is notable for its richly decorated altars (silver Altar of the Sacrament, 1632–72). The Old Cathedral of Coimbra (see A to Z), built by Afonso Henriques in 1170, has a sumptuously decorated west doorway surmounted by a balcony and a window. The richly decorated north doorway (Porta Especiosa, c. 1530), like the severe 12th c. façade, betrays French influence. The high altar, in Flamboyant style, is of polychrome carved wood (by Oliver of Ghent and John of Ypres, 1503); the Manueline font is by John of Rouen. Braga Cathedral (see A to Z), begun in 1180 was much altered in later centuries, and the Romanesque cloister (1110) was demolished in the 18th c. Évora Cathedral (see A to Z), with its beautiful tower and imposing interior, dates mainly from the 13th c. The last of the great Romanesque cathedrals, it already shows the strong influence of French Gothic.

The order of Templars, which came to Portugal in 1126, began in 1160
to build a new stronghold at Tomar (see A to Z), which in the early
12th c. had stood on the frontier between Christendom and Islam. Little
is left of this fortress but a commanding square watch-tower. After the
suppressions of the Templars the castle was taken over by the order of
the Knights of Christ, which rose to great magnificence, particularly
under the Grand Master Henry the Navigator. The wealthiest order in
Christendom during the reign of Manuel I (1495–1521), this knightly
order became a monastic one in 1523 and was dissolved in 1910. The
Convent-Castle of the Knights of Christ at Tomar is a large complex of
buildings ranging in date from the 12th to the 17th c. and in style from
Romanesque to Baroque. Following the model of the round church
originally built by Constantine the Great over the Holy Sepulchre in
Jerusalem, frequently destroyed and regularly rebuilt, the Templars
built round Churches of the Holy Sepulchre all over Europe. The Templar church at Tomar is a sixteen-sided structure of Syro-Byzantine
type on a centralised plan. It was begun in 1160 with a central octagon,
which in the time of Manuel I became the high choir (*coro alto, capela-
mór*) of the church of the Knights of Christ, the nave of which was
enlarged in Manueline style by Diogo de Arruda after 1510. The magnificent south doorway was the work of João de Castilho (1510). The
conventual buildings around the church have a number of interesting
cloisters.

Little sculpture of the Romanesque period has been preserved in Portugal, and much, even of the monumental sculpture, has been lost. The
only item calling for mention is the tomb of Egas Moniz (1144) in the
Romanesque church of the Benedictine monastery at Paço de Sousa
near Oporto.

The Cistercians, who like the Templars were summoned to Portugal by
Afonso Henriques, built a series of abbey churches which mark the
final establishment of the Gothic style in Portugal. Gothic architecture
was strongly influenced by France; but during the 13th and 14th c.
different European countries evolved their own distinctive variants of
the style.
    The cathedral at Évora, consecrated in 1204, already shows indica-
tions of the transition to a somewhat severer form of Gothic in Portugal.
The Franciscan convent at Santarém (see A to Z), completed in 1240
and now unfortunately in a state of considerable dilapidation, has a
fine cloister of the 13th–15th c. with pointed arches and charming twin
columns.

The Cistercian abbey of Alcobaça (see A to Z), founded by Afonso
Henriques in 1153, was a daughter house of Clairvaux in Burgundy and
is built on the same plan as Clairvaux. The church was consecrated in
1253 but the building of the abbey continued into the 14th c. Much
rebuilding was required to make good the devastation caused by the
1755 earthquake, flooding and Napoleon's troops. The church – an
austere hall-church in early Gothic style with pointed vaulting – contains the tombs of Pedro I and his beloved Inês de Castro, with a
profusion of figural decoration along the sides and recumbent figures
of Pedro and Inês, lying with their feet towards one another so that they
would see one another at once on the day of resurrection (14th c.).
Other notable features in the church are a 17th c. terracotta group
depicting the death of St Bernard and two fine Renaissance doors by
João de Castilho.
    On the north side of the church is the impressive two-storey Claustro
do Silêncio (or Claustro de Dom Dinis), a jewel of Cistercian Gothic
built in 1311 (upper storey 16th c.), with pointed vaulting and triple
windows, separated by twin colonettes and surmounted by rosettes,
opening into the central garden. The two-storey hexagonal fountain-
house has 16th c. relief decoration.

## Art and Culture

Other Gothic
Buildings

The octagonal Dominican church (consecrated 1267) at Elvas (see A to Z), with an azulejo-faced dome supported on columns, is the first master-work of Gothic architecture in Portugal. With its wide aisles and five chapels it is a marvel of simplicity and restrained elegance of proportion. The steadily increasing refinement of Portuguese Gothic, originally somewhat severe, can be observed in the romantic remains of the convent of Santa Clare-a-Velha in Coimbra (1286; see A to Z), now partly silted up by the flooding of the River Mondego (west wall with fine rose window, Renaissance chapels). In addition to the beautiful Gothic cloisters already referred to, which rank among the finest achievements of Gothic architecture in Portugal, with their two tiers of galleries, their sturdy pillars and their graceful arches, mention should also be made of the cloister of Lisbon Cathedral.

During this period King Dinis (1279–1325) caused a series of mighty fortresses to be built along the frontiers of his kingdom – the Torre de Menagem at Bragança, the castle of Leiria (originally founded by Afonso Henriques in 1135 and enlarged by Dinis; the Gothic chapel attributed to Master Huguet of Batalha) and the castle at Beja (see entries A to Z).

Batalha Abbey

The finest example of 14th c. Gothic architecture in Portugal is the church of Batalha Abbey (1388–1402; see A to Z), built to commemorate the decisive Portuguese victory over Castile at Aljubarrota in 1385. One of the great achievements of Christian architecture, the church is now a Portuguese national shrine. The architects involved in building the Batalha church were Afonso Domingues (d. before 1402), Master Huguet, probably a Frenchman (attested until 1438), Martin Vásques (d. before 1448), Fernão d'Évora (d. 1477) and the famous João de Castilho (d. before 1553). The interior of the church, with fine stained glass (particularly in the choir) and massive piers, is of impressive effect. The square Founder's Chapel contains a number of notable tombs – the sarcophagus, supported on lions, of João I (d. 1433) and his English queen, Philippa of Lancaster, and the monuments of the Infante Fernardo (Caldéron's "Steadfast Prince") and Henry the Navigator (d. 1460). The west front of the church with its sculptural decoration and the richly articulated south side are seen to particular effect, due to the open location of the church. Adjoining the church are three cloisters – the Claustro de João III (destroyed in 1811), the 15th c. Claustro de Dom Afonso V with its simple lines and the Claustro Real, a truly royal cloister laid out around a garden-like court which is a masterpiece and a perfect exemplar of Portuguese Gothic, with arched galleries which range from the simplest forms to fantastic riots of Manueline ornament and offer charming glimpses of the fountain-house. On the east side of the cloister is the chapterhouse, with pointed vaulting. At the east end of the church are the Capelas Imperfeitas (Unfinished Chapels), with seven funerary chapels enclosing a central octagon; the tombs include those of King Duarte I and his wife Eleanor of Aragon.

Gothic Sculpture

Cistercian Gothic paid little attention to sculpture: only funerary sculpture flourished. Notable among tombs of the 14th c. are those of Archbishop Gonçalo Pereira (1336) in Braga Cathedral, and of Pedro I and Inês de Castro at Alcobaça which have already been referred to.

**Manueline Style**

The period of prosperity and cultural flowering in the reign of Manuel I (1495–1521) led to the emergence of a "Batalha school" and the development of a distinctively Portuguese version of late Gothic. This Manueline style incorporates Early Renaissance features, elements taken over from the Moorish Mudéjar style and Oriental and Indian influences. It is notable for its delightful ornament, which – as in the Plat
eresque style of Spain – often includes naturalistic details,

with a marked preference for the world of the sea and seafaring (e.g. twisted ropes, knots, shells, coral, etc.), symbolising the territories which Portugal had won under the leadership of Henry the Navigator.

The most striking example of the Manueline style is the Hieronymite convent at Belém (now a suburb of Lisbon; see A to Z), which miraculously survived the 17th c. earthquake unscathed. Designed by an architect named Boytac (Boitac, Boytaca, Boutaca, etc.; see Famous People), probably a Frenchman, it was begun in 1502. The south doorway of the church has a profusion of sculptural decoration expressing the new power and wealth of Portugal. The west doorway, strongly reminiscent of a doorway at Champmol, near Dijon (Burgundy), was the work of Nicolas Chanterene. The interior of the church, of the type known as *igrejas salões* (saloon churches), is notable for its width and fine proportions and for the delicately carved decoration of the piers. The church contains the sarcophagus of Vasco da Gama and the cenotaph (empty tomb) of the poet Luís de Camões. Adjoining the church is a magnificent two-storey cloister. Both the church and the cloister were completed by João Castilho, the great master of the Manueline style.

*Hieronymite Convent at Belém*

Another splendid Manueline building is the Tower of Belém (Torre de Belém; see A to Z Lisbon) commanding the Tagus estuary, built between 1515 and 1521 by Francisco Arruda, brother of the famous architect Diogo de Arruda who worked at Tomar. With its flat domes, elegant loggias, Arab-style twin windows and intricate stone tracery the Tower is of strikingly Arab and Moorish style.

Other fine examples of the Manueline style at Batalha and Tomar have already been mentioned. Also of interest is the famous Manueline window of the old chapterhouse at Tomar (by Diogo de Arruda) with its striking and very typical ornament, here carried to excess.

*Other Manueline Buildings*

*Hieronymite Convent in Belém*

## Art and Culture

Sintra, once the summer residence of the Portuguese kings, has three castles – the Castelo dos Mouros, the old Moorish castle (7th–8th c., much altered in later periods), the Palácio da Pena (19th c.) and the Paço Real or Royal Palace (14th–15th/16th c.), on the foundations of an earlier Moorish castle; it is built in a Manueline style which shows clear Mudéjar influence.

Manueline
Sculpture

The Manueline style laid great stress on architectural sculpture, and Coimbra became the place of origin of two schools of sculpture, one of which, stimulated by influence from Rouen, played an important part in bringing the Renaissance to Portugal. Nicolas Chanterene was responsible for the north doorway of the abbey church at Belém and for the tombs of Afonso Henriques and his son Sancho I in the church of the Santa Cruz convent at Coimbra, while to John of Rouen (João de Ruão) is attributed the Porta Especiosa of the Old Cathedral, Coimbra. Other notable foreign sculptors working in Portugal were Loguin and Oliver of Ghent (polychrome wood sculpture in the dome of the Rotunda at Tomar). The other, more "national" school continued to work in the traditional style; a leading member of the school was Diogo Pires the Younger. Fine work was still produced in the field of funerary sculpture (tomb monuments), while the goldsmith's art which had long flourished in Portugal created some of its finest achievements.

Pelourinhos

Between the 12th and the 18th c. the stone columns known as *pelourinhos* or pillories were erected in towns and villages all over Portugal. They were not, however, primarily designed for the punishment of thieves and other criminals but were emblems of municipal or feudal authority (*pelouro* = local authority). This function explains both the form of the pelourinhos, which are often elaborately decorated, and the choice of site, usually near areas of secular or ecclesiastical

*Pelourinhos are seen everywhere: Oporto . . . . . . and in Barcelos*

60

*Pelourinho in Óbidos . . .*                    *. . . and in Elvas*

authority such as town halls and bishop's palaces. The pelourinhos erected in the 16th c. have the sumptuous decoration of the Manueline style. Columns of this type are particularly numerous, reflecting the large number of communities which were granted charters of privileges by Manuel I.

The shaft of the column, richly decorated, may be cylindrical, conical, prismatic or spiral in form; occasionally it may resemble an obelisk. The summit also has sculptural decoration, often including the sword of justice as a symbol of legal jurisdiction.

The Mudéjar style is the particular architectural and decorative style practised by the Moors who were allowed to stay on after the Reconquest and by Christians imitating them. It is basically a late Gothic style incorporating Moorish elements, and often with Manueline features. Particular marks of Moorish influence are the beautiful dark-coloured coffered ceilings and above all the use of azulejos, one of the most characteristic features of Portuguese art.

**Mudéjar Style**

Everywhere in Portugal, as well as in Madeira and the Azores, practically every church, chapel and convent, most palaces and country houses and the walls of countless other buildings are decorated with the glazed ornamental tiles known as azulejos.

**Azulejos**

Azulejos – which probably get their name from the Arabic, *az-zuleycha*, for mosaic pieces, rather than *azul*, which is Spanish/Portuguese for blue – were originally imported into Portugal in the early 16th c. from Spain, where they were made by Moorish craftsmen in blue and other ground colours, with geometric patterns in relief. After the Moors were expelled from Spain towards the end of the 16th c. and Moorish-made tiles were no longer available, numbers of azulejo factories were established in Portugal (particularly in Lisbon, Oporto and Coimbra), producing Portuguese tiles with new decorative motifs. These tiles,

*Glazed tile decoration in Estoi*

however, were no longer made in relief patterns but were flat, in the manner of Italian and Flemish majolica. They were now given a white tin glaze on which the designs were painted in metallic pigments. What is probably the oldest tile picture in Portugal, dating from 1565, is to be seen in the Quinta de Bacalhoa, to the west of Setúbal.

Characteristic of the 17th c. are the "tile tapestries" (*tapetes*), with a great variety of patterns in blue, white and yellow. Mass production of azulejos began with the establishment by King José in 1767 of the Royal Factory (Real Fábrica do Rato) at Lisbon. Every conceivable surface – the walls of churches, staircases, fountains, benches, the exterior and interior walls of palaces, kitchens, etc. – was now covered with tiles.

In the early 19th c., when the court fled to Brazil and the country was convulsed by civil war, the production of azulejos ceased almost completely, but in the middle of the century they enjoyed a revival of popularity. Following the Brazilian model, tiles now began to be used for the decoration, both externally and internally, of ordinary middle-class houses and commercial, municipal and other public buildings throughout the country. There was a final flowering of the art of the azulejo at the turn of the 19th c.

Tile-clad buildings have the advantage over stone or plaster surfaces that they retain a fresh, trim appearance – although the more recent azulejos, mass-produced in standard designs, are seldom of high artistic quality. Present-day azulejo factories – notably three large firms in Lisbon – concentrate mainly on reproductions of old designs and export most of their output (mainly to the United States, Germany and Holland).

A good impression of the range and variety of Portuguese azulejos is provided by the Azulejo Museum in the Madre de Deus convent, the cloisters of the old Augustinian house of São Vincente de Fora and the Fronteira Palace, all in Lisbon.

Portugal's political and economic decline, beginning at the end of the heroic age after the disastrous Moroccan campaign of 1580, also had its effect on the country's artistic development.

The choir of the monastic church at Belém betrays the influence of the High Renaissance (marble choir-stalls; royal tombs supported on marble elephants). But on the whole the Renaissance – its influence postponed and weakened by the great flowering of the Manueline style – never really established itself in Portugal, in spite of the country's intensive cultural and economic contacts with Italy, but remained a phenomenon of merely marginal importance.

An example of Late Renaissance architecture, though much influenced by the Manueline style, is the Claustro dos Filipes, the main cloister of the Convent-Castle of Tomar (see A to Z). This was begun by João de Castilho, but work was suspended after his death in 1551, and when it was resumed in 1562 the Neo-Classical Palladian style had come into fashion. The new architects were either trained in Italy, like Diogo de Torralva, or were themselves Italian, like Filippo Terzi. The latter built the church of São Roque in Lisbon (façade rebuilt after the 1755 earthquake; see A to Z), a fine example of the Jesuit style, with an impressive interior (trompe-l'oeil painting). The church contains a masterpiece of the most sumptuous Italian Baroque in the form of the Chapel of St John the Baptist, originally built in Rome in 1742, then dismantled and re-erected in São Roque in the reign of João V. The church of São Vicente de Fora in Lisbon (the tower of which collapsed in the 1755 earthquake) was also built by Terzi.

The influence of foreign artists remained considerable after the Portuguese revival (under the Portuguese kings of the House of Bragança from 1640): the native power of artistic creation appeared to be exhausted.

The development of Portuguese painting followed a roughly parallel course to that of Spain. The first individual artistic personality emerged in Nuno Gonçalves (active between 1450 and 1480), whose principal work is the famous altarpiece, the "Adoration of St Vincent", a polyptych with numerous figures which clearly shows the influence of Flemish models (Museu Nacional de Arte Antiga, Lisbon). There followed a flowering of late medieval painting which lasted until the middle of the 16th c., its finest achievements being in the field of portraiture.

In addition to Gonçalves, leading figures of this period included Jorge Afonso (d. after 1540) who had a studio in Lisbon, Guilherme de Belles, João Mestre (d. 1528), Luis de Velasco, António Taca and Vasco Fernandes (b. about 1542), known as Grão Vasco, who worked in Viseu (works in Museu Grão Vasco, Viseu).

During the reign of João III the Dutch "Romanist" school exerted still stronger influence on Portuguese painters including Gregório Lopes (d. 1550: "Salome", "St Augustine"), but particularly on Cristóvão de Figueiredo (attested between 1515 and 1540: retable on high altar of Santa Cruz church, Coimbra) and the Master of Santa Auta ("Martyrdom of the 11,000 Virgins", Museu Nacional de Arte Antiga, Lisbon).

The next generation of painters – represented, for example, by Cristóvão Lopes (1516–1606) – show Italian influence, now coming direct and no longer through Flemish intermediaries. The old tradition of portrait-painting, a notable practitioner of which was Cristóvão de Morais, declined in importance with the departure of A. Sanchez Coelho (1513–90) for the Spanish court.

During the Baroque period painting was of subordinate importance, being used mainly for the decoration of palaces and the vaulting of churches. Painters of this period include Francisco Vieira Lusitano (1699–1783), the fresco-painter Domingos António de Sequeira (1769–

1837), Francisco Portuense (1765–1805) and Pedro Carvalho Alexan-
drino (1730–1810).

**Baroque**

In the field of Baroque architecture a leading place is occupied by the
massive complex at Mafra (see A to Z), planned on the model of the
Spanish Escorial to include a royal palace, a church and a monastery in
a unified group and built between 1717 and 1770. This enormous
building, designed by two German architects, Johann Friedrich Ludwig and his son Johann Peter Ludwig, broke away from the severity of
Spanish Baroque with its profusion of decoration and its chinoiserie
and influenced a whole architectural generation in the late Baroque
and Rococo periods, which became steadily more luxuriant and fantastic. At the same time there was a great flowering of azulejos.

**Taljas douradas**

In the early Baroque period there first appears in Portugal an ornate
form of decorative art which was to achieve its finest flowering here,
though it was also practised in Spain and other countries. This was the
wood sculpture covered with gold leaf known as talhas douradas,
predominantly used in religious art. In many 18th c. churches in Portugal altars, walls, recesses, domes and ceilings were covered either in
whole or in part with carving of this kind, foliage and arabesques
combining with figures in rich decorative patterns.

**Foreign Influences**

Foreign architects also worked in Oporto, where an Italian, Nicoló
Mazzoni, built the church of the Clérigos with its fine Capela-mór and
famous tower (1732–48). The French architect J. B. Robillon completed
the royal palace at Queluz, which had been begun in 1758 by Mateus
Vicente (1747–86) on the model of Versailles – a likeness which is
enhanced by the park, laid out in the style of Le Nôtre. The interior is of
great magnificence, the Throne Room and the Hall of the Ambassadors
being particularly fine.

**Baroque Sculpture**

The sculpture of the Baroque period – affected, like architecture and
painting, by Portugal's cultural decline in the 17th c. – can claim few
artists of any importance apart from Joaquim Machado de Castro
(1736–1828), whose vigorous work can be seen on the sumptuous
façade of the late Baroque Basílica da Estrêla in Lisbon, built in the
Roman style at the end of the 18th c.

**Planned
Redevlopment of
Lisbon**

The great earthquake on All Saints Day in 1755, which laid Lisbon in
ruins and spread alarm throughout Europe, offered a unique opportunity for architects and town planners, which José I's chief minister the
Marquês de Pombal, ruling in the spirit of enlightened absolutism, was
quick to grasp. Rebuilt under the direction of Eugénio dos Santos,
Lisbon became one of the finest capitals in Europe.
   The new town thus created (though the wide Avenida da Liberdade
and the Praça do Marquês de Pombal, with the huge monument to
Pombal, were not completed until the end of the 19th c.) is laid out on
spacious lines. Streets intersect at right angles and there are three
superb squares: the Praça da Figueira, the even larger Praça de Dom
Pedro IV (Rossio) and the Praça do Comércio (Terreiro do Paça), one
of the most famous squares in the world, with an equestrian statue of
José I (by Joaquim Machado de Castro, 1755). The uniform layout of
the square and its three ranges of arcaded buildings with coloured
façades contrast attractively with the surprising width of the fourth
side, and with its marble steps leading down to the Tagus, is reminiscent of St Mark's Square in Venice.

**Neo-Classicism**

After the catastrophe of the 1775 earthquake there was a general
reaction against the decorative excesses of Baroque and Rococo, and a
more sober neo-classicism came into vogue. In Lisbon work began in
1802 on the Palácio da Ajuda, which remained unfinished and has been

completed only in recent years as a convention complex; the Teatro Nacional de Dona Maria II was built on the Rossio in 1846. In Oporto the church of the Third Order of St Francis was built, not to be confused with the adjoining church of São Francisco, originally Gothic, with a Renaissance doorway altered in the Baroque period.

Although the Neo-Classical school of architecture long remained dominant, the school known as Historicism, with its romantic leanings towards the past, became established in Portugal, as elsewhere in Europe, in the second half of the 19th c. French influence can be detected but so, too, can influences from Britain and Germany, as in the Palácio da Pena at Sintra (1840–50; see A to Z), built for Ferdinand of Saxe-Coburg-Koháry by Baron Eschwege in the style of a medieval castle (borrowing some ideas from the extraordinary castles built for King Ludwig II of Bavaria). This fantastic mixture of styles – Arab, Gothic, Manueline, Renaissance, Baroque – has a curious charm. A striking and typical feature is the monstrous figure above the main entrance, a riot of fancy which is half man, half fish or tree. Other examples of Historicist architecture are the Moorish-style bullring in the Campo Pequeno in Lisbon (1892) and the Palace Hotel in the beautiful Buçaco Forest (now a national park, with many rare trees), a Neo-Manueline structure built at the end of the 19th c. as a royal summer residence.

**Historicism**

Portugal is especially rich in fine parks and gardens, illustrating the development of landscape architecture from the Moorish style by way of the formal gardens of the Baroque period to the more natural English style.

Parks and Gardens

Modern art and architecture were slow to establish themselves in Portugal. Gustave Eiffel, best known for the Eiffel Tower in Paris, built the Ponte de Dom Luís I in Oporto, the famous two-storey bridge which spans the Douro at an impressive height (1877–78), and was also responsible for the Elevador de Santa Justa, the lift which links the upper and lower towns of Lisbon. About 1940 the massive complex of the University City (Cidade Universitária) was built in Lisbon. The monumental style of an authoritarian regime found expression in the huge figure of Christ the King (1959) on the left bank of the Tagus near Lisbon and the 52m/170ft high Monument of the Discoveries (Padrão dos Descrombrimentos, 1960) on the banks of the Tagus at Belém. The Ponte do 25 de Abril (originally Ponte Salazar, 1966), a suspension bridge 2227m/2436yd long which provides a rapid link between Lisbon and southern Portugal, is an impressive technological achievement.

**Modern**

Opinions are divided on the "post-modern" architecture of the Eighties. One of the country's best-known architects is currently Tomás Taveira whose Amoreiras Center in Lisbon is one of Portugal's largest and most elegant shopping malls.

In painting, developments in the 19th c. followed the general European pattern. Notable figures during this period were the portrait-painter Miguel Lupi (1826–83), Tomás de Anunciação (1818–79) and the landscape artist António Carvalho da Silva (1850–93). The "Grupo de Leão", established in 1881, had close affinities with Impressionism. The portrait and fresco painter Columbano (1867–1929) remained within the romantic tradition. Other schools also had their adherents, including Fauvism, Cubism – a leading representative of which was Amadeu de Souza Cardoso (1887–1918) – and a rather strident revolutionary Naturalism. Between the two world wars the Futurist Almada Negreiros gained a considerable reputation with his tapestries and frescoes.

19th and 20th c. Painting

*Lisbon: Monument of the Discoveries . . .*     *. . . and the bridge over the Tagus*

The Salazar regime discouraged artists with unduly progressive leanings, and only after the "Carnation Revolution" of 1974 did Portuguese art fall into line with the international movements of the day. A great reputation is enjoyed by the Franco-Portuguese woman painter Maria Helena Vieira da Silva (b. 1908). Lourdés Castro (b. 1930 in Funchalm, Madeira) is a sculptress whose figures are mounted on coloured plastic panels.

House Types in Rural Portugal

Situated as it is on the western margin of Europe, exposed to influences from other countries only on the north and east, Portugal has developed its own distinctive house types, particularly in rural areas. As in many southern countries, building is mostly in stone. The peasants' houses and farmhouses usually have no more than two storeys.

In Minho the two-storey house type is common, with stables and working areas on the lower floor and living accommodation on the upper storey, usually opening on to a balcony and reached by an external stair. Characteristic features of this northern region are the *espigueiros*, small granaries or storehouses built on piles and constructed either of granite or timber.

Farther south, where Moorish influence can be detected, the house fronts are mostly whitewashed, with the doors and window-frames painted in vivid colours. Depending on the local topography, single-storey farmhouses become more common. The doors and windows are smaller in order to keep out the heat of summer. Since the winters become more severe with increasing distance from the moderating influence of the Atlantic, open fires are more usual in the inland regions and the chimney becomes a prominent feature of the house.

In the deep south of the country, the Algarve, the single-storey house is predominant, frequently in the shape of a cube. Flat roofs are sometimes used to collect rainwater, which is then stored in a cistern.

*A farmstead in the south of Portugal (Algarve)*

Particularly characteristic of the Algarve are the richly decorated chimneys with their lantern-like tops.

In no other country in Europe are there so many water mills and windmills still working as in Portugal. There are some thousands of water mills of different types (azenhas with vertical wheels, sesicas with horizontal wheels) on rivers, streams and reservoirs all over the country, used for grinding corn but more particularly, and increasingly, for irrigating fields and gardens.

Water Mills and Windmills

In parts of the country with little water or wind power winches or gins are used, worked either by animal power or by an engine. Visitors to Portugal are more likely, however, to be impressed by the characteristic old windmills (first referred to in the 13th c.) which are still to be seen in considerable numbers, adding a picturesque touch to the landscape. The mills are usually round, with a conical roof. The triangular sails are suspended between long wooden spokes which form a giant wheel. There are sometimes clay vessels attached to the ropes which make a whistling sound as the sails turn in the wind.

## Literature

The development of literature in Portugal went in step with the formation of the Portuguese nation-state and the sense of national and linguistic identity in the Portuguese people. Throughout this period of development and down to modern times the characteristic features of Portuguese literature have been a rather melancholy sensibility, marked national feeling and a leaning towards criticism of the society of the day; and this Portuguese sensibility is underlined by the soft and gentle tonal colouring of the language.

# Literature

Middle Ages

The earliest courtly lyric poetry, found in the neighbouring region of Galicia as well as in Portugal, had its leading practitioners in King Alfonso X of Castile (d. 1284) and Kings Sancho I (1185–1211) and Dinis I (1279–1325) of Portugal. This poetry consists exclusively of songs in Provençal style, some 2000 of which – love songs (*cantigas de amor*), women's songs (*cantigas de amigo*) and satirical songs (*cantigas de maldizer*) – are preserved in three collections, the "Cancioneiro da Ajuda", the "Cancioneiro da Vaticana" and the "Cancioneiro Colocci-Brancuti".

In the 14th c. this poetry rapidly declined in quality and the first cautious beginnings of prose writing appeared, at first taking the form of works written for a practical purpose: genealogical registers recording the lineage of noble families (*livros de linhagem*) and dry chronicles of modest literary pretension but great documentary value. During this period translations of religious and edifying works from Latin, French and Spanish were also produced. Then towards the end of the century lyric poetry enjoyed an astonishing renaissance under the influence of the Galician troubadour Macias o Enamorado ("Macias the Enamoured").

The beginning of the 15th c. brought a temporary decline in the literary use of Portuguese, and Castilian usage increasingly asserted itself in the written language. The work of the "palace poets" (*poetas palacianos*) who now came into fashion was collected by Garcia de Resenda in his "Cancioneiro geral".

Humanism

With the Renaissance and the great voyages of discovery by Portuguese navigators the ideas of humanism gained entry to the court, and literature, particularly prose writing, enjoyed generous royal patronage. Prominent in this respect were King Duarte I (1391–1438) and his brother Dom Pedro (1392–1449) the authors of treatises on moral philosophy of no great literary merit. Historical writing was institutionalised by the creation of the post of historiographer royal, and Fernão Lopes (*c.* 1384–*c.* 1460), Gomes Eanes de Zurura (*c.* 1410–73), Rui de Pina (*c.* 1440–*c.* 1522) and João de Barros (*c.* 1496–1570) wrote works showing a very modern objectivity. Unofficial chronicles of a more speculative and picturesque character were written by Damião de Gois (1502–74), Caspar Correia (*c.* 1495–*c.* 1565), Fernão Lopes de Castanheda (*c.* 1500–59) and Fernão Mendes Pinto (*c.* 1510–*c.* 1583).

Other genres which now established themselves were the bucolic poems of Bernardim Ribeiro (1482–1552; "Saudades") and Cristóvão Falcão, whose existence in the first half of the 16th c. is still the subject of dispute, and the pastoral plays of Gil Vicente (*c.* 1465–*c.* 1540), who thus introduced the drama to the court and into Portuguese literature, always taking his subjects from popular life. During this period, too, Francisco Sá de Miranda (*c.* 1481–1558) introduced Italian stylistic features in his sonnets, canções and comedies; and while these, like the sensitive lyric poetry of António Ferreira (1528–69) and Diogo Bernardes (1530–1600), enjoyed great success they did not displace the more popularly written works of other contemporaries such as Gonçalo Eanes Bandarra.

Luís Vaz de Camões

In the second half of the 16th c. Portuguese literature gained international status with the appearance of the country's greatest writer, Luís Vaz de Camões (see Famous People). After a life of adventure and many vicissitudes he glorified the achievements of the Portuguese people in the national epic "Os Lusiadas" ("The Lusiads", 1572; after Lusus, the legendary ancestor of the Portuguese), which exerted a powerful influence on the Portuguese literature of the day and later periods. Camões' wide-ranging and sensitive work, often reflecting his own experiences, attracted numerous imitators, who treated similar national themes with markedly inferior talent, setting the pattern for Portuguese literature until the beginning of the 17th c.

The period of decline during the Baroque age in the 17th c. brought a return to the old forms of bucolic poetry and religious and moralising prose. The personal union with Spain, seen by the Portuguese as the imposition of foreign rule, led to an increase in the cultural and linguistic influence of Castile and a decline in the writing of Portuguese. Only Franciso Rodrigues Lobo (1580–1622), with his idyllic pastoral poems, Francisco Manuel de Melo (1608–66), Manuel de Sousa Coutinho, known as Frei Luís de Sousa (c. 1555–1632), and the Jesuit preacher António de Vieira (1608–97) achieved reputations which outlasted their own day.

At the turn of the 17th c. the Enlightenment, coming from France, began to make headway in Portugal, where it took on a curiously melancholy note. The 18th c. was the heyday of various literary societies committed to the renewal of literature, the most notable being the "Arcádia Lusitana" (1757–74) and the "Nova Arcádia" (1790–94), with such figures as Francisco Manuel do Nascimento (1734–1819), a committed opponent of rhyme in poetry, António Correia (1724–72), José Agostinho Macedo (1761–1831) and Manuel Maria Barbosa do Bocage (1765–1805). All these writers sought to renew Portuguese drama in the classical style.

The prose writing of the later 18th c. consisted mainly of reports, letters and didactic works by such writers as the diplomat Francisco Xavier de Oliveira (1702–82), António da Costa (d. 1780), António Nunes (d. 1783) and Luís António Verney (1718–92), António José da Silva (1705–39) wrote librettos for puppet operas on popular themes.

After 1825 the Romantic movement, coming from Germany, France and Britain, began to make rapid headway in Portugal. Fostered and emotionally reinforced by the serious and sentimental cast of mind of the Portuguese, it soon led to a new flowering of the national literature. The first Portuguese Romantics and the most brilliant representatives of the movement were João Baptista de Silva Leitão de Almeida Garrett (1799–1854), author of romances, epics and lyrical dramas, and Alexandre Herculano de Carvalho e Araújo (1810–77), a historian who also wrote historical novels. Historical novels and novels of manners were written by Camilo Castelo Branco (Visconde de Correia Botelho, 1825–90), Augusto Rebelo da Silva, Pinheiro Chagas and others, novels of country life and love by Júlio Dinis (pseudonym of Joaquim Guilherme Gomes; 1839–71).

The excesses of Romanticism were countered from 1865 onwards by the "Coimbra school", the leader of which was João de Deus Nogueira Ramos (1830–96). Towards the end of the century this developed into a Realist school, with such writers as Antero de Quental (1842–91), José Maria Eça de Queirós (1845–1900) and Teófilo Braga (1843–1924).

The first decades of the 20th c. were notable for their lyric poetry. Symbolism, largely concerned with patriotic themes, was represented by António Nobre (1867–1900), Camilo Pessanha (1867–1926), Eugénio de Castro e Almeida (1869–1944) and Mário de Sá-Carneiro (1890–1916), who founded the review "Orpheu" in 1915. The "Saudosismo" of Texeira de Pascoaes (1877–1952) took on an almost messianic tone. The literary review "Aguia", published between 1910 and 1932, provided a forum for the writers of the period. One of the major lyric poets of recent times was Fernando António Nogueira Pessoa (1888–1935), who grew up in South Africa and wrote some of his work in English. Like his contemporaries he had a strong sense of mission, and with his linguistic virtuosity and profundity of content he exerted an influence which extended beyond the bounds of Portugal, impinging on both the English Romantics and the French Symbolists. Together with José Régio (pseudonym of José Maria dos Reis Pereira, 1901–69) Pessoa

*Baroque Poetry*

*Enlightenment*

*Romantic Movement*

*Realism*

*20th Century*

introduced the modern movement in Portuguese literature, which found a mouthpiece in the review "Presença" (1927–40). Other representatives of this trend are Vitorino Nemésio (Vitorino Nemésio Mendes Pinheiro da Silva, b. 1901), José Sobral Almada-Negreiros (b. 1893) and Miguel Torga (pseudonym of Adolfo Correia da Rocha, b. 1907).

In more recent times there has been a trend, in both poetry and prose, towards neo-realism and social criticism. Among notable lyric poets are José Gomes Ferreira (b. 1900), Eugénio de Andrade (b. 1923) and Alberto de Lacerda (b. 1928); among novelists and short story writers Raul Brandão (1867–1930), Aquilino Ribeiro (1885–1963), José Maria Ferreira de Castro (b. 1898), António Alves Redol (1901–69), Fernando Namora (b. 1919) and Carlos de Oliveira (b. 1921).

Since the revolution of 1974, which put an end to a long period of authoritarian government, liberal and more particularly socialist ideas have increasingly found expression in literature: thus Manuel Alegre (b. 1936), while actively engaged in politics, has also made a name for himself as a writer.

Luso-Brazilian
Literature

Until the end of the 18th c. Luso-Brazilian literature was a mere off-shoot of Portuguese literature and wholly under the influence of mainland Portugal. At the turn of the century there were signs of a distinctively Brazilian approach, particularly in religious writings, and with the separation of Brazil from Portugal in the mid 19th c. this trend was strengthened.

## Music

Middle Ages

From the earliest days of Portugal's existence as an independent state there is evidence in both literature and art of a distinctive Galician/Portuguese musical culture.

Composed music (as distinct from folk music) went through the same phases of development in Portugal as in other European countries. Various song-books of the 12th–14th c. ("Cancioneiro da Ajuda", "Cancioneiro de Colocci-Brancuti", "Cancioneiro da Vaticana") have been preserved, but these give only the texts, not the music. During this period the art of the troubadours flourished at the courts, particularly in Lisbon, producing distinctively Portuguese genres in the *cantares de amigo* and *cantares de escarnio e maldizer*. The songs of the troubadours were accompanied on various instruments, including the fiddle, the psaltery, the harp, the rattle, the tambourine and the gittern (a seven-stringed plucked instrument with a cranked neck). During the 15th c. Portuguese music was exposed to increased influence from other countries (England, Burgundy, the Low Countries) as a result of the royal family's foreign alliances and the growth in trade. Singing to the accompaniment of a guitar or a keyboard instrument enjoyed a considerable vogue. Two song-books of this period, "De Palacio" and "Da Biblioteca Publia Hortênsia", contain part-songs with Galician/Portuguese texts. Music also played an important part in theatrical performances (singspiels).

Gil Vicente

At the court of Manuel I, Gil Vicente (c. 1465–1540) performed his famous autos (Corpus Christi plays) and tragi-comedies, in which both instrumental and vocal music figured prominently, using such musical forms as the *vilancico*, the *chacota*, the *folia* and the *entrada*, the forerunner of the early Baroque toccata.

16th and 17th c.

In the 16th and 17th c. polyphonic instrumental and vocal music enjoyed a great flowering (motets, cantatas, masses, psalms), influenced by the Dutch music of the period. Notable names include Damião de Goes (1502–74), António Pinheiro (c. 1530–90), Vicente Lusitano

(c. 1550–1610), Cosme Delgado (1540–1603), Manuel Mendes (c. 1547–1605), D. Lobo (1565–1646) and J. L. Rebello (1609–61).

Fine music for keyboard instruments (organ, harpsichord) was written by António Carreira (1590–1650) and Duarte Lobo (c. 1570–1643), while Manuel Cardoso (1571–1650), Pedro Vaz (c. 1585–1640) and Alejandro de Aguiar (c. 1590–1645) wrote mainly for the guitar.

In 1620 Manuel Rodrigues Coelho (c. 1580–after 1633) published his "Flores de Música para o instrumento de Tecla e Harpa" – the first printed instrumental music in Portugal.

During the 18th c., in spite of increasing Italian influence, the instrumental music of José António Carlos de Seixas (1704–42), Frederico Jacinto (1700–55) and João de Sousa Carvalho (1720–98) shows a characteristically Portuguese lyrical sensibility. 18th c.

The main contribution to the music of the 18th c. was made by opera. In 1733 the poet António José da Silva (1705–39), known as "O Judeo" ("the Jew"), and the composer António Teixeiras founded a musical puppet theatre where they put on popular shows (satires, parodies) resembling singspiels. Da Silva wrote pieces such as "Os Encantos", "O Labirinto de Creta" and the puppet opera "Guerras do alecrim e da mangerona" ("Wars of Rosemary and Marjoram", first performed during the Carnival in 1737). Accused by the Inquisition of heresy, da Silva was burned at the stake in 1739 at the age of 34.

King João V (who married Maria Ana of Austria in 1708) was a great lover of Italian opera, and accordingly this came to dominate the musical scene in Portugal as it did in other countries. The king sent Portuguese composers to Italy to study and brought Italians to his court as teachers. Among them was Domenico Scarlatti, who was court harpsichordist at Lisbon from 1721 to 1725 and composed many of his famous sonatas there.

In 1732 the first Italian touring company came to Portugal. The leading representative of Portuguese opera in the Italian style was Franciso António de Almeida (d. about 1765; "Il Pentimento de Davide", "La Finta pazza"), whose opera buffa "La Pazienza di Socrate" was performed in the Teatro Paco da Ribeira in 1733, the first opera written by a Portuguese composer. Marcos da Fonseca Portugal (1762–1830; "La morte di Semiramide", "Le nozze di Figaro", "Zaira"), long-time director of the Teatro de São Carlos in Lisbon, also made a major contribution to the creation of opera in Portuguese.

The 1755 earthquake destroyed Lisbon's five opera-houses, and it was nearly 40 years before the new Teatro de São Carlos was built on the initiative of Diogo de Pina Manique. It was opened in 1793 with a performance of Domenico Cimarosa's work "La Ballerina amante", and is still Portugal's leading opera-house. Famous foreign singers and instrumentalists (including Franz List in 1845) performed there, and by 1910 more than 60 operas by Portuguese composers had been produced. The great majority of the operas were performed in Italian, but Gounod's "Faust" was sung in French in 1884 and Wagner's "Ring" in German in 1909. Teatro de São<br/>Carlos

In the 19th c. Portuguese composers turned mainly to the romantic opera, reflecting both French and German (from 1850 Wagner) influence in their work. The foundation of the Philharmonic Academy (1838) and the Lisbon Conservatoire by João Alberto Rodrigues da Costa (1798–1870) and João Domingos Bomtempo (1775–1842) enriched the quality of Portuguese musical life in an enduring fashion. 19th c.

Francisco Xavier Migone (1811–61) wrote two operas ("Sampiero", "Mocana") which were performed in the Teatro de São Carlos; Francisco Norberto dos Santos Pinto (1815–60) composed much music for the theatre and ballet as well as church music. Eugénio Ricardo Monteiro d'Almeda (1826–98) wrote operas and sacred music, including a

"Libera me" which was highly praised by Rossini. Francisco de Freitas Gazul (1842–1925) composed one opera ("Fra Luigi di Sousa") and numerous operettas, symphonies, oratorios and overtures.

Domingos Ciriaco de Cardoso (1846–1900) ranks as the leading Portuguese operetta composer ("Girofle-Girofle").

Romantic School

Representatives of the Portuguese Romantic school were the composers Augusto Machado (1845–1924) and Alfredo Keil (1850–1907). Machado's main work was in the field of lyric opera, sometimes showing French influence ("Laureana", "Os Dorias"), and in operettas of considerable musical quality ("Ticão Negro", "O Rapto de Helena", "Venus"). Both in his piano music and his songs Keil shows strong national feeling. His song "A Portuguesa" was chosen as the national anthem on the proclamation of the republic in 1910. He also wrote operas ("Serrana", "Irene"), cantatas and symphonic poems ("Uma Caçada na Corte").

20th Century

At the beginning of the 20th c. Portuguese music was in a state of stagnation, having become unduly subject to the influence of Italian music. J. Vianna da Motta (1868–1948), a pupil of Liszt, turned away from Italianism and gave fresh vitality to instrumental music.

With Luís de Freitas Branco (1890–1955) the music of the modern age came to Portugal. In his extensive oeuvre ("Vathek 1914", "Artificial Paradises", symphonies and sonatas for violin and piano) he showed affinities with the atonality of the school of Schönberg and gave a major stimulus to the development of Impressionism in Portuguese music. Rui Coelho (b. 1892) also followed in the footsteps of Schönberg's twelve-tone music ("Camoniana"; "Inês de Castro", 1926), while Frederico de Freitas (b. 1902; "Wall of Contention", "Nazaré") adopted the linear polytonality of Milhaud and Honegger for the first time in his sonata for violin and piano.

Fernando Lopes Graça (b. 1905) represents a Portuguese classical style, devoting himself mainly to the Portuguese folk-song and developing a very personal technique of harmonisation, particularly in the treatment of a cappella voices ("Prayer for the Souls of the Departed", "Traditional Portuguese Christmas Music").

The leading figure among younger Portuguese composers is Jorge Peixinho (b. 1940), who studied in Venice with Luigi Nono and in Basle with Pierre Boulez with the aid of a scholarship from the Gulbenkian Foundation, and worked with Karlheinz Stockhausen in Darmstadt. In 1970 he founded the Contemporary Music Group in Lisbon.

The leading Portuguese orchestra, consisting exclusively of professional musicians, is the National Radio Symphony Orchestra (Emissora Nacional), established in 1934. The Lisbon Opera House, the Teatro São Carlos as well as the Gulbenkian Orchestra, the Gulbenkian Choir and the Gulbenkian Ballet also make their contribution to the musical life of Portugal.

## Folklore

In Portugal, as in all Romance countries, folk festivals, dances and music play a central part in people's lives.

Folk Music

In contrast to Spain, the folk music of Portugal shows little Arab or Moorish influence except in the southerly region of Algarve. The folk dances performed at the numerous religious and secular festivals are usually accompanied by singing and a music accompaniment on traditional instruments such as the guitar (guitarra, viola), fiddle (rabeca), flute (flauta), bagpipe (gaita), drum (tambor) and reque-reque, a percussion instrument, probably of African origin, consisting of reed pipes which struck with a wooden rod.

A specifically Portuguese form of music is the type of song known as
the *fado*. The word fado comes from the Latin fatum, "fate", with which
the Portuguese associate the ideas of misfortune, unhappiness, dis-
aster and destruction.

In many fados the word *saudade* occurs: originally derived from
the Latin *solitudo*, "loneliness", this has acquired connotations of
desolation, homesickness, nostalgia, melancholy and longing for an
apparently unattainable happiness.

The genuine fado always has a note of melancholy. The melody is
usually in a minor key, but even in the major has a tinge of sadness. The
elaborate cadences express selfless devotion on the one hand, theatrical self-pity on the other. Although it is difficult to define in words the
distinctive character of the fado, it always involves an outpouring of
passionate emotional feeling, its words recounting in unaffected bal-
lad form the needs, desires and fortunes of the people, especially the
common people. The Lisbon fado, which can be heard in late evening
sessions in the *casas de fado* of the old town, is always sung by a solo
*fadista*, either female or male. The fadista, usually wearing black, is
accompanied by two guitarists, one playing the melody on the silvery-
toned twelve-stringed guitarra, the other supplying the rhythm on the
six-stringed viola, alternating between tonic and dominant sevenths.

The fado was for long confined to the more disreputable quarters of
Lisbon, and it was only from about 1870 that it began to reach a wider
public. Its origins are still the subject of dispute: some authorities
maintain that it was derived from the Moors, others seek its beginnings
in the negro music of Africa or Brazil, while others again believe that it
originated among seamen, a theory to which the rhythms of the fado
would seem to lend some support. But since it is known that Lisbon
had a long tradition of singing and dancing to a guitar accompaniment
before the arrival of the term "fado" the most widely accepted view is
that the origins of the fado are to be looked for in the folk music of the
capital.

Thanks to its geographical situation, its importance as a seaport and
its status as the national capital, Lisbon was always receptive to influences from outside. Thus as early as the 16th c. an exotic dance
known as the *batuque* was popular in the town; and there are other
dances including the *oitavado*, the *arrepia* and the *charamba* in 1734.
About the middle of the 18th c. the *lundum* was danced in the streets of
Lisbon to the accompaniment of guitars, and this was soon afterwards
followed by a melancholy type of song called the *modinha*. The fado
may well, therefore, have developed in the late 18th c. and early 19th c.
out of these two forms.

There is also much difference of opinion about the qualities of the
fado. The writer Ventura de Abrantes calls it "the most authentic of all
Portuguese songs" and refers to "this liturgy of the popular soul",
while José Maciel Ribeiro Forte sees it as "a song of rogues, a hymn to
crime, an ode to vice, an incitement to depravity".

The most celebrated fadistas of the 19th c. were José Dias (1824–96)
and the legendary Maria Severa (around 1840). In our own day radio
and recorded music have made the fado known far beyond the frontiers of Portugal, so that it has developed into a kind of pop music. The
best known contemporary fado singer, with an international reputation, is Amália Rodrigues.

The Coimbra fado is very different from the ballad-like Lisbon fado.
In this old university town the students sing their own traditional form
of fado, reminiscent of the serenades of the southern European
countries.

The folk dances show considerable regional variation. In the northern
coastal regions between the Minho and the Douro the commonest
dance is the *vira*, a lively round dance. The Galician *gota* is danced to an
even faster tempo. In the *malhão* and *cana verde* the women wear

beautiful traditional costumes. In the hill country of Trás-os-Montes, Beira Alta and Beira Baixa the most popular dance is the *chula*. The *dança dos pauliteiros* which is also danced in these regions is performed by men bearing staves, probably substitutes for sabres used in the old warlike dances. The vira performed at Nazaré on the coast of Estremadura is a graceful fisherfolk's dance. In the Ribatejo region men dance the solo *escovinho* and *fandango*.

To the south of the Tagus, where the people are of a more serious cast of mind, the dances are stately, almost melancholy. The best known folk dances of Alentejo are the *saia* and the *balha*. In the Algarve on the other hand, the lively and vigorous *corridinho* is danced.

The old folk dances are mostly danced at the various popular festivals (*romarias, festas*) which are particularly numerous in spring and late summer. In country areas the harvest thanksgiving festival is an occasion for great celebration, based on a service giving thanks for a good harvest or on the blessing of the livestock and the fields.

Romarias

In a profoundly Catholic country like Portugal the various religious festivals are naturally of prime importance. Paricularly in the conservative north there are numerous *romarias* in honour of a particular saint or in commemoration of some miracle or apparition. The more important of these may last several days, with secular celebrations as well as religious ceremonies.

The romaria is basically a pilgrimage, with long processions of pilgrims, festively dressed, and splendidly decorated floats. Sometimes a romaria is dedicated to a particular craft (in a fishing town, for example, to the fishermen); but this does not prevent large numbers of spectators and visitors from joining in and playing their part in the celebrations.

The central feature of the religious ritual is a solemn procession accompanying some sacred symbol, which in some cases may be

*Easter procession at Graciosa in the Azores*

merely a large candle (*cirio*), to the place of pilgrimage, usually a church. On arriving at the church the procession usually walks round it several times, to the accompaniment of music and a great deal of noise, before setting up the cross or candle or other symbol by the high altar.

In order to obtain forgiveness for their sins the pilgrims perform a variety of ritual acts or offer ex-votos to the saint in gratitude for help received. The Portuguese, however, are not uncritical of their saints and if a pilgrim thinks a saint has let him down it is quite common for him to scold and denigrate that saint before placing any trust in him the following year.

The romarias are mainly financed by offerings from the community. A few days before the festival the organisers arrange for the collection of alms, accompanied by music to encourage cheerful giving.

Some of the larger romarias are widely famed, and offer an excellent opportunity of getting to know the way of life and customs of Portugal. Among the most notable are those of Viana do Castelo, Póvoa de Varzim, Amarante and Loulé.

Associated with the religious ceremonies there are usually *festas* — fairs offering a variety of attractions and entertainments, with dancing and singing, eating and drinking.

Festas

The various festas and romarias give visitors an opportunity of seeing a great range of splendid traditional costumes (*trajes*). As in many other countries, the women's costumes are particularly fine. Those of the northern provinces of Minho and Douro are notable for their richness of colouring, the brightly coloured embroidered jackets and waistcoats being set off by white blouses and stockings, with head-scarves, kerchiefs and jewellery to complete the effect.

Costumes

Black costumes, with long gold-embroidered skirts fitting closely on the hips which are reminiscent of Provençal dress, are also found in northern Portugal, and black costumes are common in the Algarve, at the other end of the country. In Alentejo the costumes are adapted to the peasants' hard work in the fields, which is often done by women, wearing trouser-like nether garments, with a kerchief or a floppy hat on their heads. In Ribatejo the *campesinos* (cattle-herders) wear breeches, brightly coloured waistcoats and stockings, light-coloured shirts and the stocking caps which are found all over Portugal.

In the little fishing town of Nazaré and the surrounding area young women and girls wear simple coloured dresses with a flower pattern in black or white and a white or black woollen jersey or shawl over their shoulders to protect them from the rough Atlantic winds which often blow in this area.

There are great processions (*procissões*) in the pilgrimage centre of Fátima twice a year (on May 13th and October 13th), with smaller pilgrimages on the 12th and 13th of every month.

Processions

There are also processions in many towns and villages at Easter, carrying figures connected with the story of the Passion.

Particularly notable is the Festa dos Tabuleiros, celebrated at Tomar in alternate years. White-clad girls walk in procession through the town bearing on their heads the elaborate tower-like structures known as *tabuleiros*, each incorporating thirty loaves of bread and a decoration of ears of corn, flowers and foliage. The tabuleiros is usually as tall as the girl carrying it. The procession is supposed to commemorate a 14th c. ceremony during which the Order of the Holy Ghost distributed food to the poor.

Portuguese folklore includes many traditions of pagan origin, and numerous everyday habits and customs which to the outsider may appear exotic or even antiquated. Among these for example is the way

Traditions

in which the fishermen of Nazaré launch their boats into the heavy surf and haul them ashore on their return by their own muscle-power or with the help of oxen. Local colour is also provided by the women sitting outside their houses doing embroidery or pillow-lace work, the women selling shellfish in the street, the fisherfolk mending nets or setting out fish to dry in the sun on special racks, and the people grilling sardines on little charcoal stoves outside their houses, producing the penetrating aroma which pervades whole villages and will be one of every visitor's memories of Portugal. The heaviest of loads are carried on people's heads, the women balancing theirs with great poise and dignity.

Bullfighting

The bullfight (*tourada*) is very much part of Portuguese tradition. It is quite different from the Spanish "corrida" which to the Portuguese is almost a swear word. Unlike Spain and some towns in the South of France, in Portugal the bull is not killed – in the arena at any rate – and there are no picadores to soften the bull up.

The central character in a Portuguese bullfight is the *cavaleiro*, a kind of mounted torero clad in an elegant costume of the time of Louis XV of France, a legacy from the days when all cavaleiros were noblemen. After some demonstrations of haute école horsemanship the bull is released into the arena and the cavaleiro begins his *faena* (the Portuguese borrow the Spanish word for the occasion), dexterously avoiding the bull's charge and planting *farpas*, or *bandarilhas* in its neck. In order to avoid injury to the horse the bull's horns are blunted by leather pads (*emboladas*).

Unmounted aides – *toureiros* or *capinhas* – sometimes enter the ring to allow the cavaleiro a short breathing-space. After the cavaleiro has planted all his farpas he withdraws from the contest and leaves the field to eight *forcados*, on foot and unarmed, who set about bringing the bull to a standstill in the phase of the fight known as the *pega*. When the bull has been defeated the *campinos* enter the arena with a small herd of oxen or young bulls, and after a brief period of hesitation the bewildered beast joins the herd and leaves the arena with them.

The bullfighting season in Portugal is from Easter to October. Bullfights are held not only in the special bullrings (*praças de touros*) in the larger towns but also in market squares and sports grounds in smaller places.

Mounted bullfighting is also practised in Spain and the South of France, where it is known as the *rejonea*. This is very similar to the Portuguese form, except that there are no forcados. In the rejonea the bull is often killed in the arena, usually by a torero on foot, rarely by the rider. In Spain, too, the bull's horns are usually not padded, increasing the hazard for both horse and rider. Portuguese cavaleiros occasionally appear in rejoneas outside Portugal.

# Portugal in Quotations

After sunrise we saw that we really were close to land. Was it the cliffs of Cintra? On to Lisbon, then? Really there was no other choice.

Christopher Columbus (1451–1506)

At midday we were already close to the shore. I tried to put in at Cassaes, but the gale drove me away from the coast time and again. Perhaps it will be possible to sail up the Tagus.

I succeeded in anchoring off Rastello. We are saved. Saved? Whether we are or not will appear by and by. Immediately after coming ashore I sent a messenger to Juan II with a detailed letter informing him of my arrival and asking for help – and also for leave to continue on my way to Lisbon. I did not let the opportunity pass of remarking that I had not been to Guinea but to India. The best way of protecting yourself against an ox is to grasp it by the horns! Perhaps he will be so surprised that he will forget to gore me.

Christopher Columbus made these entries in his ship's log book on March 5th 1492.

Lisbon, before which we now lay at anchor, is said to be built on the same number of hills with old Rome; but these do not all appear to the water; on the contrary, one sees from thence one vast high hill and rock, with buildings arising above one another, and that in so steep and almost perpendicular a manner, that they all seem to have but one foundation.

Henry Fielding (1707–54)

As the houses, convents, churches, etc., are large, and all built with white stone, they look very beautiful at a distance; but as you approach nearer, and find them to want every kind of ornament, all idea of beauty vanishes at once. While I was surveying the prospect of this city, which bears so little resemblance to any other that I have ever seen, a reflection occurred to me, that if a man were suddenly to be removed from Palmyra hither, and should take a view of no other city, in how glorious a light would the ancient architecture appear to him! and what desolation of arts and sciences would he conclude had happened between the several eras of these cities! . . .

About seven in the evening I got into a chaise on shore, and was driven through the nastiest city in the world, though at the same time one of the most populous, to a kind of coffee-house, which is very pleasantly situated on the brow of a hill about a mile from the city and hath a very fine prospect of the river Tajo from Lisbon to the sea. Here we regaled ourselves with a good supper.

From Henry Fielding's "Journal of a Voyage to Lisbon", undertaken in 1754.

Two leagues to Coimbra over a rich and lovely country. The view opened from the last eminence upon the mountains, and one snowy summit of the Serra Estrella. Halfway down the heights were floating clouds, all silver in the sunshine. The nearer ground was hill and dale, olives, oranges, quinces blossoming in the hedgerows – and cypresses peering everywhere. At the last the Mondego appeared swol'n with the rains – a broad and ample stream, winding among olive wooded hills – and a long low bridge reaching to Coimbra, whose convents and colleges were on the opposite height, large and fine buildings, of that unsullied whiteness which stone preserves only in a climate like this. I never saw a scene more magnificent, – a city more gloriously seated. The olives large and healthy shaded all the hills, in every garden the fine oranges were hung with fine fruit, and everywhere the cypress – thick as the poplars near London. There are

Robert Southey (1774–1843)

frequent openings on the bridge to let the current pass. We entered the city thro an ancient gate . . .

From Robert Southey, "Journals of a Residence in Portugal", March 13th 1801.

Duke of
Wellington, the
"Iron Duke"
(1769–1852)

PEOPLE OF PORTUGAL.

The time is arrived to rescue your country and restore the government of your lawful Prince.

His Britannic Majesty, our most gracious King and master, has, in compliance with the wishes and ardent supplications for succour from all parts of Portugal, sent to your aid a British army, directed to co-operate with his fleet, already on your coast.

The English soldiers, who land upon your shore, do so with every sentiment of friendship, faith and honour.

The glorious struggle upon which you are engaged is for all that is dear to man – the protection of your wives and children; the restoration of your lawful Prince; the protection, nay, the very existence of your Kingdom; and for the preservation of your holy religion. Objects like these can only be obtained by distinguished examples of fortitude and constancy.

The noble struggle against the tyranny and usurpation of France will be jointly maintained by Portugal, Spain and England; and in contributing to the success of a cause so just and glorious, the views of His Britannic Majesty are the same as those by which you are yourselves animated.

Proclamation issued by General Sir Arthur Wellesley (later the Duke of Wellington) when British troops landed in Portugal in August 1808.

Lord Byron
(1788–1824)

I am very happy here, because I loves oranges, and talk bad Latin to the Monks, who understand it as it is like their own. And I goes into society (with my pocket pistols) and I swims in the Tagus all across at once, and I have got a diarrhoea, and bites from the mosquitoes. But what of that? Comfort must not be expected by folks that go a pleasuring.

Lord Byron, letter to the Rev. F. Hodgson, July 16th 1809.

We sailed from Falmouth on July 2nd, reached Lisbon after a very favourable passage of four days and a half, and took up our abode in that city. It has been often described without being worthy of description; for, except for the view from the Tagus, which is beautiful, and some fine churches and convents, it contains little but filthy streets, and more filthy inhabitants. To make amends for this, the village of Cintra, about fifteen miles from the capital, is, perhaps in every respect, the most delightful in Europe; it contains beauties of every description, natural and artificial. Palaces and gardens rising in the midst of rocks, cataracts, and precipices; convents on stupendous heights – a distant view of the sea and the Tagus . . . It unites in itself all the wildness of the western highlands, with the verdure of France.

Lord Byron, letter to his mother, August 11th 1809.

Sir William
Wraxall
(1751–1831)

In the year 1772 the Court of Lisbon offered scarcely any sources of amusements to the foreigner. Neither levees nor drawing-rooms were ever held, except on birth-days, and on a few particular festivals. The King, Queen, his brother Don Pedro, his three daughters and the young Prince of Beyra, lived all under the same roof and inhabited a long wooden range of apartments at Belem, lower down the bank of the Tagus than Lisbon. The terrors and recollections of the earthquake of 1755 were so deeply impressed on their minds that they preferred residing in a wooden building, however mean or inconvenient, rather than encounter the perils annexed to a stone edifice. Joseph had never slept under a house, properly so denominated, during near sixteen years. Wherever he moved, either wooden barracks or tents were provided for his accommodation. I have seen tents pitched for his reception in the fields adjoining the palace of Maffra, while that immense and costly edifice was totally abandoned, neglected and unfurnished. These precautions, however singular and almost pusillanimous they may at first sight seem, were nevertheless necessary. Evidence had fully demonstrated that most solid, massy and well-constructed buildings of stone only exposed the inhabitant to greater and more inevitable destruction, in the event of an earthquake, because the resistance made by such materials to the undulation or shock produced their overthrow. On the contrary, any structure composed of wood, supported like the barracks inhabited by the Royal Family, on pillars of the same materials, yielding to the concussion of the earth, rocked and waved with the convulsion, thus escaping its worst effects.

From Sir N. William Wraxall's "Historical Memoirs of My Own Time", first published in 1815.

On the authority of British travellers, most of whom, like Byron, have approached by sea, Lisbon has been called the most beautiful city in Europe after Constantinople and Naples, and as an old saying asserts "quem não tem visto Lisboa, não tem visto cousa bona" (he who has not seen Lisbon does not know what beauty is). However this may be, everyone will willingly allow that nature and man have here co-operated to great advantage, and that the city, in spite of the absence of a mountain background or distinguished buildings, possesses a beauty of its own in the picturesque disposition of its terraces, its view of the wide expanses of the Tagus, and the luxuriant vegetation of its public gardens and parks.

Lisbon is now one of cleanest towns of Southern Europe, though at the beginning of the last century it was notorious for its dilapidation, insecurity and dirt.

From Karl Baedeker's Spain and Portugal: Handbook for Travellers, third edition, 1908.

Baedeker's Spain and Portugal 1908 edition

Portuguese Melody – "April in Portugal". Music by Raul Ferrao

# Suggested Routes

The following suggested itineraries are intended to help the motorist touring Portugal, without denying him freedom to make his own plans and choice of route. The routes have been chosen so that the principal places of interest in the country are visited. However, not all the places of interest in this guide can be covered without making detours. The proposed routes can be followed on the map at the back of this book which simplifies detailed planning. Preliminary note

Places and areas which are covered in the A to Z section under a main heading are printed in **bold**.

Most of the towns, villages, areas, rivers, etc. mentioned in the routes, as well as individual sights, whether they are under main headings or in the surroundings, can be found in the index at the end of the guide.

The figures in brackets after the headings are approximate distances and refer to the direct route; distances of detours or alternative roads on fairly long stretches are specially noted.

## Tour of southern Portugal (820km/510 miles)

This tour of southern Portugal is aimed at anyone wanting to combine a relaxing holiday on the Algarve with some sightseeing. It can be done in three days – in which case it would be best to stop overnight in Lisbon and Évora – but to do justice to the sights and the scenery it should really take at least a week.

Many visitors enter Portugal via the little town of **Vila Real de Santo António** on its south-eastern frontier. From here take the N 125 coast-road west as far as Portimão (this section of the route is described in detail under **Algarve**). It is definitely worth planning stops at Tavira, a little town with as yet uncrowded beaches and a look still very much all its own, and **Faro**, chief resort of the Algarve. Past Faro the landscape gradually becomes the "Rocky Algarve", and the bizarre rock formations at **Praia da Rocha**, just south of **Portimão**, are particularly worth seeing. Algarve

The detour from Portimão to windswept Cape St Vincent (Cabo de São Vicente), via the pretty town of **Lagos**, is a round-trip of about 100km/62 miles. This stretch presents quite a different picture of the Algarve. The vegetation is sparser, thanks to the much harsher climate, but this also ensures that the countryside is not overrun by tourists. Detour to Cape St Vincent

From Portimão the route runs north on the N 124 then the N 266 through the delightful **Serra de Monchique**. The winding mountain road, from which there are lovely views, skirts the old-established spa of Caldas de Monchique then goes through the little hill town of Monchique. Following the N 266 then the N 123 the route picks up the N 120 at Odemira and speeds northward to Tanganheira where it forks right to avoid the industrial port of **Sines**. Twenty km/12 miles further on lies the attractive hill-top town of **Santiago do Cacém**. From here to Grândola it is worth leaving the main road and taking the narrow country road which runs through some pretty countryside via Cruz de João Mendes. Back on the N 120 it is a further 20km/12 miles to **Alcácer do Sal**, where the best view of this ancient little town is from the bridge over the Rio Sado as you enter. From Portimão to Alcácer do Sal

◀ *An idyllic bay on the Lisbon coast*

**Suggested Routes**

*Tavira, on the Algarve coast*

Detour to the Tróia
peninsula

The tip of the Tróia peninsula, with its mile upon mile of shining sandy beaches, is about 45km/28 miles from Alcácer do Sal.

From Alcácer do
Sal to Lisbon

The route follows the busy N 5 and then, forking left, the N 10 to **Setúbal**, which remains a pleasant place despite its industry.

Although there is a motorway from here to Lisbon the lovely scenery makes it definitely well worth taking the long way round along the coast road west out of Setúbal through the Serra da Arrábida, with its wonderful views over the rocky bays and coves of the coastline (see photograph p 80). The fishing village of Portinho da Arrábida is a good place for a quick stop.

Passing through beautiful and as yet largely unspoilt scenery the road eventually arrives at Vila Nogueira de Azeitão, famous for its wineries. (**Sesimbra**, 13km/8 miles south-west, is a good place for anyone wanting to stay in this area overnight.) A few miles to the east it is possible to visit what is probably the earliest "azulejo" tile-picture in Portugal at Vila Fresca de Azeitão.

Back on the N 10 the route soon joins the motorway to **Lisbon**, Portugal's capital, which needs a visit of at least two days to do anything like justice to its many sights.

Detour along the
Costa do Sol to
Sintra

A day-trip worth taking from Lisbon is the drive along the **Costa do Sol** to **Sintra**. It's only 60km/37 miles but contains many sights of interest (more detailed description in tour of Central Portugal).

From Lisbon to
Évora

The best way south out of Lisbon is the motorway straight to Setúbal, but it is also possible to go by car ferry from the city centre over to the south bank of the Tagus. With perhaps a brief stop in **Palmela** the route then retraces the N 10 from Setúbal back 20km/12 miles east to the cross-roads just past Águas de Moura after which it turns north, still on the N 10, before soon taking the N 4 east towards Montemor-o-Novo, a small town overshadowed by its castle. **Arraiolos**, noted for its carpets, lies about 25km/16 miles east of here, and **Évora**, one of Portugal's finest cities, a further 22km/14 miles to the south.

If enough time is available it is worth only taking the N 18 direct route to Beja as far as Portel then turning left and passing through largely unspoilt scenery on the road to **Moura**, which is worth a visit for its charming old quarter and the park around its spa. The route continues southward to Serpa, a pretty place that is also worth having a look at before turning west on the N 260, soon crossing the Rio Guadiana and covering the 30km/19 miles to **Beja**, another picturesque old town.

From Évora to Beja

From Beja the route goes south about 45km/28 miles to the modest small market town of **Castro Verde**, then continues with gentle gradients to Almodôvar, a little town with a Franciscan convent. The road crosses into the Algarve from Alentejo Province just past the village of Dogueno then heads upward into the Serra do Caldeirão passing through hilly country, rich in iron-ore, with fine views. The Miradouro do Caldeirão provides a viewing place at the highest point of this stretch, then the road winds downwards to Barranco do Velho followed by the charmingly situated market town of São Brás de Alportel. Here the route joins the N 270 to Tavira and continues along the coast back to its starting point Vila Real de Santo António.

From Beja via Castro Verde and Tavira to Vila Real de Santo António

The alternative route from Beja to Vila Real de Santo António via Mértola passes through equally charming countryside. It also leaves Beja travelling southward but bends left after 15km/9 miles to cover the remaining 40km/25 miles to **Mértola** with its fortified Romanesque parish church converted from an earlier mosque. The little-travelled country road wends past lonely farmsteads and only the very occasional village. Barely 35km/22 miles past Mértola a minor road goes off to the left to Alcoutim, from where there is a superb view of the Rio Guadiana as it forms the frontier between Spain and Portugal. Once back on the main road it's another 40km/25 miles to Vila Real de Santo António.

Alternative route via Mértola

## Tour of central Portugal (730km/455 miles)

Anyone particularly wanting to visit Portugal's art treasures would be best advised to choose this tour of central Portugal and to allow about a week. It takes in two of the country's loveliest cities (Lisbon and Évora), the major abbeys and convents (Batalha, Tomar and Alcobaça), the most impressive castles (Sintra and Mafra), but also offers glimpses of smaller romantic places in unusually fine settings such as Castelo de Vide and Marvão.

Leaving Lisbon by its western suburb of Belém, with its outstanding examples of Manueline architecture, the route runs along the part of the coast known as the **Costa do Sol**, the four-lane motorway ending just before the popular resorts of **Estoril** and **Cascais**. On the left just past Cascais is "Hell's Mouth", the Boca do Inferno – cliffs hollowed out by the sea into caves – and there are also impressive views over the rocky coastline from Cabo Raso and especially Cabo da Roca.
   At Colares the route leaves the coast road and heads inland to **Sintra** which, with its two castles, many royal residences and extremely beautiful parks and gardens, requires almost a whole day in itself.
   From there the route runs north on the N 9 to **Mafra** and its enormous palace-monastery, and then turns north-west towards Ericeira, a further 10km/6 miles ahead on the coast. Continuing to hug the coastline

From Lisbon to Batalha via Sintra

*On the Costa do Sol: Estoril . . .*          *. . . and Cabo da Roca*

(sightseeing in **Torres Vedras** can be given a miss) the next destination is **Peniche**, on its rocky peninsula projecting far out to sea, then, heading inland, 25km/16 miles further on, the picturesque walled town of **Óbidos**, which, with its whitewashed houses and pretty shop-lined alleys, is now well on the tourist map, possibly making it difficult to get accommodation here at the height of the season. Keeping on the N 8, just 6km/4 miles to the north lies **Caldas da Rainha**, a centre for majolica ware, and 25km/16 miles up the road one of the great sights of Portugal, the magnificent abbey of **Alcobaça**. From here it is possible either to make a detour to take in **Nazaré**, where the pilgrimage chapel high above the town commands some of Portugal's most impressive views of its Atlantic coast, or to keep on up the N 8 and go direct to **Batalha**, which has an abbey that is one of the very best examples of Manueline architecture.

Detour to Leiria

From Batalha it is only 10km/6 miles to **Leiria**, the busy district capital, its fine castle complete with well-preserved walls and towers. Take the N 113 to get from here to Fátima.

From Batalha to Marvão via Tomar

Whether it be for its religious aspects or not, a brief visit should be fitted in to **Fátima**, Portugal's place of pilgrimage, if only for the approach on the N 356 that connects it to Batalha. From Fátima via Vila Nova de Ourem it is a bare 35km/22 miles to **Tomar** which has a massive convent, The route continues southward through very pretty countryside. About 6km/4 miles past Tomar it is possible to turn left off the main road and head for Castelo de Bode where there is a pousada in a delightful wooded lakeside setting. At Constância the country road joins the main road to **Abrantes**. Although there is nothing very special to see in Abrantes it is definitely worth making the short detour to Castelo de Almourol (turn right at Constância towards Tancos then left along a road leading to the castle which stands on an island in the Tagus).

*View of Abrantes*

*Castelo de Almourol*

Beyond Abrantes a 370m/1214ft bridge crosses the Tagus and a fine view of the town can be obtained by looking back from the village of Rossio on this side of the river. The route follows the river upstream for a time then leaves it at Gavião; rice, agave and figs gradually give way to what eventually become bleak hillsides. About 18km/11 miles beyond Gavião the N 118 forks right to **Castelo de Vide** which, like **Marvão** just a few miles to its south-east and also definitely worth a visit, is an extremely attractive little town that still retains its medieval character and atmosphere.

From Marvão the route goes south to Portalegre through the lovely mountain landscapes of the Serra do São Mamede. There is no need to spend too long in **Portalegre**, which is the rather noisy and hectic district capital. Leaving on the N 18 the southward bound route speeds up over the 60km/37 miles to **Estremoz**, with its picturesque old upper town and busy newer lower town.

From Marvão to Estremoz via Elvas

This round trip to Elvas of about 90km/56 miles begins by taking the N 4 eastwards from Estremoz. About 10km/6 miles along this road the simple white building on the left is the Museu de Cristo housing an interesting collection of crucifixes. Just over a mile further on lies **Borba**, surrounded by many big marble quarries. Take the N 255 south out of the town for 6km/4 miles, past a fine marble fountain at the junction, to **Vila Viçosa**. This otherwise unremarkable little country town is a great tourist attraction because of the vast Palace of the Dukes of Bragança. Returning to Borba and back on the N 4 again the route continues to **Elvas**. This old fortified frontier town still has many well-preserved fortifications, not to mention an amazing four-tier aqueduct, which are worth seeing.

Detour to Elvas

From Estremoz the route continues towards Évora along the N 18. After 17km/11 miles it is worth taking a brief detour along the little road to

From Estremoz to Lisbon via Évora

Évoramonte off to the right and following it for about half a mile to get right into the massive ruins of Évoramonte Castle. Back on the main road it is just 30km/19 miles to Évora and the many sights it has to offer. The way back to Lisbon is via Montemor-o-Novo (it is possible to make a trip first to **Arraiolos**, where the famous rugs are made), Vendas Novas and **Setúbal**, then on through the Serra da Arrábida (described in detail in the tour of southern Portugal).

## Tour of northern Portugal (850km/528 miles)

While the central Portugal tour is to be recommended for anyone chiefly interested in culture, the tour of northern Portugal will be the one that particularly appeals to lovers of nature, taking in some unique and still quite unspoilt scenery (especially in the north-east of the country) and two interesting but completely different national parks, not to mention several very attractive old towns and cities.

Because the bends in the road will make it necessary to travel slowly in many places, to enjoy the tour at least a week, or, if the detour to the north-east is included ten days, should be allowed.

From Oporto to Braga via Monção

The metropolis of northern Portugal, and clearly Lisbon's rival, is **Oporto**, and no visit there is complete without visiting one of the port wine lodges in Vila Nova de Gaia. From Oporto the route goes north on the N 13 to **Vila do Conde** which almost merges with **Póvoa de Varzim** further up the coast. Although there is quite a lot of industry in and around the two towns they are both very popular seaside resorts. Esposende, further north, is rather quieter. Anyone considering a beach holiday on this part of the "green coast", the **Costa Verde**, should be prepared for relatively cool sea temperatures and some strong winds off the sea.

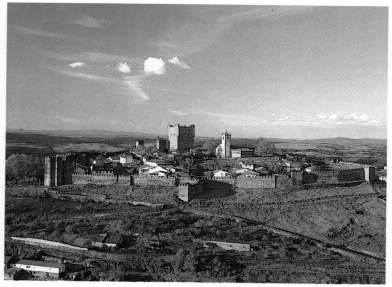

*Bragança in the north of Portugal*

Continuing along the coast on the N 13 the route crosses the wide Rio Lima on an iron bridge 560m/1838ft long (under the railway), built in 1877 by Eiffel & Co in Paris, to get to **Viano do Castelo**, the district capital with a very attractive town centre. From here it carries on northwards, through countryside that is getting prettier all the time, to its next destination, **Caminha**. The road now turns north-west, running up the valley of the Minho – the Spanish–Portuguese frontier at this point – where vineyards alternate with heath and pine-woods. After the fortress town of **Valença do Minho** the route leaves the N 13 but continues along the pleasing Minho valley to the rather sleepy-seeming spa of **Monção**.

Here the route turns south down the N 101, passing through quite well populated hilly country, dotted with many villages and home-steads. Past Barroças the road winds its way up to the Serra do Extremo (chapel with good view) then drops down again after Aboim das Chocas. Arcos de Valdevez and **Ponte da Barca** are both pictur-esque little towns worth a quick visit.

Just a few miles east of Ponte da Barca is the start of the **Peneda Gerês National Park**. For anyone pressed for time and who only wants to take a short drive through this largely unspoilt area the best route is to go from Ponte da Barca to Lindoso then drive on out into Spain and get back into the park again through the entrance at Portelá do Homem. The route then goes through the little spa of Gerês and runs south past various reservoirs to pick up the N 103, taking it west to **Braga**, with its many churches.

From Braga follow the signs to Bom Jesús do Monte, the pilgrimage church 6km/4 miles east of the town. A narrow road via Sobreposta leads from there to the Iron Age site **Citânia de Briteiros**. The road then snakes downhill to Caldelas where it joins the N 101, the main road to **Guimarães**. This historic town is known as "the cradle of the nation" and still has many of its fine old buildings. Keeping on the N 101 the route continues to **Amarante**, where it crosses the Rio Tâmega – the new bridge affording a superb view of the heart of the old town. The main road from here eastward to **Vila Real** is still full of twists and turns, but a new one is projected.

From Braga to Vila Real

Only those who have plenty of time should take on this 310km/193 mile trip which heads north from Vila Real to **Chaves** and then east to **Bragança**, traversing the rugged mountain province of **Trás os Montes**, still a largely untouched and very poor region. From Bragança the route goes south on the N 15 then after 37km/23 miles forks left onto the N 102 and crosses the Serra de Bornes, providing lovely views almost all the way. It eventually crosses the Rio Sabor and enters the ancient town of **Torre de Moncorvo**. The next destination is Vila Nova de Foz Côa, which has a fine Manueline church, then just over a mile further on the route leaves the N 102 to go left onto the N 222 to Touça and then winds its way down to the **Douro Valley**. This region is known as "País do Vinho", the land of wine, because of the vineyards on the terraced slopes which provide the rather heavy wine used for making port. The route now carries on down the valley to rejoin the main route (described below) at Peso da Régua.

Tour Extension to Bragança via Chaves

A detour 4km/2½ miles east to the Baroque country house of the Counts of Vila Real at Mateus (home of the rosé) is a must before leaving Vila Real and travelling south, crossing the Douro at Peso da Régua then heading for **Lamego**, with its pilgrimage church attrac-tively located overlooking the town. Still moving south on the N 2 the route passes through Castro Daire to **Viseu** which besides its fine cathedral and churches also boasts handsome burghers' houses and palaces of the Renaissance and Baroque periods. The next stretch westward on the N 16 to Guarda can be quite a fast one and contains a

From Vila Real to Guarda

section of new road, with work continuing on the rest of it. Its altitude of 1057m/3468ft makes **Guarda** Portugal's highest town.

From Guarda to Coimbra through the Serra da Estrela

From Guarda take the N 18 south then turn left off the main road after about 19km/12 miles to have a look at the Roman watch-tower at Centum Cellas. Back on the N 18 the turning to the charming little hill town of **Belmonte** is only a few hundred yards further on. The 20km/12 miles from Belmonte to **Covilhã** is a fast run before the tour enters the **Serra da Estrela**, renowned for the beauty of its mountain scenery. From Covilhã take the road to Tortosendo and turn west along the N 230 which twists and turns until it eventually connects up with N 17 to **Coimbra**.

From Coimbra to Oporto

Although there is a motorway from Coimbra to Oporto it is worth doing at least the first part of the trip off the main road, leaving Coimbra on the N 110 heading eastward towards Penacova, passing through particularly pretty countryside on the north bank of the Rio Mondego. Just before Penacova there is a turning on the left to the convent of Lorvão a little way off the road. On narrow little roads follow the signs to Buçaco National Park where the dense network of paths allows visitors to explore the beauties of the forest. After Luso, the little spa on the northern edge of the park, head back west to the motorway and stay on it until the turn-off to **Aveiro**. Although it is an exaggeration to compare this little fishing town with Amsterdam or Venice, its canals make it a pleasant place in which to finish off this tour by taking a stroll around the town before rejoining the motorway back to Oporto.

# Grand Tour of Portugal (2000km/1243 miles)

The three tours of Portugal can easily be joined together to make one grand tour. Anyone who wanted to acquaint themselves with the best of Portugal's towns, sights and scenery would need to take at least four weeks.

The individual stops on the tour are only touched on in greater detail when this tour deviates from the other three. Since many visitors from abroad enter Portugal through Faro, the main town of the Algarve, that is where this tour begins.

Tour Stages

From **Faro** head west through the flourishing countryside of the **Algarve** to the busy town of **Portimão**, then turn inland and traverse the charming **Serra de Monchique**. The next destinations are Odemira (at this juncture Vila Nova de Milfontes is a good place to rest for a day), **Santiago do Cacém**, Grândola and **Alcácer do Sal**. From the port of **Setúbal** it is definitely worth making a detour to sample the charming scenery of the Serra da Arrábida. From here it is not far to **Lisbon**, Portugal's capital. No tour would be complete without **Sintra** and **Mafra** either. (If another rest day is needed nearby Ericeira has a good swimming beach.) Next it is northwards via **Óbidos** to **Alcobaça**, from where it is only 15km/9 miles to the pretty beach resort of **Nazaré**. Further on, at **Batalha**, the abbey is one of the great sights of Portuguese architecture. Turning inland the tour takes in **Fátima** and **Tomar** before heading north to **Coimbra**. The stretch from here via Penacova to the **Buçaco National Park** is full of lovely views. Next on the route is **Aveiro** then **Oporto**. The route follows the coastline north of the **Costa Verde** as far as **Viana do Castelo** (which also has some very good beaches). Here the route turns inland up the valley of the Rio Lima, via **Ponte da Barca**, to **Peneda Gerês National Park**. Next on the programme comes **Braga**, city of churches, not forgetting a small detour to **Citânia de Briteiros**. Subsequent destinations are **Guimarães** and **Amarante**. Deviating from the earlier tour of central Portugal it would be possible to follow the Rio Tâmega downstream for a stretch, cross the Douro at Entre os Rios, then follow the Douro upstream as far as Cinfães so as eventually to get to Castro Daire through the Serra de Montemuro. **Viseu** is next on the sightseeing itinerary, followed by **Guarda**, Portugal's highest town, and eventually **Belmonte**. A detour from here into the **Serra da Estrela** should not be missed. The tour heads south through Fundão and **Castelo Branco**, with its lovely gardens, to **Castelo de Vide** and **Marvão** which must be highlights of any tour of Portugal. After only a brief stop in **Portalegre** the route continues south to **Elvas** or direct to **Estremoz**. Further on lies Évoramonte with its fine views from a splendid setting, and from there it's not far to one of Portugal's major cities, **Évora**. From here the route speeds across the uplands of **Alentejo** heading for **Beja** and ultimately, via **Castro Verde** and the Serra do Malhão, returns to the starting point at Faro.

# Portugal A to Z

## Abrantes

Historical province: Ribatejo. District: Santarèm
Altitude: 190m/623ft. Population: 6000

An old-world little town of white houses and flower-bedecked streets perched high above the north bank of the Tagus, Abrantes occupies an exposed situation which made it a keypoint in the defence of the old Beira provinces. Until now the town has been able to retain its original character. A local speciality is "palha de Abrantes", a sweet egg floss.

*Situation and Importance*

## Sights

Above the town are the remains of the once mighty Castelo, built by King Dinis in 1301. It was destroyed by an earthquake in 1533 and finally demolished in 1807 by French troops under Marshal Junot, whom Napoleon created Duke of Abrantes. Within the castle precincts is the church of Santa Maria do Castelo (originally built in 1215; restored in the 15th c.), now housing the Museu Dom Lopo de Almeida, which contains, in addition to the fine late Gothic monuments of the Almeida family (15th–16th c.), valuable old tiles (16th c.), Gothic sculpture, a Gothic head of Christ and two Roman statues of the 1st c. A.D. A visit to the castle is worthwhile because of the magnificent view over Abrantes and the Tagus valley. From the partly restored keep, the Torre de Menagem, the view is even more extensive.

*Castelo*

Other features of interest in Abrantes, to be found in the picturesque alleyways of the old town below the Castelo, are the church of São João Baptista (founded 1300, rebuilt 1589), with a Renaissance coffered ceiling and rich woodcarving, and the church of the Misericórdia (16th c.) which has a Renaissance doorway and paintings of the 16th c. Portuguese school. Also worth seeing is the nearby Convento de São Domingos (originally 1472; much altered and rebuilt), with a beautiful two-storey cloister. The church of São Vicente, in the northern part of the old town, near the road to Sardoal, dates almost entirely from the late 16th c.

*Old Town*

## Surroundings

12km/7½ miles west on a beautiful road with splendid views Constância, the Roman Pugna Tagi, is charmingly situated at the junction of the Rio Zêzere and the Tagus. The Church of the Misericórdia, with tile decoration, and a parish church (1636; restored in the 19th c. with a ceiling painting from 1890) are both worth seeing.

*Constância*

5km/3 miles south-west of Constância, on a rocky islet in the Tagus, stands the Templar castle of Almourol. Built on Roman and Moorish foundations, with eleven towers, it is undoubtedly one of Portugal's finest 12th c. castles (restored in the 19th c.).
  There is a ferry over to the castle during the tourist season.

*★Castelo de Almourol*

Tancos, just 2km/½ mile west of the castle, has a pretty Renaissance-style parish church.

*Tancos*

Castelo do Bode (pousada), 10km/6 miles north of Constância, is particularly popular with the Portuguese for its water sports and leisure facilities.

*Castelo do Bode*

◀ *The Torre de Belém in Lisbon*

*Castelo de Almourol*

Its 115m/377ft high dam forms an enormous lake (Barragem do Castelo do Bode) and is the lowest of a series of dams on the Rio Zêzere creating a string of lakes stretching for more than 50km/31 miles.

Sardoal

The most interesting feature of Sardoal, about 12km/7 miles north of Abrantes, is the altarpiece (polyptych) by an unknown 16th c. master in the parish church.

Belver

The little town of Belver (alt. 220m/720ft; pop. 2000) on the right bank of the Tagus 30km/19 miles east of Abrantes is dominated by a castle begun in 1194, in the reign of King Sancho I, completed in 1212 and restored in the 14th c. There is a beautiful carved 13th c. reredos in the castle chapel and "Sancho I's balcony" affords a splendid view of the Tagus valley.

## Albufeira

B7

Historical province: Algarve. District: Faro
Altitude: 0–35m/0–115ft. Population: 17,000

Situation and Importance

In a bay on Portugal's south coast and beautifully located, like an amphitheatre in the shelter of bizarrely shaped cliffs (Ponta da Baleeira), Albufeira has developed in recent years into one of the major seaside resorts of the Algarve.

It has lost much of its former character as the haunt of painters and would-be artists – in the sixties and seventies it was known as the "St Tropez of the Algarve" – but, offsetting this, provides a whole range of sport and recreation facilities (water-skiing, windsurfing, tennis riding, golf, etc.).

Townscape

Despite the dual carriageways and big new hotels, holiday complexes, etc. constantly springing up in its outskirts Albufeira has still managed to retain, in its old town, something of its original Moorish character as a picturesque little town of white houses and steep, narrow streets where visitors can enjoy a stroll among inviting cafés, shops and little boutiques. The 18th c. church of Santana (St Anne) is worth seeing, as is the church of the Misericórdia, originally Gothic, with a beautiful doorway in Manueline Renaissance style.

There is marvellous view of the town and the beach from the Bem Parece terrace.

Viewpoint

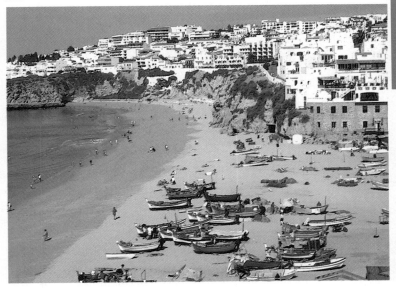

*Albufeira on the Algarve coast*

Beaches

Below the town, reached by steps or by a tunnel 50m/55yd long, is the beach. Usually very crowded, its east end also serves as harbour for the many brightly painted fishing boats. The busy activity of the local fishermen and the more leisurely pursuits of the holidaymakers complement each other in this attractive setting.

Other beaches include Praia Baleeira, Praia de São Rafel and Praia do Castelo (picturesque cliffs) to the west and, east of the harbour, Praia da Oura.

Surroundings

A pleasant boat-trip can be made to the Xorino Grottos west of Albufeira. For other places in the area worth visiting see Algarve.

## Alcácer do Sal                                                      B6

Historical province: Alentejo. District: Setúbal
Altitude: 30m/100ft. Population: 16,000

Situation and Importance

The ancient little town of Alcácer do Sal ("castle of salt"), the Roman Salacia, lies above the right bank of the Rio Sado, which here opens out into a wide estuary. The banks of the river are lined with the salt-pans which have given the town its name.

A number of fine old buildings bear witness to the town's earlier prosperity, achieved from medieval times onwards by its flourishing trade in salt and corn, and the growing of rice in the warm low lying marshland along the river, a crop that has increased in importance since recent decades have seen many of the salt-pans around the town abandoned.

## Sights

Castelo

Above the town the ruins of the castle, still ringed round by its walls, afford fine views of the town and river.

*Alcácer do Sal*

The Romanesque church of Santa Maria next to the castle dates from the 12th/13th c. and has a Renaissance doorway to the Chapel of the Sacrament and beautiful 17th c. tile decoration.

To the north of the town centre is the former Convent of Santo António (16th c.), which also has an impressive Renaissance doorway, as well as lavish marble decoration in the Chapel of the 11,000 Virgins (16th c.).

Near the Town Hall, which stands on the riverbank and houses the tourist information centre, is the former church do Espírito Santo (Manueline window) containing the town museum, the Museu Municipal, with Stone Age and Roman material, relics of the Moorish period and coins.

The Romanesque and Gothic church do Senhor dos Mártires (13th/14th c.) on the western edge of town contains the stone sarcophagus of Diogo de Pereira (1427) who, as Grand Master of the Knights of São Tiago, played a crucial role in recapturing the city from the Moors (1217).

## Surroundings

Located on the banks of the Barragem de Vale de Gaio reservoir some 30km/19 miles south-east of Alcácer do Sal, Torrão is the birthplace of Bernardim Ribeiro (c. 1482–c. 1552), famous for his poem "Saudades", published in 1554, probably posthumously. The Manueline church contains 17th c. azulejo tiling.

The little country town of Grândola (alt. 95m/312ft; pop. 10,000) 23km/14 miles south of Alcácer do Sal is an important centre for the Portuguese cork industry. It is also the town that featured in the song that in April 1974 heralded the "Carnation Revolution" ("Grândola, vila morena" = "Grândola, brown town").

See Costa de Lisboa

# Alcobaça

Historical province: Estremadura. District: Leiria
Altitude: 42m/138ft. Population: 5000

Situation and
Importance

Alcobaça, about 20km/12 miles south of Batalha and known by the Romans as Eburobriga, is charmingly set between two little rivers, the Alcoa and the Baça, below the ruins of a Moorish castle. Its principal attraction is its magnificent Cistercian abbey, Real Abadia de Santa Maria de Alcobaça, once one of the most prosperous and influential religious houses in Portugal and now one of its outstanding architectural monuments.

Alcobaça is the cultural and economic heart of a large and fertile agricultural region (fruit canning), first brought under cultivation by St Bernard's monks in the 14th c.

The town is noted for its blue painted pottery which, with other handicrafts, can be found on sale in the square fronting the abbey.

## ★★Real Abadia de Santa Maria de Alcobaça

History

In 1154 King Afonso (Henriques) I granted land in this area, recovered during the liberation of Santarém from the Moors (March 15th 1147), to Bernard of Clairvaux, who had supported him in the long-drawn-out negotiations for Papal recognition of the newly established kingdom of Portugal, for the foundation of a Cistercian abbey. The king had himself already laid the foundation stone of a first church in 1148, and 1154 saw the first monastic buildings. The influx of monks from Burgundy soon necessitated larger quarters and the building of a new abbey was begun in 1178 and largely completed by 1222. It was to be much altered in subsequent centuries, the new buildings combining with the old to form an ensemble of notable harmony.

In accordance with the rules of the order there were always 999 monks ("one less than a thousand"), who cultivated fruit and vines in the valleys of the Alcoa and the Baça, thus laying the foundations of what is still the largest area of orchards and vineyards in Portugal. Here, too, in the 13th c., the monks established the first public school in the kingdom, and this later played a part in securing the establishment of the first Portuguese university at Coimbra. The abbot of Alcobaça, who styled himself "Counsellor to His Majesty and Almoner of the Crown", had dominion over thirteen towns and villages, three ports and two castles; and between the 13th and the 18th c. the abbey was one of the country's leading intellectual and spiritual institutions, providing the Portuguese kings not only with a refuge in case of need but also with a place for retreat and meditation.

The 1775 earthquake severely damaged the abbey, and in 1811 it was occupied by French troops under Marshal Junot and plundered of many of its treasures. In 1834 the abbey was secularised and the buildings converted to various uses (barracks, stables, etc.). Finally, in 1930, the importance of this national monument was recognised and it was given statutory protection.

General layout

The abbey layout is modelled on that of the mother house at Cluny, and its excellent state of preservation makes it the finest example of Cistercian architecture in Europe. Basically Gothic in structure, the abbey is approximately square in plan. In addition to the mighty church and the usual offices it contains five cloisters, seven dorters (dormitories), accommodation for guests, a library and a huge kitchen. Some parts of the building are occupied by government offices and a school, and hence not open to the public.

*The Church of Alcobaça Abbey* ▶

# Alcobaça Abbey

**Real Abadia de Santa Maria de Alcobaça**

1 Tomb of Pedro I
2 Tomb of Inês de Castro
3 Choir
4 "Death of St Bernard" (terracotta)
5 Sala dos Túmulos (funerary chapel)
6 Chapel of the Sacrament
7 Manueline doorways
8 Sacristy
9 Chapterhouse
10 Dorter (upper floor)
11 Kitchen
12 Pantry
13 Refectory
14 Fountain-house

© Baedeker

Abbey church

The main front of the abbey, 221m/725ft long, is dominated by the Baroque façade (1725) of the church with its two low towers and its numerous statues. Of the original Gothic façade there survive only the doorway (also decorated with Baroque sculpture) and the large rose window.

The interior of the early Gothic hall-church is of Cistercian clarity, austerity and simplicity. The most spacious church interior in Portugal (106m/348ft long, 21.5m/71ft wide and 20m/65ft high), it is divided into three aisles of equal height, the lateral aisles being very narrow. Twenty-four massive piers, recessed on the inner side to take the choir-stalls (which were burned by the French), support twelve bays of Gothic vaulting. Around the choir are nine chapels and the high altar is surrounded by eight columns.

In the transepts are the sumptuous tombs of King Pedro I (south transept) and his beloved Inês de Castro (north transept), who was murdered at the behest of Pedro's father King Afonso IV. After his accession Pedro had her exhumed and crowned in due form at Coimbra as queen. The tragic story of the unhappy lovers and the bloody vengeance which Pedro exacted on the murderers after he became king, earning him the sobriquet of Pedro the Cruel, are celebrated by Camões in the third canto of his "Lusiads".

At Pedro's wish the tombs were so placed that when they arose on the Day of Judgment the two lovers would see each other at once. The sarcophaguses, hewn from soft Ançã sandstone, with rich figural decoration, are in the Flamboyant style of the second half of the 14th c. They were much damaged by Junot's troops in 1811.

On the sarcophagus of Inês de Castro, which is supported by crouching figures, is the recumbent figure of the dead woman, surrounded by six praying angels. Along the sides are scenes from the life of Christ, at the foot the Last Judgment, at the head Christ on Calvary. The stone sarcophagus of King Pedro, borne by six lions, has the recumbent figure of the king, also surrounded by praying angels. Along the sides are scenes from the life of St Bartholomew, and at the head is a wheel of fortune with 18 episodes from the life of the two lovers, including the murder of Inês.

In the transept chapels are painted terracotta figures of unnamed monks (17th c.) and a fine representation of the death of St Bernard. To the east of the ambulatory the two fine Manueline doorways (16th c.) are by João de Castilho. In the antechamber of the sacristy is the only example of reticulated vaulting in the abbey.

On the west side of the south transept is the Sala dos Túmulos, a funerary chapel containing a number of tombs.

On the north side of the church are the medieval monastic buildings. A doorway in the north aisle leads into the beautiful two-storey Claustro do Silêncio or Claustro de Rei Dinis. The lower cloister was built by Domingo and Diogo Domingues between 1308 and 1311; the upper gallery (by the Castilho brothers) was built for King Manuel in the 16th c.

Monastic buildings

On the north side of the cloister stands the Gothic fountain-house. Here, too, is the entrance to the refectory (fine reading-desk), one of the oldest parts of the abbey. Adjoining is the large kitchen, 18m/60ft high, with a huge open fireplace and a fish-tank supplied with water from the Alcoa which was once an important feature of the abbey, since the Cistercians were forbidden to eat meat.

On the south-east side of the cloister is the chapterhouse (Sala do Capítulo, 14th c.), at the south-west corner the Sala dos Reis (Hall of Kings), the walls of which are decorated with azulejos depicting scenes from the history of the abbey. Also on the walls are terracotta statues (probably by monks) of most of the Portuguese kings down to José I. On the upper floor are the dorters, the library, etc.

## Surroundings

Located on the road to Batalha leading eastward out of Alcobaça this "national wine museum" illustrates the regional winemaking methods and traditions.

Museu Nacional do Vinho

Aljubarrota, 7km/4½ miles further along the same road, is the scene of a famous battle on August 15th 1385 in which a Portuguese army com-

Aljubarrota

*Claustro do Silêncio (cloister of silence) . . .   . . . and well-house*

manded by Nuno Alvares Pereira won a decisive victory over the Spaniards. In token of thanksgiving King João I founded Batalha Abbey (see entry). The town has a number of handsome 17th and 18th c. houses and the church of Nossa Senhora dos Prazeres (originally Romanesque).

Vestiaria

The village of Vestiaria, 2km/1¼ miles south-west of Alcobaça, has a church with a fine Manueline doorway.

Termas da Piedade

Termas da Piedade is a little spa 2km/1¼ miles north of Alcobaça specialising in cures for diseases of the stomach and intestines.

## Alenquer
A5

Historical province: Estremadura. District: Lisboa
Altitude: 160m/525ft. Population: 10,000

Situation and Importance

The seemingly rather sleepy little town of Alenquer is tucked away about 45km/28 miles north of Lisbon. Its population is mainly employed in the woollen and papermaking industries.

It was the birthplace of the navigator and pilot Pero de Alenquer who was with Bartolomeu Dias when he discovered the Cape of Good Hope and with Vasco da Gama on his expedition to discover the sea route to India. Pero, a man of humble origin, won a great reputation for his extraordinary achievements, earning himself the nickname "prince of pilots" and access to the court. His exploits were vividly described in the writings of the diplomat and chronicler of Manuel I, Daimão de Góis (1507–71), scion of a noble Alenquer family.

Townscape

Alenquer's particular charm lies in its setting, with even the simplest of its houses clinging picturesquely to the slopes of the hillside on which it stands.

The local museum is the Museu de Hipólito Cabaço containing archaeological (particularly Stone Age) material.

Above the town, and only partially accessible, is the Convent of São Francisco, the oldest Franciscan house in Portugal, founded in 1222 during the saint's lifetime.

## Surroundings

Vila Franca de Xira

Vila Franca de Xira, some 10km/3 miles south of Alenquer, is the centre of Portuguese bullfighting where most of the fighting bulls are bred and where the "Agrinxira" agricultural and livestock show is held annually in May and the lively "Festival of the Red Waistcoat" (Colete Encardo), with processions and bullfights, is celebrated every July.

## Alentejo
B/C 6/7

Historical province: Alentejo
Districts: Portalegre, Évora, Beja and Setúbal
Area: 28,747 sq.km/11,096 sq.miles
Population: 370,000. Chief town: Évora

General Information

The southern Portuguese province of Alentejo extends to the south-east of the Tagus ("além Tejo", beyond the Tagus) over a seemingly endless tableland as far as the Algarve, bounded on the east by the Spanish frontier and on the west by the Atlantic Ocean. The chief town of Alto Alentejo (Upper Alentejo, to the north) and of the province as a whole is Évora (see entry). The main town of Baixo Alentejo (Lower Alentejo, to the south) is Beja (see entry).

The lonely, barren and almost featureless landscape is reminiscent of more northerly latitudes, and a remarkable contrast to the hilly terrain and luxuriant vegetation of most of the Portuguese provinces.

Geologically Alentejo is a continuation of the Castilian Meseta, a residual expanse worn down and levelled by erosion, resting on Palaeozoic rocks of the Iberian basement. The land rises to average heights of between 150 and 350m/500 and 1150ft, reaching barely 400m/1300ft at its highest point in the south-west and with its only "real" mountains in the north-east, the Serra de São Mamede (1025m/3365ft).

The climate is Mediterranean, but with some continental features: a cold but snow-free winter, a short spring with little rain, a hot, dry summer and frequent showers of rain in the autumn. The rainfall is relatively low, an annual average of 600–700mm/24–28in.

Given this climatic pattern, the natural vegetation is confined to modest evergreen heaths and oaks and sclerophyllous evergreens (woody plants with small leathery leaves). The few trees mostly grow in isolated clumps. The cork-oak is widely distributed, and makes an important contribution to the economy of the region.

With only 370,000 inhabitants – barely 4% of Portugal's population – spread over at least a fifth of the country's area, Alentejo is very sparsely populated, with a density of 21 to the sq.km/54 to the sq.mile. There are concentrations of population in a few smallish towns and large villages, but for the rest the rural population is widely dispersed, living in and around large isolated farms (*montes*). These are often on low hills and consist of the farmhouse itself, the houses of the farm workers and the various farm buildings and are usually surrounded by great expanses of farmland. The buildings, with walls of beaten earth, are carefully white-washed, and with their flat roofs and intricately decorated openwork chimneys have preserved many Moorish features.

*Mértola in the Alentejo*

Farms of this kind, which with the addition of day labourers and seasonal workers can amount to settlements of considerable size, are characteristic of the old type of large estate which has long given rise to social tensions in Portugal. The expropriation measures introduced after the 1974 revolution – some of them since revoked or mitigated by compensation payments – still present the government with serious domestic problems.

Culture

Alentejo is a region of very ancient settlement, with numerous remains of Stone Age occupation (standing stones and megalithic chamber tombs, known as *antas*, being particularly common in Alto Alentejo) and of the Roman and Moorish periods.

The purely agricultural character of the region is reflected in the architecture: here the seafaring motifs common in the architectural ornament of the Manueline period give place to agricultural motifs (ears of corn, plants, farm implements).

Economy

Although Alentejo has a fifth of Portugal's total coastline the life and activities of the region revolve around the interior. Less than 1% of the country's total catch of fish comes from here, and the endless stretches of broad beach are empty and scarcely known to tourists. The people of the Alentejo region live almost exclusively from agriculture. In spite of the sparse population and the extreme aridity, almost the whole area is carefully cultivated. In the west, on poor soils, extensive monoculture predominates (corn, grown by dry-farming methods); in addition grazing farming (with a third of the total Portuguese stock of cattle) is carried on throughout the year, together with the growing of cork-oaks (*montados*), pig-farming and charcoal-burning. The wet and fertile coastal areas and the land on the weather side of the hills in the north-east are the granary of Portugal, growing in addition to grain (wheat, rye, maize) large quantities of fruit and olives.

Alentejo is also the home of a celebrated breed of horses, the Alter Real, which has been reared here since the mid 18th c. and is particularly prized for dressage.

The problem of irrigation is of fundamental importance in this agricultural province. The rivers which flow through the region are almost dry in summer and are thus of little use for irrigation; but there is an ambitious plan to build a series of dams on the Tagus and Guadiana and the Guadiana's left-bank tributary, the Rio Chança, and pump the water throughout the region in a dense network of canals.

## Algarve

B/C 7/8

Historical province: Algarve. District: Faro
Area: 4960 sq.km/1915 sq.miles
Population: 323,500. Chief town: Faro

General

The southern Portuguese province of the Algarve, lying in the extreme south-west corner of Europe, is a broad strip of land, some 155km/95 miles long and up to 50km/30 miles wide, on the southern Atlantic coast of Portugal, extending from Cabo de São Vincente (Cape St Vincent) in the west to the Rio Guadiana, the frontier with Spain, in the east. Sheltered on the north by a mountain range, which increases in height from east to west and isolates it from the rest of Portugal, the Algarve has preserved its own distinctive character and is very different in scenery, climate and culture from the more northerly parts of the country. It is also the province of Portugal where tourism has had the greatest impact on the landscape.

Although the Algarve is much poorer in art and architecture than other parts of the country, it has developed into the most popular tourist and holiday region in Portugal thanks to its equable climate, its luxuriant sub-tropical vegetation and its beautiful beaches of fine sand.

Recent decades have seen rapid growth in this tourism and although building excesses have not been on the scale that has marred the Spanish

Mediterranean coast the Algarve, especially its "rocky" parts, also has its share of blots on the landscape from intrusive hotels and holiday complexes.

Nevertheless there has been a real attempt to preserve the natural beauty of the landscape, and to blend hotels into their surroundings. Most of the new developments are spaciously and attractively laid out, often in the Moorish style. Clearly there is a price to be paid for this luxury and comfort, and rates are considerably higher in the Algarve than elsewhere in Portugal, pricing this part of the coast beyond the reach of most Portuguese.

The name Algarve comes from the Arabic "Al-Gharb", "the West", referring to this region's location at the western edge of the Islamic empire (see History).

Name

The sparsely populated northern part of the province, the Alto Algarve (Upper Algarve), is a hilly region of schists and sandstones, overlaid in the west by the intrusive rocks of the Serra de Monchique. Apart from one or two features there is little here to interest the holidaymaker.

★★ Topography

The coastal strip, the Baixo Algarve (Lower Algarve), a Mesozoic tableland of limestone and sandstone, has two parts. The western half, from Cabo São Vicente to Vale do Lobo (just west of Faro), is the better known and scenically more striking Rocky Algarve, world-famous for its picturesque golden-yellow cliffs, slashed by crevices and caves, its sheltered beaches of fine sand, its emerald-green water and its deep blue sky.

To the east, from Faro to the Spanish frontier, is the Sandy Algarve, with endless expanses of sandy beach, dunes and pine-groves but without any outstanding scenic beauties. This area has seen less tourism development.

The Algarve has one of the most settled climates in the world, with 3000 hours of sunshine in the year. The climate on the coast is similar to that of North Africa. Sheltered on the north and north-west by the hills of the Alto Algarve and exposed to the moderating influence of the Atlantic, the Algarve escapes climatic extremes.

Climate

Winter temperatures rarely fall below 10°C/50°F; the summers are dry and hot, but there is always a light sea breeze to bring a pleasant coolness. Temperatures fall rapidly in the evening, and visitors are advised to take some warm clothing. Rainfall is low (an annual 350–600mm/14–24in.) and mostly concentrated in November; but there are abundant resources of groundwater which is used for irrigation, making it possible to get three or four crops a year off the land.

In choosing where to go for a holiday visitors should consider wind conditions. The farther west they go the less protection there is from the winds blowing off the Atlantic and the more bracing the climate. The bathing resorts in the most westerly quarter of the Algarve are for the hardy, or for diving enthusiasts and anglers, since in this area there is usually a brisk, cool wind and the sea tends to be rough.

The purplish-red soil of the Algarve supports flourishing plantations of almond-trees, olives, figs and carob-trees. The carob-tree grows to heights of 15–20m/50–65ft, with a short trunk and dense foliage; the carob beans are edible. In the irrigated valleys are orange-groves, cotton plantations and fields of rice and sugar-cane. Most of the gardens and orchards are enclosed by hedges of agaves. Camellias and oleanders make an attractive show, and the almond-trees, which flourish in the mild Mediterranean climate, come into blossom as early as January or February.

Vegetation

Shut off by a barrier of hills in the north, the Algarve developed on its own. The fertility of the soil and the pleasant climate attracted human settlement from an early period. It is known that the Phoenicians and later the Greeks established colonies here, though only scanty remains have survived. In the 6th and 5th c. B.C. Celts settled in this region, followed soon afterwards

History

by Carthaginians: it is said that Portimão was founded by Hannibal. In Roman times the Algarve, then known as Cyneticum, was a prosperous and flourishing region, and evidence of the busy trade carried on here has been recovered by excavation.

After the Romans came the Visigoths, who controlled the region for almost 300 years. The Visigoths in turn gave way to the Moors, who remained for 500 years and left an enduring mark on the population and way of life of the Algarve. The physical type of the inhabitants – swarthy, short and stocky – bears witness to a Moorish ancestry, the local style of building and the traditional costumes show clear Moorish features, and the language and place-names, not least the Algarve itself, include many elements of Arab origin.

The capture of Faro by King Afonso III of Portugal in 1249 marked the first stage in the recovery of the territory from the Moors. The Algarve then became the last element to be incorporated in Portugal, an independent kingdom subject to the Portuguese crown in a personal union.

In the 15th c. the Algarve attracted worldwide interest when Henry the Navigator founded his famous school of seamanship at Sagres and with his systematic technical research laid the foundations for the great voyages of discovery of the following century.

Economy

The inhabitants of the Algarve are concentrated in the towns and villages along the coast, earning their living from three main sources of roughly equal importance: tunny and sardine fisheries, processed locally, although this has declined of late; agriculture, with up to four crops a year, principally of citrus fruits, vines, vegetables, almonds, rice and cotton; and the tourist trade, which continues to grow in importance, with about half of all visitors to Portugal holidaying on the Algarve.

## Along the Algarve coast

★Cabo de São Vicente

At the western tip of the coast is the windswept Cabo de São Vicente, a rocky headland rising 60m/200ft above the sea, familiar in British history as the scene of the naval victory of Cape St Vincent over a Spanish fleet in 1797. On the cape is a lighthouse 24m/80ft high, with a light which is visible at a distance of 35km/22 miles.

Here in the 12th c. a ship bearing the body of St Vincent (martyred in 304) came ashore, accompanied by two ravens. The mortal remains of the patron saint of seafarers and vinegrowers were subsequently interred in Lisbon (see entry) in a silver shrine in Sé Patriarcal.

From Cape St Vincent the coast road runs north-east over a windy heath for 1km/¾ mile to Fort Beliche with its former sea fort housing a restaurant.

From here it is 5km/3 miles to the port of Sagres (see entry) with the ruins of Henry the Navigator's famous School of Seamanship.

Martinhal excavations

At Martinhal, just east of Sagres, archaeologists have uncovered the remains of a Roman village, revealing an interesting settlement with a population of about 3000 who, judging from the coloured decoration of the houses and the complicated drainage system, were probably members of a prosperous village community.

Vila do Bispo

The "Bishop's town" of Vila do Bispo (pop. 1400), 10km/6 miles north of Sagres, has a 17th c. parish church richly decorated with blue azulejos and gilded woodcarving.

The Torre de Aspa, 3.5km/2 miles to the west, is the highest cliff on the Algarve coast at 156m/512ft and affords a magnificent view.

The 13th c. Romanesque and Gothic chapel of Nossa Senhora de Guadalupe 4km/2½ miles east of Vila do Bispo is where Henry the Navigator is

*Rock formations on the Algarve coast* ▶

# Algarve

Praia da Rocha, etc. = Names of Algarve beaches

supposed to have prayed for the successful outcome of his projected voyages of discovery.

**Salema, Burgau, Luz**

Further along the N 125 sideroads lead to the coastal resorts of Salema, Burgau and Luz, all with good beaches although Luz tends to be the most exclusive.

Beyond Luz the main road continues through increasingly sheltered and fertile countryside to Lagos (see entry). Solitude has become a thing of the past with the advent of modern hotels and holiday complexes, but Lagos has nevertheless managed to retain much of its special charm.

**Alvor**

Alvor, or Portus Hannibalis, as it was known to the Romans and Albur as it was called by the Moors, lies just 20km/12 miles east of Lagos on the Rio Alvor estuary. Its people lived mostly from fishing until well into the 1970s but nowadays tourism is the main industry and the countless hotels and holiday chalets bear witness to that fact. Visitors are also catered for with golf courses (the Penina Golf Hotel) and a casino.

King João II died here in 1495 after seeking a cure at Caldas de Monchique (see Serra de Monchique).

From Alvor a small road runs close to the coast to Praia da Rocha (see entry), famous for its magnificent beaches between picturesque cliffs.

The port of Portimão (see entry), just north of Praia da Rocha, although not picturesque or boasting any particular sights, is a good shopping centre with some quite original bars and restaurants.

From here the road to Porto de Lagos leads up into the Serra de Monchique (see entry).

Leaving Portimão by the suburb of Vila Nova de Portimão the coast road crosses the Rio Arade on a long viaduct, with the fishing village of Ferrugado (see Portimão) at the other end.

Lagoa (pop. 6000), 8km/5 miles east of Portimão, is a modest little country town with wine-making establishments. From here a road goes off left to Silves (see entry) and right to Carvoeiro.

Lagoa

The nearby Slide and Splash water pleasure park (see Practical Information, Water Pleasure Parks) has plenty of giant waterslides and other attractions to keep the children amused!

Carvoeiro is frequently cited as a particularly successful example of the new-style coastal resort but development of exclusive vacation homes, etc. on the rocky hills above the old town centre has reached such a pitch that the beautiful craggy coast and hinterland is almost completely smothered with Moorish style holiday villas. Further tourism development, including an 18-hole, possibly 36-hole, golf course, is planned.

Carvoeiro

At the eastern end of the resort is the picturesque rock arch the "Algar Seco", where the sea has scoured strange shapes and caves out of the white limestone.

There is another big water pleasure park, "the Big One", at Porches, on the N 125 (see Practical Information, Water Pleasure Parks).

Porches

From Porches and Alcantarilha roads lead south from the N 125 to Armação de Pêra. The uniformity of its plain multi-storey buildings, and its limited, more simple accommodation than that offered by Carvoeiro is offset by its excellent and seemingly endless beach. It is popular with both Portuguese and foreign holidaymakers.

Armação de Pêra

*Coast near Lagos (aerial photo)*

About 2km/1¼ miles west, on a high crag, is the 13th c. chapel of Nossa Senhora da Rocha.

Barely 5km/2 miles east of Alcantarilha a road leads to the Algarve's biggest and best-known holiday resort, Albufeira (see entry).

**Vilamoura**

About 10km/6 miles east of Albufeira is a planning development straight off the drawing board. The little holiday villages dotted over the hilly countryside offer every conceivable leisure activity – golf-courses, casinos, marinas, etc.

Building works near Vilamoura's marina revealed the remains of the original Roman settlement Cerro da Vila, and the "mosaic house" dating from the 3rd c. A.D. is particularly worth seeing.

**Quarteira, Vale do Lobo, Quinta do Lago**

Quarteira, 3km/2 miles south of Vilamoura, is less attractive with its serried ranks of hotels and apartment blocks.

Vale do Lobo (wolf valley) and Quinta do Lago (estate by the sea), a few kilometres south-east of Quarteira, revert to exclusive holiday complexes, with comfortable villas and hotels in a park landscape. This pleasant scenery was the setting for the 1989 session of the NATO assembly in Quinta do Lago.

**Loulé**

Just before Almansil a road leaves the N 125 for Loulé (see entry) which is supposed to have the best decorated chimneys in the region.

**São Lourenço**

Just past Almansil, still on the N 125 to Faro, the Baroque church of São Lourenço de Matos on the left of the road contains splendid azulejos depicting the life of St Lawrence.

Faro (see entry), the chief town of Algarve province, lies about 10km/6 miles beyond São Lourenço.

The coast road runs east from Faro over the irrigated plain, which resembles one enormous fertile garden. From here to the Spanish frontier

*View of Carvoeiro*

extends a long succession of broad sandy beaches. This part of the coast is not as popular with tourists as the rocky Algarve and the hotels and holiday settlements are fewer and further between so that, outside the high season, secluded beaches are still to be found.

The next place of any size is Olhão (see entry), which cannot be appreciated from the road – it takes a stroll around this little fishing town to sense something of its Moorish atmosphere.

No tour of the Algarve should overlook Tavira (see entry), 22km/14 miles east of Olhão.

The little fishing villages of Cabanas and Cacela, just east of Tavira, are still relatively free of mass tourism, with only a limited amount of holiday accommodation among their small white square-stone houses. They are good places for getting away from the crowds, and anyone wanting to enjoy a quiet swim from the offshore spit can get there on foot at low tide or be ferried out by fishing boat.

Cabanas, Cacela

20km/12½ miles beyond Tavira a road forks right to the resort of Monte Gordo, much favoured by British and Dutch visitors, with its casino and promenade, complete with gardens, running alongside the broad beach.

Monte Gordo

Vila Real de Santo António (see entry), 3km/2 miles east of Monte Gordo, is on the Rio Guadiana, the frontier between Portugal and Spain.

# Amarante

B3

Historical province: Duoro Litoral. District: Porto (Oporto)
Altitude: 125m/410ft. Population: 5000

## Amarante

**Situation and Importance**

The little town of Amarante, well known for its wine, lies picturesquely on both sides of the Rio Tâmega, on the north-west slopes of the Serra de Marão, about 70km/43 miles east of Oporto.

**Civic Festival**

The annual festival of Romaria de São Gonçalo on the first Saturday in June is a very popular event. In honour of the town's patron saint, who is also patron of married couples and lovers, it may well be a survival of a pre-Christian fertility cult, phallic-shaped biscuits are traditionally exchanged during the festival.

**★Townscape**

The old part of the town has a number of fine burghers' houses of the 16th–18th c., most of them roofed with shingles and surrounded by wooden balconies. The best view of this part of town and the beautiful 18th c. bridge over the Rio Tâmega, the Ponte de São Gonçalo, is from the new bridge or one of the café terraces on the south bank of the river.

## Sights

**Ponte de São Gonçalo**

The Ponte de São Gonçalo is a fine three-arched granite bridge over to the old town and was built in 1790 to replace an earlier river crossing.

**Convento de São Gonçalo**

The bridge brings the visitor into the 16th c. Convento de São Gonçalo, dominated by its tile-clad central dome. The convent, originally founded by King João III and his queen, Catherine of Castile, was enlarged in the reign of Filipe III in the "Philippine" style of the Renaissance period. The exterior, with arcades decorated with sculpture on the granite façade, is reminiscent of Italian Renaissance architecture. Inside the church and to the left of the high altar is the tomb of São Gonçalo (d. about 1260), in an over-decorated chapel. The organ has a fine carved case (17th c.). In the sacristy are paintings (damaged by Napoleon's troops) of scenes from life of the saint.

*The Convento de São Gonçalo in Amarante*

There are two adjoining cloisters. The first is rather dilapidated but the second has been restored and contains the Museu de Albano Sardoeira and some municipal offices.

The Museu de Albano Sardoeira on the upper floor of the cloister is a museum of Portuguese art from 1900 onwards, and includes works by the Cubist painter Amadeu de Sousa Cardoso, a native of the town. There is a special archaeological section as well.

Museu de Albano Sardoeira

The round church of São Pedro, above the convent church, is 17th c. apart from its façade which dates from 1725. The interior is richly decorated with talha dourada and azulejos.

São Pedro

## Surroundings

Freixo do Baixo, 6km/4 miles north-west, has the fine Romanesque church of São Salvador (1210).

Freixo de Baixo

In a valley about 25km/15 miles north-west of Amarante, Travanca is worth visiting for its fortified church belonging to the former Benedictine convent. The church (three-aisled), originally founded in 970, was rebuilt in Romanesque style in the 12th c. and has remained substantially unchanged since then apart from the apse added in the 16th c. It has preserved very fine 12th c. sculpture and the main portal abounds with mythical and animal carving.

Travanca

The little spa of Marco de Canaveses is about 17km/10 miles south-west and has hot springs containing sulphur and arsenic applied to treat rheumatism, skin complaints and diseases of the lymphatic system.

Marco de Canaveses

A very attractive excursion winds its way eastward over about 50km/30 miles through the wooded Serra do Marão (1415m/4643ft), reaching a height of 1020m/3347ft at the Alto do Espinho pass then descending past the Pousada de São Gonçalo (885m/2904ft), where there is a magnificent view, despite the ravages of forest fires and road-building.

★Serra do Marão

There are fine views all along the rest of the route which carries on to Vila Real (see entry).

## Arraiolos

C6

Historical province: Alto Alentejo. District: Évora
Altitude: 275m/900ft. Population: 6000

The ancient little town of Arraiolos about 20km/12 miles north of Évora, referred to by the Alexandrian geographer Ptolemy under the name of Arandia, is set in delightful surroundings on a low hill above the wide Alentejo plain, with magnificent views.
    The town is noted for its brightly coloured woollen carpets which are made in a kind of cross-stitch.
    This form of carpetmaking, presumably inherited from the Moors, has been practised here since the 17th c. The early designs were mainly Persian imitations, subsequently becoming geometric and more local. Arraiolos carpets, still mostly in strong colours, have been back in fashion since the mid 1970s, and are sold in other Alentejo towns, such as Évora, as well as in Arraiolos itself.

*Carpet*

# Arraiolos

*View of Arraiolos*

## Sights

**Castelo**

Above the white houses of the town, with their coloured (mostly blue) window-frames, rise the massive ruins of the 14th c. castle, with two gates and six square towers and, within its walls, a 16th c. church.

From here there is a superb view over the town and the fertile Alentejo plain.

**Town hall/Carpet exhibition**

The late 19th c. town hall, next to the tourist office, houses a permanent exhibition of Arraiolos carpets (also on sale).

**Igreja da Misericórdia**

The church of the Misericórdia, just south of the town hall, dates from the 16th c. and contains beautiful azulejo decoration (18th c.) and some notable paintings.

**Quinta dos Lóios**

Outside the town, to the north, stands the old Convento (now Quinta) dos Lóios (16th c.), now used by a commercial estate. Its church has a Manueline doorway and is completely faced with azulejos (c. 1700); the size of the interior is apparently increased by trompe-l'oeil painting. In the two-storey cloister is a beautiful marble basin of 1575.

## Surroundings

**Santana do Campo**

The village church of Santana do Campo 6km/4 miles north-west of Arraiolos was built on the site of a Roman temple.

**Montemor-o-Novo**

The little town of Montemor-o-Novo (alt. 291m/955ft) 23km/14 miles south-west has a Moorish appearance, with its white houses rising up the slopes of a hill. High above the town are the ruins of a medieval castle, occupying the site of a Roman fortress. In the archaeological museum can be seen reproductions of drawings and finds from the Gruta do Escoural (open: Tues.–Sun. 10am–5pm.

## Aveiro

Historical province: Beira Litoral. District: Aveiro
Altitude: sea level. Population: 30,000

About half way between Oporto and Coimbra, the old port and fishing town of Aveiro is attractively situated on the east side of the Ria de Aveiro, a lagoon 47km/29 miles long and up to 7km/4½ miles wide, well stocked with fish, with many branches and windings which earn it the local name of the *pólipo aquático* (sea polyp). Chief town of the district, Aveiro is the see of a bishop and one of Portugal's main west coast ports. The people of Aveiro and the surrounding area live chiefly from the production of salt, obtained from the salt-pans on the shores of the Ria de Aveiro, the gathering of seaweed for use as a fertiliser, and the manufacture of porcelain and ceramics, an industry established here in the early 19th c.

White pyramids of salt can be seen in the area, some covered with straw to withstand storms.

*Situation and Importance*

In Roman times the town, then known as Talabriga, lay directly on the sea. In the course of time, however, alluvium brought down by the Rio Vouga built up a spit of land off the coast, leaving only a narrow channel to the sea, the Barra. The town thus acquired one of the most sheltered harbours on the west coast of the peninsula, and enjoyed a period of high prosperity in the 15th and 16th c. as a result of the voyages of discovery which set out from here. The town still preserves many fine old buildings dating from this period.

In 1575 a violent storm devastated the town and closed its outlet to the sea. The harbour was now landlocked and useless, and all attempts to

*History*

Figueira da Foz, Coimbra

*Aviero: Barcos moliceiros are the characteristic craft*

reopen the passage to the sea were unsuccessful; the fishermen, deprived of their livelihood, migrated in the 18th c. to the new port of Vila Real de Santo António at the mouth of the Guadiana, founded by Pombal. A further storm in 1808 opened up the old channel to the sea, and this is now protected from silting-up by dykes and weirs. Aveiro harbour now ranks once again among the finest harbours in Portugal.

Seaweed-fishers

An unusual harvest is gathered by the *moliceiros* of Aveiro, the seaweed-fishers with their characteristic boats, the *barcos moliceiros*; they fish up seaweed (*moliço*), used as a natural fertiliser, from the Ria de Aveiro.

The moliceiros sail their wooden boats, with naïve pictures painted in bright colours on the high prow and stern, through the many branches of the estuary, gathering the seaweed with large rakes. When the shallow vessels have a full load the "crop" is landed or loaded into ox-carts in the shallows. The boats are up to 15m/50ft long and 2–2.2m/6½–7ft wide. If there is sufficient wind a trapezoid sail is hoisted; otherwise the boats are propelled by long poles or towed along narrow channels by long cables.

In recent times the number of boats has fallen from its original total of over a thousand to about thirty. The once busy and profitable trade of seaweed-gathering is now gradually dying out because of the increasing use of artificial fertilisers. As the demand for seaweed has fallen the moliceiros have begun to harvest wrack-grass (*junco*) which is dried and used as litter for livestock. The difficulty of making a living and the drift of young people to the towns, however, mean that few young men are now prepared to take up this ancient trade.

During the Festa da Ria, held annually in the second half of July, the last of the moliceiros take part in a regatta, with contests of skill and a competition for the finest paintings on the boats.

★Townscape

Aveiro is often compared with Amsterdam or Venice, despite having only three canals, but the many medieval features it has managed to preserve do make it very attractive. This is due in no small measure to the *barcos moliceiros* and a canal trip on one of these boats shows Aveiro at its most appealing.

## Sights

In the Praça da República, opposite the town hall, stands the church of the Misericórdia (16th–17th c.), with a fine Baroque doorway and beautiful 19th c. azulejo decoration on the façade.

Igreja da Misericórdia

To the south-east is the Catedral de São Domingos, presented to the Dominicans by the Infante Dom Pedro and consecrated in 1464. It was much altered in the 18th c., and the Baroque porch on the granite façade dates from 1719. The Cathedral contains the tomb of Catarina de Atalíde (d. 1551), who was celebrated by Camões in his sonnets under the name of Natércia. The verses were so passionate that in 1546 the poet was forced to flee from Lisbon.

Catedral de São Domingos

In front of the Cathedral is one of Portugal's finest calvaries, the Gothic Cruizeiro de São Domingos.

Opposite the Cathedral is the former Dominican convent, the Convento de Jesús, which houses the Museu de Aveiro. The daughter of King Afonso V, Infante Joana, entered this convent in 1472 against her father's wishes. She died here in 1490 at the age of only 38 and was buried in the convent church. Her readiness to endure privation and her renunciation of all privileges won her many admirers, and she is now much revered as the town's patron saint.

★Museu de Aveiro

The Museu de Aveiro was installed in the church, cloisters and other convent buildings in 1911. It provides an excellent and almost complete survey of Portuguese Baroque art, as well as showing pictures of the 15th to 20th c., sculpture and archaeological material. In the vestibule of the church, which is richly decorated with talha dourada and azulejos, is the Baroque tomb of St Joana (1699–1711, by João Antunes).

In the north of the town is the octagonal chapel of Senhor das Barrocas (1730), also the work of João Antunes. As is usual with Baroque it has richly decorated portals.

Capela do Senhor das Barrocas

## Surroundings of Aveiro

Along the Atlantic coast west of Aveiro stretch the beautiful sandy beaches of the "Silver Coast", the Costa de Prata (see entry). These include São Jacinto, about 8km/5 miles west of Aveiro, and, further south, Barra and Costa Nova, one of the region's finest coastal villages. They offer not only good sea bathing but excellent water sports facilities in the lagoon (sailing, rowing, motorboats, water-skiing).

Beaches

A boat-trip round the Ria de Aveiro lagoon is well worth undertaking (angling, wildfowling) as it provides an opportunity to see buildings on piles to cope with varying water levels, and the racks for drying the cod (stockfish) landed by the deep-sea fishermen. It also may be possible to get a glimpse of the remaining boats of the seaweed-gathering moliceiros in Bico harbour at Murtosa.

★Ria de Aveiro

25km/16 miles north-east of Aveiro, at Avanca, there is a little museum about Portugal's only Nobel prizewinner, António Egas Moniz, a doctor who won his Nobel Prize in 1949 for his contribution to medicine.

Avanca

At the north end of the Ria de Aveiro is Ovar (pop. 14,000, timber), famous for its Carnival with splendid processions through the streets of the town.

Ovar

The Calvário, with six chapels, is a scheduled national monument. The interesting local museum contains modern painting, folk art and ethnographical material.

4km/2½ miles further north-west is the pretty little resort of Praia do Furadouro (good beach), where, as at Nazaré (see entry), the fishermen use oxen to haul in their full nets.

Farther south, also on the spit of land between the estuary and the sea, are the village of Torreira and the Pousada da Ria.

Vila da Feira    About 12km/7½ miles north-east of Ovar, the little market town of Vila da Feira (pop. 3000) is dominated by the imposing ruins of a castle built in the 11th c. and later much altered and enlarged.

Ilhavo    In the old fishing port of Ilhavo (pop. 6500 and now completely silted up) about 7km/4½ miles south of Aveiro there is an interesting regional and maritime museum (Museu Marítimo e Regional) which also has exhibits of Vista Alegre procelain.

Vista Alegre    The best way to see Vista Alegre porcelain is to visit the town itself, 2km/1¼ mile south of Ilhavo. Famous throughout Portugal, the local porcelain has been made here since 1824 and factory has its own sales outlet and adjacent museum showing the long tradition of porcelain manufacture.

In the nearby little chapel of Nossa Senhora da Penha de França (17th c.) is the tomb of Bishop Manuel de Moura (1699) by the French sculptor Claude Laparde.

## Avis    C5

Historical province: Alentejo. District: Portalegre
Altitude: 200m/655ft. Population: 2000

Situation and Importance    The little town of Avis (formerly spelt Aviz) lies at the junction of the Ribeira de Avis and the Ribeira de Sêda which about 10km/6 miles south-west of the town is dammed by the Maranhão hydro-electric station, converting the river into a long, straggling lake with numerous arms.

Now an unpretentious little place Avis nevertheless can look back on a glorious past.

History    Avis became important in 1211 when Afonso II moved the headquarters of the military order of the Freires de Évora, which he had founded in 1147 to fight the Moors, to the town. The first knightly religious order in Europe it became the order of "São Bento de Aviz" and its splendour and influence lasted into the late 18th c.

With the coronation of the Grand Master of Avis as King João I in 1385 Avis became the cradle of a royal dynasty which ruled Portugal until 1580, during which period (particularly in the regency of João II and the reign of Manuel I) the country flourished as never before and became the leading seafaring nation in the world.

## Sights

Castle of the Knights    Of the simple curtain wall of the former Castle of the Knights (founded 1214) only one gateway, the keep (reconstructed in the 15th c.) and two other towers still remain.

Church of the Order    The Order's church (rebuilt in the 17th c.) contains a number of 15th c. tombs and a valuable gilt reliquary.

## Surroundings

Fronteira    The little town of Fronteira (pop. 2500) is 25km/15 miles east and has a late 16th c. parish church and burghers' houses of the 17th and 18th c. In

**Situation of the Azores**

FRANCE
ANDORRA
PORTUGAL
SPAIN
Azores
Balearics
Mediterranean Sea
Ceuta (E)
Gibraltar (GB)
Melilla (E)
Atlantic Ocean
Madeira
MOROCCO
ALGERIA
Canary Islands (E)
Western Sahara
MAURETANIA
© Baedeker

500 km

the main square stands a handsome 17th c. marble pillory column. There are fine views over the town from the Town Hall tower.

Above the town is the church of Nossa Senhora da Vila Velha, entirely clad with 17th c. azulejos.

This 20km/12 mile reservoir about 40km/25 miles west of Avis has a holiday centre with many sporting facilities.

Barragem de Montargil

## Azores (Ilhas dos Açores)

Autonomous Region of the Azores. (Região Autónoma dos Açores)
Area of islands: 2247 sq.km/867 sq.miles. Population: 252,000

The archipelago of the Azores (Ilhas dos Açores, "islands of the hawks"), still little involved in tourism, lies in the Atlantic 1400–1800km/870–1120 miles west of the Cabo da Roca on the mainland of Portugal and 1800–2500km/1120–1150 miles east of Newfoundland, between lat. 39°43′ and 36°55′ north and long. 24°46′ and 31°16′ west.

Situation and General

The nine largest islands lie in three widely separated groups. To the east are Santa Maria, with the little Formigas Islands, and São Miguel, the principal island of the whole archipelago; in the middle are the islands of Terceira, Graciosa, São Jorge, Faial and Pico, with Portugal's highest mountain (Pico, 2351m/7714ft); and to the north-west are Flores and Corvo. Two broad arms of the sea, more than 2000m/6500ft deep and respectively 137km/85 miles and 222km/138 miles wide, separate the three groups, the farthest points of which are 635km/395 miles apart.

Like other groups of islands in the Atlantic, the Azores are of volcanic origin, consisting of basaltic lavas, mainly of Tertiary date, and trachytes overlying the Central Atlantic anticline. There are numbers of huge caldeiras, and some of these craters (particularly on São Miguel) contain lakes of considerable size. The general topography of the islands is strikingly impressive, with a variegated pattern of hills and uplands, deeply slashed gorges, steep coastal cliffs and numerous hot springs.

Topography

Some islands have frequent earthquakes (São Miguel was completely destroyed in 1522, and there were severe earthquakes on Terceira, São Jorge, Faial and Pico on New Year's Day 1980), while others (Santa Maria, Graciosa) are almost free from seismic activity. Sea-quakes are of frequent occurrence in the offshore waters.

Thanks to their oceanic location and the influence of the Gulf Stream, which flows past the islands to the north, the Azores have a very equable sub-tropical climate. The annual variation of temperature is scarcely greater than on the more southerly island of Madeira (see entry; January average at Ponta Delgada 14.1°C/57.4°F, August 21.9°C/71.4°F), but the rainfall is higher than on Madeira and the summers in particular are not so dry (average rainfall at Ponta Delgada 1083mm/43 in.; average duration of sunshine in the year 1580 hours). The islands are exposed throughout the year to strong winds, in summer blowing mainly from the north-east (trade winds), in winter often violent, mostly coming from the south-west.

Climate

The Azores are of great importance to weather forecasters, since very stable zones of high pressure frequently build up in the area, particularly to the south and west, from which they move north-east towards Europe, bringing a settled period of good weather.

The vegetation of the Azores, thanks to the high humidity content of the air, is of almost tropical abundance, though it falls short of the luxuriance and variety found on Madeira. The flora is mainly of either European or African origin.

Vegetation

In spite of excessive felling of trees since the colonisation of the islands the hillsides are still covered with fine coniferous forests. Plans are now under way for replanting the deforested areas. Laurels, chestnuts and eucalyptuses are frequently found, either in fair-sized stretches of woodland or in smaller groves. The undergrowth includes bamboos and ferns. Palms are rare, and olive-trees are found in large numbers only on Terceira.

Apart from a few native species of birds and bats the animal life is of European origin. Curiously, the sparrow so ubiquitous elsewhere has never established itself in the Azores. Rabbits, mice and rats – common everywhere, and in some places so numerous as to have become pests – were brought in by ships.

Fauna

The population of the Azores is predominantly of Portuguese origin, with some admixture of Irish, Flemish and Breton blood and small numbers of negroes and mulattoes.

Population

The overwhelming majority of the population is Roman Catholic. In the past an unduly high population density and the unequal distribution of the land, most of which has remained since the colonial period in the hands of a few large landowners, led to a high rate of emigration, particularly to North and South America.

The Azores were known to the Phoenicians in the 6th c. B.C., and many centuries later were visited by Norsemen. Thereafter they were forgotten for centuries, first reappearing on an Italian map of 1351. The islands were rediscovered in 1427 by Portuguese seafarers sent out by Henry the Navigator. In 1432 Gonçalo Velho Cabral landed on Santa Maria, in 1444 a Portuguese vessel put in at São Miguel, and by 1452 the other islands were also known. From 1439 the archipelago, until then uninhabited, began to be settled and colonised by the Portuguese. In 1466 Afonso V made the islands of Faial and Pico over to his aunt Duchess Isabella of Burgundy, and thereafter there was a considerable influx of Flemish settlers. As an important port of call on the voyages of exploration in the 15th and 16th c. the islands enjoyed a period of great prosperity. From 1580 to 1640 the Azores, like the rest of Portugal, were under Spanish rule. They played an important part in the constitutional conflicts in Portugal between 1829 and 1832.

History

During both world wars, in spite of Portugal's neutrality, the United States established important naval and air bases in these strategically situated islands, and these appear set to continue under relatively recent treaties between the two countries.

◀ *São Miguel, the "green island" in the Azores*

The political movements for independence from the Portuguese mainland (Frente de Libertação dos Açores, FLA, and other groups) lost their importance when the Azores acquired autonomous region status in 1976.

The islands are currently represented by five members of Parliament in Lisbon.

**Economy**

The economy, now as in the past, depends mainly on agriculture. All the islands are well cultivated, producing grain (wheat, maize), fruit (apricots, pomegranates, bananas, figs, citrus fruits; pineapples on São Miguel), tea and tobacco for export, chiefly to mainland Portugal. Wine is produced on all the islands. There is also a considerable amount of stock-farming (cattle, pigs, sheep, goats). There are productive fisheries off the coasts. Whaling, long based on Faial and Pico, is now very much in decline. A contribution is also made to the economy by the gathering of seaweed, which produces the agar-agar used in the manufacture of gelatine.

There is practically no industry in the Azores apart from a few recently established textile plants on Terceira and São Miguel. Linen and woollen goods, lace and pottery are made at home or in small workshops, and – like the brandies which are distilled at a number of places in the islands – make popular souvenirs. Everything else, other than agricultural produce, has to be imported. For some years tourism has also been seen as a source of income but, with about 85,000 visitors a year, mostly from mainland Portugal, the Azores remains for the time being a destination for the individualist.

**Transport**

All the islands except Corvo have their own airport. Terceira and São Miguel take international flights and Santa Maria is also a transatlantic staging post. There are scheduled flights and ferry services between the islands, while the individual islands have bus services (again, not Corvo), and taxis or hire cars for reaching the more remote spots.

## São Miguel/Ilha de São Miguel

**Situation and general**

São Miguel (St Michael) is in the east of the archipelago and the largest and most heavily populated of the islands (area 747 sq.km/288 sq.miles; 65km/40 miles long and up to 16km/10 miles wide; pop.133,000). It is the economic and cultural hub of the Azores, with more features of tourist interest and better facilities for visitors than any of the other islands, and its extraordinary fertility means it is also known as the "green island".

Most of its people live on the steep south coast and are engaged in agriculture, producing maize, figs, pineapples, oranges, wine and tea.

The highest points on the island are the Pico da Vara (1105m/3626ft) in the east and the Pico da Cruz (846m/2776ft) in the west; in the middle of the island, between these two peaks, are many basalt cones ranging in height between 200m/650ft and 500m/1650ft. The volcanic character of this hilly island is reflected in the countless extinct craters, large and small, and the severe earthquakes and volcanic eruptions which have racked São Miguel since the 15th c. Some of the largest craters are now occupied by beautiful mountain lakes (Caldeira das Sete Cidades, Lagoa das Furnas, Lagoa do Fogo) which are now among the island's main tourist attractions. Warm and mineral springs are found, particularly in the valleys of Ribeira Grande near the north coast, and at Furnas near the south coast.

*Topography*

## ★Ponta Delgada

Ponta Delgada, capital of the autonomous region of the Azores and the chief town and port of the whole archipelago, is at sea level, has a population of 29,000 and lies in a wide bay on the south coast of the island of São Miguel. West of the town is one of the two international airports in the Azores.

*Situation and importance*

The pride of Ponta Delgada is its small university, opened in 1975 and boasting about a thousand graduates to date.

The town is built on gently rising ground between green hills, and with its many churches, its trim white houses and the lush gardens on its outskirts presents an attractive spectacle to visitors arriving by sea.

*Townscape*

*Ponta Delgada (São Miguel), the capital of the Azores*

Sights   The harbour, which mainly handles fruit and vegetables, is protected by a breakwater 1544m/1690yd long, from which there are fine views. At the landward end of the breakwater is Fort São Braz (1553), behind which stands a former Franciscan convent (now a hospital), with the beautifully decorated church of São José (15th–18th c.).

In the middle of town there are three linked squares. The first of these, as one comes from the harbour by way of the triple-arched Town Gate (1783), is the Praça de Gonçalo Velho, with a monument to Gonçalo Velho Cabral, discoverer and first governor of the Azores; then comes the Praça da República, with a statue of St Michael (São Miguel) in front of the Paço do Concelho (Town Hall, 17th–18th c.); and finally the Largo da Matriz, with the church of São Sebastião (founded 1533, in the reign of Jõao III), mainly Baroque, with a tall tower which is a prominent landmark. The beautiful main doorway, on the west front, is in Manueline style. The church has a beautiful high altar of carved cedarwood (18th c.) and fine choir-stalls. The adjoining museum is devoted to religious art, especially 16th c. vestments. The former convent of Santo André (16th c.; chapel with azulejo decoration) now houses the interesting Museu Carlos Machado, with extensive collections illustrating the folk traditions, culture and natural history (birds, fishes) of the Azores. From here Rua Guilherme Poças leads to the Igreja do Colégio (1592), built for the Jesuits (who were expelled in 1759). The church has a sumptuous Baroque doorway and a magnificent Baroque altar.

On the outskirts of the town are a number of attractive gardens and parks, some of them privately owned (viewing by request), including the municipal park, formerly the Jardim António Borges (wild-life enclosure). Also worth a visit are the pineapple hothouses just outside the town.

# Other sights on São Miguel

Views   There are superb panoramic views from the hills around the town: the Pico Salomão (3km/2 miles north), the Pico da Lima (6km/4 miles north-east) and the Pico do Fogo (10km/6 miles north-east).

★Caldeira das Sete Cidades   About 17km/11 miles north-west of Ponta Delgada is the Caldeira des Sete Cidades ("Cauldron of the Seven Cities") in which, according to legend, seven towns founded by expelled Spanish bishops were sunk. This is a volcanic crater which collapsed during some mighty eruption in prehistoric times and was given its present form with a diameter of some 7km/4½ miles and a circumference of 17km/10½ miles, by another violent eruption in 1445. The caldera is occupied by three small and two large crater lakes, the latter two – the Lagoa Grande or Lagoa Verde, with clear green water, and the Lagoa Azul, with deep blue water – being separated only by a narrow strip of land. The walls of the crater, falling steeply down for some 300m/1000ft, are surrounded by a fringe of woods, ferns and laurels.

Ribeira Grande   18km/11 miles noth-east of Ponta Delgada, on a lava plateau above the north coast of São Miguel, is the town of Ribeira Grande (pop. 9000), with a town hall of the 16th–18th c. and a 17th c. parish church.

★Lagoa do Fogo   From Ribeira Grande a road climbs to the south-east via Caldeira da Ribeira (6km/4 miles), a small spa with hot mineral springs containing carbonic acid and hydrogen sulphide, and Lombadas (11km/7 miles), which produces a mineral water esteemed throughout Portugal, to the Lagoa do Fogo ("Lake of Fire"), a crater lake 2km/1¼ miles long by 1km/¾ mile wide, surrounded by high hills, which was formed during an eruption in 1563.

It is worth climbing the Pico da Barrosa (949m/3114ft) to enjoy the panoramic view it affords over the whole island.

Vila Franca do Campo   About 25km/15 miles east of Ponta Delgada, on the south coast, is the former capital of the Azores, Vila Franca do Campo, birthplace of the navigator Bento de Góis, which was completely destroyed by an earthquake in 1522 (several 16th c. churches; potteries).

*Hot springs at Furnas (São Miguel) . . .*          *. . . Povoação, one of oldest settlements*

From Vila Franca do Campo a road runs inland, passing the Lagoa das ★Furnas
Furnas, a crater lake 2km/1¼ miles long, to Furnas, a popular summer
resort (fine gardens, villas, golf course) in a beautiful forest-fringed valley
basin (alt. 200–275m/650–900ft). Here after a violent volcanic eruption in
1630 there emerged a whole series of springs of various kinds (hot springs,
mud springs, sulphur and mineral springs), some of which are used for
medicinal purposes, either internally or in baths. There is magnificent
luxuriant vegetation.

12km/7½ miles south-east of Furnas on a beautiful road is Povoação (pop.   Povaoção
4000), one of the oldest settlements in the Azores, situated in a wide bay on
the south coast. Above the little town stands the Ermida de Santa Bárbara,
the first church to be built in the archipelago.

## Santa Maria/Ilha de Santa Maria

Santa Maria, the most southerly of the Azores, lies 85km/53 miles south of   Situation and
São Miguel in lat. 37° north and long. 25°5′ west.   general
   This rocky but fertile island, 17km/11 miles long and up to 8km/5 miles
wide, has an area of 97 sq.km/37 sq.miles and a population of about 6500,
who live mainly by crop-farming, stock-rearing and fishing, with pottery
often as a sideline. Santa Maria has a well-equipped airport which dates
from the Second World War when it was used as an American base.

The island is hilly, becoming flatter towards the west, with steep coasts   Topography
fringed by long stretches of cliffs. The highest point is the double summit
of Pico Alto (590m/1836ft). There are no calderas on Santa Maria.
   Some 35km/22 miles north-east of Santa Maria is the Formigas Bank, an
undersea ridge which emerges from the water to a height of up to 11m/36ft
in a series of bare cliffs known as the Rocas Formigas.

**Azores**

Sights

Vila do Porto (pop. 6000), the chief town on the island, is a small port in a wide, open bay on the south coast, surrounded by cliffs. The town, defended by two forts, is believed to have been the first settlement founded by Portuguese colonists in the 15th c. It has a number of 16th and 17th c. churches, including the church of Nossa Senhora da Assunção (15th c.; partly rebuilt in 1832), with a fine tower.

From Vila do Porto an attractive excursion (12km/7½ miles south) can be made, passing below the Pico Alto, to São Lourenço, which enjoys a beautiful setting above a sheltered bay on the east coast.

## Terceira/Ilha Terceira

General

Terceira, i.e. the "third" island, was the third to be discovered and is also the third largest in the Azores. The most important of the islands after São Miguel, it lies 157km/98 miles north-west of that island and 56km/35 miles east of the neighbouring island of São Jorge. Like São Miguel Terceira is relatively well developed for tourism. However, its 60,000 inhabitants, many of them descended from the first Flemish settlers in the 15th c., live by arable farming (thanks to the extraordinary fertility of its soil Terceira is the Azores' largest cereals producer) stock-rearing and seaweed-gathering. Some of them work on the Lajes airforce base in the north-east of the island. The island's airport, which has been greatly extended, also plays an important international role.

Topography

The island is 31km/19 miles long and up to 18km/11 miles wide, with an area of 397 sq.km/153 sq.miles. Its highest point is the Caldeira de Santa Bárbara (1067m/3501ft), in the western half of the island. The eastern half consists mainly of a great volcanic plateau surrounded by high mountains. The coasts are steep, with many stretches of cliff, protected here and there by forts.

## ★★Angra do Heroísmo

Situation and Importance

Angra do Heroísmo, the fortified chief town of its district and of the island of Terceira and the see of the Bishop of the Azores, lies in an open bay 2km/1¼ miles wide on the south coast of the island. On the west side of the bay is a peninsula, with Monte Brazil (210m/689ft). The attractive little town, which has a good harbour, was founded in 1534 and owes the second part of its name to its heroic resistance to the Spanish conquerors in the late 16th c., falling into Spanish hands only in 1583. Until 1832, when it was displaced by Ponta Delgada on São Miguel, Angra do Heroísmo was the capital of the Azores, and it still ranks as the cultural heart of the archipelago.

Townscape

The town layout was originally planned in the first half of the 16th c. and it still boasts some imposing 17th and 18th c. Baroque buildings, due in no small measure to the substantial restoration carried out after UNESCO gave it International Heritage status.

Sights

From the harbour the busy Rua de Lisboa (or Rua Direita) leads past the church of the Misericórdia, an imposing twin-towered Renaissance church, to the Praça da Restauração, the hub of the town's life. On the east side of the square is the 19th c. Câmara Municipal (town hall). The Rua de Lisboa ends in the Largo Prior do Crato, to the north of the Praça da Restauração, in which stands the former Jesuit College; the church (1652) has a richly decorated Baroque interior.

To the east of the Praça da Restauração, in the Rua de João de Deus, can be found the church of São Francisco (15th c., rebuilt in 17th c.). The convent buildings of the former Franciscan friary now house the municipal museum (Museu Municipal: folk traditions, coins, militaria, ships and the sea, art). The Franciscan friary is believed to contain the remains of Paulo da Gama (d. 1499), brother of the great navigator Vasco da Gama, who fell ill during the return voyage from the West Indies and died on Terceira; his tomb has not been identified. South-west of the Praça da Restauração, in Rua da República, is the twin-towered cathedral (Sé), built in 1568 on the site of an earlier church. Partially destroyed by fire in 1983 it was subsequently rebuilt according to the old plans. North-east of the Praça da Restauração, higher up, is an obelisk commemorating Pedro IV; from here there are far-ranging views of the town.

To the east of the Praça da Restauração, at the end of Rua Rainha Dona Amélia, is the 17th c. church of the Conceição (Conception), with rich talha dourada decoration in the interior.

Fort São João Baptista, above the town to the north-west, at the foot of Monte Brazil, is worth a visit. It was built by the Spaniards in the 17th c. and affords a magnificent panoramic view of the town. From the fort it is an easy climb up Monte Brazil (210m/689ft), a crater formed in a submarine eruption. From the rim of the crater there are superb views.

## Other sights on Terceira

About 21km/13 miles north-east of the town, in a wide bay on the east coast of Terceira, lies the old fortified port of Praia da Vitória (pop. 9000), named in honour of the Liberals' victory over the Royalists on August 11th 1829. The town has several times suffered earthquake destruction (1641, 1841; severe damage in 1980) and only two old buildings survive: the church (15th c.) in the upper part of the town, which has a rich Manueline doorway, and the 16th c. town hall. There is a fine long sandy beach. | Praia da Vitória

The busy little town of Lajes (pop. 6500) about 25km/16 miles north-west of Praia da Vitória depends almost entirely on the nearby airbase for its subsistence. | Lajes

An attractive trip can be made to the volcanic western part of Terceira and the Caldeira de Santa Bárbara (1022m/3353ft; view), the highest point on the island, a volcano with a number of explosion vents and collapsed craters. North-east and east of the volcanic plateau, between Pico Alto, Pico da Bagacina and Furnas do Enxofre, are several crater lakes and fumaroles. | Caldeira de Santa Bárbara

On a broad lava flow in the north of Terceira is the little wine-making town of Biscoitos. | Biscoitos

## Graciosa/Ilha Graciosa

Graciosa (the "lovely"), the most northerly island in the central Azores group, lies some 70km/45 miles north-west of Terceira and 55km/35 miles north of São Jorge in lat. 39°3′ north and long. 28° west. It owes its name to the abundance of its flowers. The island's 5500 inhabitants live by arable and fruit farming, and by raising livestock. | General

The island is 13km/8 miles long and up to 7km/4½ miles wide, with an area of 62 sq.km/24 sq.miles. Unlike the other islands in the Azores, it is not particularly hilly but, like them, it has steep and rocky coasts. Its highest point is the rim of the Caldeira do Enxofre (411m/1348ft). | Topography

## Sights on Graciosa

Santa Cruz (pop. 2000), chief place on the island and its principal port, lies in a small plain on the north-east coast. The little town was founded in 1485. The parish church (1701) is worth seeing and has a fine altar. | Santa Cruz

About 5km/3 miles south-east of Santa Cruz is the little port of Praia da Graciosa, from which it is a 1½ hour climb to the Caldeira do Enxofre, | ★Caldeira do Enxofre

4km/2½ miles south. This crater, from which there are extensive views, is 1200m/1300yd long, 600m/650yd across and some 300m/1000ft deep, with a crater lake and several eruption vents. On the floor of the crater is the Furna do Enxofre, a cavern some 150m/165yd long, 100m/110yd wide and over 20m/65ft high formed by the collapse of a layer of solidified lava after the outflow of the molten lava below. In the cavern are a small warm lake and several fumaroles of carbonic acid.

Termas do Carapacho
At the foot of the Caldeira, in the extreme south of the island, is the little spa of Termas do Carapacho, with subterranean healing springs for rheumatic ailments.

## São Jorge/Ilha de São Jorge

General
Roughly in the middle of the central group of the Azores is the long narrow island of São Jorge (St George), 55km/35 miles west of Terceira and separated from the islands of Pico to the south-west and Faial to the west by the 18km/11 mile wide Canal de São Jorge.
    The 11,000 inhabitants live by livestock rearing and crop husbandry, fishing and exporting timber.

Topography
São Jorge has an area of 238 sq.km/92 sq.miles and consists of one long narrow ridge of forest-covered volcanic hills, 45km/28 miles from end to end, which reaches its highest point in the Pico da Esperança (1066m/3498ft) and falls down to the sea in steep and rugged cliffs.

## Sights on São Jorge

Vila das Velas
The chief settlement on the island is the little port of Vila das Velas (pop. 2000) lying in a sheltered bay on the south-west coast.

Calheta/Pico da Esperança
About 22km/14 miles south-east of Vila das Velas is Calheta (pop. 1500; canning plant), a modest coastal village with a small harbour, from which the Pico da Esperança (1066m/3498ft) can be climbed. This is a now dormant volcano which last erupted in 1808; from the top there is a superb view of the whole archipelago.

Topo
At the eastern tip of the island is Topo, which is noted for its brighly coloured woollen blankets and cloth.

## Faial/Ilha do Faial

General
Faial, the most westerly island in the central group of the Azores, gets its name from a beech-like shrub, myrica faya, which grows all over the island. Faial is separated from the neighbouring island of Pico to the south-east by the 7km/4¼ mile wide Canal de São Jorge.
    The 16,000 inhabitants live by arable and livestock farming; Faial's centuries old whaling industry has ceased to be profitable.
    In the early years of this century the island was important as a station for several transatlantic cables but this has ceased with the advent of satellites. Faial has frequently been devastated by earthquakes, as in 1759/60, 1862, 1926, 1958 and most recently on New Year's Day 1980.
    The Nuremberg cosmographer Martin Behaim (1459–1507), who made major contributions to nautical and geographical knowledge in the age of the great discoveries, lived on Faial from 1486 to 1490.

★Topography
This hilly island, with a greatest length of 22km/14 miles and a greatest width of 15km/9 miles, has an area of 172 sq.km/66 sq.miles. Its highest

*Agriculture and cattle-rearing are the chief occupations of the inhabitants of Faial (Azores)*

point is the Pico Gordo (1043m/3422ft), a volcano which has been dormant since 1672.

The island has a soil of remarkable fertility and is covered with a luxuriant growth of vegetation. It is famous for its mass of hydrangeas which flower in June and July, and line the island's roads and tracks. The best way to get an idea of the beauty of the scenery is to go on a round-trip of the island.

## ★Horta

Horta, the fortified main town of Faial, lies facing the imposing cone of Pico in a wide bay on the south-east coast of the island, with a beach of black volcanic sand. The town is attractively situated on gently rising ground, surrounded by handsome villas and beautiful gardens. The inhabitants, many of them of Flemish descent, live by trade and the sale of fine embroidery and basketwork.

Situation and Importance

The town is probably named after Josse van Hutere, who settled Flemish colonists here at the behest of the Infante Dom Henrique. A less likely theory is that Horta is derived from the island's hydrangeas (hydrangea hortensia) although the plant is actually East Asian in origin. The Parliament of the Azores usually meets in Horta. The town with its well-protected harbour is the most frequent port of call in the North Atlantic for transatlantic sailors of every nation.

The harbour, one of the best in the Azores, is protected by a breakwater 750m/820yd long (note the "painting wall", on which the seamen immortalise themselves). The bay is closed on the south by the Guia peninsula (148m/486ft), formed by a submarine crater, which is linked to the island by a narrow isthmus. There is an attractive walk or boat trip from the harbour around the peninsula to the water-filled Caldeira do Inferno on the south

Sights

side, continuing to the former whaling station of Porto Pim on the seaward side of the isthmus.

## Other sights on Faial

★Caldeira do Pico Gordo

A road 18km/11 miles north-west ascends to the rim of the Caldeira do Pico Gordo, in the middle of the island. On the floor of the crater, which is 2km/1¼ mile in diameter and some 400m/1300ft deep, is a small lake. There is an attractive walk with magnificent views around the rim.

Volcão dos Capelinhos

The western tip of Faial is formed by the Volcão dos Capelinhos, a submarine volcano which emerged from the sea in 1957, burying under its ash the fishing village of Comprido and partly covering the old lighthouse. When the volcano subsided in 1958 the island was larger than before.

There is a small museum containing relics of the eruption and explanations of the formation of the volcano.

## Pico/Ilha do Pico

General

Pico, the most southerly island in the central group of the Azores, lies east of Faial and south-west of São Jorge, from which it is separated by the 18km/11 mile wide Canal de São Jorge.

The volcanic soil, of recent formation and spread over large areas without any covering of humus, affords little scope for agriculture, and the 15,500 or so inhabitants have to import much of their food from the neighbouring islands. The only extensive areas of cultivation are the vineyards which have been created with much labour on the slopes of the Pico Alto. The once considerable whaling industry has now much declined and its processing plant is seldom in operation.

*Fishing is almost the only occupation on Pico (Azores)*

The rugged and mountainous island of Pico, 48km/30 miles long and up to 15km/9 miles wide, with an area of 433 sq.km/167 sq. miles, rises at its western end to the prominent Pico Alto (2351m/7714ft), the highest peak not only in the Azores but in the whole of Portugal. The highest point in the eastern half of the island is the Pico Topo (1633m/5358ft). Topography

## Sights on Pico

The chief town of the island and its oldest settlement is the whaling port of Lajes (pop. 2500) on the south coast, with a town hall and parish church built of black lava. The whaling museum in Lajes graphically demonstrates just how perilous whaling has been even in our high-tech age. Two other little ports are Cais do Pico (or São Roque, fish-canning plant) on the north coast, and Madalena (regular boat services to Horta on Faial) on the north-west coast. The three places are linked by a road encircling the island which also gives access to a number of stalactitic caves, some only recently discovered, of which the Furna de Frei Matias at the north-west foot of the Pico Alto is the best known. Lajes/Cais do Pico/Madalena

The main tourist attraction on the island is the Pico Alto (2351m/7714ft), a still active volcano with an unusually steepsided summit which is frequently shrouded in cloud. The most violent recorded eruptions took place in 1562 and 1718. The ascent of the volcano (guide advisable) should be undertaken only in clear weather. The best starting-point is Madalena. From the summit there is a superb view of the whole of the central group of the Azores. In the caldera, some 300m/330yd in diameter and 30m/100ft deep, are numerous hot fumaroles (temperatures up to 74°C/165°F) and the Pico Pequreno, a bare eruption cone 70m/230ft high (difficult but rewarding climb on south-east side). ★Pico Alto

## Flores/Ilha das Flores

Flores, the "island of flowers", the most westerly of the Azores, lies 230km/145 miles north-west of Faial and 20km/12½ miles south of the neighbouring island of Corvo in lat. 39°25' north and long.31°15' west. The 4500 inhabitants live by arable and livestock farming, producing abundant yields for domestic consumption and for export. General information

The island owes its name to its masses of flowers – including, like Faial, the many hydrangeas – which make it one of the most beautiful of the Azores. 17km/11 miles long and up to 14km/9 miles wide, Flores has an area of 142 sq.km/55 sq.miles. Its highest point, the Morro Grande (942m/3091ft), is in the northern part of the island. The whole of the central and southern parts is made up of volcanic heights, with numerous crater lakes, waterfalls and hot springs. ★Topography

The main town on the island is the port of Santa Cruz das Flores (pop. 2000) halfway along the east coast, which has several small 18th c. Baroque churches. Another little port is Lajes (pop. 800) in a bay on the south-east coast. It is well worthwhile taking a trip into the lush interior of the island with its numerous crater lakes (Funda, Lomba, Rasa, etc.) and their carp which are used as bait for deep-sea fishing. Sights on Flores

## Corvo/Ilha do Corvo

Corvo ("crow island"), the most northerly and the smallest (17.5 sq.km/ 6¾ sq.miles) of the Azores, lies 15km/9 miles north-east of Flores in lat. 39°42' north which is in roughly the same latitude as Palma de Mallorca in the Balearics and Corfu in the Ionian Islands. General information

The 400 or so inhabitants of the island gain a modest subsistence from fishing and rearing livestock. The women weave excellent woollen cloth for domestic consumption. In recent years the gathering of seaweed for the production of agar-agar (gelatine) has made an increasing contribution to the economy.

Virtually untouched by tourism, Corvo is the only island in the Azores not to have an airport.

Topography

The island, 7km/4½ miles long and up to 4.5km/3 miles wide, is made up of a single extinct volcano, Monte Gordo (777m/2549ft), the crater of which, over 1.5km/1 mile wide, contains a lake with nine small rocky islets.

Sights

With its rugged and cliff-fringed coasts, which are particularly steep on the west side of the island, Corvo has no proper harbour. Boats put in at Rosário on the south coast, the island's only settlement, with a radio station and meteorological observatory on the hill above the village.

# Barcelos

B3

Historical province: Minho. District: Braga
Altitude: 40m/130ft. Population: 4000

Situation and Importance

The very picturesque old town of Barcelos, once capital of the first County established in Portugal (1298), lies on the right bank of the Rio Cávado 18km/11 miles west of Braga. It is famous for the brightly coloured pottery cockerels which have become a ubiquitous symbol of Portugal.

Barcelos Cockerel

The story goes that a pilgrim travelling to Santiago de Compostela who had been wrongly accused of theft and condemned to death was saved from the gallows when he appealed to St James to make the hangman's roast

*Barcelos: view of the Old Town*

*In the Market of Barcelos : the cockerel . . .     . . . and many ceramic articles*

cockerel crow in proof of his innocence. The grateful pilgrim then offered a pottery cockerel to St James in token of thanksgiving.

## Sights

The life of the town revolves around the spacious Campo da República, one of the largest squares in Portugal. Visitors flock to its Thursday market, which is much bigger than those held on the rest of the week, and where the goods on sale range from fruit, vegetables, meat and wine, to handicrafts and carved furniture.

★Campo da República

Next to the square is the flower-filled park of the Passeio dos Assentos.

On the north side of the square is the church of Nossa Senhora do Terço, belonging to a Benedictine house founded in 1705. It has a fine coffered ceiling with many painted panels and azulejo-clad walls (18th c.).

Nossa Senhora do Terço

The handsome Baroque church of the Bom Jesús da Cruz (16th–17th c.), an octagonal structure on a centralised plan with an imposing granite dome and a richly decorated interior, shows clear Italian influence.

Bom Jesús da Cruz

Near the church is the Torre de Menagem or Porta Nova, a relic of the town's 16th c. fortifications which today houses the tourist information centre and an exhibition of local arts and crafts.

Torre de Menagem

Opposite stands the former Capuchin convent of the Misericórdia (1649), now a hospital.

The central point of the old town, uphill from the Torre de Menagem, are the ruins of the Paço dos Duques de Bragança, seat of the Counts of Barcelos and later of the Dukes of Bragança (15th–16th c.). With its wide terrace the palace is the setting for the Archaeological Museum (Museu

★Paço dos Duques de Bragança

Arqueológico), an open-air lapidarium with inscribed stones and sculpture from the Roman period to the Middle Ages. A particularly notable item is the Cruzeiro do Senhor do Galo, a 14th c. wayside cross.

On the lower floor of the palace the Museu Regional de Cerâmica provides a wide-ranging display of the town's colourful pottery, including, needless to say, many different versions of the "Barcelos cockerel".

Igreja Matriz

Next to the palace stands the Romanesque and Gothic parish church (Igreja Matriz) dating from the 13th–14th c. and remodelled in the 18th c. It has a Romanesque doorway with an impressive rose window and fine azulejo decoration in the interior.

Solar dos Pinairos

Opposite the Paço dos Duques de Bragança is the Gothic Solar dos Pinairos (1448), a granite-built mansion with two towers and a beautiful arcaded courtyard.

In the middle of a grassed open space between the former duke's palace and the Solar dos Pinairos stands a 15th c. Gothic pelourinho, a pillory column, symbolising the jurisdiction of the municipal authorities.

Stone bridge

Below the former palace a five-arched stone bridge crosses the Rio Cávado. Originally built in the 14th c. it was rebuilt in the 16th c. and fully restored in the 19th c.

From the gardens on the other side of the bridge there is a fine view over Barcelos old town.

## Surroundings of Barcelos

Abade de Neiva

About 5km/3 miles north-west of Barcelos is the Romanesque and Gothic Abade de Neiva, with a well-preserved church and a free-standing fortified belfry.

Esposende

The seaside resort of Esposende (pop. 2200) lies where the Cávado meets the Atlantic, about 14km/9 miles west of Barcelos. Its beach of fine sand has in recent years helped to put this rather unassuming little place on the tourist map, but despite a number of new hotels and a bungalow complex on its edge the town still tends to attract visitors who favour peace and quiet rather than wanting all kinds of leisure activities.

Ofir

South of the estuary of the Cávado is the newly developed resort of Ofir, which until quite recently was a small fishing village.

Monte Franqueira

Situated on the summit of Monte Franqueira (298m/978ft) about 6km/4 miles south-west of Barcelos is the pilgrimage church of Nossa Senhora da Franqueira. Built in the 12th c. and much altered in subsequent centuries it offers fine views over the surrounding countryside.

Near the summit are the ruins of the Castelo da Faria (1373) and remains of a pre-Roman settlement.

Areias de Vilar

At Areias de Vilar about 8km/5 miles east of Barcelos is the Benedictine abbey of Vilar de Frades, now a home for the mentally handicapped. Here, too, is the Manueline church of São Lóios, with 18th c. azulejo pictures in two side chapels and a 15th c. Gothic copper cross in the sacristy.

Termas de Eirogo

The spa of Termas de Eirogo, 3km/2 miles north-east of Barcelos, has alkaline and radioactive sulphur springs which are used in the treatment of disorders of the digestive system and high blood pressure.

Manhetes

On a hill above the Cávado at Manhetes, 6km/4 miles north-east of Barcelos, stands a fine 12th c. Romanesque church.

# Batalha

Historical province: Beira Litoral. District: Leiria
Altitude: 70m/230ft. Population: 8000

The unpretentious little town of Batalha, in a fertile basin of the Lena valley between Lisbon and Coimbra, would probably attract scarcely a visitor were it not for its internationally famous Dominican abbey.

Situation and Importance

Nowadays Batalha is well equipped to cater for its visitors. Close to the abbey, around the newly built pousada, there can be found a small shopping centre and various cafés, with a permanent market on the square behind the abbey.

Townscape

Apart from the abbey Batalha also boasts a number of 17th/18th c. houses and the parish church of Santa Cruz (1512), which has a superb doorway.

## ★★Mosteiro de Santa Maria da Vitória

Batalha Abbey, the Mosteiro de Santa Maria da Vitória, on the north side of town, was founded in 1388 by King Jão I in fulfilment of a vow he had made on August 14th 1385, at the beginning of the battle of Aljubarrota (see Batalha, Surroundings), in which he defeated King Juan I of Castile and re-established Portuguese independence. Hence the name "Battle Abbey", or Mosteiro da Batalha as it is usually called.

Origins

The Abbey's first architect, who was responsible for the overall plan, was Afonso Domingues who by the time of his death in 1402 had completed the church choir and nave, the Claustro Real and some of the other monastery

History

*Batalha Abbey*

## Batalha Abbey

1 West doorway
2 Founder's Chapel (Capelo do Fundador)
3 Nave
4 Choir
5 Entrance to cloisters
6 Tomb of the Unknown Soldier
7 Fountain-house (Pavilhão)
8 Refectory (Museum of Unknown Soldier)
9 Exit
10 Entrance to Unfinished Chapels (Capelas Imperfeitas)
11 Vestibule
12 Unfinished Chapels (Capelas Imperfeitas)

Claustro de Dom Afonso V

Claustro Real

© Baedeker

30 m

### Mosteiro de Santa Maria da Vitória

buildings. His successor was David Houet (or Huguet or Huet) under whose direction until 1438 the church was finished and the Capella do Fundador built. He then started on what were later to be known as the unfinished chapels, the Capelas Imperfeitas. The work on these and the second cloister was continued by Martin Vásquez (d. before 1448) and Fernão de Évora (d. 1477). After a pause in activity building was resumed, with the vestibule between the choir and the unfinished chapels, under King Manuel I by Mateus Fernandes the Elder (d. 1515) and Mateus Fernandes the Younger (d. 1528). This period also saw the sculptor Diogo Boytaca (d. c. 1525) carry out much of the magnificent decoration that graces the abbey buildings. The last of the major architects to be involved in building Batalha Abbey was João de Castilho, creator of the the Hieronymite convent at Belém (see Lisbon). 1533 saw the last of the works carried out on the building.

Batalha Abbey suffered to some extent in the 1755 earthquake, but was far more badly damaged by French troops in 1810. The Dominican monastery was dissolved in 1834 and in 1840 it was declared a national monument. Subsequently carefully restored this great memorial to the liberation of the Portuguese people is in excellent condition today.

Abbey church

The church, built during the reign of João I, is a finely conceived example of the noblest Gothic style. Particularly notable are the west front with its rich sculptural decoration (partly restored) and the lively articulation of the south side.

The interior (80m/260ft long, 32.5m/107ft high) is very impressive, with its high stained-glass windows (some of them very old, particularly in the choir) and its massive piers. Set in the floor immediately inside the main entrance is the flat tombstone of Mateus Fernandes the Elder.

From the south aisle a magnificent doorway leads into the Founder's Chapel (Capela do Fundador), almost 20m/65ft square, with many fine tombs. In the middle is the sarcophagus, supported on eight lions, of João I (d. 1433) and his English wife Philippa of Lancaster (d. 1416). In recesses on the south side of the chapel are the tombs of four of the royal couple's children: at the left-hand end the tomb of the Infante Dom Fernando, the

*Batalha: West façade of the Abbey Church, and the Claustro Real*

"steadfast prince" of Calderon's tragedy, who died in Moroccan captivity in 1443; next to this the double tomb of the Infante João (d. 1442) and his wife Isabella; and the tombs of the Infante Dom Henrique (1394–1460; see Famous People), known to history as Henry the Navigator, although he himself never took part in any voyages of discovery, and the Infante Dom Pedro (1392–1449). On the west wall of the chapel are the tombs of King Afonso V (d. 1481) and his wife, and King João II (d. 1495) and his son Afonso.

On the north side of the church is the Royal Cloister, the Claustro Real, a masterpiece of Portuguese Gothic with its richly decorated arcades over-looking a garden-like courtyard. Here can be seen the whole range of Gothic in Portugal, from the simplest and plainest forms to the fantastic profusion of ornament of later periods. The stone tracery is mostly modern. From the cloister there is a fine view of the richly decorated north side of the church.

Claustro Real

In the north-west corner of the cloister is the chapel-like fountain-house (Pavilhão), from which, too, there are attractive glimpses of the abbey.

The Chapterhouse (Sala do Capitulo), on the east side of the cloister, has an imposing doorway and fine stained glass depicting the Passion of Christ. The tomb of two unknown soldiers from the First World War has a permanent guard of honour.

The former Refectory, on the west side of the cloister beyond the foun-tain-house, now houses the Museum of the Unknown Soldier.

A doorway at the north-west corner of the Claustro Real gives access to the Claustro de Dom Afonso V, with simple double windows and a plain pillared gallery (15th c.) on the upper floor.

Claustro de Dom Afonso V

To the east of this cloister is the Claustro de João III, destroyed by fire in 1811.

A door leads from the Claustro de Dom Afonso V to the square in front of

135

the abbey and past the Chapterhouse to the entrance of the Capelas Imperfeitas.

Capelas Imperfeitas

The Unfinished Chapels, the Capelas Imperfeitas, were built on to the east end of the church in the reigns of Duarte and Manuel I in the richest Manueline style. Surrounding a central octagon are seven large chapels, one of which contains the tomb of King Duarte (Eduard, son of João I) and his wife Eleanor of Aragon. The massive buttresses around the inside of the octagon were designed to support the dome, which was left unfinished. On the west side is a large vestibule, with a magnificent doorway almost 15m/50ft high and above this a gallery opening on to the octagon.

Equestrian statue

The equestrian statue placed before the southern façade of the church in 1961 is of Nuno Alvares Pereira, João I's commander at the battle of Aljubarrota.

## Surroundings of Batalha

São Jorge

About 5km/3 miles south-west, on the edge of the battlefield of Aljubarrota, the little chapel of São Jorge was built on the spot from which Nuno Alvares Pereira directed the conflict. At the entrance to the chapel there still stands a jug of fresh water, originally set there for the thirsty warriors.

Porto de Mós

On the slopes of an isolated hill above the Rio Lena, 9km/5½ miles south of Batalha Abbey, is Porto de Mós, dominated by a massive castle, the origins of which go back to the 9th c. After recovering the castle from the Moors King Sancho I had it restored, but much of it was again destroyed in the 1755 earthquake. Since then it has been restored on a number of occasions, most recently in 1956. From the castle there are magnificent panoramic views.

Stalactitic caves

About 10km/6 miles south-east of Porto de Mós, near the village of Mira de Aire, are three remarkable stalactitic caves (open to the public). The Grutas dos Moinhos Velhos contain interesting stalactites and stalagmites and an underground lake. A flight of steps leads down into the caves; the return is by elevator. The Grutas de Alvados, on the north-west side of the Pedra do Altar, contain numbers of small lakes in which the golden-brown walls of the caves are reflected. The caves can be seen only on a conducted tour. The Grutas de Santo António, on the upper slopes of the south face of the Pedro do Altar, contain large numbers of curiously shaped stalagmites; in three of the chambers the rock face has a reddish gleam. These caves, too, can only be seen on a conducted tour.

Alcobaça | See entry

Fátima | See entry

Leiria | See entry

Nazaré | See entry

# Beira

B–D 3–5

Historical provinces: Beira Alta, Beira Baixa and Beira Litoral
Districts: Viseu, Guarda, Catelo Branco, Aveiro and Coimbra
Area: 27,398 sq.km/10,578 sq.miles. Population: 1,923,000
Principal towns: Guarda, Castelo Branco and Coimbra

Situation and Topography

The region of Beira in northern Portugal is a great tract of land between the Douro in the north and the Tagus in the south, consisting mostly of rugged

*Beira Alta: Serra da Estrela*     *Beira Litoral: marshland near Aveiro*

mountain country and bleak plateaux. In this frontier territory, long disputed between Christians and Moors, the towns were always stoutly fortified.

Beira is made up of three old provinces of very different characters.

Beira Alta (Upper Beira) takes in the wooded highlands, geologically the continuation of the cordilleras of central Spain, which extend from the highest peaks on the Portuguese mainland, the Serra da Estrêla (see entry; 1991m/6532ft), to the valleys of the Douro (see entry) and Mondego. The climate is hot and dry in summer and cold in winter, with a great deal of snow at the higher altitudes.

This is a region of extensive agriculture and pastoral farming (sheep). Excellent wine is produced, particularly in the Dão and Mondego valleys.

The population is sparse, reflecting the low fertility of the soil and the limited area of land suitable for cultivation. The main town of Beira Alta is Guarda (see entry) with a population of only 15,000, and its largest town is Viseu (see entry), with a population of at least 21,000.

*Beira Alta*

Beira Baixa (Lower Beira), with Castelo Branco (see entry) as its capital, extends over an infertile plain between the southern foothills of the Serra da Estrêla and the Tagus.

The economy is similar to that of Alentejo; the predominant type of farming is monoculture (single-crop farming, in this case grain) on large estates, with mixed farming of Mediterranean type (grain, vegetables, fruit, including citrus fruits, olives) in the river valleys. In the extreme western part of the region the fragmentation of land holdings makes it difficult to achieve efficient and profitable working of the land. The rivers of Beira Baixa are famous for their abundance of fish.

*Beira Baixa*

Beira Litoral (coastal Beira) occupies a swathe of land extending along the coast from Ovar to Monte Real, relatively narrow in the north but becoming

*Beira Litoral*

137

broader about the latitude of the chief town Coimbra (see entry). It is bounded on the east by the heights of the Serra do Caramulo, the Serra da Estrêla and the Serra de Lousã. This is a landscape of dunes with pine-woods planted to consolidate them, marshy river estuaries (Vouga, Mondego) and salt-pans (Ria de Aveiro). Only in the inland parts of the region are grain and vegetables grown.

## Beja

C6

Historical province: Baixo Alentejo. District: Beja
Altitude: 282m/925ft. Population: 20,000

Situation and Importance

The old town of Beja, the Roman Pax Julia (of which some remains survive: foundations of walls on the north side of the town and a gate on the south side), is commandingly perched on a hill in the fertile plain of Baixo Alentejo. It is the largest town in Alentejo after Évora and is chief town of the district and an important commercial centre, especially for agricultural produce.

★Townscape

Although the little town of Beja has no very remarkable sights to boast of its many fine old buildings and winding alleys lined with gleaming white houses, some of them with charming iron grilles, windows, doorways and covered arcades, make its old town well worth a visit on any tour of Portugal. The best place to rest after a sightseeing walk is the pretty little park on the ring road where there is a café and car parking.

## Sights

★Convento N.S. da Conceição

The starting point for a tour of Beja's old town is possibly the Praça da Concaição, embellished with a modern statue (1958) of Queen Eleanor

Beja: Convent of the Conception

Beja: the Castelo

(1458–1525). In this square is the surviving part of the Convent of the Conception (Nossa Senhora da Conceição), a small house of Poor Clares founded by the Infante Dom Fernando and his wife Dona Brites and built between 1459 and 1506. It shows clear Manueline features and currently houses the regional museum.

In this convent lived the nun, Mariana Alcoforado (1640–1723; see Famous People) who, in 1665, from her window first saw the Chevalier de Chamilly. After getting to know her through her brother she embarked on an affair that ended with Chamilly's return to France in 1667. She is supposed to have sent her lover five passionate letters that were first published in 1667. These love letters which are enshrined in international literature as the "Lettres Portugaises" (letters of a Portuguese Nun) were probably, in fact, written not by the nun but by the Frenchman Gabriel-Joseph Guillerague (1636–1715).

The former convent church, richly decorated with talha, and the cloister with its beautiful 16th c. azulejo decoration, form part of the Museu Regional. Its collections, which are well worth seeing, include archaeological exhibits, paintings, one of Portugal's finest private collections of azulejos, coins, folk art, costumes and furniture.

Diagonally opposite the convent is the church of Santa Maria (13th c.). Its main façade is decorated with four small towers linked by Gothic arches.

*Santa Maria*

Opposite the entrance to the cloisters an alley leads through the old town to the Praça da República, the focus of life in Beja and the site of a fine Manueline pelourinho (pillory column).

*Praça da República*

At the north-west end of the square stands the church of the Misericórdia, which was originally built by the Infante Dom Luís in 1550 as a market hall and was later converted, by the addition of a chapel, into a church with a very spacious portico. The original function of the building, with its nine bays of vaulting which are borne on columns, can still be recognised.

*Igreja da Misericórdia*

Past the church and above the town to the north is the massive Castle, built by King Dinis I about 1300 on the remains of a Roman fortress; it has a handsome crenellated tower, built partly of marble, from which there is a fine view. In the inner courtyard is the Military Museum of Lower Alentejo (Museu Militar do Baixo Alentejo).

*Castelo*

Near the castle, beyond the Roman Évora Gate, stands the early Romanesque church of Santo Amaro. This oldest church in the town now houses a Visigothic Museum.

*Capela de Santo Amaro*

Below the castle, to the east, is the former Cathedral, in Renaissance style (1590; restored 1940).

*Sé*

South-west of the town centre, on the main road to Lisbon, is the Ermida de Santo André, founded in 1162 in thanksgiving for the recovery of the town from the Moors.

*Ermida de Santo André*

## Surroundings of Beja

About 8km/5 miles south-west of Beja on the N 18 to Aljustrel and taking the right fork at Penedo Gordo are the excavated remains of a Roman settlement at Pisões (baths, with mosaics, atrium, etc.).

*Pisões*

25km/15 miles west lies the little town of Ferreira do Alentejo (alt. 141m/462ft; pop. 6000) with a 16th c. parish church and the church of the Misericórdia with a 16th c. retable.

*Ferreira do Alentejo*

30km/19 miles south-east is the quaint little walled town of Serpa (alt. 230m/755ft; pop. 8000), still known by the name it bore in Roman times. Above the town are the ruins of a 13th c. castle which affords a superb view

*★Serpa*

of the town and surrounding countryside. The narrow lanes of the old town are lined with white houses, many of them faced with azulejos. Other features of interest are the Gothic church of Santa Maria (13th c.; polychrome azulejo decoration, 17th c., in the interior), the former convents of São Paulo and São António (15th–16th c.; cloister) and the remains of an ancient aqueduct at the Porta de Beja.

## Belmonte                                                                    C4

Historical province: Beira Baixa. District: Castelo Branco
Altitude: 610m/2000ft. Population: 2000

Situation and Importance

The charming little hill town of Belmonte, on a commanding eminence at the foot of the Serra da Estrêla and about halfway between Covilhã and Guarda, was the birthplace of the navigator Pedro Álvares Cabral (1467–1520), who discovered Brazil in 1500.

★Townscape

Skilfully restored mansions grouped around the square in the centre of Belmonte bear witness to its past prosperity and status.

In the main street stands a monument to the town's great son which was erected in 1963 on the 500th anniversary of Pedro Álvares Cabral's birth.

## Sights

Castelo

Above the town are the remains of the massive castle, built at the beginning of the 13th c., in the reign of King Dinis (restored 1940), from where there are extensive views of the Beira hills. The gate still bears the arms of the Cabral family.

*Belmonte: the Castle*

Opposite the castle gate, is the little Romanesque and Gothic chapel of Santiago (restored 1971). The interior of the church is notable for its simplicity. It contains the tomb of Cabral's mother, the remains of old frescoes in the choir and the tombs of Fernão and Henrique Francisco Cabral (17th c.). It also preserves the Gothic image of Nossa Senhora da Esperança (Our Lady of Hope) which Cabral took with him on his voyage to Brazil and later bequeathed to a Franciscan friary he founded near Belmonte. On the dissolution of the friary the image was transferred to the church of Santiago.

Chapel of
Santiago

## Surroundings of Belmonte

To get to Centum Cellas, a well-preserved Roman tower, follow the main road from Belmonte towards Guarda. About 1.5km/1 mile north of the centre of the village a signposted road bears off to the right and in about 200m/220yd comes to the remains of the tower which stands in the middle of fields. Centum Cellas was built square in plan, with two storeys and a crenellated roof and may have been just a watch-tower, or have served in the 2nd c. A.D. as a place of banishment for the Roman Bishop Cornelius.

★Centum Cellas

See entry

Serra da Estrela

## Berlenga Islands/Ilhas Berlengas · A5

Historical province: Estremadura. District: Leiria
Altitude: 0–88m/0–289ft. Population: 50

The Ilhas Berlengas, 12km/7½ miles north-west of the rugged and imposing Cabo Carvoeiro (see Peniche), rear out of the shimmering green sea as bleak and bizarrely shaped masses of granite apparently cast asunder from the mainland.
   This little archipelago consists of the main Ilha da Berlenga (4.5km/3 miles long and up to 800m/½ mile wide), the neighbouring islands of Estelas, Forcadeas and Farilhes, and numerous reefs and isolated rocks, offering magnificent opportunities for scuba divers. The main island can be reach by boat from Peniche in about an hour (regular services in summer).

Situation and
Importance

On the highest point of the main island stands a prominent lighthouse, and below this, on a crag above the sheltered bay on the south-east side of the island, is a castle (Forte de São João Baptista) built in the reign of João IV, now containing an inn (the only accommodation on the island apart from the campsite).
   From here a waymarked footpath (1½ hours) runs round the island, giving access to picturesque caves and tunnels, deep gorges and rocky coves lashed by the sea. Particularly fine is the Blue Grotto below the castle, which can stand comparison with the better known Blue Grotto on Capri. To the south of the castle is the Furado Grande, a natural tunnel 70m/75yd long which leads to the Cova do Sonho, a tiny rocky cove.
   A boat trip around the island (enquire at the harbour or the inn) is highly recommended for the many fine views.

Sights

## Borba · C6

Historical province: Alto Alentejo. District: Évora
Altitude: 416m/1365ft. Population: 4500

The attractive old-world little town of Borba, about halfway between Évora and Elvas, owes its evident prosperity to the white marble quarried in the nearby Montes Claros. A popular building material throughout Borba itself the marble is even used on the bus-shelters.
   Excellent wine is produced in the area.

Situation and
Importance

*Borba: Fonte das Bicas*

## Sights

The life of the town revolves around the Praça do Cinco de Outubro, in which are the Town Hall (1797) and parish church. The Renaissance church of São Bartolomeu (16th c.) is worth a visit with its fine doorway, brightly painted stone vaulting and rich azulejo decoration. Also of interest is the two-storey cloister of the Convento das Servas de Cristo in the middle of which is a fountain faced with azulejos.

Near the town centre, at the junction with the road to Vila Viçosa (see entry), stands the Fonte das Bicas (1781), a magnificent marble fountain in its own little park.

## Braga                                                                    B3

Historical province: Minho. District: Braga
Altitude: 185m/607ft. Population: 63,000

Situation and
Importance

The old-world town of Braga in northern Portugal and situated in an extensive depression between the rivers Cávado and Este, is one of the largest towns in the country and the seat of the Primate of Portugal. It has long been an important religious centre and its many churches have earned it the flattering title of the "Portuguese Rome".

Braga is also a busy industrial town producing motor vehicles, electrical goods, leather goods and textiles.

History

The site seems to have been inhabited in prehistoric times. Later it was the Roman Bracara Augusta, chief town and military headquarters of the territory of the Callaeci Bracarii, linked by five military highways with other military posts in Lusitania. During the Great Migrations Braga became

*Braga: Rua do Souto . . .*          *. . . fountain outside the Archbishop's Palace*

capital of the Suevic kingdom. In 716 it was occupied and devastated by the Moors. In 1040 Fernão I, the Great, recaptured the town for Castile and Christendom and at the beginning of the 12th c. it became the residence of the Portuguese kings. This was the beginning of an age of splendour, to which many buildings of the period still bear witness. When, after the great voyages of discovery, attention was increasingly focused on the coastal ports and the sea, the power and prosperity of the town began to decline and it sank back into the role of a provincial town.

Besides the notable number of churches, everywhere in the old town visitors will encounter fine old burghers' houses and noble mansions built of granite in an imposing style characteristic of Braga.

★Townscape

## Sights

The sturdy Torre de Menagem (1378) is a relic of the medieval fortifications.

Torre de Menagem

About 150m/164yd along the Rua de Souto stands the former Archbishop's Palace, the Antigo Paço Episcopal, fronting a little square with a pretty fountain (1723).
    The Palace is made up of three ranges of buildings dating from the 14th–17th c.; these now house the District Archives and one of the finest old libraries in Portugal, with more than 300,000 volumes and over 10,000 valuable manuscripts, the earliest dating from the 9th c.

★Antigo Paço Episcopal

The west façade of the Paço Episcopal faces the Praça do Municipio, relatively recently the site of the 18th c. pelican fountain, with the Baroque Town Hall, the Câmara Municipal, at the western end of the square; a collection of azulejos from the town's old buildings is housed on the first floor.

Câmara Municipal

# Braga

| | |
|---|---|
| Igreja do Pópulo | The Igreja do Pópulo, north of the square, was built in the 16th c. but its fine Baroque façade is 18th c. |
| Palácio dos Biscainhos | No walk through the town centre should miss the Palácio dos Biscainhos, west of the Town Hall. This Palace, which dates from the 16th c. but was subsequently much altered, today contains a small municipal museum. |
| Arco da Porta Nova | Just a few yards further south is the Arco da Porta Nova, the 18th c. gateway that for centuries served as Braga's main point of entry. |
| ★★Sé | Returning through the pedestrian precinct, this time a few yards to the east and then through the Rua do Cabido, we can see the main façade of the Cathedral, the Sé or Catedral. This jewel in Braga's crown was built in the 11th c. on the site of an earlier Romanesque church, enlarged in later centuries and remodelled in Manueline style in the early 16th c. |

Its most striking external features are the west porch, with three bays of groined vaulting and a beautiful iron grille, and a charming figure of Nossa Senhora do Leite (Our Lady of Milk), probably by the French sculptor Nicolas Chanteren, on the rear wall of the choir. Inside, above the richly ornamented Manueline font, is a magnificently carved organ-case. In the Coro Alto (high choir) are fine 15th c. choir-stalls. On the high altar is a 14th c. figure of the Virgin. Among the many monuments in the church is the very fine tomb in a side chapel of the Infante Dom Afonso, João I's natural son (15th c.).

An exit on the north side of the nave leads to the cloister built to replace a Gothic vestibule in the 18th c. From here a flight of steps leads up to the Treasury, richly stocked with precious objects, and a small Museum of Religious Art (fine talha dourada and azulejo decoration of the 17th–18th c., etc.).

From the cloister it is also possible to gain access to three chapels adjoining the cathedral. In the Capela dos Reis, built directly onto the nave, are the 16th c. tombs of Henry of Burgundy (d. 1112) and his wife Dona Teresa, and, behind glass, the mummified body of Archbishop Lourenço Vicente Coutinho (14th c.).

*Braga: the pilgrimage church of Bom Jesús do Monte* ▶

The Capela de São Geraldo has azulejos depicting scenes from the life of St Gerald, the first Archbishop of Braga (1096–1108). The next chapel, the Capela da Glória, decorated with azulejos and heraldic frescoes, contains the tomb of Archbishop Gonçalo Pereira (1336), commander of the Minho forces in the battle of Rio Salado against the Moroccans.

**Igreja da Misericórdia**

Behind the Cathedral is the Renaissance church of the Misericórdia (1562).

**Other Sights**

Braga has about 30 churches and also worth seeing are the church of São João do Souto (18th c.), just south of the Rua do Suoto, with the adjoining Capela da Conceição or Capela dos Coimbra, founded by João Coimbra in 1525 (fine statues), and the church of Santa Cruz, with its 17th c. Rococo façade.

West of the church of Santa Cruz, on the Campo de São Tiago, is the Arco de São Tiago; a nearby building houses the Museu Pio XII with displays of archaeology and religious art.

The 18th c. Palácio do Raio, or Casa do Mexicano, in the south-eastern part of the centre, has a tiled Rococo façade, and the nearby Fonte do Idolo is worth seeing. This sculpture-bedecked fountain on the edge of a garden ranks as a "national monument".

## Surroundings of Braga

**★Capela de São Frutuoso**

In the suburb of São Jerónimo Real, 3km/2 miles north-west of the town, is one of the oldest Christian buildings in Portugal, the Capela de São Frutuoso, founded by and named after an early bishop of Braga, Frutuoso de Dume (second half of 7th c.). The central part of the chapel and the east end date from the late 7th c. and show Byzantine influence – an unusual feature in Portugal. Other parts of the chapel were rebuilt or added after its destruction by the Moors in the 11th c. The simple interior shows a variety of styles (Visigothic, Romanesque, Lombard). Against the rear wall of the chapel is the sarcophagus of São Frutuoso.

The saint's remains are now in the adjoining Baroque church of the former Franciscan convent, in which the chapel, which has a fine carved pulpit, was incorporated in the 18th c.

**★Bom Jesús do Monte**

East of Braga are three well-known places of pilgrimage. The one most worth seeing is the church of Bom Jesús do Monte (alt. 401m/1316ft), 6km/4 miles east of Braga in a park on the western slopes of Monte Espinho (564m/1850ft). The beautiful gardens, little boating lake and pretty walks make it a favourite spot for picnics and excursions. There is a road up to Bom Jesús do Monte but the actual church is reached by a funicular or on foot up a Way of the Cross leading to a terrace from which a monumental Baroque staircase ascends to the church (originally 15th c.; rebuilt in 18th and 19th c.). The effort of the climb is rewarded by a panoramic view.

**Sameiro**

About 3km/2 miles farther south, on Monte Sameiro (582m/1910ft), is another pilgrimage church (20th c.). This is Portugal's second most visited pilgrimage site after Fátima (see entry). It is reached by an enormous modern flight of steps, with a statue of Pope Pius IX (1954) at the foot.

**Santa Maria Madalena**

Another 3km/2 miles beyond this is the Baroque chapel of Maria Madalena (mid 18th c.) with a pleasing granite façade.

**Citânia de Briteiros**

It is worth combining a visit to the pilgrimage churches with a trip just a few miles to the east to the Ice Age settlement of Citânia de Briteiros (see entry).

**Barcelos**

See entry

**Guimarães**

See entry

# Bragança                                                               D3

Historical province: Trás-os-Montes. District: Bragança
Altitude: 670m/2198ft. Population: 15,000

The attractive old town of Bragança, the Roman Iuliobriga, lies in a pleasantly cool setting on a hill above the valley of the Rio Sabor, in the extreme north-east corner of Portugal.
    The town is the original seat of the House of Bragança, which ruled in Portugal from 1640 to 1910 (for the last part of the period in the female line of Saxe-Coburg-Bragança) and in Brazil (as Emperors) from 1822 to 1889.
    As capital of the district of Bragança (area 6608 sq.km/2550 sq.miles; pop. 185,000) it is the cultural and economic heart of the surrounding country, which is mainly given over to farming, although in the town the traditional local craft of silk-weaving still flourishes.

*Situation and Importance*

The medieval upper town is encircled by fortified walls about 2m/6½ft thick, while the newer lower town boasts many fine burghers' houses and noble mansions of the Renaissance period, with handsome granite façades.

★Townscape

## Sights

In the middle of the newer part of the town, in the long Largo da Sé, stands the Cathedral, the Sé de São João Baptista, originally a Jesuit church, a plain and sturdy Renaissance building with the air of a secular building rather than a church. The aisleless interior is partly clad with azulejos. The choir has reticulated vaulting with bosses bearing coats of arms. The sacristy has a coffered ceiling and painted panels with scenes from the life of St Ignatius Loyola on the walls. Adjoining the church is an unusual brick-built cloister.

Sé de São João Baptista

Outside the main entrance to the Cathedral is a pelourinho (pillory column) of 1689, the symbol of municipal authority.

Pelourinho

From the Cathedral Rua do Conselheiro Abilio Beça leads to the former Bishop's Palace, now occupied by the interesting Museu do Abade de Baçal (archaeology, fine art, folk traditions, handicrafts).
    Nearby is the church of the Misericórdia.

Museu do Abade de Baçal

Above the town stands the massive Castle (Fortaleza), an imposing stronghold, long regarded as impregnable, which was built by King Sancho I in 1187 and later strengthened by João I. Originally the castle enclosed within its double circuit of walls and eighteen towers the whole of the medieval town. Contemporary views, however, show that by the 15th c. the town had expanded well beyond the castle walls.
    In front of the castle gateway is a modern statue of Dom Fernando, Duke of Bragança and governor of Ceuta, erected to commemorate the 500th anniversary of the ceremonial granting of a charter to the town in 1464.
    Within the walls are the remains of the Ducal Castle (12th c.), seat of the Dukes of Bragança. The 34m/112ft high keep, the Torre de Menagem, with two fine Gothic twin windows on the south and east sides, was built in the 15th c. Nearby is a 6m/20ft high pelourinho (pillory column), its Gothic shaft resting on the back of a wild boar carved from granite, probably dating from the late Iron Age. Also within the precincts of the castle is the church of Santa Maria do Castelo (16th c.), with a fine Renaissance doorway.
    The most interesting building within the castle walls is the Romanesque Domus Municipalis (Town Hall), a severe granite structure of the 12th c., built over a Roman cistern. In form an irregular pentagon, it has a dwarf gallery under the roof ridge (recently restored). This is one of the few secular buildings of the Romanesque period in Portugal.

★Fortaleza

Buçaco
National Park
Parque Nacional
do Buçaco

300 m

1 Capela de Caifas
2 Porta de Siloé
3 Porta de Cedron
4 Capela de Annas
5 Ermida de Nossa Senhora
 da Assunção
6 Fonte da Samaritana
7 Ermida de São José
8 Casa de Pilatos
9 Porta Judiciária
10 Ermida de Nossa Senhora
 da Conceição
11 Ermida und Fonte de São Elias
12 Ermida do Sepulcro
13 Ermida do Calvário
14 Ermida de São Miguel
15 Ermida de São João Baptista
16 Fonte de São Miguel

Battlefield
of 1810

© Baedeker

## Surroundings of Bragança

The Capela de São Bartolomeu, 5km/3 miles south of the town, offers an unusually fine panoramic view over the town and castle.

Capela de São Bartolomeu

The Montezinho Natural Park extends north of Bragança to the Spanish frontier and is still quite unspoilt and virtually free of settlement.

Parque Natural de Montezinho

6km/4 miles north-east, in the village of Castro de Avelãs, are the remains of a 12th c. Benedictine abbey. Parts of the abbey church, the only brick-built church in Portugal, have been incorporated in the present parish church.

Castro de Avelãs

## Buçaco National Park (Parque Nacional do Buçaco)    B4

Historical province: Beira Litoral. District: Aveiro
Altitude: 220–541m/722–1775ft. Area: 105 hectares/260 acres

Buçaco National Park, which lies 25km/15½ miles north-east of Coimbra on the northern slopes of the Serra do Buçaco, is virtually unrivalled in its scenic beauty and richness of vegetation. The older spelling, Busaco, is familiar in British history as the scene of Wellington's victory over Napoleon's troops in 1810.

Situation and General

Although it is possible to drive through the Buçaco Forest's 105ha/260 acres – enclosed by a wall over 5km/3 miles long – it is well worth taking the time to explore them using the network of attractive footpaths leading to idyllic glades, picturesque fountains and springs, and magnificent viewpoints. A good starting point inside the park is the Palace Hotel do Buçaco, accessible by car through the Porta das Ameias, Porta da Serra or Porta da Rainha.

In the 6th c. the Benedictine monks of Lorvão established a hermitage in the forest on the eastern slopes of the Cruz Alta hill. In the 11th c. this passed into the hands of the Augustinian canons of Coimbra, who always strenuously upheld their claim to the area and maintained it with great care. In 1622 women were forbidden to enter the area.

History

In 1628 a Carmelite convent was established in the forest and enclosed by the wall, with nine gates, which is still to be seen today. Here the monks planted an arboretum which quickly became famous and was continuously enriched by exotic species brought back by the Portuguese navigators from their worldwide voyaging.

A papal decree of 1643 prohibited the felling or damaging of any of the trees.

After the secularisation of all religious houses in Portugal in 1834 the property passed to the crown.

## Sights

The forest now contains some 400 native and 300 exotic species. Its special pride is its array of enormous cedars of Lebanon, and from Mexico, India and Africa; other outstanding specimens include mighty cypresses, ancient ginkgo trees, sequoias, araucarias and palms.

★★Topography

Besides its trees the park is also well worth a visit for its grottoes, pools, fountainheads, chapels, hermitages, oratories and walks. The springs, carefully constructed by the monks, are particularly worth seeing. These include, north of the hotel, the Fonte Fria ("cold spring"), with a cascade of 144 steps descending to a basin surrounded by beautiful flowering shrubs and conifers, and the Fonte do Carregal, flowing out of a grotto, to the south of the hotel.

In the centre of the park, surrounded by flowerbeds ablaze with colour, stands the former summer residence and hunting lodge of Carlos I, the

★Palace Hotel do Buçaco

*Buçaco National Park: Palace Hotel*

palace which he had the Italian architect Luigi Manini build between 1888 and 1907 alongside what had become the dilapidated remains of the convent. This sumptuous palace in Neo-Manueline style, with a great deal of sculpture and azulejo decoration, now has a certain nostalgic charm. Since 1909 it has been the luxurious Palace Hotel do Buçaco.

Convento

All that remains of the old convent is the little church (with sculpture and paintings illustrating the history of the convent), the cloister and a number of cells (small Wellington memorial).

★Cruz Alta

From the hotel a Way of the Cross (and a road via the Porta da Cruz Alta) leads up the hill to the Cruz Alta ("High Cross", 541m/1775ft), from which there are superb panoramic views extending to the Serra da Estrela (see entry) and the Atlantic Ocean.

Obelisk and Museum

An obelisk just outside the park walls near the Porta da Rainha and the small military museum both commemorate the battle of Buçaco, when Napoleon's third attempt to take Portugal was thwarted.

## Surroundings of Buçaco National Park

Luso

On the north-western edge of the park, in a picturesque setting at the foot of the Cruz Alta, are the attractively located spa hotels of Luso (alt. 380m/1247ft), where the chalybeate and radioactive mineral springs are used in the treatment of rheumatic and bronchial disorders.
Luso's bottled mineral water is Portugal's most popular brand.

Curia

Curia (pop. 3000, alt. 40m/130ft), about 10km/6 miles north-west of the park, is another well-known spa. Its hot springs containing calcium sulphate are favoured for ailments of the joints and metabolism. Curia has modern treatment facilities a variety of sport and recreational amenities and an attractive spa park.

## Caldas da Rainha                                                    A5

Historical province: Estremadura. District: Leiria
Altitude: 50m/165ft. Population: 20,000

About 100km/62 miles north of Lisbon and only about 10km/6 miles from the Atlantic, Caldas da Rainha is one of Portugal's leading spas, with hot sulphur springs (34.5°C/94.1°F) which are particularly recommended for the treatment of rheumatism.

Situation and Importance

Visitors flock from far and near to its Monday market in the central square, the Praça da República, where the tourist information centre is also sited. There are always some stalls selling the local majolica ware. This bright and often rather crudely coloured ware, which is also obtainable throughout the town, is very different from that found in the north.

The story to which the town owes its name – "the Queen's hot baths" – is that the virtues of the mineral springs were discovered by Queen Leonor, wife of João II, who observed the local peasants bathing in the water to cure pains in their joints. She then sold her jewels and used the money to found a hospital (1484), to which she herself often came to take the cure.

History

## Sights

This bath-house in the old town centre was founded by Queen Leonor and rebuilt in the mid-18th c. under King João IV, who also frequented the spa.

Hospital Termal

*Caldas da Rainha: a majolica factory*

*Caminha: Ingreja Matriz collegiate church*

| Igreja Nossa Senhora do Pópulo | Adjoining the bath-house, to the east, is the Igreja Nossa Senhora do Pópulo. This too was founded by Queen Leonor, and built in 1500 by the famous architect Boytaca. It has a separate tower, the lower part of which is square and the upper part octagonal. Notable features of the interior are a fine triptych and a Manueline chancel arch. The little baptistery and the font are richly decorated with azulejos. |
|---|---|
| Parque Dom Carlos I | The origins of the spa park, the Parque Dom Carlos I, also go back to Queen Leonor. Nowadays it has beautiful gardens, fine old trees, and a small lake in the centre. Near the eastern rim of the park are the buildings of the majolica works dating from the 19th c. and currently empty apart from exhibitions and other cultural uses. |
| Museu de José Malhôa | The pavilion in the park houses the Museu de José Malhôa containing modern Portuguese sculpture and paintings, including works by Malhôa who was born in Caldas da Rainha in 1855, with a ceramics section entered from the side. |

## Caminha                                                     B3

Historical province: Minho. District: Viana do Castelo
Altitude: 30m/100ft. Population: 2000

| Situation and Importance | The frontier town of Caminha, once strongly fortified, is charmingly set on a tongue of land between the rivers Coura and Minho, just above the mouth of the Minho.
Once a bulwark in the defence of northern Portugal against Galicia, strategically situated south-west of the Spanish stronghold of Santa Tecla, Caminha is now a modest little fishing town, with handicrafts and lace-making as flourishing subsidiary activities. |
|---|---|

## Sights in Caminha

| Praça do Conselheiro Silva Torres | In the main square, the Praça do Conselheiro Silva Torres, stands the town hall (Paços do Concelho, 15th c.), with a beautiful coffered ceiling in the council chamber. The adjoining 15th c. clock-tower is a relic of the town's medieval fortifications. On the south side of the square can be seen the Gothic Palácio dos Pitas (1490), and in the middle of the square, opposite the town hall, is a Renaissance granite fountain (16th c.). |
|---|---|
| Igreja Matriz | The town's most notable building, located about 150m/164yd beyond the arch in the clock-tower, is the three-aisled Collegiate Church, the Igreja Matriz, built between 1488 and 1565 and combining Gothic with early Renaissance elements. It has a Renaissance façade with an imposing main doorway and a beautiful rose window. Inside there is a wood ceiling carved in Mudéjar style by a Spanish master, while the apse and the charming octagonal font are Manueline. |

## Cascais                                                     A6

Historical province: Estremadura. District: Lisboa
Altitude: 0–20m/0–65ft. Population: 30,000

| Situation and importance | Situated 25km/15½ miles west of Lisbon on the Costa do Sol, Cascais is one of Portugal's most popular seaside resorts, with a correspondingly wide range of sporting and recreational facilities. Partly owing to the shelter from north winds afforded by the Serra de Sintra this former quiet fishing port swiftly expanded to become an elegant, almost cosmopolitan, coastal resort but little of this elegance remains today. Although prosperous |
|---|---|

folk from Lisbon still live here Cascais is thronged in the summer months by an endless stream of sunseekers.

History
There was a settlement here in Roman times. Cascais was granted a charter in the 14th c., but it was devastated by the 1755 earthquake which destroyed most of its old buildings.

As the summer residence of the kings of Portugal (from 1870) and the President of the Republic, the turn of the century saw Cascais becoming a meeting-place for high society.

Townscape
In recent years Cascais has grown at a furious rate and has now almost joined up with Estoril (see entry). The old town centre is the only place where there are still a few narrow alleys lined by pretty white houses.

The road west out of the town is like a permanent market, complete with stalls.

## Sights

Above the south-west side of the bay stands the 17th c. citadel, now the President's summer residence (no admittance).

Just north of the citadel is the Manueline church of Nossa Senhora da Assunção, with 18th c. azulejos, and, somewhat further up the road, the Baroque-style church of Nossa Senhora dos Navegantes, which has a remarkable portal and fine azulejos in the interior.

To the west of the citadel extends the Parque do Marechal Carmona,

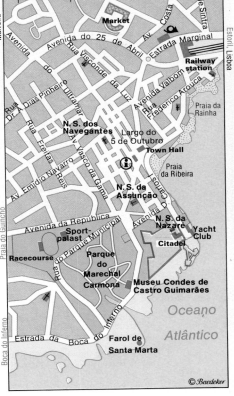

and on the south-east side of the park is the Palace of the Condes de Castro Guimarães, dating from the beginning of the century, which the family conveyed to the State in 1927. It houses a small museum containing family portraits and other paintings, as well as furniture, china, silver and gold objects, etc.

At the western exit from Cascais is the viewpoint above the ★Boca do Inferno, the "mouth of Hell", a cliff 15–20m/50–65ft high in which the sea has hollowed out a number of caves in which the pounding of the waves gives an impressive demonstration of the power of the Atlantic.

From the north side of the citadel the Avenida de Dom Carlos I promenade winds north-east above the Praia da Ribeira (sandy beach), affording beautiful views of Cascais Bay. Beyond this are the little beach of Praia da Rainha, picturesquely framed by rocks, and, still farther north-east in the

Beaches

153

*Cascais: the "Boca do Inferno" (mouth of hell)*

direction of Estoril (see entry), the beach of Praia da Duquesa, with fine sand and good facilities for bathers. In the summer all these beaches are overcrowded.

## Surroundings of Cascais

Ibn Mukau monument

About 5km/3 miles north of Cascais on the road to Alcabideche is a monument to Ibn Mukau, the 10th c. Arab poet who was born here, the first writer to celebrate the windmills of Portugal.

Costa do Sol

The trip along the Costa do Sol (see entry) from Lisbon (see entry) via Estoril (see entry) to Sintra (see entry) is well worth making.

## Castelo Branco                                                   C5

Historical province: Beira Baixa. District: Castelo Branco
Altitude: 375m/1230ft. Population: 25,000

Situation and Importance

Castelo Branco, in central Portugal near the Spanish frontier, is the former capital of the old province of Beira Baixa and now chief town of the district which bears its name.

It has been celebrated since the 17th c. for the brightly coloured embroidered bedspreads known as colchas. Other local products much esteemed in Portugal are goat's milk cheese and olive oil.

History

Lying so near the Spanish frontier, the town was of great military and strategic importance. Of the medieval Templar castle, the "castelo branco" or white castle, probably built in the reign of King Dinis, only scanty remains survive. In spite of its defensive walls Castelo Branco suffered

154

*Jardim Episcopal*

throughout its history from enemy assaults and raids, most recently in 1807, when Napoleon's troops did much damage.

Apart from the lovely Jardim Episcopal Castelo Branco has no particularly notable sights or unusual townscape features. Today's Castelo Branco is centred around the broad Alameda da Liberdade and the adjacent square, with gardens and the tourist information centre. West of this newer part of town are the 16th c. town hall and some 16th–18th c. townhouses, grouped around the Praça Luís de Camões.

Townscape

## Sights

The town's principal attraction is the Jardim Episcopal, formerly the Bishop's gardens and certainly one of the loveliest Baroque gardens in Portugal. The terraced gardens, laid out in the early 18th c. for Dom João de Mendoça, are a showpiece of Baroque extravagance and fantasy, with carefully clipped trees and shrubs, elaborately patterned flowerbeds and a profusion of basins and fountains. There is also a lavish display of Baroque sculpture – archangels, evangelists, apostles, allegorical figures, animals and, flanking a flight of steps, the complete series of Portuguese kings with the Spanish Hapsburg kings (1580–1640) rather pointedly represented by much smaller figures.

★Jardim Episcopal

The old Bishop's Palace, on the northern edge of the park, which was originally Gothic and remodelled as Baroque in 1726, houses the Museu de Francisco Tavares Proença Júnior, with prehistoric and Roman material from the Castelo Branco area, pictures by Portuguese artists of the 16th, 18th and 19th c., tapestries, coins, furniture, armour, etc.
In front of the palace is a pelourinho (pillory column) with a twisted shaft.

Antigo Paço Episcopal

The church of the Misericórdia (1519), opposite the Bishop's Palace, has a Manueline doorway, while the main attractions of the church of Nossa Senhora da Piedade are the azulejos, and of the church of Santa Isabel, the paintings.

Other sights

155

*Jardim Episcopal – the Baroque stairway . . .   . . . and a Fortaleza figure*

Above the town are the ruins of the 12th c. Templar castle and the little church of Santa Maria do Castelo. From here a flight of steps leads up to the Miradouro de São Gens, a viewpoint from which there is a far-ranging prospect of the town and surrounding area.

## Surroundings of Castelo Branco

| | |
|---|---|
| Nossa Senhora de Mércoles | About 5km/3 miles east is the Gothic pilgrimage church of Nossa Senhora de Mércoles (15th c.). |
| Idanha-a-Velha | The little village of Idanha-a-Velha some 50km/31 miles north-east of Castelo Branco boasts an illustrious past. Founded by the Romans it was the episcopal see under the Visigoths in the 6th c. before sinking back into obscurity following the Moorish invasion in the 8th c. It still has parts of a Roman street and gateway and further excavation would doubtless reveal traces of many other buildings. |
| ★Monsanto | About 10km/6 miles north-east of Idanha-a-Velha, below the summit of a rocky hill, is the picturesque little town of Monsanto da Beira (alt. 758m/2487ft), dominated by the ruins of a castle. With its trim white houses, sometimes hewn out of the rock, its steep and narrow lanes and its Celtic remains it is one of the most visited and most characteristic places in Beira Baixa – and in fact emerged from a competition in 1940 as "the most Portuguese village". |
| Portas de Ródão | About 30km/19 miles south-west of Castelo Branco the Tagus has carved out a magnificent rocky gorge, 45m/150ft wide, the Portas de Ródão. The best view of the gorge is from the bridge over the Tagus at Vila Velha de Ródão to the east. |

Castelo Branco is a good base for excursions in the Serra de Gardunha, a range of hills north of the town which in places take on an almost Alpine character, with bizarrely shaped rock formations bearing such names as the Cabeça de Frade ("monk's head") and Pedra Sobreposta ("rockpile").

★Serra da Gardunha

The pleasant little hill-town of Alpedrinha (alt. 555m/1855ft), about 30km/ 19 miles along the Castelo Branco road to Covilhã (see entry), is a good starting point for walks in the Serra da Gardunha. There is a lovely walk from here to the Penha da Senhora da Serra (hermitage), with beautiful panoramic views, and then on to the Pirâmide (1223m/4013ft), the highest point in this range of hills.

The Pirâmide can also be climbed from the picturesque hill village of Castelo Novo (700m/2300ft), below the hermitage and boasting an 18th c. town hall and a Manueline pelourinho both of which are worth seeing.

The chief place in the Serra da Gardunha is the little town of Fundão (alt. 496m/1627ft; pop. 6000), 45km/28 miles north of Castelo Branco in a fertile fruit-growing region on the northern slopes of the hills, with an old-established textile industry. It has two attractive churches, the parish church of the Misericórdia (18th c.) and the chapel of São Francisco.

Fundão

## Castelo de Vide

Historical province: Alto Alentejo. District: Portalegre
Altitude: 460–628m/1509–2060ft. Population: 2600

On the north-west side of the bleak Serra de São Mameda, clustering in steps and stairs around the hilltop on which stands its castle, Castelo de Vide is 20km/12½ miles north of Portalegre, near the Spanish frontier. Although one of Portugal's most picturesque places, tourism is still within reasonable bounds, and the townsfolk mostly still earn their living from agriculture and handicrafts, as well as from visitors to the cold mineral springs containing Glauber's salt and taken for the treatment of diabetes and skin and liver ailments.

Situation and Importance

Castelo de Vide has managed to preserve its medieval townscape virtually intact, with its picturesque maze of narrow streets and trim whitewashed houses with their characteristic chimneys, and many charming little squares and nooks and corners. Flowers are everywhere and just about every house in the old town centre is resplendent with window boxes and rows of flowerpots.

★★Townscape

## Sights

The centre of Castelo de Vide, and the best starting point for a walk round the town, is the Praça de Dom Pedro V, a well-proportioned square bounded by Baroque palaces, churches and the town hall with a statue of Dom Pedro V in the middle. Dominating the square is the Baroque church of Santa Maria with its squat pyramidal central tower.

Praça de Dom Pedro V

From the Praça de Dom Pedro V signs point the way along picturesque lanes up to the Castelo do São Roque, built in 1327 on the remains of a Moorish castle, from which an ingenious ventilation system still survives. Its massive keep was damaged by an explosion in 1705 but can still be climbed to obtain superb views over the town and countryside.

Castelo

Within the castle perimeter stands the church of Nossa Senhora da Alegria, completely covered with 17th c. azulejos.

Just left of the exit from the castle is the old Jewish quarter, the Judiaria, where time seems to have stood still. The narrow steep alleyways are pedestrian only. Many of the little houses have fine Gothic and Manueline

Judiaria

windows and doors. Easily viewable, the 14th c. synagogue on the main street is barely distinguishable from the other houses.

The main street ends in an attractive square with the covered Renaissance town fountain, the Fonte da Vile.

North-east of the Praça de Dom Pedro, in the opposite direction to the castle at the other end of town, and reached via gardens and the "Fonte do Montorinho" fountain, is the former Franciscan convent, the Convento de São Francisco, now a home for the visually handicapped.

Convento de São Francisco

## Surroundings of Castelo de Vide

4km/2½ miles south-west is the Monte da Penha (700m/2300ft; chapel), from which there is a charming view of the town.

Monte da Penha

The little town of Nisa, 25km/15 miles north-west of Castelo de Vide, has a 13th c. ruined castle, the remains of its walls, with two 14th c. towers, and a fine Baroque parish church.

Nisa

To the west of Nisa flows the Ribeira de Nisa, a tributary of the Tagus, which is dammed about 10km/6 miles south-east of the town to form the Barragem da Póvoa (water sports).

Ribeira de Nisa

Within easy reach of Castelo de Vide and definitely worth a visit are Marvão, with its castle (12km/7½ miles south-east – see entry), and Portalegre (20km/12½ miles south – see entry).

Marvão, Portalegre

## Castro Verde                                           B7

Historical province: Baixo Alentejo. District: Beja
Altitude: 245m/804ft. Population: 6000

The modest little market town of Castro Verde (green castle) lies about 60km/37 miles south-west of the chief town of the district, Beja, and is surrounded by pastureland and forests of cork-oak.

Situation and Importance

## Sights

The aisleless church of Nossa Senhora da Conceição has an interior completely clad with early 18th c. azulejos depicting scenes from the battle of Ourique (see Surroundings).

Igreja da Conceição

Also of interest is the church of the Chagas do Salvador, decorated with azulejos in a style typical of the region, which was built by Philip II of Spain in the 16th c. on the site of an earlier church.

Igreja das Chagas do Salvador

## Surroundings of Castro Verde

Tradition has it that the battle of Ourique, when Afonso I Henriques won a decisive victory over the Moors in 1139, took place near the modest little village of Ourique, about 15km/9 miles south-west of Castro Verde. The actual site of the battle is supposed to be Campo de Ourique, between Castro Verde and the village, although historians cast doubt on whether the battle actually happened so far south.

Ourique

About 6km/4 miles south of Aldeia dos Palheiros a little road branches off (4km/2½ miles) to the remains of a settlement of the early historical period,

Castro de Cola

◀ *Castelo de Vide: the view from the castle*

the Castro de Cola (known in Roman times as Ossonoba). Roughly rectangular in shape, it is surrounded by a rampart 5m/16ft high.

Almôdôvar
Almôdôvar (alt. 289m/948ft; pop. 2500), 21km/13 miles south of Castro Verde, has a 17th c. Franciscan convent with a beautiful cloister, and a Gothic and Manueline parish church which are worth seeing.

Aljustrel
23km/14 miles north of Castro Verde lies the busy little town of Aljustrel (alt. 200m/655ft; pop. 10,000), with copper-mines, some of which have been worked since ancient times.

## Chaves                                                                    C3

Historical province: Trás-os-Montes. District: Vila Real
Altitude: 324m/1063ft. Population: 13,000

Situation and Importance
The old-world little town of Chaves, the Roman Aquae Flaviae, lies on a plateau in northern Portugal near the Spanish frontier, in an area watered by the Rio Tâmega which has been intensively cultivated since ancient times. As far back as the Romans there has been recourse to the town's hot springs (73°C/163°F) for the treatment of rheumatism and internal ailments.

History
The town has a history dating back to pre-Roman times. With a substantial stone bridge over the Rio Tâmega built in the reign of Trajan (98–117), it became an important staging point on the road between Asturica Augusta (Astorga) and Bracara Augusta (Braga). During the Middle Ages it was a stronghold defending Portuguese territory against Spain in the north.

Townscape
The town still presents a sturdy defensive face to the world, its powerful castle rearing above the white houses with their balconies and arcades.

## Sights

Ponte Romana
The Rio Tâmega is spanned by a well-preserved Roman bridge of twelve arches, 140m/155yds long, dating from the 2nd c. A.D. The two Roman milestones, with inscriptions, in the middle of the bridge are copies of the originals which are in the town museum.

São João de Deus
Near the bridge, on the left bank of the river, stands the Baroque church of São João de Deus, an octagonal structure made particularly impressive by its fine granite façade.

Igreja Matriz
The life of the town revolves around the Praça da República, with a Manueline pelourinho (pillory column) and the parish church, the Igreja Matriz. Originally Romanesque, this was rebuilt in the 16th c., only the tower and part of the doorway surviving from the earlier church.

Igreja da Misericórdia
Behind the parish church the Baroque church of the Misericórdia (17th c.) has azulejo pictures (Biblical scenes) covering the interior walls and fine 18th c. ceiling paintings.

Museu Municipal
The nearby municipal museum in the 17th c. palace of the Dukes of Bragança contains archaeological material found locally, coins, azulejos and folk art.

Castelo
The massive castle above the town was built on the site of a Roman fortress. It was strengthened after the Moorish conquest, badly damaged during the Reconquista and rebuilt by King Dinis in the 13th/14th c. The medieval castle was the residence of the first Duke of Bragança, a natural son of King João I. In the 17th c. Vauban-style bastions were built on to the castle, but these were later destroyed. The imposing keep, the Torre de Menagem, houses a small military museum.

## Surroundings of Chaves

About 4km/2½ miles north of Chaves stands the church of Nossa Senhora da Azinheira, an aisleless Romanesque building with unusual figural decoration on the façade, and medieval frescoes (much altered) in the interior.

Nossa Senhora da Azinheira

The interesting feature of Santo Estêvão, 3km/2 miles east of Chaves, is its 13th c. castle ruins.

Santo Estêvão

About 15km/9 miles south-west of Chaves, Vidago (alt. 350m/1148ft) has hot springs used to treat internal ailments.

Vidago

Carvalhelhos, about 30km/19 miles west of Chaves, is also a little spa. Nearby are the remains of an Iron Age settlement.

Carvalhelhos

## Citânia de Briteiros                                                    B3

Historical province: Minho. District: Braga
Altitude: 336m/1102ft

About 12km/7½ miles east of Braga on Monte São Romão, surrounded by the pleasant hills of the Serra Falperra, are the remains of the Citânia de Briteiros, an Iron Age settlement. Together with Castro de Sabroso it is Portugal's oldest known settlement to date. Fragments of pottery (much of it painted), carved stones, weapons, implements and jewellery recovered during the excavations are now in the Museu de Martins Sarmento in Guimarães (see entry).

Situation and General

It is well worth taking the time to look round Citânia de Briteiros, climbing slowly up from the entrance located below the main excavation area to the two reconstructed round huts and then on to the small chapel of São

**Citânia de Briteiros**

Crematorium

São Romão

Reconstructed huts

Meeting-house

Look-out

© *Baedeker*                    50 m

——— walls        ▢ rectangular huts        ● round huts

*View of the excavation site*

Romão on top of the hill where there is an excellent general view over the site.

History

The Celtic-Iberian settlement, discovered in 1874 and excavated from 1875 onwards under the direction of Franciso Martins Sarmento (1833–99), was probably established about 500 B.C.; its most flourishing period was in the 4th c. B.C. and, as the excavations have shown, it continued to be occupied into late Roman times.

★★Site

The ancient town was enclosed within three rings of ramparts and contained some 150 single-roomed dwellings, round, oval or rectangular in plan, and built from stone cut to fit so snugly and firmly that no mortar was needed. The water conduits can still be seen, as well as traces of the streets, already paved with stone slabs.

Two of the round huts were reconstructed on the model of the trulli of Apulia or the Sardinian nuraghi, on the theory that the circular dwelling with a conical roof was the basic type of human habitation. There remains considerable doubt, however, about the authenticity of the reconstructions.

A much bigger house (about 11m/36ft in diameter) is believed to have been used for meetings, and an isolated building outside the perimeter, near the Guimarães–Braga road, was probably a cremation site.

## Castro de Sabroso

Also on a hill (278m/912ft), a short distance from Citânia de Briteiros, are the remains (less well preserved) of another prehistoric settlement, the Castro de Sabroso, which gets its name from the massive surrounding wall of dressed stone.

Sabroso, which was also excavated by Francisco Martins Sarmento, is older (*c.* 800–300 B.C.) and smaller than Briteiros.

*Reconstructed houses of the Citânia de Briteiros*

There are remains of numerous circular huts on this site, too, some of them with a block of stone in the middle which may have supported the roof.

## Coimbra

Historical province: Beira Litoral. District: Coimbra
Altitude: 75–100m/250–330ft. Population: 80,000

Rich in tradition, the old University town of Coimbra, principal town of its own district and the see of a bishop, lies halfway between Lisbon and Oporto in the hilly country of Beira Litoral. It is built on the right bank of the Rio Mondego, here skirting the chalk hills of the Serra de Lorvão.

Situation and Importance

The 13,000 or so Coimbra University students are very much a feature of life in the town. Bareheaded, they wear a long black robe (batina) under a black cape (capa), with facings of different colours for the various faculties.

With its fine old buildings, many of them dating from the time of Manuel I, and many other art treasures Coimbra should be included in any visit to Portugal. There is a very real shortage of hotel beds, however, and no really quiet, comfortable hotels in the centre. This may mean having to go some 25km/15½ miles further afield for accommodation to the environs of the Buçaco National Park (see entry).

Archaeological material found on the site carries the history of the town back to prehistoric times. It was known to the Romans as Aeminium, but later, having become the see of a bishop, it took the name of the nearby Roman town of Conimbriga (see Surroundings), which was destroyed by the Suevi in 468. The area fell into the hands of the Moors in the 8th c., but the town was temporarily won back in 872 and finally recovered by

History

*Coimbra: panorama of the old university city*

163

## Coimbra

Fernando the Great of Castile in 1064. In the 12th c. Coimbra became capital of the new Portuguese kingdom. It lost this status to Lisbon in 1260, but was compensated by the foundation (1307–08) of the University which, with interruptions, was until 1911 the only university in Portugal and which became a major element in the town's cultural and intellectual life.

★★Townscape

From the more modern Lower Town on the right bank of the Mondego steep lanes climb to the Upper Town, with the extensive buildings of the University, on a hill 100m/330ft above the river. On the left bank is the district of Santa Clara with two former convents and a miniature village.

A good starting point for a tour of the town is the Largo da Portagem, which is also where the tourist information centre is located and which, like the broad Avenida Emidio Navarro, is resplendent with greenery. After enjoying the fine view of the town from the bridge opposite, the Ponte de Santa Clara over the Mondego, the best route is to stroll along the Rua Ferreira Borges/Rua Visconde da Luz, Coimbra's main shopping street.

## Sights

★Praça do
Comércio

To the left of the Rua Visconde da Luz lies the Praça do Comércio, the town's old market place. Nowadays one of the most impressive squares in Portugal, it is well worth lingering in a street café and looking at the façades of the nearby houses which have long been home to artisans and craftworkers.

São Tiago

At the northern end of the square stands the Romanesque church of São Tiago, founded by Fernando the Great in the 11th c. in thanksgiving for the

Santa Clara convent, stadium
Condeixa (Conimbriga), Lisboa

Guarda

reconquest of the town from the Moors. The church has a plain timber ceiling.

The Rua Eduardo Coelho, on the north side of the Praça do Comércio, leads eventually to the Praça 8 de Maio, focal point of life in the town. On the east side of the square is the Convento de Santa Cruz. This former Augustinian monastery was founded in 1131 and much altered and enlarged in later centuries. Fundamental innovation work was carried out in the 15th/16th c. in the reign of Manuel I by his celebrated architect Boytaca, and after his death by Nicolas de Chantarène.

★ Convento de Santa Cruz

The whole of the north wing is now occupied by the town hall, the Câmara Municipal.

The south wing contains the aisleless convent church (1131–32), which has a Manueline façade with rich sculptural decoration, and a vaulted interior with side chapels. On the north wall is a magnificent pulpit (1522), a relic of the rich furnishings which are referred to in historical documents. In the Gallery are fine 16th c. stalls, the only ones of that period in Portugal, carved with representations of Vasco da Gama's voyages and scenes from Camões' "Lusiads".

In the Sacristy, entered from the right-hand side of the church and a Renaissance structure of 1622 with coffered barrel vaulting and poly-chrome azulejo decoration on the walls, are a number of notable pictures by Portuguese artists ("Pentecost" by Cristóvão de Figueiredo; "Calvary" by São Bento).

In the Choir, reached through the Sacristy, are the tombs (mainly in late Gothic style) of the first Portuguese kings; they were commissioned by Manuel I from Nicolas de Chantarène: on the left the recumbent figure of Afonso I Henriques (1139–85), on the right Sancho I (1185–1211), each surrounded by seven saints.

Also reached from the Sacristy, via the Chapterhouse, is the picturesque Claustro do Silêncio (16th c.), a two-storey Manueline cloister with three

*Cloister of the Monastery of Santa Cruz*

magnificent reliefs (scenes from the Passion) in the south-west and north-east corners and on the south side, and in the centre a beautiful Renaissance fountain.

**Jardim da Manga**

Adjoining the monastery complex to the east is the Jardim da Manga, all that is left of a second, later cloister built by João III according to a design drawn on his sleeve, hence the name "Manga". The domed building in the centre is surrounded by water and four small round chapels, to which access used to be by drawbridge only. Once these were raised there was nothing to disturb the monks' meditation.

**Arco de Almedina**

The Upper Town is reached on foot by turning south down the Rua Visconde da Luz and then turning left, beside number 75, through the Arco de Almedina. The arch is a relic of the Moorish town walls. The Gothic two-storey tower built over it in the 15th c. was occupied by a municipal court in the 16th c. and now houses a Museum of Ethnography.

**Paço de Sobre-Ripas**

North of the Arco de Almedina in the Rua de Sobre-Ripas is the 16th c. palace of the same name which has a fine Manueline portal.

**★Sé Velha**

A stepped lane leads up to Sé Velha, the old cathedral, a fortress-like structure built in the reign of Afonso I Henriques (12th c.), with a plain exterior, crenellated walls and a massive Romanesque west doorway. Only the Porta Especiosa, a richly decorated early Renaissance doorway on the north side of the church, relieves the sombre effect of the exterior.

The Romanesque interior, with three aisles, is strikingly impressive. The most notable features are a number of fine tombs, including that of Bishop Almeida (16th c.); the large Late Gothic high altar, with representations of the Assumption by two Flemish masters, Oliver of Ghent and John of Ypres; and the Renaissance font (16th c.). From the south aisle a flight of steps leads up to the Early Gothic cloister (13th c.).

In the square in front of the Old Cathedral Dom João was proclaimed King of Portugal in 1385.

**Sé Nova**

From the north side of the Old Cathedral the steep Rua do Cabido goes up to the Largo da Feira, which has been considerably enlarged in recent years. On the north side of the square stands the Sé Nova, the new cathedral. Originally constructed for the Jesuits, building was begun in the late 16th c. but work continued well into the 17th c. and, with the banishment of the Jesuits, it was raised to cathedral status in 1772. It has a handsome Early Baroque façade and, inside, barrel vaulting, Baroque altars and a 17th c. organ.

**★Museu Nacional de Machado de Castro**

On the west side of the Largo da Feira, in the former Bishop's Palace (rebuilt in the late 16th c.) and in the church of São João, is the Museu Nacional de Machado de Castro, named after the Coimbra-born sculptor Machado de Castro (1736–1828) and containing Roman material from excavations, medieval sarcophaguses, Romanesque and Gothic sculpture in stone and

**Coimbra**
**Old Cathedral**
**Sé Velha**

1 Porta Especiosa
2 North apse (tomb of Bishop Almeida)
3 Choir
4 South apse
5 Font
6 Crossing

© Baedeker

wood, goldsmiths' work, furniture, tapestries, porcelain, paintings of the 16th–18th c. (including some notable Flemish pictures), a special section devoted to work by modern Portuguese painters and a department of religious art..

From the double loggia in the beautiful courtyard there is a very fine view of the town.

To the south of the Largo da Feira, within the area once occupied by the castle, are the imposing modern buildings of the University; to the east the Faculty of Medicine, adjoining it on the right the Faculty of Arts, with a small archaeological museum, and the Library (Biblioteca Geral).

Modern University buildings

To the west, on the highest point of the upper town, where the royal palace (now represented only by a Manueline doorway) once stood, is the Old University, partly rebuilt in the 17th and 18th c., with the earlier Porta Férrea ("iron gate", 1634) leading into the fine courtyard. Enclosed on three sides by buildings, it has a terrace on the south side from which there is a magnificent view. The general impression of the courtyard is spoilt, however, by its use as a carpark.

★★Old University

On the north side is the actual Old University building, the Colégio, with the Chancellery and the Law Faculty, and, up flights of steps, the "Via Latina" colonnade where once only Latin was allowed to be spoken. On the east side of the courtyard is the observatory (Observatório) and on the west the University Church, built in 1517–52 as the palace chapel, with a 33m/110ft high tower (1733) and an adjacent small museum of sacred art.

Adjoining the church is the sumptuous Old Library, built 1716–23 on the model of the Court Library in Vienna (João V's queen, Ana Maria, being Austrian). It has ceiling and wall paintings by António Simões Ribeiro and valuable furniture with intarsia decoration. Its one million or so books and manuscripts come from all parts of Portugal and since 1910 can only be viewed with a special permit.

Go back through the Porta Férrea and straight on to the Praça de Dom Dinis then down the steps and under the 16th c. aqueduct to arrive at the entrance to the Jardim Botânico, the botanic gardens, commissioned by Marquês de Pombal (see Famous People) and laid out in terraces on the slopes of a side valley of the Mondego, with large numbers of subtropical plants. Unfortunately the gardens are only partly open to the public since they also form part of the University.

★Jardim Botânico

North-east of the botanic gardens is Penedo da Saudade, traditionally a meeting place for the students but above all a superb viewpoint.

Penedo da Saudade

On the left bank of the Mondego, to the left of the Lisbon road, are the partly sunken ruins of the Gothic Convent of Santa Clara-a-Velha, founded in 1286, which has gradually been destroyed by the flooding of the river. Here the saintly Queen Isabel (1271–1336) spent the last ten years of her life and here she was buried, as was the murdered Inês de Castro (see Alcobaça), Pedro I's secret bride. Their remains were moved elsewhere after the destruction of the convent.

★Convento de Santa Clara-a-Velha

About 1km/½ mile east of the old convent along the Rua António Augusto Gonçalves is Quinta das Lágrimas, the "villa of tears", where Inês de Castro is said to have been murdered in 1355.

The Fonte dos Amores, the "lovers' fountain", in the park recalls her tragic love story.

Quinta das Lágrimas

Opposite the old Santa Clara Convent can be found Portugal dos Pequenitos, a miniature village established in 1940, with reproductions of the country's most important buildings and of typical homes and buildings from the former colonies. The garden setting makes a visit here enjoyable for adults as well as children.

★Portugal dos Pequenitos Parque

*Miniature buildings in the Pequenitos Parque*

| | |
|---|---|
| Convento de Santa Clara-a-Nova | Since the old Convent of Santa Clara was almost completely destroyed in the 17th c. a new convent, the Convento de Santa-Clara-a-Nova, was built between 1649 and 1696 to the right on the Monte da Esperança. It is possible to visit the convent church, cloister and the rooms containing a small military museum. The other buildings now serve as a barracks. The Renaissance convent church is dedicated to St Isabel, wife of King Dinis and Coimbra's patron saint, and contains her silver shrine (1614) which was originally in the old convent and was transferred here to its current position in the choir by Pedro II at the end of the 17th c. St Isabel's empty stone sarcophagus is also worth seeing. Dating from the early 14th c. it is borne on six crouching lions, with the recumbent figure of the queen dressed in the simple habit of the Poor Clares but wearing a crown to show her rank. |

## Surroundings of Coimbra

| | |
|---|---|
| Celas | About 1.5km/1 mile east of Coimbra, in the suburb of Celas, is the former Benedictine abbey of Celas, founded in the 13th c. by Dona Sancha, daughter of King Sancho I, and much altered in the 16th c. It has a fine late 13th c. cloister which is worth seeing. |
| Santo António dos Olivais | Farther east is the church of the former Franciscan convent of Santo António dos Olivais, which was burned down in the middle of the 19th c. St Antony is said to have lived in the convent (founded at the beginning of the 13th c.) in about 1220. |
| Condeixa | Condeixa, 15km/9 miles south-west of Coimbra, has some fine palaces, including the 17th c. Palácio dos Lemos. |
| ★★Conimbriga | Only 2km/1¼ miles south-east of Condeixa lies the extensive site of the Roman town of Conimbriga, founded in the 2nd c. B.C. and destroyed by the |

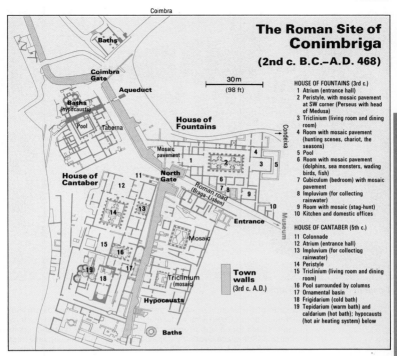

Coimbra

# The Roman Site of **Conimbriga**
## (2nd c. B.C.–A.D. 468)

Baths

Coimbra Gate

Aqueduct

30m
(98 ft)

Baths (hypocausts)

Pool    Taberna

Mosaic pavement

House of Fountains

Condeixa

North Gate

House of Cantaber    11

Roman road (Braga–Lisbon)

12

Mosaic pavement

Entrance

Museum

13    14

Mosaic

15

16

19    17

18

Triclinium (mosaic)

Town walls (3rd c. A.D.)

Hypocausts

Baths

HOUSE OF FOUNTAINS (3rd c.)
1 Atrium (entrance hall)
2 Peristyle, with mosaic pavement at SW corner (Perseus with head of Medusa)
3 Triclinium (living room and dining room)
4 Room with mosaic pavement (hunting scenes, chariot, the seasons)
5 Pool
6 Room with mosaic pavement (dolphins, sea monsters, wading birds, fish)
7 Cubiculum (bedroom) with mosaic pavement
8 Impluvium (for collecting rainwater)
9 Room with mosaic (stag-hunt)
10 Kitchen and domestic offices

HOUSE OF CANTABER (5th c.)
11 Colonnade
12 Atrium (entrance hall)
13 Impluvium (for collecting rainwater)
14 Peristyle
15 Triclinium (living room and dining room)
16 Pool surrounded by columns
17 Ornamental basin
18 Frigidarium (cold bath)
19 Tepidarium (warm bath) and caldarium (hot bath); hypocausts (hot air heating system) below

Suevi in A.D. 468. Although still being excavated, it is already clear that this settlement, to which present-day Coimbra owes its name, constitutes the largest Roman site in Portugal.

The town was secured by a wall about 2km/1¼ miles long, and some of it, dating from the 3rd c. A.D., still remains. The many ruins of houses, baths and fountains, and their mosaics, some of which are quite well preserved, are testimony to the wealth and good taste of Conimbriga's inhabitants. The 3rd c. "House of Fountains" is especially well worth seeing. The mosaics depict hunting scenes, dolphins and Perseus with the head of Medusa (it may be possible to persuade the attendant to turn on the fountains which date from Roman times).

In the Museu Monográfico adjoining the site is displayed material recovered by the excavators (mosaics, pottery, marble busts, a colossal head of Augustus, etc.).

About 15km/9 miles south-east of Condeixa, picturesquely situated on a spur of high ground, is Penela, with a massive castle (11th/12th c.).    Penela

About 15km/9 miles west of Coimbra can be found the convent church (1510) of St Mark, containing some notable 15th and 16th c. sculpture, and all that is left of the Hieronymite Convento de São Marcos which was destroyed by fire in 1860.    Convento de São Marcos

In this case it is almost better to travel than to arrive, since the journey from Coimbra towards Penacova passes through the beautiful, virtually unspoilt    ★Lorvão

*Conimbriga: House of Fountains*

landscape of the Mondego valley, turning at Rebodosa towards Lorvão, which lies about 25km/15 miles further on. The last part of the route is through woods (good opportunities for walks) then the first buildings in this remote little place suddenly appear, together with the convent, first recorded in 878. The present buildings, originally dating from the 10th c., were remodelled at the Renaissance. Only the church and cloister can be visited since the rest of the complex is a mental health institution. The imposing church (late 16th c.) has interesting choir-stalls and 18th c. silver shrines, with elaborate intarsia decorations, containing the remains of Sancho I's daughters Sancha and Teresa (13th c.). The cloister is enclosed by an intricately wrought grille.

This trip can easily be combined with a visit to the Bucaço National Park (see entry) which lies north of Lorvão.

Lourosa

Lourosa, a little place about 75km/47 miles east of Coimbra, has a pre-Romanesque, early 10th c. church. The belfry has been relocated because it was found to be on top of a very old burial site.

## Costa de Lisboa      A/B 6

Historical province: Estremadura. District: Setúbal

Location and General

The Costa de Lisboa, or "Lisbon coast", is the name given to the coast of the peninsula formed by the Serra da Arrábida and its northern outliers between the estuaries of the Tagus and the Rio Sado. Although still largely untouched by international tourism the area is very popular in summer with the people of Lisbon and is especially attractive because of its beautiful scenery and fine beaches. The southern section in particular still has appealing and relatively unspoilt places and empty beaches, although accommodation is limited.

## Sights

Once a small fishing village, Costa da Caparica, 15km/9 miles south-west of Lisbon, has developed in recent years into a none too attractive resort, complete with concrete apartment blocks and fast-food outlets.

Costa da Caparica

The Convento dos Capuchos above the town was fully restored in 1960 enabling concerts to be staged in the former Capuchin convent in the summer.

The Praia do Sol, a broad beach fringed by dunes, with wooded hills lying just inland, runs south from Costa da Caparica for some 22km/14 miles. Access to the remoter beaches is by a narrow-gauge beach railway that runs as far as Fonte da Telha.

★Praia do Sol

Cabo Espichel is the western tip of the peninsula, formed by a westerly outlier of the Serra da Arrábida. This bleak landscape affords impressive views of the coastal scenery, the cliffs falling sheer into the sea. Just north of the lighthouse warning seafarers of the dangers is the Baroque pilgrimage chapel of Nossa Senhora do Cabo, flanked by long two-storey buildings to accommodate the pilgrims. A very popular annual fishermen's festival takes place here on the last Sunday in September.

Cabo de Espichel

The fishing town of Sesimbra (see entry) is about 13km/8 miles east of the cape, and the port of Setúbal a further 25km/16 miles east.

Sesimbra, Setúbal

A tiny fishing village, now attracting increasing numbers of foreign visitors, Portinho da Arrábida is idyllically situated in a small sandy cove below the south side of the Serra da Arrábida, which here falls steeply down to the sea. There is excellent scuba diving to be had in the many little rocky coves, such as Praia de Galápos and Praia da Figuerinha, along this section of coast.

Portinho da Arrábida

Tucked away above Portinho da Arrábida on the southern slopes of the Serra da Arrábida is the Franciscan convent, the Convento Novo da Arrábida, founded in 1542, surrounded by a wall and now in private hands.

About 500m/¼ mile west of Portinho da Arrábida in the little grotto of Lapa de Santa Margarida are early traces of man's existence (access by steps).

Tróia holiday village, its high-rise buildings making it visible from afar, is at the northern tip of the Peninsula de Tróia, a spit of land extending into the lagoon at the mouth of the Rio Sado, south-west of Setúbal (ferry and fast motor-launch services).

Tróia

About 6km/4 miles south-east are the remains of the Roman town of Cetobriga, destroyed by a tidal wave in A.D. 412 (open: Tues.–Sun. 9am–6pm).

The peninsula, which boasts the longest sandy beach in Portugal (30km/19 miles), great stretches of dunes and areas of woodland but few roads, is ideal for walking.

There are pleasant excursions into the solitude of the hills in the beautiful Serra da Arrábida, where the luxuriant vegetation includes many rare species.

★Serra da Arrábida

The highest point is the Alto do Formosinho (501m/1643ft), and there are fantastic views from the N 379.1 which winds through the hills.

## Costa de Prata

A/B 3–6

Historical provinces: Beira Litoral and Estremadura
Districts: Aveiro, Coimbra, Leiria and Lisboa

The Costa de Prata, the "silver coast", the central stretch of the Portuguese Atlantic coast between the Cabo da Roca and the mouth of the Douro, has long been favoured for summer holidays by the people of Portugal.

Location and General

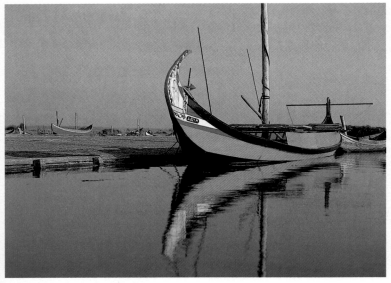

*Fishing boats on the Costa da Prata*

The attractive landscape is one of broad beaches, fringed by dunes or edged by cliffs, of pinewoods and olive-groves, with its working windmills adding a touch of the picturesque.

Its cold sea temperatures and bracing, if not windy, climate make the Costa de Prata less than ideal for anyone wanting a holiday spent solely on the beach.

## Sights on the Costa de Prata

Ericeira

Picturesquely located above the steep and rocky coast, full of clefts and caves, Ericeira (pop. 3000), which has a long tradition as a little port and fishing village, is 50km/31 miles north-west of Lisbon. Nowadays the fishing is mostly for crayfish and its decline as a port earlier this century has meant Ericeira has come increasingly to rely on earnings from tourism generated by the nearby beaches.

Praia de Santa Cruz, Praia do Porto Novo

Around Praia de Santa Cruz and Praia do Porto Novo are extensive beaches of fine sand, bordered by rocks and green hills.

Vimeiro

About 4km/2½ miles inland is the spa of Vimeiro, with a golf-course.

Peniche, Nazaré

Further north are Peniche (see entry) and the famous seaside resort of Nazaré (see entry).

São Pedro de Muel

The pretty beach resort of São Pedro de Muel is set in pinewoods some 20km/12 miles north of Nazaré.

Figueira da Foz, Aveiro

Aveiro (see entry) is still full of character, and Figueira da Foz (see entry) is another popular resort.

Espinho

A seaside resort 15km/9 miles south of Oporto, Espinho is dominated by foreign tourists, and has a broad beach of coarse sand and a fine seafront promenade. It has a wide range of recreation facilities, including an 18-hole golf-course, a landing-field for light aircraft, and a casino.

## Costa do Algarve

See Algarve

## Costa do Sol                                                              A6

Historical province: Estremadura. District: Lisboa (Lisbon)

The Costa do Sol, the "sunshine coast", the coastal stretch west of Lisbon and known with some justification as the Portuguese Riviera, is undoubtedly one of the loveliest sections of Portugal's west coast. The attractive scenery, good beaches and pleasant climate, with correspondingly lush vegetation, mean that the towns and resorts on the Costa do Sol attract large number of visitors, especially from among the Portuguese, but this also means that at the height of the season the beaches are overcrowded and traffic on the coast road is extremely heavy.

*Location and General*

### Sights

The route west out of Lisbon, through the suburbs of Belém, Algés and Dafundo (see Lisbon), ends after 10km/6 miles in the centre of Caxias. The fortress high above this little place housed political prisoners until 1974. Another fort, the Forte de São Bruno, is a youth hostel.

*Caxias*

Oeiras (pop. 14,000), 4km/2½ miles west of Caxias, is a popular resort with the summer residence of the Marquês de Pombal (see Famous People), a

*Oeiras*

*Cabo da Roca on the Costa do Sol, Europe's most westerly point*

handsome 18th c. villa set in beautiful gardens (statues, fountains and cascades). The building now belongs to the Gulbenkian Foundation (see Lisbon).

Forte Julião da Barra

About 2km/1¼ mile beyond Oeiras, on the left of the road, is the Fort São Julião de Barra, a 17th c. fortification complete with tower and bastions.

Estoril, Cascais

The well-built dual carriageway ends just before the much expanded resorts of Estoril and Cascais (see entries).

The road out of Cascais passes the viewpoint over the Boca do Inferno (see Cascais).

Cabo Raso

Cabo Raso, with its lighthouse, is about 5km/3 miles beyond Cascais, and there is a superb view from here of the Cabo da Roca.

Praia do Guincho

Praia do Guincho is a magnificent dune-fringed beach sheltered by pinewoods, about 3km/2 miles from Cabo Raso. It gets very crowded in the high season and its general appearance is marred by a new hotel complex.

★Cabo da Roca

About 7km/4¼ miles beyond Praia do Guincho a left-hand turn from the main road leads down a little road to Cabo da Roca, the most westerly point in Europe, rising to a height of 144m/472ft above the Atlantic (a visitor's certificate is offered).

The headland, known to the Romans as Promontorium Magnum, is a granite outlier of the Serra de Sintra (see Sintra). The view from the lighthouse is not to be missed.

Colares

Back on the main road and going north just before Colares, famous for its wine (see Sintra), there is a road off to the right to Convento dos Capuchos (see Sintra).

## Costa Dourada                                            B 6/7

Historical province: Baixo Alentejo. Districts: Sétubal and Beja

Location and General

Portugal's "golden coast", the Costa Dourada, extends along the open Atlantic between the Ponta da Arrifana in the south of the country and the mouth of the Rio Sado. Although very scenic, with its cliffs and seemingly endless beaches, it is still virtually undeveloped in terms of tourism. This is because of its fairly raw climate and the wind blowing constantly off the sea, so that only a few sheltered coves are suitable for swimming.

## Sights

Aljezur

Aljezur (pop. 4000), 30km/19 miles north of Lagos, is dominated by the ruins of a Moorish castle. Narrow side-roads run down from the little town to the beaches of Praia de Arrifana (south-west) and Praia de Monte Clérigo (north-west).

Vila Nova de Milfontes

About 50km/31 miles north of Aljezur, Vila Nova de Milfontes is a fishing village and developing seaside resort, picturesquely situated above the mouth of the Rio Mira. Its 17th c. castle was built under King João IV. South of the river there are some fine beaches.

Porto Covo

The little fishing port of Porto Covo, 20km/12½ miles further north, is surrounded by fine beaches but with formidable breakers.

Sines

See entry

## Costa Verde                                               B3

Historical provinces: Douro Litoral and Minho
Districts: Porto (Oporto), Braga and Viana do Castelo

*Vila Nova de Milfontes*

*Covilhã: Praça do Municipio*

### Covilhã

<table>
<tr><td>Location and<br>General</td><td>The Costa Verde, the "green coast" and the stretch of the northern Portuguese Atlantic coast between the mouths of the Douro and the Minho, has long been a favourite holiday area for the Portuguese, together with the adjoining Costa de Prata (see entry) to the south. Its long beaches of fine sand are fringed by dunes or sheltered by cliffs. With its relatively cold water and its frequent high winds off the sea this is not the place for simply swimming and sunbathing but it is a good base for enjoyable trips inland to such destinations as Braga, Guimarães and Peneda-Gerês National Park (see entries).</td></tr>
<tr><td>Resorts</td><td>The route north from Oporto (see entry) passes through a number of neighbouring resorts – first Vila do Conde and Póvoa de Varzim (see entries), with a good deal of industry inland, followed by the quieter Ofir and Esposende (see Barcelos), and finally, the attractive little town of Viana do Castelo (see entry). Seemingly endless beaches then extend northwards to the Spanish frontier, and the only tourist bases in this area are the little resorts of Vila Praia de Âncora and Moledo do Minho (see Caminha).</td></tr>
</table>

## Covilhã                                                                      C4

Historical province: Beira Baixa. District: Castelo Branco
Altitude: 700m/2300ft. Population: 22,000

<table>
<tr><td>Situation and<br>Importance</td><td>Picturesquely situated on the south-east slopes of the Serra da Estrela, the hill town of Covilhã is a popular base with the Portuguese for exploring the Serra da Estrela. The look of the town is marred somewhat by the surrounding industrial development, since Covilhã is the focus of the Portuguese textile industry, producing woollen goods under British licence for the international market.</td></tr>
<tr><td>Townscape</td><td>Covilhã presents a charming picture, with its steep and winding little streets. The town's life is focused on the flower-bedecked Praça do Município with the Câmara Municipal (town hall, and location of the tourist information centre) and, above the square, the 15th c. church of Santa Maria, its façade decorated with azulejos depicting scenes from the life of the Virgin. Also of interest are the Romanesque chapel of São Martinho and the 16th c. chapel of Santa Cruz, with pictures and woodcarvings. Within the walls that once enclosed a Franciscan convent is the Municipal Park, and there are fine views from the Monumento de Nossa Senhora da Conceição.</td></tr>
<tr><td>Nearby<br>destinations</td><td>As already mentioned, Covilhã is a good base for drives and walks in the Serra da Estrela (see entry). To the south of the town, between the Serra da Estrela and Serra da Gardunha (see Castelo Branco), is the Cova da Beira, the wide and fertile valley of the Zêzere. The evident prosperity of this area stems from its woods, cornfields, orchards, vineyards and, above all, its wool.</td></tr>
</table>

## Douro Valley                                                                 B–D 3

<table>
<tr><td>Course of the river</td><td>The Douro (Spanish Duero), known to the Romans as the Durius, one of the great waterways of the Iberian peninsula, rises on the Pico de Urbión (2252m/7389ft) in the Spanish province of Soria and flows into the Atlantic after a total course of 925km/575 miles through Spain and Portugal. In its upper reaches it traverses the plateau of Old Castile and León; it then forms the frontier between Spain and Portugal for a distance of 122km/76 miles, flowing through a gorge up to 400m/1300ft deep; and finally cuts through the Portuguese highlands between Trás-os-Montes and Beira in a wild and scenic valley, to reach the Atlantic at Oporto.</td></tr>
</table>

*Valley of the Douro near Oporto*

Along the stretch of the river between Spain and Portugal there is a series of impressive dams providing hydro-electric power, built under an agreement between the two countries. The Portuguese also generate hydro-electricity in the Duoro's lower reaches, with the dams beyond Pinhão turning it into a slow, broad river.

Dams

Hitherto the extreme seasonal variations in water level (highest in autumn and spring, lowest usually in summer) have meant that the stretch around the mouth of the river, below Oporto, was the only one navigable by regular shipping. Above Oporto the only vessels were the rabelos, skiffs with a shallow draught used for shipping port (although this is now conveyed to Oporto by road tanker). However, an ambitious project has been under way for some time to make this section of the river navigable as well.

Navigation

The steep valley of the Douro, plus those of a few tributaries, is the world's oldest legally defined wine-producing region (see Practical Information, Wine), starting 100km/61 miles east of Oporto and covering 120km/75 miles in the direction of the Spanish frontier. Port wine may only be produced in this region, the "Pais do Vinho" – "wine country".

Wine production

The steep slopes of the Douro Valley have been terraced to make vineyards as narrow as 2m/6½ft, where mechanisation is very limited indeed. Hopefully this landscape, which it has taken centuries of cultivation to create, will not be put at risk by the quest for greater agricultural efficiency.

## Elvas

C6

Historical province: Alto Alentejo. District: Portalegre
Altitude: 300m/985ft. Population: 14,000

Approximately in the same latitude as Lisbon, Elvas is an old fortress town near the Spanish frontier and set amid rich fruit orchards and olive groves.

Situation and Importance

To counter its Spanish opposite number, Badajoz, the town was ever more strongly fortified from the late medieval period onwards, and in the 17th and 18th c. was still further reinforced by powerful forts, which are among the best preserved and most impressive of their period in Portugal.

Nowadays the centre for marketing the agricultural produce of the fertile surrounding area, Elvas is also popular with tourists and has several fairly large hotels in the middle of town, set in pleasant gardens.

While in Elvas it is worth trying the local delicacy of candied plums.

★Townscape

Within its massive walls Elvas has retained much of its original Moorish character, and in and around the alleys of the old town there are still houses with elegant iron window grilles, fine archways and many picturesque squares.

The town revolves around the Praça da República; on its south side stands the old 16th c. town hall with a small regional museum and the tourist information centre.

## Sights

Igreja de Nossa Senhora da Assunção

On the north side of the Praça da República is the church of Nossa Senhora da Assunção which served as a cathedral from 1570 to 1882 when Elvas was the episcopal see.

Originally Late Gothic, the church was rebuilt in the 16th c. in Manueline style. The main façade, with its classic portico, stems from the 17th/18th c. It has a beautiful three-aisled interior with polychrome azulejo decoration.

*Elvas: Igrela de Nossa Senhora da Assunção*

Uphill from the former cathedral is the church of Nossa Senhora da Consolação. Its unusual octagonal central building is part of a Dominican monastery founded in the mid 16th c. The church was substantially altered in the mid 17th c. The dome, borne on columns, is entirely covered with azulejos.

Adjoining the Dominican church is the picturesque Largo Santa Clara, surrounded by handsome houses with elegant iron window grilles. In the middle of the square is a fine 16th c. pelourinho (pillory column).

*Igreja de Nossa Senhora da Consolação*

Just north-east of the Largo Santa Clara stands the castle built by the Moors in the 13th c. on the site of an earlier Roman fortress and enlarged in the 15th c., with a massive keep. There are fine views from the bastions.

*Castelo*

South of the Praça da Repúblic, in the former Jesuit convent, the Convento dos Jesuitas, is the town library and its museum, the Museu de António Tomás Pires, containing a collection of religious art, archaeology (Roman mosaics), coins, pictures and sculpture of the 13th–16th c. and folk art. The library's 55,000 volumes include some very rare editions (e.g. a 16th c. bible).

*Convento dos Jesuitas*

To the east of the Jesuit convent is the former Dominican convent (Convento de S. Domingos), founded in 1267 and frequently modified in the 15th, 16th and 17th c. The convent church, which is open to the public, has impressive stellar vaulting in the chancel.

*Convento de S. Domingos*

To the north of the town rises the 18th c. fort of Nossa Senhora da Graça, also known as Forte de Lippe after Count Wilhelm von Schaumburg-Lippe, who commanded the Portuguese army in 1762–64.

*Forte de Nossa Senhora da Graça*

To the south of the town is the Santa Luzia fort, an excellent and well-preserved example of 17th c. Portuguese military engineering.

*Forte de S. Luzia*

## Estoril

★Aqueduto da Amoreira

The road into Elvas from Estremoz or Lisbon enters the town alongside the Aqueduto da Amoreira, an aqueduct more than 7km/4½ miles long, built between 1498 and 1622 on the foundations of a Roman aqueduct, which still supplies water to the 17th c. Misericórdia fountain on the western edge of the town centre. The aqueduct's 843 arches – about half of them still from the original construction – are in up to four tiers, reaching a maximum height of 31m/100ft.

## Surroundings of Elvas

Campo Maior

About 20km/12½ miles north-east of Elvas is the picturesque little town of Campo Maior (alt. 277m/909ft, pop. 9000), still enclosed within a complete circuit of walls (17th/18th c.), with a 14th c. castle built by King Dinis and a Gothic parish church (charnel-house).

## Estoril      A6

Historical province: Estremadura. District: Lisboa
Altitude: sea level. Population: 25,000

Situation and Importance

Once a modest fishing village on the Costa do Sol, Estoril (pronounced shturíu) has expanded to merge with nearby Cascais (see entry). Thanks to its equable climate and beautiful subtropical gardens, it had by the end of the 19th c. become an elegant resort and winter spa, frequented by the rich and famous of the international set, and in fact its residents still include some illustrious figures, a number of crowned heads among them. In the peak holiday season its exclusivity is very much a thing of the past, as it is swamped by day-trippers from nearby Lisbon. Its radioactive hot springs (33°C/91°F), containing carbonic acid, are recommended for the treatment of rheumatism and diseases of the joints.

Townscape

Estoril itself has no particularly outstanding features of interest; it is visited primarily for its atmosphere of international elegance, its fine villas, its palm-lined promenades and the magnificent park, full of tropical and exotic plants, around the spa and the casino.

About 1.5km/1 mile west of the park is Monte Estoril (109m/358ft) which has become the new smart residential district. There are fine beaches nearby, but these are usually crowded.

*Estoril: the Casino*

There are plenty of trips that can be made from Estoril (e.g. to Lisbon, Sintra, or along the Costa do Sol – see entries).

Surroundings

## Estremadura

A/B 5/6

Historical province: Estremadura. Districts: Leiria, Lisboa and Setúbal
Area: 11,430 sq.km/4413 sq.miles
Population: 3,000,000. Chief town: Lisbon (Lisboa)

The historical Portuguese province and region of Estremadura (from the Latin "extrema durii" – "farthest land on the Douro"), consists of the districts of Lisboa (Lisbon), Leiria and Setúbal, together with the national capital Lisbon, comprising in its centre the estuary area of the Tagus as far as the basin of the Ribatejo. It extends to the north by way of the Serra de Sintra and the south-western outliers of the Serra da Estrela, dropping steeply to the sea just south of Coimbra. To the south it includes the Setúbal peninsula (Serra da Arrábida) as far as the mouth of the Rio Sado.

General

Because of its fertility and diversity of landscape within a relatively small area, Estremadura, together with Ribatejo (see entry) adjoining it on the east has since Roman times been central to the development of Lusitanian and later Portuguese culture. This area contains Lisbon, the intellectual focal point, as well as the religious centres of Alcobaça and Batalha, and the former royal seats of Queluz, Mafra and Sintra (see entries).

Another thing that Estremadura has in common with Ribatejo is the fact that between them they contain the largest single wine-producing area in Portugal.

The intricate geological and landscape makeup of this region, affected in many places by tectonic action, is reflected in a degree of economic and cultural diversity scarcely to be found in any other province of Portugal.

Landscapes

181

The northern uplands, part of a massif of Mesozoic limestones, show typical karst landscape features, with poljes and swallowholes, sparse undergrowth in the depressions and mainly the herding of sheep and goats.

To the west of this area is a chain of hills of fertile clay and sandstone, the agricultural heartland of the province where, around Alcobaça, there is mostly mixed Mediterranean-type farming (wheat, maize, citrus fruits, vegetables, olives, wine).

To the south of this rises the Serra de Sintra, a range of volcanic hills where the fertile soils and mild, damp maritime climate have resulted in a beautiful park-type landscape which, with the many thermal springs (Caldas da Rainha, Estoril, etc.; see entries), has helped this to become one of Portugal's leading holiday regions.

The narrow coastal strip in the north and the areas around the mouths of the Tagus, the Sado, the Mondego and the Vouga, with areas of marshland, lagoons and long sandspits, are chiefly orientated towards the sea. Here are the old-established fishing ports which are used by the deep-sea fishermen sailing to distant waters, especially Newfoundland, with their fish-canning and drying establishments and their extensive saltpans. The marshy land in the river basins is also good for rice-growing.

## Estremoz                                                                    C6

Historical province: Alto Alentejo. District: Évora
Altitude: 430m/1410ft. Population: 8000

Situation and Importance

The little old-world town of Estremoz lies 50km/31 miles north-east of Évora, in the undulating landscape of the Alto Alentejo, and is particularly notable for the number of buildings made from the locally quarried white marble, which was already widely renowned in the Middle Ages.

Estremoz is also important as a centre for pottery, wood-carving and leatherwork, although agriculture continues to be the main occupation.

Townscape

The older part of Estremoz is the upper town, with its picturesque narrow lanes clustered on the hill around the castle. The lower town, which goes back to the 16th c., is centred on the "Rossio", the Praça do Marquês de Pombal, the enormous square where the principal weekly market is held on Saturdays, although there are usually a few stalls here throughout the week, selling the characteristic red Estremoz pottery.

## Sights

Lower town

At the southern end of the Rossio is the town hall, the Câmara Municipal, originally built (1698) as a convent, and containing fine azulejo depictions of scenes from the life of St Philippus. The folk-art museum on the east side of the Rossio is worth a visit.

Adjoining the Rossio on the north is the Largo do General Graça with the 17th c. Tocha Palace (azulejo pictures) and the former Franciscan convent, originally 13th c., in which King Pedro I died in 1367. Although this is now used as a barracks the Gothic convent church can be visited.

★Upper town

The upper town, enclosed within 17th c. Vauban-style fortifications with several massive towers, still has a rather Moorish aspect, and its white-washed houses, with their small window-openings, are designed to afford protection against the fierce heat of the summer.

The highest point of the town is the castle, the Castelo, built in the first half of the 13th c. All that remains of the original building is the massive keep, 27m/89ft high, and topped by splendid battlements. The royal palace was built onto this keep in the early 14th c. and, with the castle, served as the residence of King Dinis I and his wife, St Isabel, who died here in 1336

*Estremoz: the castle keep . . .*                    *. . . and a pousada in the Upper Town*

and is commemorated by a monument in the castle square. The palace was restored in the 18th c. and is now a luxurious pousada.

Opposite the palace is the three-aisled church of Santa Maria do Castelo which was built on the site of a Gothic predecessor in 1559 and contains two paintings of the Virgin by El Greco. Adjoining the church is the Manueline, but originally Gothic, royal audience chamber.

The castle square is also bordered by the old town hall and the municipal museum (furniture, pottery, azulejos, etc.).

## Surroundings of Estremoz

About 10km/6 miles east on the Borba road in a simple, white house on the right-hand side is the Museu de Cristo, with an interesting collection of crucifixes.

Museu de Cristo

25km/16 miles south of Estremoz on a road which runs through the Serra de Ossa (653m/2142ft), passing the Convento da Berra, lies Redondo (alt. 305m/1000ft; pop. 7000), a pleasant little town with the ruins of a 14th c. castle built in the reign of King Dinis I and, higher up, the church of the Misericórdia, which has a Manueline choir.

Redondo

Sousel (pop. 2000), 18km/11 miles north-west of Estremoz, founded by Nuno Álvares Pereira (see Batalha) in 1387, has a 16th c. parish church and another 16th c. church, the Misericórdia, with 18th c. azulejo decoration.

Sousel

The village of Veiros, 15km/9¼ miles north-east of Estremoz, prides itself on having produced the Bragança line since it is the birthplace of Afonso, illegitimate son of King João I and later Duke of Bragança. Very little remains of the old castle.

Veiros

Other places worth visiting from Estremoz include Evoramonte (see Évora), Borba and Vila Viçosa (see entries).

Other destinations

183

# Évora

Historical province: Alto Alentejo. District: Évora
Altitude: 300m/985ft. Population: 36,000

**Situation and Importance**

Évora, built on a low hill surrounded by rolling plains, was the old capital of the upland region of Alentejo and is now the chief town of its own district, the see of an archbishop and, since 1979, a University once more. In economic terms, it is the trading centre for the agricultural produce of Alentejo (wool, cloth, cork) and has its own important electrical goods industry.

Its many sights and lovely townscape make it a highlight of any tour of Portugal, although it is worth noting that the town centre hotels, although good, are all relatively small, and are frequently full in the holiday season. The local speciality is "porco á alentejana" – pork with mussels.

**History**

Évora is one of the oldest trading posts on the Iberian peninsula. In Roman times it was a very important town, first called Ebora, under the praetorship of Sertorius, then renamed Liberalitas Iulia under Julius Caesar.

In 715 the town fell into the hands of the Moors and became known as Yebora. It was reconquered by Giraldo Sempavor (Gerald the Fearless) in

Évora

200 m

© Baedeker

1165 and reunited with the kingdom of Afonso Henriques. From the 14th to the 16th c. it was intermittently the residence of the Portuguese kings and hence the focus of political and cultural life; however, with the permanent transfer of the seat of government to Lisbon and the eventual closing of its university, Évora's splendour and influence declined. and it is only in recent decades that this has partially been recovered, owing to some extent to its importance as a tourist centre – in 1986 Unesco awarded Évora international heritage status.

With its walls of the Roman, Moorish and later periods, still largely preserved, and its narrow lanes, sometimes lined with arcades, Évora's townscape still has a Moorish and medieval appearance, hence its entitlement to the term "cidade museu" – museum city. ★★Townscape

A good starting point for a tour of the town is the square by the cathedral (limited parking).

## Sights

The Cathedral – Catedral or Sé – is a severe and fortress-like structure in Early Gothic style which was begun in 1186 and completed in the 13th and 14th c. The façade is dominated by the two asymmetrical towers flanking the massive doorway. Above the crossing is an octagonal belfry with a helm roof of scale-like tiles. The twelve figures of apostles on the doorway are masterpieces of Portuguese Gothic sculpture. ★★Catedral

The interior, notable for its regular masonry with white mortar joints, is of impressive simplicity and harmony. The gently sweeping lines of Baroque are only apparent in the raised Choir, entered by a flight of steps in the south aisle. This was remodelled in the 18th c. by Johann Friedrich Ludwig, architect of the convent of Mafra (see entry), and lavishly decorated with marble. The fine carved choir-stalls date from 1562.

*Évora: The roof-terrace of the Cathedral . . .  . . . and the Cloister*

Also in the south aisle is the entrance to the Gothic cloister, with statues of the evangelists. Several dark narrow corridors lead from the cloister up to the roof terrace (intermittent access), affording a close look at the tower helm roof, as well as fine views over the town and surrounding countryside.

The Cathedral Treasury, which used to be kept in the Sacristy, is now housed in the Museu de Arte Sacra in the cathedral's south tower. Its precious items include a 13th c. ivory triptych of the Virgin and Child, as well as many outstanding examples of 16th and 17th c. gold and silver and enamel work.

**Museu de Évora**

The former Archbishop's Palace, on the north side of the Cathedral, now houses the well-stocked Museu de Évora, the regional museum, displaying Roman archaeological finds, Romanesque and Gothic architectural fragments, Portuguese and Flemish pictures of the 16th–18th c., applied and decorative art, and two cenotaphs by Nicolas Chanterène for Dom Álvares de Costa (1535) and Dom Afonso de Portugal (1537).

**★Templo Romano**

Opposite the museum entrance is what has become the symbol of Évora, its Roman temple (Templo Romano). Dating from the 2nd or 3rd century A.D., it is one of the best preserved Roman structures in Portugal and is popularly known as the Temple of Diana, although it is not clear to which deity it was actually dedicated. On the 3m/10ft high base, which is almost completely preserved, there still stand 14 of the original 18 Corinthian columns, with part of the architrave. During the Middle Ages the temple was converted into a fortress, and later served for many years as a slaughterhouse, a use which ultimately saved it from demolition.

The gardens behind the temple overlook a terrace with good views over the northern part of Évora.

**Convento dos Lóios**

Opposite the temple, to the east, is the church of the Convent dos Lóios, which was built between 1485 and 1491 and much altered in the following centuries. The Manueline porch was part of the original building, and bears the arms of the de Melos who founded the church and chose to be buried there.

Parts of the former convent have been converted into a pousada, and the beautiful cloister now serves as a charming garden for its guests, with the restaurant located in the galleries. The former chapterhouse, through the cloister, has Manueline stellar vaulting.

The Biblioteca Pública, the public library, is in another part of the building and contains about 2000 incunabula and manuscripts.

**Paço dos Duques de Cadaval**

There used to be direct access from the north front of the convent church to the Paço dos Duques de Cadaval, the palace that King João I presented to the de Melos, ancestors of the Cadavals, at the end of the 14th c. Because of its pentagonal north tower – originally part of the medieval town fortifications – it is also known as the pentagonal palace, the "Palácio das Cinco Quinas".

**Paço dos Condes de Basto**

The Paço dos Condes de Basto is several hundred yards to the right beyond the Paço dos Duques de Cadaval. This Gothic-Manueline palace of the Counts of Basto which was intermittently the residence of various kings contains part of the Romanesque cum Visigothic town walls.

**Universidade**

On the other side of the street is the extensive University complex. The Universidade, in Italian Renaissance style, was founded in 1551 as a Jesuit college, raised to the status of a university in 1558 and closed in 1759, after the dissolution of the Jesuit order in Portugal. After Évora acquired its university status again in 1979 lecture rooms were reinstated around the cloister, many of them embellished with azulejos and marble.

The university church (Nossa Senhora da Conceição) was consecrated in 1574, and also boasts marble and talha in its single-nave interior.

A route down the alleys leading southward from the university then westward along the Rua de Machede brings the visitor to the Largo das Portas de Moura, which owes much of its picturesque, quaint character to the Renaissance fountain (1556) in its centre, with a globe looming over its marble basin as the symbol of the dawn of a new age.

★Largo das Portas de Moura

On the south side of the square stands the Casa Cordovil, an elegant 16th c. palace in Moorish and Manueline style, catching the eye with its loggia and four graceful pillars.

Opposite the Casa Cordovil a double flight of steps leads down into the forecourt of the early 17th c. church of the former Carmo convent and bearing over its portal the bold motto of the Dukes of Bragança "depois de vós – nós", after You (i.e. the King), us!

The Igreja da Graça, west of the Largo das Portas de Moura, was founded by João I in the 16th c, and its façade is reminiscent of the Italian Renaissance. The interior and adjoining convent buildings contain an officers' mess and are not open to the public.

Igreja da Graça

Quite close by stands the church of São Francisco, a former convent church dating from the second half of the 15th c. and perhaps the finest example of Manueline architecture in southern Portugal. The severe white interior, with the same white mortar joints as in the Cathedral, creates an effect of greater spaciousness than the latter.

Igreja Real de São Francisco

Adjoining the south aisle is the Casa dos Ossos, a 17th c. charnel-house. Those of a more sensitive disposition should think twice before venturing inside, since the walls are formed by carefully arranged layers of human bones. The macabre effect is heightened by the skeletons of a man and a child hanging from this gruesome wall, and to top it all the motto over the door reads "our bones that lie within are waiting for yours to join them".

*Largo das Portas de Moura with Renaissance fountain*

## Évora

**Museu de Artesanato Regional**

Opposite the side of the Igreja Real de São Francisco is what purports to be a regional handicrafts museum, the Museu de Artesanato Regional, but is in fact more of a sales outlet.

**Jardim Público**

Farther south lies the town park, the Jardim Público, with its inviting shady walks and lovely flowers. The Galeria das Damas inside the park was part of the 15th/16th c. royal palace and its Moorish arcades today serve as exhibition areas. Together with the rest of the now demolished palace buildings it once enjoyed the glittering life of Manuel I's court, and was where the King received Vasco da Gama.

**Ermida de São Brás**

Further south along the Rua da República there is a monument, topped by an angel, commemorating the soldiers of Évora who fell in the First World War. This is within sight of the Ermida de São Bras, the hermitage of St Blaise, a fortress-like building in a Late Gothic style showing Moorish influence which was erected in 1485 in thanksgiving for survival from the plague. The flat roof is crenellated and flanked by six conical pinnacles along each side, and the interior is unusually plain.

**Igreja das Mercês**

The tour of the town continues by returning to the walls around the Jardim Público, built in the 17th c. according to the Vauban system, then turning west along the fortifications as far as the Rua do Raimundo, and the Igreja das Mercês, the church of the Mercês, which now houses the museum of decorative arts, the Museu das Artes Decorativas, containing arts and crafts as well as religious art.

**★Praça do Giraldo**

A couple of hundred yards to the north-east, in the centre of the town, is the elongated Praça do Giraldo, the picturesque square that was once a place of execution where many victims of the Inquisition went to the stake. Its street cafés provide a good opportunity to appreciate the scenic effect of the beautiful houses and arcades surrounding the square. The Renaissance

*Galeria das Damas in the Jardim Publico*

*Praça do Giraldo and Santo Antão*

fountain in Estremoz marble (by Afonso Avares, 1581) stands on the site of a Roman triumphal arch demolished in 1570. On the north side of the square is the collegiate church of Santo Antão, built in 1557 by the archbishop who later became King Henrique II; it has a clearly defined Renaissance façade.

The Rua 5 de Outubro, full of souvenir shops and the favourite precinct for promenading, soon brings the walk round the city back to its starting point.

The other sights worth visiting, if staying longer in Évora, include the former convent of Santa Clara, west of the Praça do Giraldo. Founded in 1452, it was substantially altered in the 16th c. and its church, with its elegant belfry, is worth seeing. Another interesting convent, further north, is the Convento do Calvário, its church and 16th c. cloister open to the public. North-east, nearby, are the remains of an aqueduct, built in the 16th c. probably to replace a Roman equivalent.

*Other sights*

## Surroundings of Évora

About 3km/2 miles north-west of Évora is the Convent of Nossa Senhora d'Espinheiro (15th–16th c.), with a beautiful cloister.

*Convento d'Espinheiro*

The Convento de São Bento de Castris, 4km/2½ miles north-west of Évora on the N114-4 to Arraiolos, stands at the foot of Mt São Bento (367m/1203ft; fine views). The convent was founded in 1274 and has a church of the 14th/15th c. containing 18th c. azulejo decoration; there is also a fine 16th c. cloister.

*Convento de São Bento de Castris*

Évoramonte, about 35km/22 miles north-east of Évora, is worth a visit. Prominently situated above the newer town on a hill (474m/1555ft), the old town centre, with its winding alleys and little white houses, is still surrounded by its walls, with at its highest point Évoramonte Castle, built in the 14th c. on the ruins of a Moorish predecessor and rebuilt after an earthquake in 1531. The recently restored, yellow-painted fort can be visited (ask for the key if necessary). A plaque on the wall of a house on the left side of the main street, past the walls, commemorates the fact the Treaty of Évoramonte concluding the "Miguelist" wars (see History) was signed here on May 26th 1834.

*★Évoramonte*

About 11km/7 miles south-west of Évora is the Quinta de Valverde, once belonging to the Capuchins and now an agricultural college; it has a round church (16th c.), a two-storey cloister and some fine marble sculpture in the gardens.

*Quinta de Valverde*

22km/14 miles farther south-west, at the foot of the Serra de São João, lies Alcáçovas, with a handsome 15th c. palace of the Counts of Alcáçovas and a notable 16th c. parish church.

The chapel of Nossa Senhora da Esperança (16th c.), above the village, 3km/2 miles west, is all that is left of a former Dominican convent. From the hill on which it stands there are fine views.

*Alcáçovas*

Viana do Alentejo, 30km/19 miles south of Évora, has a 15th c. castle and a 16th c. parish church with a magnificent Manueline doorway and azulejo decoration inside.

*Viana do Alentejo*

The little country town of Alvito, 10km/6 miles south of Viana do Alentejo, boasts a parish church with magnificent 17th c. azulejo decoration and a fine fortified castle (15th c.) built by the Marquês de Alvito.

A little road north-east out of Alvito leads to Agua de Peixes, where the Dukes of Cadaval (see above, Paço dos Duques de Cadaval) sited their fine 16th c. Hispano-Mauresque country mansion.

*Alvito*

189

*Monsaraz*

Portel

About 41km/25 miles south-east of Évora is the small country town of Portel. Its 13th c. Bragança castle was rebuilt under Manuel I (view). The little chapel of Santo António is lavishly decorated with polychrome azulejos.

★Monsaraz

Monsaraz, 50km/31 miles east of Évora, near the Spanish border, still has a very medieval look, and is worth a visit. Its fortifying walls date from the 14th c., and a walk round the sleepy little town should take in the Gothic parish church, the 17th c. pelourinho, the Gothic palace of justice and, above all, the castle.

Other destinations around Évora

Other places to visit include Arraiolos (see entry), north of Évora, famous for its townscape and its rugs, and Montemore-o-Novo (see Arraiolos) 25km/15½ miles to the west. Estremoz (see entry), about 45km/28 miles north-east of Évora, is definitely worth seeing, while Redondo (see Estremoz) offers yet another castle.

# Faro                                                                                           C7

Historical province: Algarve. District: Faro
Altitude: sea level. Population: 29,000

Situation and Importance

The busy industrial town and port of Faro, chief town of its district in the south of Portugal, lies at the north end of a lagoon dotted with saltpans and islands. Wine, fruit, cork and fish are shipped out through its small, sheltered harbour. Its airport (7km/4½ miles south-west) has made it the focal point of the whole of the Algarve's tourist trade, especially since a new, three million passenger capacity terminal was opened. Despite the nearby beaches Faro is no holiday resort as such, and its immediate vicinity is

São Brás de Alportel

Rua Cidade de Hayward

Praça
de Tânger

Rua do Sport Clube Farense

Praceta
Colégio
Militar

E.N. 125

Rua Aboim Ascensão

Rua Gen. T. Trindade

**Mercado**

**Igreja
do Carmo**

Largo
do Carmo

Largo
das Mouras
Velhas

Santo
António
do Alto

**Estação**

**Igreja
de São Pedro**

Praça
F. de
Almeida

Avenida 5 de Outubro

**Museu
Marítimo**

Praça
D. F.
Gomes

Rua S. António

**Museu
Etnográfico**

Jardim
Manuel
Bivar

**Igreja da
Misericórdia**

Rua do Bocage

**Arco da Vila**

**Câmara
Municipal**

**Arco do
Repouso**

**Paço
Episcopal**

**Sé**

**Museu
Arqueológico**

**Colecção
Ferreira
de Almeida**

**Igreja
de São
Francisco**

Oceano
Atlântico

Largo
de São Francisco

**Faro**

300 m

© *Baedeker*

lacking in comfortable hotels with adequate grounds. Nor can Faro boast
any outstanding sights since a devastating earthquake in 1755 robbed this
originally Moorish city of most of its major buildings.

The main attraction of any stay in Faro is its good shopping. Some of the
smaller streets in the centre around the Rua de Santo António, east of the
Praça de Dom Francisco Gomes, have been made pedestrian precincts and
offer plenty of restaurants and cafés to relax in.

## Sights

To the north-east of the harbour is the Praça de Dom Francisco Gomes, with
the adjoining palms of the Jardim de Manuel Bivar. The traffic that flows
round the square encircles the 15m/50ft high obelisk commemorating the
diplomat Ferreira de Almeida.

Praça de Dom
Francisco Gomes

The Igreja da Misericórdia on the east side of the Manuel Bivar gardens
dates originally from the 16th c. and was restored after 1755.

At the south end of the square stands the 18th c. Arco da Vila, an arched
gateway with a statue of Faro's patron saint, St Thomas Aquinas; this gate
leads to the Cathedral, the Sé. Originally Gothic, this suffered severe destruction in the 1755 earthquake, with only the tower still standing. The
interior is predominantly Renaissance.

Sé

191

**Faro**

Faro: a pedestrian zone . . .

. . . and the Cathedral

In the square in front of the Cathedral, the Largo da Sé, stand the town hall (Câmara Municipal) and the old and new Bishop's Palaces (Paço Episcopal).

Museu Arqueológico

In the nearby Praça Afonso III, just south of the cathedral square, is the archaeological museum, housed in the former Convent of Nossa Senhora da Assunção, a house of Poor Clares founded in 1518. Apart from the exhibits (especially finds from Ossonoba, see Surroundings), the two-storey cloister is particularly notable.

Colecção Ferreira de Almeida

Also housed in the same buildings is the collection of various curios and arts and crafts assembled by Ferreira de Almeida.

Igreja de São Francisco

The church of St Francis, on the spacious Largo de São Francisco, is reached through the Arco do Repouso. The 17th c. church is part of what was a Franciscan convent, and is today occupied by the military.

Museu Etnográfico

The Museum of Regional Ethnography, just north of the Franciscan church, affords an insight into the way of life and folk art of the local people.

Other sights

The Maritime Museum in the Harbourmaster's office, north of the harbour, gives a good general picture of seafaring and fishing in the Algarve.

North-east of the museum are the 16th c. Igreja de São Pedro and the Igreja do Carmo, a twin-towered Baroque church. In the cemetery behind the church can be seen the walls of its charnel-house, the Capela dos Ossos, built, as its name suggests, from human bones.

In the eastern outskirts of the town, on a hill commanding far-ranging views, stands the little church of Santo António do Alto (1754), with a museum devoted to St Antony.

## Surroundings of Faro

North-west of the town, beyond the airport, on an offshore island connected to the mainland by a bridge, is the extensive sandy beach of Praia do Faro.

Praia de Faro

About 10km/6 miles north of Faro, on higher ground, is Estói, with the privately-owned palace and park of the Counts of Estói.

Estói

Only 1km/½ mile west of Estói, near the village of Milreu, are the remains of the Roman town of Ossonoba, where excavations carried out from 1876 onwards brought to light baths with mosaic pavements, a basilica and several houses. Most of the finds can be seen in Faro's Archaeological Museum.

Milreu/Ossonoba

See entry

Olhão

Other places worth seeing around Faro can be found under the entry for the Algarve.

Algarve

## Fátima                                                                       B5

Historical province: Ribatejo. District: Santarém
Altitude: 800m/2625ft. Population: 7300

Fátima, internationally famous as a place of pilgrimage, is in central Portugal a good 20km/12 miles south-east of Leiria and on what was once the barren plateau of Cova da Iria. Every year it attracts thousands of believers from far and wide to beseech forgiveness for their sins or pray for a cure. Fátima also figures in every organised excursion or coach tour of this part of Portugal.

Situation and Importance

*Fatima: Place of Assembly and Basilica*

**Fátima**

© Baedeker

Basilica

Chapel of the Epiphany

Meeting-place

Rua de Santa Ana

Rua de

Rua F. Marto

Santa Isabel

Tomar
Batalha, Leiria

Rua Anjo di Portugal

Rua de São José

Waxworks

Praceta
Santo
António

Rua de Santo António

Batalha, Leiria

Rua de São

Rua Conego Formigão

Avenida D. José Alves Correia da Silva ⓘ

On the eve of the chief annual pilgrimages (May 13th and October 13th) there are large torch-light processions.

"Miracle of Fátima"

On May 13th 1917, and again on the 13th of each subsequent month until October in that year, the "Virgin of the Rosary" is said to have appeared to the three peasant children, Lúcia de Jesús and Francisco and Jacinta Marto. At first sceptical about these visions, on the last appearance, October 13th 1917, the Church saw over 70,000 people making the pilgrimage to Fátima where they are supposed to have witnessed not only the appearance of the Virgin but also an amazing natural phenomenon – in pouring rain the sun suddenly began to revolve on its axis and throw out multi-coloured rays of light. There were also a number of miraculous cures in the days that followed. The Church authorities investigated the incidents for several years before finally giving the Fátima cult of the Madonna the official seal of approval in 1930.

Speculation continues to this day about the three "revelations" that the children – who were seven, nine and ten at the time – said had been vouchsafed them by the Virgin on July 13th 1917. The first two are public knowledge, the first being a description of "Hell", and the second prophesying a speedy end to the First World War, but also foretelling a dreadful war if the world did not cease offending God.

The third prophesy was confided in writing to the Vatican in 1941 by Lúcia, who had entered a convent in 1928, but she also stipulated it should not be made public before 1960 and to date no Pope has unveiled the secret.

## Sights

Esplanade

The esplanade that serves as the rallying point for the kneeling pilgrims is of huge proportions (150,000 sq.m/37 acres). It is dominated by the Neo-Baroque Basilica, with its 65m/215ft high central tower. Building was begun on May 13th 1928 and it is flanked by colonnades linking it with the extensive conventual and hospital buildings. Inside the Basilica are the tombs of Francisco and Jacinta Marto, who died in 1919 and 1920 respectively. The place where the Virgin Mary is supposed to have appeared to the children in the branches of an oak in 1917 is marked by the little chapel of the apparitions, the Capela das Aparições, in front of the Cathedral. The first chapel built here in 1918 was later destroyed by an explosion.

West of the esplanade is a wax museum, the Museu de Cera de Fátima, opened in 1984 and depicting the miraculous events at Fátima in a series of 29 scenes.

Wax museum

## Surroundings of Fátima

About 10km/6 miles north-east of Fátima, on an isolated hill rising out of the valley, is the little medieval walled town of Ourém, a huddle of narrow lanes and picturesque nooks and corners in the shadow of the 15th c. castle of the Margraves of Ourém.

Ourém

In the crypt of the collegiate church, originally Gothic but rebuilt in the 18th c., is the magnificent tomb of Dom Afonso de Ourém, a descendant of João I, who rebuilt and enlarged the original Moorish castle. Ourém also has a beautiful Gothic fountain and a pelourinho, both of the 15th c.

Many of the inhabitants of Ourém have moved to Vila Nova de Ourém, 2km/1¼ miles to the east.

| | |
|---|---|
| See entry | Alcobaça |
| See entry | Batalha |
| See entry | Leiria |
| See entry | Tomar |

## Figueira da Foz                                                                B4

Historical province: Beira Litoral. District: Coimbra
Altitude: sea level. Population: 15,000

**Figueira da Foz**

Situation and Importance

At the mouth of the Mondego, the regularly laid out little port town of Figueira da Foz, the "fig-tree on the estuary", is one of the principal bases of the cod fisheries off the Portuguese Atlantic coast – the fish market is held every morning on the south bank of the Mondego. Because of its broad beach of fine sand, stretching for 3km/2 miles, Figueira da Foz is also one of the most popular resorts on Portugal's west coast, with a range of sport and leisure facilities to match, including a marina and casino.

Townscape

The park on the coast road divides the new hotel district from the old town of Figueira da Foz, near the harbour and mostly 19th c.

## Sights

Forte Santa Catarina

At the mouth of the river stands the old Santa Catarina fort, dating from the 17th c.

Casa do Paço

Another 17th c. building is the Casa do Paço in the old town, near the main post office, much of it decorated with Delft tiles showing biblical themes, landscapes and riding scenes.

Museu Municipal do Dr Santos Rocha

The municipal museum, together with its library, is housed in a building surrounded by a park, and has displays of prehistoric finds as well as Roman exhibits, applied and decorative art, pottery, furniture, religious art, ethnography of the Portuguese overseas territories, etc.

Santo António

Just east of the museum is the Franciscan convent of Santo António, founded in 1527 and much altered in the 18th c., its walls decorated with scenes from the life of St Antony.

*Figuaira da Foz: the beach, shared by fishermen and visitors*

## Surroundings of Figueira da Foz

The fishing village of Buarcos to the north-west, now almost a suburb of Figueira da Foz, is partly surrounded by a wall, and has two 16th c. Manueline pelourinhos.

Buarcos

About 3km/2 miles farther on is Cabo Mondego, a rocky headland falling sheer down to the Atlantic in a mighty cliff. Adjoining the lighthouse is an observatory and nearby there are abandoned lignite mines and limestone quarries.

Cabo Mondego

The Serra de Boa Viagem (up to 258m/846ft), a few miles north of Figueira da Foz, is an area of scattered woodland which offers some very good walks.
   From the summit of the Alto da Vela (209m/686ft) there are superb panoramic views.

Serra de Boa Viagem

## Figueira de Castelo Rodrigo                                    D4

Historical province: Beira Alta. District: Guarda
Altitude: 627m/2057ft. Population: 2000

The frontier town of Figueira de Castelo Rodrigo lies 60km/37 miles north-east of Guarda in a beautiful setting on a plateau covered with fruit orchards.
   In the 19th c. the population of the nearby fortified town of Castelo Rodrigo, an important stronghold during the Middle Ages, began to move to Figueira, which soon overshadowed its older neighbour.

Situation and Importance

Figueira de Castelo Rodrigo has managed to retain something of a medieval aspect. The 18th c. Baroque parish church has numerous carved and gilded altars.

Townscape

## Surroundings of Figueira de Castelo Rodrigo

The 13th c. privately-owned former Cistercian Convent of Santa Maria de Aguiar, about 3km/2 miles south-east, has a three-aisled Gothic hall-church and a beautiful chapter-house. The loggia is supported by Tuscan columns.

Santa Maria de Aguiar

On a hill 3km/2 miles south of Figueira de Castelo Rodrigo lies Castelo Rodrigo, now a decayed village but in the Middle Ages a fortified town of considerable importance, with a ruined 15th c. castle and keep, an old palace and a cistern. Also worth seeing are the little Gothic church and Manueline pelourinho, but undoubtedly best of all is the view from the castle.

Castelo Rodrigo

From Castelo Rodrigo a road runs south for 16km/10 miles through the wild and rocky Serra de Marofa, with superb views, to the little town of Almeida, which is still surrounded by Vauban-style fortifications laid out like a twelve-pointed star.

Almeida

About 20km/12 miles south-west of Figueira de Castelo Rodrigo is the little town of Pinhel, still enclosed within stout defensive walls with six towers. Within the ruined castle, built by King Dinis, stands the 14th c. church of Santa Maria do Castelo, with a cycle of 14 paintings of scenes from the life of the Virgin (17th c.). The town has many typical old houses and a monolithic pelourinho. Outside the walls are the ruins of the Romanesque da Trinidade church.

Pinhel

Some 6km/4 miles west of Figueira de Castelo Rodrigo, the village of Freixeda de Torrão has an old castle and a church, with a Romanesque doorway. The local wines have a good reputation.

Freixeda do Torrão

## Guarda

Freixo de Espada á
Cinta

On the edge of a fertile valley basin, 45km/28 miles north-east of Figueira de
Castelo Rodrigo, is the little town of Freixo de Espada á Cinta, birthplace of
the navigator Jorge Álvares and of the poet Guerra Junqueiro (1850–1923;
museum). Its 16th c. parish church has a richly decorated interior.

## Guarda                                                                    C4

Historical province: Beira Alta. District: Guarda
Altitude: 1057m/3468ft. Population: 15,000

Situation and
Importance

The old district
capital of Guarda,
the see of a
bishop and once
an important
stronghold in the
province of Beira
Alta, lies on a
plateau in the
north-east of the
Serra da Estrela.
As Portugal's
highest town,
with a healthy
and very pleasant
climate, it has
become a pop-
ular health resort.

History

There was al-
ready a stongly
fortified town on
this strategically
important site in
Roman times. In 80 B.C. it sided with Quintus Sertorius in his attempt to
break away from Rome, and thereafter withstood many years of assaults
and sieges by Caesar's forces. After the town was devastated by the Moors
its inhabitants fled and the remaining buildings became derelict. Much
later, in the 12th and 13th c., Guarda was rebuilt by Sancho I and Dinis I and
strongly fortified against attack by the Moors and Castilians.

Townscape

At first sight the town, built largely of granite, has a rather grey appearance,
but a closer look reveals finely decorated old patrican houses, particularly
in the Cathedral Square and the Rua de Dom Luis I.

Of the town's 12th and 13th c. fortifications there remain the keep, three
town gates and parts of the town walls.

## Sights

★Catedral

The Catedral (cathedral), which is in the middle of the town, is a granite
building of fortress-like appearance, with crenellated walls. It was begun in
Gothic style in 1390 and completed in the 16th c., although the portal on the
northern transept still looks Gothic. The Manueline additions, notably the
west front and doorway, were built by Manuel I's great architect, Boytaca,
on the model of Batalha Abbey (see Batalha).

The magnificent three-aisled interior achieves its effect by its harmo-
nious proportions and simplicity of line. The stone retable (1550), on which
over 100 figures enact scenes from the life of Christ, was the work of John
of Rouen (João de Ruão); the gilding was added in the 18th c. It is well
worth climbing up to the roof terrace to see the method of construction of

*Guarda Cathedral*

the roof, spanned by flying buttresses, and to enjoy the superb view over the town to the Serra da Estrela.

In front of the northern façade of the cathedral is the Praça de Luís de Camões, or Praça da Sé, containing a modern monument to Sancho I, to whom the town owed its economic and cultural advancement in the Middle Ages. The tourist information centre is in the 16th c. Manueline town hall, the Câmara Municipal.

Praça de Luís de Camões/Praça da Sé

The former Bishop's Palace (15th/16th c.) now houses the Regional Museum, where the exhibits range from archaeological finds and pictorial archives to paintings and sculpture.

Museu Regional

Also worth seeing are two Baroque churches, the 17th c. Misericórdia and 18th c. São Vicente. Though perhaps somewhat provincial in style, they are no less attractive for that.
    About 1km/¾ mile from the town centre is the Romanesque Ermida de Nossa Senhora da Póvoa de Mileu, with finely carved capitals.

Churches

## Surroundings of Guarda

Celorico da Beira (alt. 550m/1804ft), 28km/17 miles north-west of Guarda, is a little town with a ruined castle (view), destroyed by French troops in the early 19th c., and several old houses with some Manueline windows.

Celorico da Beira

Trancoso, which is at an altitude of 880m/2886ft about 20km/12 miles north of Celorico da Beira, is encircled by walls that were still being extended in the 16th c., signifying its former importance as a fortress. Trancoso castle, now a ruin, was where King Dinis I married his Queen, later Saint, Isabel in 1282. Also worth seeing are several houses of the nobility, complete with

Trancoso

199

coats of arms, a Manueline pelourinho, and the 13th c. church of Santa Luzia.

Fornos de Algodres

Fornos de Algodres, 10km/6 miles west of Celorico da Beira, is an unpretentious little town in the upper valley of the Rio Mondego.

Serra da Estrela

Guarda is also a good base from which to explore the Serra da Estrela (see entry) stretching away to the south.

Sabugal

Sabugal, about 30km/19 miles south-east of Guarda, is increasingly given over to modern buildings but it has a well-preserved 13th/14th c. castle.

## Guimarães                                                                                    B3

Historical province: Minho. District: Braga
Altitude: 200m/655ft. Population: 23,000

Situation and Importance

Guimarães, in the north of Portugal at the foot of the Serra de Santa Catarina, is reverentially known as the "cradle of the nation", the berco da nação, owing to the fact that it was the first capital of the newly established kingdom of Portugal, as well as being the birthplace of its first king, Afonso Henriques, not to mention the celebrated poet and dramatist Gil Vicente. Its well-preserved old town and profusion of historic monuments and art treasures make it a worthwhile destination for the visitor.

★Townscape

There is a welcoming feel about Guimarães, with so much greenery everywhere. Town life revolves around the Praça Toural, lined with shops, houses and banks and the beginning of the town's main shopping street, the Rua de S. António, but tourists tend to be drawn more towards the picturesque old town, with its imposing granite houses. Many have wrought-iron balconies, smothered with flowers, and the finest are to be found in the Rua de Santa Maria, around the Largo da Oliveira and to the west of it.

## Guimarães

1 Capela de São Miguel do Castelo
2 Convento do Carmo
3 Paço do Concelho
4 Pousada
5 Collegiate church Nossa Senhora da Oliveira
6 Museu de Alberto Sampaio
7 Church of São Francisco
8 Church of Santos Passos

200 m

© Baedeker

## Sights

Above the town rears the grey bulk of the 10th c. castle (Castelo), with its high, slender battlements, one of the most complete and best preserved medieval strongholds in Portugal. As the birthplace on June 24th 1110 of the first Portuguese king, Afonso Henriques, it is also something of a national shrine.

★Castelo

In the middle of the oval courtyard rises the tall and massive keep, the Torre de Menagem, which could hold out on its own if need be. This is believed to have housed in the 11th c. a Benedictine convent founded by the Galician Countess Mumadona.

The curtain walls of the castle, with their eight towers, afford magnificent views, including those of the battlefield of Mamede.

Below the castle entrance stands the small chapel of São Miguel (1105), built of massive courses of dressed stone, in which Afonso Henriques was baptised.

Capela de São Miguel do Castelo

Mass is celebrated here annually on the king's birthday to commemorate the event.

At the foot of the castle hill, surrounded by greensward, is the large Paço Ducal, the Palace of the Dukes of Bragança, a magnificent Gothic residence originally built by Afonso, first Duke of Bragança, in the French style fashionable in his day (completed 1442). After the seat of the Bragança family was transferred in the early 16th c. to Vila Viçosa (see entry) the palace lost its earlier importance, and over the centuries fell into ruin. It was extensively restored and rebuilt in the 1930s, suffering considerable alteration (for example to the chapel) in the process.

★Paço Ducal

Its fine interior, with 16th–18th c. furniture, Flemish tapestries and valuable porcelain, is open to the public.

The route back to the old town passes below the ducal palace through the Praça de Mumadona, with a modern monument to the Duchess and, somewhat further west, the former Carmelite convent, the Convento do Carmo, its little church in an unpretentious local version of Baroque.

Convento do Carmo

The impressive Largo da Oliveira, in the heart of the old town, has been particularly successful in managing to retain its medieval aspect.

★★Largo da Oliveira

The story goes that the square, and the church, Nossa Senhora da Oliveira, owe their name – "Oliveira" means olive-tree – to Wamba the Visigoth. Called on to be King, Wamba refused to accept unless a dry olive twig stuck in the sand put forth green shoots again. No sooner was the twig in the ground, presumably where the Gothic/Manueline canopy now stands, than it began to turn green.

The old town hall, the Paço do Concelho, on the north side of the square contains the town archives. With its Gothic arcades, it was begun in the 14th c., during the reign of João I, and radically altered in the 17th c. The adjoining building contains a luxurious pousada.

In the centre of the square is the Gothic/Manueline alpendre (a canopy sheltering a crucifix) erected to commemorate victory in the battle on the Rio Salado in 1340, when the allied Portuguese and Spanish forces defeated the troops of the Sultan of Morocco.

The Largo da Oliveira is dominated by the collegiate church of Nossa Senhora da Oliveira. The church, originally founded by Afonso Henriques in the 12th c., in thanksgiving for his victory in the battle of Ourique, stands on the site of an earlier convent founded by Countess Mumadona in the 10th c. It was considerably enlarged in 1387–1400 by João I to commemorate the battle of Aljubarrota, when most of the original Romanesque cloister was demolished. The church as it appears today is largely 16th c.; the Manueline tower was added in 1505.

★Nossa Senhora da Oliveira

Features of the interior of the church include a Gothic stone altar and the Romanesque baptismal font from the Capela de São Miguel do Castelo, where Afonso I Henriques is said to have been christened.

*Guimarães: Square and Church of Nossa Senhora da Oliveira and the Hall of Victory*

★Museu de
Alberto Sampaio

The adjoining cloister and part of the former Dominican convent now house the very impressive Museu de Alberto Sampaio, with pictures and sculpture, mainly by Portuguese artists of the 14th–16th c., goldsmiths' work and a valuable collection of historical costume and furniture. Outstanding among the exhibits are the splendid sarcophagus of Constança de Noronhas, first Duchess of Bragança (in the cloister), a superb silver processional cross (16th c.) and the cloak which João I wore over his armour at the battle of Aljubarrota.

Santos Passos

From the collegiate church the long Largo da República do Brasil leads to the twin-towered Baroque church of the Santos Passos (18th c.), richly decorated with azulejos and sculpture showing Italian influence on the façade.

São Francisco

To the west stands the church of São Francisco, founded by João I about 1400 and remodelled in Baroque. The spacious interior is entirely faced with azulejos. The sacristy has a massive coffered ceiling.

Museu de Martins
Sarmento

In the west of the town centre it is worth visiting the Museu de Martins Sarmento, an archaeological museum in a former Dominican convent (13th c.) containing finds from the prehistoric settlements of Citânia de Briteiros (see entry) and Castro de Sabroso.

## Surroundings of Guimarães

Penha de Santa
Catarina

About 5km/3 miles south-east above the town, reached by a lovely mountain road, is the Penha or Serra de Santa Catarina (617m/2024ft), a rocky height with a pilgrimage church (1898) and a statue of Pope Pius IX. There are superb views from the summit south-east to the Serra de Marão (see Amarante) and, on a clear day, north to the Serra do Gerês (see Peneda-Gerês National Park) and west to the Atlantic.

10km/6 miles south-west of Guimarães, attractively situated on both banks of the Rio Vizela, is the spa of Caldas de Vizela (pop. 3000), with sulphurous springs which were already being frequented in Roman times. There are altogether 55 springs with an abundant flow of water at temperatures ranging from 16°C/61°F to 65.6°C/150°F, used for the treatment of bronchial and skin ailments, rheumatism, and conditions of the joints. There is an attractive park on the banks of the river (swimming, rowing) where a week of events is staged annually at the end of August, including folk-dancing, various sporting competitions, clay-pigeon shooting, etc.

Within easy reach of Caldas de Vizela are the late 17th c. pilgrimage chapel of São Bento (4km/2½ miles) and the 12th c. Romanesque church of São Miguel de Vilarinho (3km/2 miles), with a 12th c. Gothic cloister adjoining the church.

Another spa, Caldas das Taipas, about 7km/4½ miles north-west of Guimarães, was also known to the Romans. It too has hot sulphurous springs (30°C/86°F), used for treating bronchial and digestive system ailments, as well as rheumatism, etc. Here, too, there is an attractive park, this time on the banks of the Rio Ave.

## Lagos                                                                 B7

Historical province: Algarve. District: Faro
Altitude: sea level. Population: 10,000

Once capital of the old province of the Algarve, Lagos lies on the west side of a bay of the Rio Alvor, here fully 2km/1¼ miles wide, which is sheltered on the east by the Ponta dos Três Irmãos and on the west by the Ponta da Piedade (see below) and the broad estuary of Ribeira de Bensafrim. The excellent beaches nearby have led to a great deal of recent hotel development around the town, but the people of Lagos continue to make part of their living from fishing (tuna, sardines).

"Lacóbriga" to the Romans, Lagos became "Zawaya" under the Moors, who built the walls that originally fortified the town. These eventually succumbed to the Portuguese kings and Sancho II was able to take the town in the mid-13th c. In the centuries that followed it developed into an important ship-building town and port, thanks partly to Henry the Navigator. It was also from here that Gil Eanes, who was born in Lagos, set sail in 1434 to become the first seafarer to round Cape Bojador in West Africa. The voyages of discovery brought Lagos fame and fortune. Trade flourished, and the slave-trade with it – the first slaves from Africa were auctioned in 1443 in a building on the present Praça da República. Lagos became the capital of the historical province of Algarve in 1577 and remained so until 1756, the year following the destruction of much of the town by an earthquake. Its subsequent decline in importance was only halted in the late 20th c. when tourism has brought new prosperity.

Although Lagos has developed in recent years into a typical tourist centre it still has the feel of a compact, pleasant town about it. Around the town on the south-west are parts of the old walls (14th–16th c.), enclosing the former Governor's Palace (restored) and ending at the 17th c. Fortaleza, jutting far out into the sea. The wide seafront promenade of the Avenida dos Descobrimentos, the "Avenue of the Discoveries", 1961, demarcates the north-east edge of the old town centre. The hub of the town is the Praça de Gil Eanes which, with the surrounding streets, has been made a pedestrian precinct and in the summer months has the appearance of a big outdoor café.

## Sights

Focal point of the square is a modernistic statue (1973) of King Sebastião who set out from Lagos on a voyage of discovery never to return. Also in

## Lagos

Lisboa, Portimão, Railway station

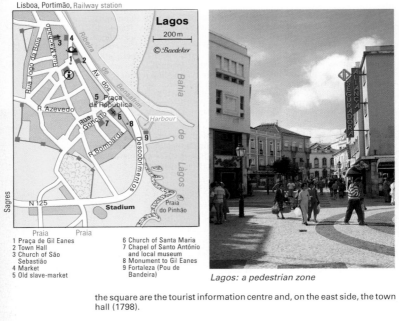

1 Praça de Gil Eanes
2 Town Hall
3 Church of São Sebastião
4 Market
5 Old slave-market

6 Church of Santa Maria
7 Chapel of Santo António and local museum
8 Monument to Gil Eanes
9 Fortaleza (Pou de Bandeira)

*Lagos: a pedestrian zone*

the square are the tourist information centre and, on the east side, the town hall (1798).

**São Sebastião**

The church of São Sebastião, north of the Praça de Gil Eanes, has a fine Renaissance doorway, with an adjoining chapter-house.

**Praça da República**

On the Praça da República, open to the seafront promenade, is a statue of Henry the Navigator, erected in 1960 to commemorate the 500th anniversary of his death. On the south side of the square stands the church of Santa Maria where Henry the Navigator was originally buried before his remains were transferred to Batalha Abbey (see entry). The 16th c. church was restored in the 19th c.

Opposite the church is the Delegação da Alfândega (customs house). Its arcades were where the slave market was held, the slaves shackled to the massive iron posts. A small memorial on the town wall south of the square commemorates seafarer Gil Eanes.

**Santo António**

Just south-west of the Praça da República is the Baroque chapel of Santo António, built in 1769 on the site of an earlier church; it has a magnificent talha dourada Baroque altar covering the whole choir wall.

**Museu Regional**

Adjoining the chapel is the regional museum with exhibits ranging from archaeological finds and folk and sacred art to all kinds of curios from the town's history, including a remarkable collection of Germany's inflation banknotes.

## Surroundings of Lagos

**★★Ponta da Piedade**

About 3km/2 miles south of Lagos is one of the most spectacular sections of the Algarve coastline, abounding in caves and superb rock formations,

*Praia Dona Ana, near Lagos*

including the rugged promontory of the Ponta da Piedade (lighthouse). A boat trip from Lagos harbour is a good way of appreciating the full impact of the scenery.

On either side of the mouth of the Ribeira de Bensafrim are sheltered beaches – to the east the Meia Praia, to the south the Praia do Pinhão and the Praia da Dona Ana (hotel colony).

Beaches

Odiáxere, 6km/4 miles north of Lagos, has a parish church with an outstanding Manueline portal. It was rebuilt after the 1755 earthquake in red sandstone from Silves (see entry).
   A pleasant trip can be made from here to Bravura Lake, 10km/6 miles north-west.

Odiáxere

## Lamego

C3

Historical province: Beira Alta. District: Viseu
Altitude: 490m/1610ft. Population: 10,000

The little episcopal town of Lamego, charmingly situated amid vineyards and fields on the slopes of Monte Penude about 100km/62 miles east of Oporto, has been since medieval times an important market for the agricultural produce from the fertile countryside around it. It was here that the Portuguese Estates met for the first time in 1143 to proclaim Afonso Henriques king of the newly established state. Lamego is also famous for its sparkling wine (Caves da Raposeira can be visited).

Situation and Importance

Lamego is a relatively undistinguished little town but does have some fine 16th–18th c. townhouses.

Townscape

# Sights

**Sé**

In the centre of town rises the massive Gothic Cathedral (Sé), founded by Afonso Henriques in 1129 and much altered in the 16th and 17th c. Of the original building there survives only the sturdy square tower. The interior was completely remodelled in the 18th c. The adjoining Renaissance cloister has several fine chapels.

**Museu Regional**

The Regional Museum is housed in the former Bishop's Palace (18th c.), on the Largo de Camões diagonally opposite the Cathedral. Its interesting collection includes 16th c. Flemish tapestries that once furnished the palace itself, Portuguese painting of the 16th–18th c., sculpture of the 13th–17th c., and religious and folk art.

**Capela do Desterro**

Another interesting feature of the town is the Capela do Desterro (1640) south of the cathedral on the main road to Guarda. Richly decorated with 17th c. azulejos and talha dourada, it has a Renaissance portal and a fine painted coffered ceiling.

**Castelo**

On a hill above the town is the 11th–13th c. castle, originally Moorish, with only its 13th c. keep and some of the walls still standing.

**Igreja de Almacave**

Just below the castle, to the west, is the Romanesque Igreja de Almacave with fine carved capitals and a 16th Renaissance pulpit.

**★Santuário Nossa Senhora dos Remédios**

The main sight of Lamego is undoubtedly the pilgrimage church of Nossa Senhora dos Remédios. From the town a magnificent Baroque staircase with 14 Stations of the Cross leads up to the sumptuous 18th c. twin-towered church on the Monte de Santo Estêvão. (It is also accessible by car, forking right at the entrance to Lamego coming from Viseu.) Thousands of pilgrims gather here at the beginning of September every year to seek healing and consolation.

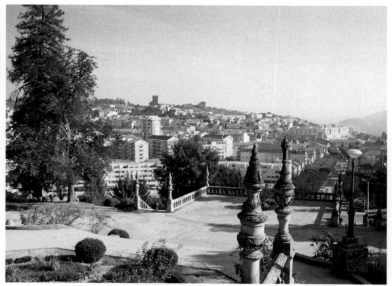

*Lamego, seen from the pilgrimage church of N.S. dos Remédios*

The terrace below the church holds statues of kings and biblical figures, with an obelisk in the centre, and affords an impressive view over Lamego and the surrounding fertile countryside.

## Surroundings of Lamego

About 3km/2 miles north-east of Lamego (right fork just before reaching Lamego on the Guarda road), in the valley of the Rio Balsemão, stands the Visigothic church of São Pedro de Balsemão, which is believed to be the oldest church in Portugal (7th c.). The church was restored in 1643 and given a coffered ceiling. It contains the sarcophagus of Afonso Pires, a 14th c. bishop of Oporto.

São Pedro de Balsemão

Barrô, 16km/10 miles north-west of Lamego on the N222, is delightfully situated above the Douro valley (see entry) and has a 12th c. Romanesque church.

Barrô

5km/3 miles further along the N222, as it winds its way along the Douro valley, São Martinho de Mouros has a Romanesque church (9th–11th c.) at the end of the village and is notable for its richly carved capitals and a picture of St Martin ascribed to Vasco Fernandes.

São Martinho de Mouros

Resende is a further 8km/5 miles along the road to the west. It is a trim little town, with above it the Romanesque church of São Salvador (view).

Resende

A side-road at Anreade (2km/1 mile further west) leads, after 8km/5 miles, to the Manueline church Santa Maria de Cárquere, which belonged to a convent founded in the 11th c.

Santa Maria de Cárquere

The little spa of Caldas de Aregos, 5km/3 miles west of Anreade, is beautifully situated on a wooded hill above the Douro valley. It has hot sulphur springs (50–61°C/122–142°F) used to treat ailments of the joints and bronchial diseases. It has a lovely park and there are fine views from the Penedo de São João, a crag above the town.

Caldas de Aregos

Famed for its vinho verde, Cinfães is 15km/9 miles further west and has an 18th c. mansion, the Quinta da Fervança.

Cinfães

Tarouquela, 15km/9 miles west of Cinfães, has a well-preserved hilltop Romanesque church, Santa Maria Major, which belonged to a 12th c. Benedictine convent. Close by is the Romanesque/Gothic chapel of São João Baptista.

Tarouquela

10km/6 miles further along the road Castelo de Paiva, or Sobrado de Paiva as it is also known, is a little town surrounded by hills and famous for its wine. A good centre from which to explore the surrounding area, it boasts an attraction of its own in the Quinta da Boa Vista, an 18th c. country house.

Castelo de Paiva

13km/8 miles north of Lamego on the N2, Peso da Régua (pop. 6000; alt. 380m/1246ft), Régua for short, is a pretty little town situated at the point where the little rivers Corgo (right bank) and Baroso (left bank) flow into the Douro. It is the focal point of the "País do Vinho" (the wine country – see Douro valley), and the busy centre of the port wine district. The town is particularly lively during the vintage (end of September to end of October) when helpers arrive from far and near.

Peso da Régua

Off the road to Guarda, 10km/6 miles south of Lamego, is the pretty village of Tarouca, in a beautiful setting at the head of a valley flanked by rugged walls of rock. In the church of the former Cistercian convent of São João de Tarouca, probably founded by Afonso I in 1171, is the imposing tomb of Conde Pedro de Barcelos (d. 1354), illegitimate son of King Dinis I and

Tarouca

author of the "Livro das Linhagens", a register of the nobility. The sarcophagus of his wife, formerly in the church, is now in the museum in Lamego.

Sernancelhe    Sernancelhe, about 50km/31 miles south-east of Lamego, has a Romanesque parish church with a separate belfry and a 16th c. pelourinho.

## Leiria                                                                 B5

Historical province: Beira Litoral. District: Leiria
Altitude: 30–113m/100–370ft. Population: 12,500

Situation and    Leiria is a busy district capital and market town in central Portugal, 10km/
Importance    6 miles north of Batalha (see entry). The Rio Liz flows through its centre.
Called Collipo by the Romans, the little town was a royal residence for a
time under King Dinis I and since 1545 has been the see of a bishop.
The fertile farming area around Leiria and its rural population still practice many old crafts and customs (basketwork, pottery, woven blankets, glass-blowing; traditional costumes).

Townscape    The heart of the town is the Praça de Rodrigues Lobo, surrounded by
gardens, handsome burghers' houses and noble mansions (also the site of
the tourist information centre).
The arcades are the remains of the cloister of the former Convent of St Martin.

## Sights

★Castelo    High above Leiria towers its castle, built originally by Afonso Henriques in
1135 on the remains of a Moorish castle, which itself had succeeded an
earlier Roman fortress. When Portugal's frontier shifted further south in
1147 the castle lost its strategic importance. Its dilapidation was halted,
however, in the early 14th c. when King Dinis had it rebuilt and extended to
make a palace that would serve as a residence for himself and his queen, St
Isabel. The keep (1324), from which there is a magnificent view, and part of
the castle walls are well preserved. The rest of the royal castle has been
restored, and from the loggia there are also good views over the town. The
early Gothic church of Nossa Senhora da Pena (1314) remains a ruin.

São Pedro    Below the castle is the 12th c. church of São Pedro, originally Romanesque
but much altered in later centuries.

Sé    The Cathedral (Sé) is a plain Renaissance building in the old part of Leiria
(16th c.; restored in 18th c.).
The small adjoining museum contains pictures, furniture, pottery and
glass.

Santuário de    Opposite the castle mound, on another hill, is the Santuário de Nossa
Nossa Senhora da    Senhora da Encarnação (1588), reached by an 18th c. staircase, with
Encarnação    panoramic views from the top.

## Surroundings of Leiria

Milagres    About 7km/4½ miles north of Leiria is the little town of Milagres with pretty
houses and a popular 18th c. pilgrimage church.

Monte Real    The little spa of Monte Real, 15km/9 miles north of Leiria, is used for
treatment of liver and stomach ailments (park).

Pombal    About 27km/17 miles north-east of Leiria, in the valley of the Rio Soura, is
the busy town of Pombal (pop. 11,000; alt. 221m/725ft). It owes its fame to

*Leira: the Castelo*

José I's powerful minister Sebastião José de Carvalho e Mello, Marquês de Pombal (see Famous People), who died here in exile in 1752. A monument to the Marquês de Pombal stands in the main square near the church of São Martinho (founded 1323, rebuilt 1520). There is a castle (renovated in the 16th c.) above the town together with the 12th c. church of Santa Maria do Castelo.

About 8km/5 miles east of Leiria is an impressive gorge on the Rio Caranguejeira, with rock faces fully 100m/330ft high.

Rio Caranguejeira

Marinha Grande is about 12km/7½ miles west of Leiria amidst the Pinhal de Leiria, or Pinhal Real, the pinewoods which were planted by King Dinis I using maritime pines from the south of France to provide protection against the drifting sand. Nowadays the trees yield resin and turpentine. Marinha Grande developed in the mid-18th c. when the glass-works, now one of the most important in the country, were set up here.

Marinha Grande/
Pinhal de Leiria

## Lisbon (Lisboa)

A6

Historical province: Estremadura. District: Lisboa (Lisbon)
Altitude: 23–112m/75–365ft
Population: 825,000 (Greater Lisbon: 2.1 million)

Lisbon, in Portuguese Lisboa (pronounced "Lishbóa"), capital of Portugal and its principal port and business centre, the see of an archbishop, and a university city, lies some 17km/10½ miles from the Atlantic on the north bank of the Tagus, which here opens out into the Mar de Palha ("sea of straw"), 7km/4½ miles wide. To the west of the city the estuary narrows again to 2–3km/1–2 miles across, forming a fine sheltered natural harbour.

Situation and
Importance

**Lisbon (Lisboa)**

Plan of the
Inner City

210

Plan of the
Inner City

© *Baedeker*

– – –○– – – Metropolitana

## Lisbon (Lisboa)

Thanks to its wonderful setting Lisbon is rightly numbered among the world's most beautiful cities. Even though the city has very recently lost something of its former glory through internal political events, such as an influx of often penniless refugees from the former overseas territories, nevertheless the many treasures of art and architecture still testify to its glorious past and, together with the charm of the old town and its steep narrow streets, make a stay here a memorable experience for any visitor.

History

The Phoenicians were the first to take advantage of this excellent harbour-age at the mouth of the Tagus, establishing a settlement which they called Alis Ubbo. Later the Lusitanian port of Olisipo, it was taken over by the Romans, surrounded by walls and, as Felicitas Iulia, became the adminis-trative capital of the Roman province of Lusitania, the second most impor-tant town (after Mérida) in the Iberian peninsula.

In A.D. 407 the town was taken by the Alani; from 585 to 715 it was under Visigothic rule; and after the battle of Jerez it fell into the hands of the Moors, who called it Al Oshbuna or Lishbuna. Under the Moors (until 1147) it enjoyed economic prosperity and a great flowering of culture.

Lisbon became of major importance again in 1260, when King Afonso III made it his capital. The great discoveries of the late 15th c. and the con-quest of the East Indies principally benefited the capital, which rapidly developed into one of the wealthiest cities in Europe.

On November 1st 1755 most of the town was laid in ruins by a devas-tating earthquake, but rebuilding soon began under the direction of the Marquês de Pombal. The new city was laid out on a magnificent scale, which is still visible today, to the plans of Manuel da Maira, incorporating such of the older Gothic and Manueline buildings as had survived.

The transfer of the capital to Rio de Janeiro from the French invasion (1807–08) until 1821, followed by the loss of Brazil as a colony, were considerable setbacks to Lisbon, from which it only gradually recovered in the second half of the 19th c. The twentieth century has seen Lisbon develop into a modern and enlightened city whilst generally retaining its individuality, despite the impact on its history by the fire that destroyed 7500 sq.m/8970 sq.yd of the centre in August 1988.

★★Cityscape

Lisbon's sea of whitish-grey houses extends over twenty hills on the south-ern slopes of the Estremadura plateau, with considerable variations in height, the different parts of the city being linked by steep streets and a number of lifts and funiculars.

At the heart of the city is the Baixa, the lower town, completely rebuilt in a depression just above the level of the Tagus after the quarter had been destroyed by the 1755 earthquake. It is full of gardens and broad prome-nades, along with narrow streets lined by great business houses. East of the Baixa, on the slopes of the castle mound, are Lisbon's oldest quarters, the Alfama and Mouraria, with their mass of secretive, medieval-seeming alleys that survived the earthquake virtually unscathed. The same was true of the other old part of town, the Bairro Alto, the upper town west of the Baixo. This is bordered on the west by Lapa, one of Lisbon's smartest residential suburbs and also the diplomatic quarter, where many countries have their embassies and the homes of their diplomats, while the suburb of Belém, farther west, has its own impressive buildings that serve as remin-ders of Portugal's past greatness.

The most radical changes to the face of Lisbon in recent decades have been in the north and east with the building of enormous housing estates such as Alvalade, in the north, designed to accommodate 50,000, while modern office and retailing complexes such as the Amoreiras shopping centre have also made their mark on the city's skyline.

Mosaic pavements

Artistically composed mosaic pavements are a feature of any walk around Lisbon – on the Rossio, simulating hills and valleys, on the Praça do

*View of Baixa and the Castelo de São Jorge* ▶

**Lisbon (Lisboa)**

Império, famous for its signs of the zodiac, or on the Avenida da Liberdade. The 1755 earthquake is supposed to have caused the people of Lisbon to have their promenades and squares plastered over, using the marble rubble as foundations. Nowadays the impressive mosaic pavements are increasingly being superseded, on cost grounds, by asphalt, and the 400 or so *calceteiros* who lived and worked in Lisbon at the start of this century have dwindled today to no more than 30, and they have to work for a pittance, usually only on repair jobs. If there is a new design the calceteiros get out the old, carefully archived wooden patterns which are then laid on the smoothed ground and filled with black and white stones, knapped so meticulously that only the smallest of joins remain.

A city's problems

In the "bairros da lata" in the northern and eastern outskirts of Lisbon the poorest of the community live in shanties, often without electricity or running water. Many of these deprived people have come from the former Portuguese colonies or from other parts of Portugal, or are simply unable to afford higher rents. The housing shortage in the inner city is another pressing problem, and most people who work in the capital have to commute daily. In its turn this has led to chaotic traffic conditions, especially in the rush-hours. Attempts are now being made to alleviate the housing shortage and to control rents, but it will be some time before the effects of these measures can be assessed.

## Description of the city

Anyone who can only manage a brief stay in Lisbon should at least spend a little time on the Rossio, go for a walk around the Alfama and get out to the suburb of Belém.

## Lower Town (Cidade Baixa)

Praça dos Restauradores

The best place to start a walk around the Lower Town is the Praça dos Restauradores, where the tourist information centre is situated. This busy square contains the Monumento dos Restauradores de Portugal, an obelisk almost 30m/100ft high erected in 1882 to commemorate the rising on December 1st 1640 which ended sixty years of Spanish rule.

Estação do Rossio

At the south-west corner of the square is the Rossio Station, the Estação do Rossio, looking more like a theatre or a monumental building than a station. It is in fact the local station for trains to Sintra and Leiria, which leave the city via a tunnel 2600m/2850yd long.

Teatro Nacional de Dona Maria II

Diagonally opposite the station is the side of the national theatre, the Teatro Nacional de Dona Maria II, which has its frontage on the Rossio. The Classical building, completed in 1846, was burnt down in 1964 and not reopened, after modernisation, until 1978.

★Rossio

The Rossio, or the Praça de Dom Pedro IV, as it's officially known, is the real centre of Lisbon, where it is worth taking the time to relax in one of the street cafés and watch the passers-by, streetsellers, shoe-shine boys, etc. In the middle of the square stands a marble column, 23m/75ft high, put up in 1870 and topped by a bronze statue of King Pedro IV. It also boasts two lovely fountains, some fine mosaic pavements (see above) and is surrounded by elegant 18th c. houses. South of the square, leaving by the Rua do Ouro or Aurea, the right of the street is in the shadow of the iron Elevador de Santa Justa (see upper town).

Quarter between Rossio and Praça do Comércio

The grid of streets between Rossio and Praça do Comércio was laid out like a chessboard on Marquês de Pombal's orders after the 1755 earthquake. The streets were arranged to accommodate certain guilds, hence the Rua

*View of the Rossio*

da Prata (silver street for the silversmiths), Rua Aurea, or Rua do Ouro (goldsmiths) and the Rua Augusta for the cloth merchants. Although this system is no longer discernible today this is still Lisbon's trading and shopping quarter.

At the far end of these streets, looking out onto the Tagus, is the Praça do Comércio, also known as the Terreiro do Paço after the royal palace (da Ribeira), which was destroyed in the 1755 earthquake. Its traditional English name is Black Horse Square, after the bronze equestrian statue of King José I (erected 1775) in the middle of the square. The square is surrounded by arcades and by various public buildings (mainly government departments), most of which were built by Santos de Carvalho after the earthquake. On the north side of the square towers a huge triumphal arch completed in 1873, the Arco Monumental da Rua Augusta, with statues of famous Portuguese figures.

Praça do Comércio

The general impression is unfortunately spoilt by all the parked cars, but the redesigning of the square has already gone out to an architectural competition.

Boats for Cacilhas (see Surroundings of Lisbon) on the opposite bank of the Tagus regularly leave from the embankment at the south end of the square; the boat trip provides a superb view of the gently rising terraces of houses that make up Portugal's capital.

## Old town

A short distance along Rua da Alfândega from the north-east corner of the Praça do Comércio is the church of Nossa Senhora da Conceição Velha, rebuilt after the earthquake but preserving a richly decorated Manueline façade from an earlier church.

Igreja da Conceição Velha

## Lisbon (Lisboa)

**Casa dos Bicos**

A little further east, and worth looking at, is the Casa dos Bicos, "the house of points", which owes its name to the diamond-shaped ashlar blocks that clad its striking façade. The ground floor of the 16th c. palace was all that survived the earthquake, but the upper storeys have since been rebuilt according to the old plans but with modern materials. Nowadays the building is used for exhibitions.

**★ Sé Patriarcal**

To the north-west, after a relatively short walk up through the narrow lanes of the old town, we reach the Cathedral, the Sé Patriarcal, the oldest church in the city. The greater part of it dates from 1344 onwards, when it replaced an earlier church which is believed to have been converted from a mosque in 1150. The fortress-like west front with its two towers was built in 1380.

Although the interior of the Cathedral appears predominantly Romanesque, the choir and ambulatory are Gothic. The font immediately left of the entrance is where St Antony is supposed to have been baptised in 1195. In the first chapel on the left is a beautiful terracotta Nativity group by Joaquin Machado de Castro. The choir contains the tombs of King Afonso IV and his queen, Brites. St Vincent's Chapel, at the near end of the ambulatory, used to hold the reliquary of St Vincent. Another chapel off the ambulatory contains the interesting sarcophagi of Lopo Fernandes Pacheco, a supporter of King Afonso IV, and his wife. The valuable treasures in the Sacristy include the silver reliquary of St Vincent.

A visit to the church should include the fine two-storey 14th c. cloister, with a superb Romanesque wrought-iron screen.

**Igreja de Santo António da Sé**

On the west side of the square opposite the cathedral is the church of Santo António da Sé, rebuilt between 1757 and 1812 following the earthquake, and said to mark the site of the house in which St Antony of Padua was born. The saint, who is supposed to have cured the lame and raised the dead, is commemorated by a monument and small museum nearby.

**★ Alfama**

The slopes east and north-east of the Cathedral are taken up by the Alfama, Lisbon's highly picturesque old quarter. Its stepped lanes and romantic squares attract lots of visitors, particularly in the evening when locals and tourists alike come to hear the fados sung in some of the cafés and restaurants.

The name Alfama comes from the Arabic "al-Hama", meaning hot springs. In the Middle Ages this quarter was home to Lisbon's nobility and prosperous bourgeoisie. Later came the craftspeople, fisherfolk and sea-farers and in the 18th c. the Alfama was also the red-light district. Nowadays Lisbon's old town is where those at the bottom of the income ladder live, and it is questionable whether life has the quaint charms for them that appeal to the tourist.

The best course is to wander aimlessly through the maze of narrow lanes, steep steps and hidden backyards. Despite the obvious poverty the place has a lively feel, with canaries trilling in each alley and plants trailing

**Lisbon**

**Cathedral**
**Sé Patriarcal**

1 Font
2 Crib (Nativity group)
3 Sacristy
4 High altar
5 Patriarchal throne
6 Tomb of Lopo Fernandes Pacheco
7 Entrances to cloister
9 St Vincent's Chapel
9 Chapel of the Sacrament

*View of the Alfama*                    *A typical street in the Old Town*

from every façade. The busiest street is the Rua de São Pedro, with its little shops, tabernas and street vendors.

On the north-west edge of the quarter, by the Rua do Limoeiro, the Mira-douro de Santa Luzia (Belvedere) offers a superb view from its terrace of the jumble of houses.

Miradouro de Santa Luzia

Opposite the terrace, in the former palace of the Visconde de Azurara (17th c.), on the Largo das Portas do Sol, is the Museum of Decorative Arts, with a school and workshops as well as a fine collection of 18th and 19th c. furniture, silver, carpets and ceramics (open: Tues.–Sat. 10am–1pm, 2.30–5pm).

Museu de Artes Decorativas

On top of the hill, once the middle of the Moorish town, is the Castelo de São Jorge. The oldest parts of the castle date from the 6th c. In the 12th c. the Moorish fortress was converted into a royal palace and until the 16th c. it served as a royal residence, then was used as an armoury and prison. It was severely damaged in the 1755 earthquake and what was left of the castle walls was restored in 1938–40, when the courtyard was made into gardens. From the tree-planted terrace on the south side of the castle and from the wall-walks and towers there are fine views of the city and the Tagus Mar de Palha (orientation table). (Open: daily 9am–5pm.)

★Castelo de São Jorge

Immediately east of the castle mound, on the Largo Rodrigues de Freitas, there is a small marionette museum (open: Tues.–Sun. 11am–1pm, 3–6pm).

Museu de Marionetas

There are good views of the castle from the Convento da Graça, a former convent now used as a barracks, to its north-east. The church of this former convent, Nossa Senhora da Graça, dates from 1556 and was rebuilt after 1755. Its south transept contains an image of Christ, Nosso Senhor dos Passos, that is revered as miraculous.

Convento da Graça

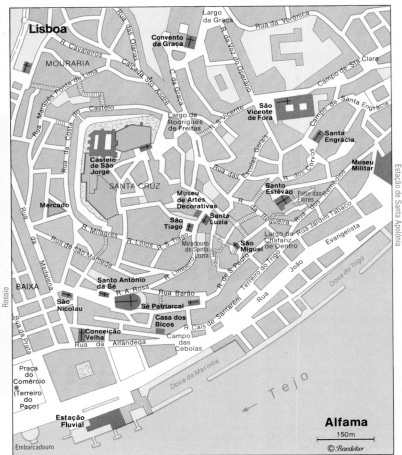

| | |
|---|---|
| Ermida Nossa Senhora do Monte | On a ridge some 300m/328yd north is the Ermida de Nossa Senhora do Monte (alt. 100m/330ft), built in 1243. Its terrace (orientation table) also has a panoramic view of Lisbon. |
| São Vicente de Fora | About 500m/550yd east of the castle mound is the imposing church of São Vicente de Fora by the Italian architect Filippo Terzi; it was built between 1582 and 1627 and has a rather severe twin-towered façade which contrasts markedly with the rich Baroque of the interior.<br><br>In the adjoining convent, a former Augustinian house, the entrance and cloisters boast a profusion of 18th c. azulejos. In the former refectory is the Panteão Real (Royal Pantheon), installed here in 1855, with the tombs of members of the House of Bragança from João IV (d. 1656) to Queen Amalia (d. 1951). |

Below São Vicente is the church of Santa Engrácia, or the Panteão Nacional, which has an unusual history. An earlier church was demolished in 1630 after theft of the host caused its deconsecration, only for the new building to collapse in 1681. Building of the present church was begun in 1682 but had taken almost three centuries to complete when it was finished with the dome in 1966.

    Its interior is on the plan of a Greek cross, and serves as a pantheon for such famous Portuguese as Vasco da Gama and Henry the Navigator.

Santa Engrácia

The Military Museum on the banks of the Tagus is in the former Army Arsenal (Arsenal do Exército), which was producing armaments up until the early 20th c. Nowadays the public can visit its large collection of arms and trophies which include 14th c. cannon and Vasco da Gama's sword. Some of the rooms have rich Baroque decoration (open: Tues.–Sat. 10am–4pm; Sun. 11am–5pm).

Museu Militar

The Santa Apolónia Station east of the Military Museum is the terminus for trains to Oporto and France.

Estação de Santa Apolónia

About halfway between the Apolónia Station and the azulejo museum is the civic waterworks museum, the Museu da Agua Manuel da Maia, opened in 1987. Displays in the former pumping station tell the story of Lisbon's water supply (open: Tues.–Sat. 10am–12.30; 2–5pm).

Museu da Agua Manuel da Maia

About 500m/550yd east of the Apolónia Station is the Museu do Azulejo which is housed in part of the Madre de Deus, the former convent of the Poor Clares, founded in 1509.

    This building was also largely destroyed in 1755 and rebuilt in the second half of the 18th c. The ornate main portal of the church was reconstructed in 1872 in its original Manueline style.

    Although most of the interior of the church is post-1755, the two cloisters survived the earthquake almost unscathed, with the larger being Renaissance in appearance and the smaller ranking as Manueline in style. These cloisters and other convent buildings contain the azulejo museum. This has a very extensive collection of Portuguese and foreign ceramic tiles, and includes an enormous azulejo portrait of Lisbon before the 1755 earthquake with the royal palace and the Casa dos Bicos easily recognisable (open: Tues.–Sun. 10am–12.30pm and 2–5pm).

★Madre de Deus/Museu do Azulejo

## Upper Town (Bairro Alto)

The Lower Town (see above) and the Upper Town (Bairro Alto) adjoining it on the west are rather bizarrely linked by the Santa Justa Elevator, near the Rossio. This wrought-iron structure is often ascribed to Gustave Eiffel but was in fact built between 1898 and 1901 according to the designs of Mesnier de Ponsard, a Portuguese of French descent.

    On alighting from the Elevador de Santa Justa in the Upper Town the eye is met with the dreadful sight of the ravages wrought on the streets by the fire of August 1988. There is, however, also a magnificent view of the lower town and the Alfama.

Elevador de Santa Justa

The elegant pedestrian precinct of the Rua do Carmo and its western adjunct the Rua Garrett – usually together known as Chiado – were partly destroyed by the fire in 1988. This not only badly damaged innumerable homes and business premises, it also wiped out a part of the city that had many literary and political associations for it was in its cafés that Portugal's poets and scholars had argued over their work. In order that this part of the national identity should not be completely forgotten it was decided that the Chiado quarter should be rebuilt incorporating the former façades.

Chiado

Near the upper exit from the Santa Justa Elevator is the former Convento do Carmo. Built between 1389 and 1423, most of it was destroyed in 1755,

★Convento do Carmo

*The Rua do Carmo, destroyed by fire*        *The Convento do Carmo*

and never rebuilt. However, even the ruins of what was once Lisbon's largest church are still impressive as a Gothic monument. The open nave of the church now houses an Archaeological Museum (Museu Arqueologico), showing classical and medieval tombs and architectural fragments as well as arms and coins (open: from Apr. 1st to Sept. 30th: Mon.–Sat. 10am–6pm; from Oct. 1st to Mar. 31st: Mon.–Sat. 10am–1pm and 2–5pm).

In front of the ruins of the church, in the middle of the Largo do Carmo, stands the Chafanz do Carmo, a lavishly designed fountain decorated with figures of four dolphins.

★Igreja São Roque

North-west of the Convento do Carmo is the Igreja São Roque. Its sumptuous Baroque interior makes it Lisbon's most magnificent church. Built for the Jesuits with the assistance of Filippo Terzi it dates from the second half of the 16th c. The sober façade is in stark contrast to the azulejos, paintings, marble and talhas douradas (gilded wooden carving) that adorn the interior. This embellishment reaches its apotheosis in the fourth side chapel on the left, the Capela de São João Baptista, built in Rome in 1742 for King João V from the most precious of materials – marble, alabaster, semi-precious stones, gold and silver – and brought to Lisbon by sea in 1747.

Museu de Arte Sacra

Near the church in the former Misericórdia almshouses and orphanage is the Museu de Arte Sacra, the museum of sacred art, with exhibits that include outstanding work by Italian goldsmiths (open: Tues.–Fri. 10am–5pm).

The Rua de S. Pedro de Alcântara leads northwards to a terrace with a fine view over the city and the Tagus (orientation table).

From here the Calçada da Gloria funicular descends to the Avenida da Liberdade (see Northern Districts) and the Praça dos Restauradores (see Lower Town). Further north-west, along the Rua de Dom Pedro V, is the highest point of the new town, the Praça do Principe Real; there is another excellent view of the city from the western corner of the square.

Even finer gardens than the Praça do Principe Real can be found in the Jardim Botânico opposite, dating from 1873 and richly stocked with tropical and subtropical plants. The botanical gardens are part of the Faculdade das Ciêncas, the science faculty of the university, which is located in the Classical building on the west side of the park.

Jardim Botânico

The centre of the Upper Town is the Largo do Chiado, where the Rua Garrett ends. It owes its second name, "Largo das duas Igrejas", to the two churches on it, Nossa Senhora da Encarnação (1784) in the south and the Loreto church (1517) in the north.

Largo do Chiado

Fortunately the historic Café Á Brasileira, rich in tradition, in the Rua do Carmo survived the fire unscathed. Its rooms have been declared a national monument of the architecture of the turn of the century. One of its regulars was Fernando Pessoa (see Famous People), whose statue was placed in front of the Café in 1988 on the centenary of his birth.

Café Á Brasileira

The Largo do Chiado opens into the tree-lined Praça de Camões, with a monument erected in 1867 to the famous Portuguese poet Luis de Camões (see Famous People).

Praça de Camões

From the Praça de Camões a walk north-west through a succession of streets beginning with the Rua do Loreto ends at the Igreja dos Paulistas, or Santa Catarina. The church was built in the mid-17th c. and its woodcarvings are particularly worth seeing.

Igreja dos Paulistas

Still further west is the Parliament building (Palácio de São Bento; Assembleia da República), converted from a 17th c. convent in 1834 and subsequently much altered. It also contains the National Archives, dating back to 1375.

Palácio de São Bento

On the north-west edge of the inner city stands the Basílica da Estrela. The "star basilica" was built between 1779 and 1790 and its imposing twin-towered façade and high dome over the crossing make it a prominent cityscape feature. There is a good view from the dome over the city.
Queen Maria I, who died in Brazil in 1816, is interred in the church. She commissioned the building after the birth of the heir to the throne but he died before it was complete.

Basilica da Estrela

Opposite the church is the Jardim da Estrela, attractive gardens with a profusion of flowers, ponds, fountains and grottoes.

Jardim da Estrela

The district of Lapa, south-west of the Jardim da Estrela, is the hub of diplomatic life and one of Lisbon's smartest residential areas.

Lapa

In the south of the Upper Town is Lisbon's famous opera-house, the Teatro Nacional de São Carlos, built in Classical style between 1792 and 1795 and recently restored.

Teatro Nacional de São Carlos

Opposite the opera-house is a former Franciscan convent containing the Academia de Belas Artes and the Museu Nacional de Arte Contemporânea, the national museum for contemporary art, with works, mainly by Portuguese artists, from 1850 onwards. The national museum collection includes pictures by Tomás da Anunciação, Marquês de Oliveira, Silva Porto, José Malhoa ("Outono"), Alfredo Keil, Columbano Bordale Pinheiro ("A Chávena de Chá", "O Concerto de Amadores"), Henrique Pousão, Carlos Reis, Eduardo Viana ("A Viola"), Francisco Smith, Amadeu de Sousa-Cardoso, Abel Manta, Dordio Gomes, António Soares, Carlos Botelho, Costa Pinto, Eduardo Malta, Mário Elói and Vieira da Silva, as well as sculpture by Soares dos Reis, Teixeira Lopes ("A Viúva"), Francisco Franco, Diogo de Macedo, Canto da Maia ("Juventude") and Auguste Rodin.

★Museu Nacional de Arte Contemporânea

## Northern Districts

Lisbon's main traffic artery is the Avenida da Liberdade, the broad (90m/100yd) avenue, with its ten rows of trees and its gardens, and lined

Avenida da Liberdade

221

# Lisbon (Lisboa)

*Praça do Marquês de Pombal*

with shops, hotels, banks and government buildings, that runs for 1.5km/1 mile through the city from the Praça dos Restauradores (see Lower Town) to the Praça do Marquês de Pombal.

**Praça do Marquês de Pombal**

At the northern end of the Avenida da Liberdade, the Praça do Marquês de Pombal is an important traffic intersection with a huge monument to the Marquês de Pombal (see Famous People) at its centre.

**Parque de Eduardo VII**

The circular Praça merges to the north into the Edward VII Park, so named in honour of the King Edward VII's visit to Lisbon in 1903. In the upper part of the park is the Estufa Fria (cool house), an open-roofed greenhouse with slats, for sub-tropical trees and cacti. There is also a smaller hot house for tropical plants. Pools, grottoes, rocks, waterfalls and streams abound in the park and from the terrace higher up there are extensive views of the city and the Tagus estuary.

**★★Museu Calouste Gulbenkian**

About 1km/¾ mile north of the Parque de Eduardo VII is the 17 acre-park of the Gulbenkian Foundation, the Fundação Calouste Gulbenkian, an institute of culture with a theatre, concert and conference halls, a library of some 400,000 volumes and the Gulbenkian Museum, one of the world's greatest private collections. The museum was opened on the centenary of the birth of its founder, the Armenian oil magnate Calouste Sarkis Gulbenkian, who lived in Lisbon from 1942 until his death in 1955.

The modern open-plan buildings of the Gulbenkian Museum, covering an area of 25,000 sq.m/30,000 sq.yd, were built between 1964 and 1969 and the architects were Alberto Passoal, Pedro Cid and Ruy Athouguia. The museum highlights include the extensive and outstanding collections of Oriental art, especially from Egypt, Mesopotamia, Islam and the Far East (China and Japan), an unusually rich collection of ceramics, and important Greek and Roman antiquities, particularly a fine collection of coins.

The picture gallery has works by German artists, including a "Presentation in the Temple" (1445) by Stefan Lochner, artists from the Low Coun-

## Museu Calouste Gulbenkian

PERMANENT EXHIBITIONS

1 Egyptian art
2 Greco-Roman art
3 Mesopotamian art
4 Oriental-Islamic art
5 Armenian art
6 Art from the Far East
7 Work in ivory; illuminated manuscripts
8 15th, 16th and 17th c. painting and sculpture:
   Germany, Holland, Flanders, Italy
9 Renaissance art

10 18th c. decorative art: France
11 18th c. painting and sculpture:
    France
12 18th and 19th c. silverwork: France
13 18th and 19th c. painting: England
14 18th c. painting: Italy
15 19th c. painting and sculpture:
    France

tries, such as Rubens ("Portrait of Hélène Fourment"), Thierry Bouts ("Annunciation"), Van Dyck ("Portrait of a Man"), Gossaert, Frans Hals and Rembrandt ("Pallas Athene"), the French artists Fragonard, Corot, Manet, Monet, Renoir and Degas (self-portrait), the English painters Hoppner, Gainsborough, Romney, Lawrence and Edward Burne-Jones ("Mirror of Venus"), the Venetian Carpaccio ("Virgin and Child with Donor"), and the Florentines Ghirlandaio and Guardi (ten pictures on Venetian themes).

There is also sculpture by Houdon (Diana) and Rodin (Burghers of Calais, in the park), textiles, 18th c. French furniture and more modern jewellery (Art Nouveau by Lalique). In the tropical park around the buildings of the foundation there is a 3m/10ft high seated bronze of Calouste Gulbenkian (by L. de Almeida) in front of a stone Horus falcon. The Calouste Gulbenkian Museum is open from June to September Tues., Thur., Fri. and Sun. 10am–5pm, Mon. and Sat. 2–7.30pm; October to May Tues.–Sun. 10am–5pm.

The Centro de Arte Moderna in the south-west corner of the Gulbenkian Foundation site dates from 1984 and is a lively cultural centre with a Museum of Modern Art which completes the original Gulbenkian collection which ended with Impressionism. Artists represented include Jaime Azinheira, with his sculpture "The Kiss", Jorge Pinheiro, with "The Bishop", 1981 and an unusually disrespectful work for Catholic Portugal, Costa Pinheiro, with an image of the author Fernando Pessoa (see Famous People), José Almada Negreiros, with three interesting self-portraits, etc. In addition to the comprehensive collection of contemporary Portuguese art the Museum also has many works by modern artists from outside Portugal. Adjoining the museum there is a sculpture park as well as a multi-purpose hall, studios, etc. (open: Tues.–Sun. 10am–5pm; from July to Oct. Wed. and Sat. till 7pm).

Centro de Arte
Moderna

The Zoological Gardens, the Jardim Zoológico, are in the north of the city, about 3km/2 miles from the Parque de Eduardo VII via the Avenida de

Jardim Zoológico

# Lisbon (Lisboa)

António Augusto de Aguiar and the Estrada de Benfica (open daily: summer 9am–8pm; winter 9am–6pm).

**Campo Grande**

East of the Zoo, along the Avenida das Forças, is the lovely park of Campo Grande with boats and outdoor cafés. Here also are the national library (Biblioteca Nacional; over 1 million volumes), the university city (Cidade Universitária) and the National Archive, completed in 1990.

**Museu da Cidade**

The Museu da Cidade, also in the Campo Grande, tells the story of the development of Lisbon. The museum is in the 18th c. Palácio Pimenta, at one time a gift from João V to his mistress. Particularly interesting is the scale model of Lisbon before the 1755 earthquake (open: Tues.–Sun. 10am–1pm, 2–6pm).

**Museu Rafael Bordalo Pinheiro**

Opposite the Museu da Cidade is the Museu Rafael Bordalo Pinheiro, the museum dedicated to the artist Rafael Bordalo Pinheiro (1846–1905) who was particularly famous for his ceramics (open: Tues.–Sun. 10am–1pm, 2pm–6pm).

**Museu Nacional de Trajo**

The National Costume museum, north of the Campo Grande in the Lumiar district (Museu Nacional de Trajo, 12 Estrada do Lumiar) is worth a visit. It is in the Palácio do Monteiro-Mor, surrounded by a large park, and features costumes throughout the ages in appropriate settings; there is also a collection of dolls and dolls' houses (open: Tues.–Sun. 10am–1pm, 2.30–5pm).

**Museu Nacional do Teatro**

The Theatre Museum (Museu Nacional do Teatro) is also in the Parque de Monteiro-Mor at Estrada do Lumiar 10. Displays include theatrical costumes, sets, tickets, etc., and give an overall view of theatrical history. Open: Tues.–Sun. 10am–5pm.

**★Amoreiras Shopping Center**

The Amoreiras Shopping Center on the Sintra/Estoril road in the northwest of the city has, since its advent in the early Eighties, added a whole new dimension to the Lisbon scene. For its architect, Tomás Taveira, the Armoreiras (mulberry trees) is his most important, and most controversial, work to date, reflecting his "neomodern" approach and, with its interplay of colours and shapes, the idea that there is more to architecture than pure utilitarianism. Behind the bright tower block façades there are houses, offices and, of course, shopping arcades.

The fully air-conditioned Shopping Center covers 86,000 sq.m/103,000 sq.yd and is open daily from 10am to midnight.

## Western Districts

**Praça do Municipio**

To the west of the Praça do Comércio is the Praça do Municipio, City Hall Square, which, because of the 18th c. pelourinho with a twisted shaft in the middle, is also known as Largo do Pelourinho.

The City Hall (Câmara Municipal) on the west side of the square was built between 1865 and 1880.

A short distance west of the Praça do Município is the Estação do Cais do Sodré, the station for trains to Cascais, and the quay for the Tagus ferries. From here, passing the market (Mercado) on the right, it is 2km/1¼ miles along the Avenida Vinte e Quatro de Julho, via the Tagus quays, to the Museu Nacional de Arte Antiga, Portugal's National Gallery.

**★★Museu Nacional de Arte Antiga (See plan page 226)**

Popularly known as the "Casa das Janelas Verdas" – house of the green windows – the National Museum of Ancient Art occupies a palace that belonged to the Marquês de Pombal and its modern extension (open: Tues.–Sun. 10am–1pm, 2.30–5pm).

The greater part of the Museum is taken up by the large picture gallery in rooms on the main floor, notable particularly for one of the great masterpieces of 15th c. Portuguese art, the famous polyptych from St Vincent's altar, formerly in the church of São Vicente de Fora, painted by Nuno Gonçalves between 1460 and 1470, with sixty portraits of leading figures in Portuguese history, including St Isabel (Queen Isabel) and Henry the Navigator.

16th c. artists represented in the collection include Vasco Fernandes (Grão Vasco) from Viseu, with "Adoration of the Virgin", Gregório Lopes, Cristóvão de Figueiredo and Frei Carlos. The 17th c. is represented by Josefa de Óbidos and Vieira Portuense ("Dona Isabel de Moura"), the 18th and 19th by Domingos António de Sequeira ("Family of the first Viscount of Santarém" and "The Painter's Daughter playing the Piano"). German masters represented include Albrecht Dürer ("St Jerome"), Lucas Cranach ("Salome") and Hans Holbein the Elder ("Virgin and Child with Saints"). Famous Spaniards include Velázquez ("Maria of Austria"), Zurbarán ("St Peter") and Murillo. Among outstanding works by Flemish artists are Hieronymus Bosch's triptych "Temptation of St Antony", Hans Memling's "Mother and Child", and Pieter Coek's "Descent from the Cross". French painting is represented by Fragonard ("Two Cousins"), Courbet, Poussin and others; English painting by Reynolds, Lawrence and Romney, the Italian schools by Piero della Francsca ("St Augustine"), Raphael ("St Eusebius Raising Three Men from the Dead"), Tintoretto ("Descent from the Cross"), Guardi and others.

Besides its outstanding picture gallery the Museum also has a collection of Egyptian, Greek and Roman sculpture (torso of an Apollo, 9th c.), a notable collection of pottery and porcelain (including work by António Ferreira and Machado de Castro, 18th c.), magnificent examples of goldsmith's and silversmith's work, including the cross of Sancho I (13th c.) and monstrances from Belém (16th c.) and Bemposta (18th c.), and a large collection of French table silver. The museum also has furniture, oriental rugs, tapestries, Portuguese, Spanish and Italian embroidery, plus graphics, drawings and illustrations.

About 1km/¾ mile north-west of the Museu Nacional de Arte Antiga is the Palácio das Necessidades, built in 1743–50 on the site of the Ermida Nossa Senhora da Necessidades. It was a royal palace until 1910 and is now occupied by the Ministry of Foreign Affairs. The adjoining park, the Tapada das Necessidades, is not usually open to the public.

*Palácio das Necessidades*

## Polyptych "Veneração a São Vicente"
### Painted by Nuno Gonçalves c. 1460–1470

## Museo Nacional de Arte Antiga, Lisbon

© Baedeker

| Cistercian monks from Alcobaça | Nuno Gonçalves | Isabel of Aragón | Henry the Navigator | Infante João (João II) | Archbishop of Lisbon | Gomes Eanes de Azurara | Moorish knight | Beggar | Jew |
|---|---|---|---|---|---|---|---|---|---|
| Fishermen and pilots | Queen Isabel | St Vincent | King Afonso V | Infante Fernão | St Vincent | Knight of Bragança | Fernão, 2nd Duke | | Cleric with St Vincent's skull |

**Lisbon (Lisboa)**

**Museu Nacional
de Arte Antiga
of Lisbon**

**Casa das Janelas Verdes**

**National
Museum of Art
Lisbon**

© Baedeker

1 Sala Calouste Gulbenkian
  (sculptures)
2 14th–15th c. painting
3 15th–16th c. painting (Flemish,
  Spanish)
4 15th–16th c. painting (Bosch
  altar, Cranach, etc.)
5–6 15th–16th c. painting (Dürer,
  Holbein the elder, etc.)
7 16th c. painting
8 17th c. painting
9 15th–18th c. portrait painting

10–12 16th–18th c. applied art
13–17 Temporary exhibitions
18 18th c. portrait painting
19–22 18th c. applied art
23 Christmas crib
24–26 Ecclesiastical vestments and
  tapestry
27 Namban art
28, 29 17th/18th c. Indo-
  Portuguese handicraft;
  17th c. Afro-Portuguese
  furniture

30 18th c. Chinese and Japanese
  porcelain
31, 32 16th–19th c. Oriental
  porcelain
33 Portuguese porcelain
34 16th–19th c. Portuguese
  ceramics
35, 36 15th–19th c. glass
37, 38 17th–19th c. gold and
  silversmiths' work
39 14th–16th c. gold and
  silversmiths' work

**LOWER FLOOR**

© Baedeker

★Ponte 25 de
Abril

*

The road westward along the river bank soon comes to the Ponte 25 de
Abril, or Ponte Suspensa, as the bridge is also known. The 945m/1034yd
long approach-road to this toll-bridge over the Tagus rests on massive
pillars. The actual suspension bridge, one of the longest in the world, was
opened in 1966. It is 2277m/2471yd long, with a span of 1013m/1108yd
between the piers which are 190.5m/625ft high; the carriageway is 70m/
230ft above the water. The bridge currently only takes road vehicles, but
there are plans to extend it for rail traffic.

## Belém

Belém, short for Bethlehem, the south-western suburb of Lisbon, is on the right bank of the Tagus at the point where the river begins to open out again as it enters the sea. Its fine old buildings and fascinating museums probably warrant a whole day there (map on p. 229).

On the north side of the spacious Praça do Império, with its large illuminated fountain (Fonte Luminos) surrounded by formal gardens, is the crowning glory of Belém, the world-famous Hieronymite monastery, the Mosteiro dos Jerónimos de Belém. This is the supreme achievement of Manueline architecture and the most impressive symbol of Portugal's power and wealth in the age of the great colonial conquests (open in the summer: Tues.–Sun. 10am–6pm; in the winter: Tues.–Sun. 10am–5pm).

★★Mosteiro dos Jerónimos de Belém

The origins of the monastery go back to a chapel for seamen built here by Henry the Navigator, within easy reach of the harbour at Restelo from where the voyages of discovery set out, and served by the Knights of Christ. Tradition has it that Vasco da Gama spent the nights before sailing for India in 1497 praying in this chapel; and here, too, he was received by the king on his triumphant return. To commemorate and give thanks for the voyage Manuel I built on the site of the little chapel one of the most splendid buildings in Portugal, and indeed the whole of Christendom. The building of the monastery began in 1502 to the plans of Boytaca (probably a native of Languedoc), who was also concerned in the construction of Batalha Abbey (see entry). The detailed work was carried out in 1517–22 under the direction of João de Castilho, who also built the cloister. After the dissolution of the monastery in 1834 it was occupied by the Casa Pia orphanage.

At the south-east corner of the complex is the three-aisled church of Santa Maria, with a magnificent south front. The south doorway (by João de Castilho) and the west doorway (by Nicolas Chanterène) are particularly fine. The choir, in High Renaissance style, was added in 1571–72.

In the spacious interior (92m/302ft long, 22.6m/74ft wide and 25m/82ft high) the octagonal piers are richly decorated with reliefs. In the magnificent transepts and apse are the tombs, borne on elephants, of Manuel I and his successors and relatives – a total of five kings, seven queens and nineteen princes and princesses of the House of Avis. Under the organ-loft are the sarcophaguses of Vasco da Gama and Luís de Camões (who died of the plague in 1580). In the Coro Alto (access from cloister) are fine Renaissance choir-stalls (1560).

On the north side of the church is the splendid two-storey Cloister (Claustro) around a square courtyard, each side 55m/180ft long and the masterpiece of João de Castilho. In the north-west corner is a Lion Fountain, which once stood in a basin in the middle of the cloister. Here, too, is

**Mosteiro dos Jerónimos de Belém (Lisboa)**

**Hieronymite Monastery of Belém (Lisbon)**

1 South door
2 Church of Santa Maria de Belém
3 Choir
4 Sacristy
5 Chapterhouse
6 Refectorium
7 Fountain of Lions
8 West door
9 National Museum of Archaeology in former Dormitorium (Dorter)

© Baedeker

Praça do Império

# Lisbon (Lisboa)

*The Praça do Império with the façade of the Mosteiro dos Jerónimos*

the entrance to the former Refectory which has beautiful reticulated vaulting and rich azulejo decoration (17th c.) on the walls. At the north-east corner of the cloister is the former Chapterhouse, which contains the tombs of the writer and politican João Baptista da Silva Leitão de Almeida Garrett (1799–1854), the historian Alexander Herculano (1810–77) and Oscar António de Fragosa Carmona (1869–1951), President of Portugal from 1928 until his death.

**Museu Nacional de Arqueologia e Etnologia**
In the unfinished south wing of the cloister is the Dorter (dormitory), which now houses the National Museum of Archaeology and Ethnology (Museu Nacional de Arqueologia e Etnologia; open: Tues.–Sun. 10am–noon, 2–5pm). The extensive collection of prehistoric and early historical material and impressive works of art and other material of the Moorish and medieval periods has now been completely re-organised.

**Museu da Marinha**
The west wing of the monastery is the interesting Naval Museum (Museu da Marinha). Here and in the modern extension to the west a series of models of ships tell the story of Portuguese navigation. The two 18th c. ceremonial barges are particularly worth seeing (open: Tues.–Sun. 10am–5pm).

**Planetário Calouste Gulbenkian**
Between the two parts of the Naval Museum is the Calouste Gulbenkian Planetarium (1965; performances from Oct. to March: Sat., Sun. 4 and 5pm; from April to Sept. 4, 5 and 6pm; from July to Sept. also Wed. 4, 5 and 6pm).

**Praça de Afonso de Albuquerque**
Nearby, to the east of the Convento dos Jerónimos, is the Praça de Afonso de Albuquerque, with a monument in the middle to Afonso de Albuquerque (c. 1450–1515), the second Portuguese Viceroy of the East Indies.

**Palácio de Belém/Museu dos Coches**
On the north side of the square stands the former royal palace, the Paço de Belém, built by the Conde de Aveiro in 1700, which is now the residence of the President of Portugal.

*Cloister of the Hieronymite convent*

On the ground floor of the east wing the former Riding School (built 1726) now houses the National Coach Museum (Museu Nacional dos Coches), one of the largest and most valuable collections of its kind, with some 60 state and ceremonial coaches and carriages from the 17th to the 19th c. (open: Tues.–Fri. 10am–5pm).

To the south of the Praça do Império, on the banks of the Tagus, towers the 54m/175ft high Monument of the Discoveries (Padrão dos Descobrimentos), in the form of a ship's prow, erected in 1960, the 500th anniversary of the death of Prince Henry the Navigator. It commemorates the Portuguese

Padrão dos
Descobrimentos

seamen who set out from here in the 15th c. on their voyages of discovery. At the head of the row of people on the prow stands Henry the Navigator, a model ship in his hands. Inside there is a lecture theatre and several smaller rooms with displays, including one of photographs relating to the discovery period. A lift takes visitors up to the observation platform on top of the monument. The mosaic in the square in front of the monument is of a compass with a map of the world. West of the Praça do Império, in spite of some popular opposition, a new Cultural Centre (Centro Cultural) is being built.

Museu de Arte Popular

To the west of the Monument of the Discoveries the Museu de Arte Popular is a museum of folk art with a large collection of Portuguese costumes, tools, furniture, domestic utensils, pottery, etc. arranged according to provinces; there are also displays of embroidery, ceramics and jewellery (open: Tues.–Sun. 10am–12.30, 2–5pm).

★★Torre de Belém

**Opening times**
Jun.–Sept.:
Tues.–Sun.
10am–6.30pm;
Oct.–May:
Tues.–Sun.
10am–5pm

Some 500m/550yd farther west, on the Tagus, is the Belém Tower, the Torre de Belém, in the purest Manueline style, built in 1512–21 to protect the harbour of Restelo at the entrance to the Tagus. The tower was long used as a state prison. After the capture of Lisbon in 1807 French troops destroyed the top two storeys of the tower but these were restored to their original splendour in 1845. Facing the Tagus the tower has a bastion with embrasures and, below the waterline, powder and storage chambers.

The tower itself contains the "King's Chamber" taking up the whole width of the main façade, and the Governor's room. The furnishings are not the originals.

There are fine views from the tower platform over Belém and the Tagus.

Palácio Nacional da Ajuda

**Opening times**
Sun.–Tues. and
Thur.–Sat.
10am–5pm

To the east of the Paço de Belém the Calçada da Ajuda leads 1km/¾ mile upstream to the Palácio Nacional da Ajuda. This former royal palace was begun in 1802 but never completed. Finely situated above Belém, it now contains the Monument Protection Office and the Ajuda Library, and there is an architectural competition under way for a design to complete it. On the way there the road passes the Adjuda Botanic Garden (on left: view), with a dragon tree planted in 1598.

Museu de Etnologia

About 600m/656yd west of the Palácio Nacional da Ajuda, in the Avenida Ilha da Madeira, is the ethnological museum, the Museu de Etnologia. Although the museum was only opened in 1985 there is room for no more than the most important exhibits to be put on display, so there are changing exhibitions on various themes (open for pre-arranged visits: Tues.–Sun. 10am–12.30pm, 2–5pm).

Parque Florestal de Monsanto

North of the Ajuda district is the extensive Monsanto Forest Park (Parque Florestal de Monsanto, campsites) which is traversed by the western motorway. In the northern half is an old fort, the Forte de Monsanto.

Aqueduto das Águas Livres

Along the north-west edge of the park runs the Aqueduto das Águas Livres (1728–48), an aqueduct 18km/11 miles long which supplies Lisbon with its drinking water.

# Benfica

Benfica, once an elegant suburb on the north-west edge of Lisbon, has undergone rapid expansion in recent decades and today its townscape is predominantly one of highrise and shopping centres.

Estádio do Benfica

The suburb is known far beyond the frontiers of Portugal as the home of Benfica, Lisbon's famous football club, whose large stadium, the Estádio do Benfica (completed in 1944) on the Avenida do Marechal Carmona, holds 60,000 spectators.

*Torre de Belém*

In the Largo de São Domingos stands the church of São Domingos, belonging to a Dominican convent which was founded in 1399 and rebuilt after the 1755 earthquake.

Igreja São Domingos

It contains azulejo pictures by António de Oliveira. The marbles in the Capela de São Gonçalo are also worth seeing.

Near the church is the Casa dos Marqueses de Fronteira, a palatial 17th c. mansion. In the beautiful gardens is a pool surrounded by blind arcades decorated with azulejo pictures. The palace is privately owned but is open to the public, as are the gardens (from Apr. 1st to Oct. 31st: Mon., Wed. 10am–noon, Sat. 3–6.30pm; from Nov. 1st to Mar. 31st.: Mon. 10am–noon, 2–4pm).

Casa dos Marqueses de Fronteira

## Surroundings of Lisbon

### South of Lisbon

Visible from Lisbon centre, the Christ the King Monument (Monumento Cristo Rei) stands on the south bank of the Tagus. Erected in 1959, it consists of a base 82m/270ft high (containing a chapel) topped by a 28m/90ft high reinforced concrete figure of Christ.

Monumento Cristo Rei

A lift takes you up to a platform from which there is a sweeping view of Lisbon.

The little port of Cacilhas is on a promontory below the town of Almada and can be reached by ferry from Lisbon. Its good fish restaurants make it very popular with visitors and there is also a fine view from here of the terraces of houses on the north bank of the Tagus.

Cacilhas

**Loulé**

Costa da Caparica | From Cacilhas a road runs along the Tagus and then a little way inland to the west coast and the resort of Costa da Caparica (see Costa de Lisboa).

## North of Lisbon

Odivelas | 12km/7½ miles north of Lisbon, at Odivelas, is the Cistercian Convento de São Dinis e São Bernardo (1295–1305), which was partly destroyed in the 1755 earthquake and rebuilt in Baroque style from 1757 onwards. In the church is the tomb of King Dinis, founder of this convent.

Loures | 15km/9 miles north of Lisbon, on the Rio Trancão, is the little town of Loures, where the wooden carving in the 17th c. parish church (Igreja Matriz) is worth seeing. The nearby Quinta do Correio-Mór, a palace with a Baroque main block and two wings, contains azulejos, stucco decoration and paintings by José da Costa Negreiro; the kitchen (18th c.) has azulejo pictures.

Lousa | In Lousa, 10km/6 miles farther north-east, the church of São Pedro has a fine Manueline doorway and azulejo decoration; in front of the church is a large fountain.
    Near the church of São Miguel is the Manueline doorway of a demolished church, now incorporated in a house.

Mafra | From Lousa it is about 15km/9 miles to Mafra (see entry) with its enormous convent palace.

## West of Lisbon

Aquário Vasco da Gama | The Vasco da Gama aquarium in the suburb of Algés holds the oceanographic collection of King Carlos I, as well as all kinds of fish from Portugal's coastal waters and the former overseas territories (open daily: 10am–6pm; in winter 5.30pm).

Costa do Sol, Estoril, Cascais | It makes a pleasant trip to travel westward along the Costa do Sol, with the popular resorts of Estoril and Cascais (see entries).

Sintra, Queluz | It would also be a pity to leave this part of Portugal without visiting picturesque Sintra (see entry), with its two palaces, and the castle of Queluz (see entry).

---

**Loulé**                                                                    B7

Historical province: Algarve. District: Faro
Altitude: 170m/560ft. Population: 8600

Situation and Importance | Set in fertile countryside Loulé, just 17km/10½ miles north-west of Faro, chief town of the district, is an important market centre; its big Saturday market attracts many local and foreign visitors. Handicrafts are also an important part of its economy and the narrow alleys of the old town are full of potters, saddlers and coppersmiths.
    The town's main claim to fame, however, is its carnival that takes place every year on the four days before Ash Wednesday, and the almond blossom festival.

Townscape | A detour to Loulé is worthwhile for the many beautifully decorated chimneys on the white-washed houses. No two are alike, and most householders have given their imagination free rein to produce minor works of art. The town walls and castle (12th c.) date from Moorish times. Near the castle is the pilgrimage chapel of Nossa Senhora da Conceição, with 17th c.

azulejos of scenes from the life of the Virgin. The 13th c. parish church contains Renaissance altars and azulejo-clad chapels, but its finest feature is the view over the town and surrounding countryside. The Manueline doorway of the Misericórdia Church, and the ruins of the Convento da Graça are also worth seeing.

## Surroundings of Loulé

About 2km/1¼ miles above Loulé is the 16th c. pilgrimage church of Nossa Senhora de Piedade.

Nossa Senhora da Piedade

The mountain village of Alte about 25km/15½ miles north-west of Loulé offers the visitor a rural idyll, disturbed only by the bustle of the big market once a month, making it hard to believe it is only a few miles from the modern hotel cities of the coast.

Alte

See entry

Faro

For other places worth visiting around Loulé see Algarve.

Other destinations

## Macao/Macau/An Men

Chinese territory under Portuguese administration
Area: 15.7 sq.km/6 sq.miles
Altitude: 0–174m/0–571ft. Population: 430,000

The former Portuguese overseas province of Macao (Portuguese Macau, Chinese An Men), now a territory under Portuguese administration, lies some 70km/45 miles south-west of the British Crown Colony of Hong Kong on the west side of the wide estuary of the Pearl (Canton) River. The territory consists of the Macao peninsula (area 6 sq.km/2¼ sq.miles), with the capital, Macao (originally Cidade do Santo Nome de Deus de Macau), and two islands to the south, Taipa (3.4 sq.km/1¼ sq.miles) and Coloane

Situation and Importance

(6.6 sq.km/2½ sq.miles) which are linked to the mainland by bridges and causeways.

Macao attracts many day trippers and weekend visitors from Hong Kong, who come for its beautiful scenery, its six casinos (including the water-borne Macau Palace) and its reputation as a shoppers' paradise, offering goods of every conceivable kind, particularly antiques which are available in great quantity and variety and at very reasonable prices.

Climate

Macao has a subtropical climate, with warm to hot temperatures (averaging 28°C/82°F for the year), with rainfall at its heaviest from April to October. Cool winds off the sea make the hot season more bearable than in Hong Kong. The winters have less rainfall and colder temperatures (under 20°C/68°F) and the weather is at its most agreeable in November and December.

History

The first Portuguese trading post and fort was established in Macao in 1516, and in 1557 the Chinese granted Portugal a lease of the territory, in gratitude for Portuguese assistance in combating piracy. Macao thus became the first European colony in China. The most celebrated Portuguese poet, Luís de Camões, lived in Macao from 1556 to 1558 as a financial and property executor, and completed the first six cantos of his "Lusiads" here.

The settlement soon developed into an important entrepôt in East Indian trade, a focal point of political and diplomatic activity and a base for Catholic missionary work in the Far East. However, from the middle of the 19th c. Macao's importance declined as a result of the economic rise of Hong Kong. A treaty with China in 1887 confirmed the status of Macao as a Portuguese colony.

From 1951 to 1976 Macao was a Portuguese overseas province with its own governor and full financial and administrative autonomy (currency unit the pataca). The political influence exerted by the Chinese People's Republic, which increased in intensity from 1968 onwards, and the impossibility of effectively suppressing such tendencies by a Portuguese military presence demonstrated, however, that Macao had in fact retained the age-old links with the culture and economy of China. The realisation of this, combined with financial considerations, led in 1974 to the withdrawal of all Portuguese troops and in 1976 to the grant of full autonomy in domestic affairs to the territory, Portugal remaining responsible only for its external relations. However, a change in the status quo is in sight. A treaty concluded between China and Portugal in 1987 provides that on December 20th 1999, two years after Hong Kong, Macao will be ceded to China, although up until 2050 social, political and economic relations in Macao should remain unchanged.

Population

About 97% of Macao's 430,000 population is Chinese, the rest (about 12,000) being mostly Macao-born Portuguese or of mixed race (Macaenses). About 85,000 are Portuguese passport-holders. Many of the population are refugees who fled from the Japanese forces occupying China and Hong Kong during the Second World War, or left China during Mao Tse Tung's Cultural Revolution.

Economy

The territory's economy is largely based on the production and export of textiles, particularly embroidery, matches, fireworks, small boats and, increasingly, electronic and optical goods. Tourism also plays a big part, particularly the Hong Kong Chinese who come to gamble in the casinos which are banned in the Crown Colony. Of the 5 million visitors a year 90% come to play in the six casinos, so it is no surprise that half Macao's budget is made up of its gambling income.

Cityscape

Macao is a city of contrasts, where East meets West to give a mixture of native Chinese shops and dwellings, monumental European and Asian holy buildings for the various religions and elegant villas in a style reminiscent of southern Europe. The oldest parts of town in the low-lying areas safe from typhoons look like a Portuguese country town, with squat rows of houses lining cobbled streets. The rain-bleached façades of these one-time prosperous 18th c. houses, with their Rococo dormer-windows, graceful pillars and ornate balconies, hint at their past elegance. In the packed shopping streets, with ideographs strung from house to house, there are craftsmen's and tailors' modest little workshops, where scholars who can also cast horoscopes set up their tiny tables beside modern shopping arcades that bear witness to the boom times of the twentieth century.

The symbol of the town is St Paul's Church (Ruinas de São Paulo), the ruins of what was once the greatest church in the Far East, of which only the imposing Renaissance façade remains. The Museu Luis de Camões holds one of East Asia's most highly prized art collections, and other major sights include the Portas do Cerco, the border gate with the People's Republic of China, Kun Iam Tong, a labyrinthine Buddhist temple, and the cathedral, built between 1844 and 1850.

## Madeira/Archipélago da Madeira

Autonomous Region of Madeira (Região Autónoma da Madeira)
Area of islands: 794 sq.km/306 sq.miles. Population: 252,800

The archipelago of Madeira lies in the Atlantic some 535 nautical miles south-west of Lisbon and 240 miles north of Tenerife in the Canaries, between latitude 33°7' and 30°1' north and between longitude 15°51' and 17°15' west.

**Location and General**

The group consists of the main island of Madeira, rising from a depth of 4000–5000m/13,000–16,500ft below sea level to an average height of something over 800m/2600ft, with an area of 741 sq.km/286 sq.miles (length 57km/35 miles, width 22km/14 miles), together with the island of Porto Santo (highest point 507m/1663ft), 23 miles north-east, and the three almost uninhabited islets of Ilhéu Chão, Deserta Grande and Ilhéu do Bugio, 11 nautical miles south-west. Also belonging to the group are the five uninhabited Ilhas Selvagens ("Wild Islands"; area 4 sq.km/1½ sq.miles) which lie some 170 miles south on the northern fringe of the Canaries.

All the islands in the archipelago are hilly and, like the Spanish Canaries, of volcanic origin. The oldest diabase formations have thus been overlaid since the Miocene period by many volcanic craters, now extinct (lagoas).

**★ ★ Topography**

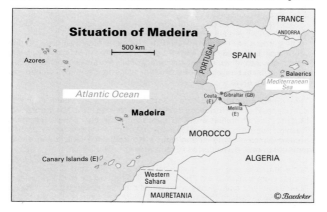

Situation of Madeira

500 km

Azores

Atlantic Ocean

Madeira

Canary Islands (E)

FRANCE
ANDORRA
PORTUGAL
SPAIN
Balaerics
Mediterranean Sea
Ceuta (E) Gibraltar (GB)
Melilla (E)
MOROCCO
ALGERIA
Western Sahara
MAURETANIA

© Baedeker

The later upthrust of the underlying rocks to some 400m/1300ft above their original level also parallels that of the Canaries.

The backbone of Madeira is a range of mountains with jagged ridges reminiscent of the Dolomites which runs in an east–west direction, reaching its highest point in the Pico Ruivo (Red Peak) de Santana (1861m/6106ft). In the west of the island is the Paúl de Serra plateau, in the east the smaller plateau of Santo António da Serra.

On the southern and northern slopes of the range are the magnificent rugged valleys, enclosed within high cliffs, known as *currais* (singular *curral*), which make their way down to the sea in deep eroded gorges, patterned with alternating layers of volcanic ash and lava. The gorges on the north coast are particularly impressive.

The coasts of Madeira are steep and rocky, with narrow strips of coastal plain only here and there as the lava flows reach the sea.

Climate

Madeira owes its mild and equable climate to its southern latitude and its location in the open Atlantic. The daily and annual ranges of temperature on the sunny and sheltered south coast are lower than in any Mediterranean resort. The average January temperature in Funchal is 16.2°C/61.2°F, the average for July 29.8°C/85.6°F. The average annual rainfall is 590mm/23 in., with five times as much rain in the north as in the south. Most of the rain falls between October and January or March in the form of cloudbursts. The number of hours of sunshine for the year averages 2124 (minimum of 97 hours in January, maximum of 251 hours in August). In spite of the nearness of the sea the relative humidity of the air is low (68%).

Water temperature averages 17.4°C/63.6°F in February, 22.4°C/72.3°F in September. From time to time there is a hot east wind, the *leste*, that blows from Africa carrying dust with it. Here it remains within tolerable limits, driving away the banks of cloud which regularly form in the middle of the day at a height of 1200–1500m/4000–5000ft.

Vegetation

Madeira's vegetation – the *flor do oceano*, flower of the ocean – is of almost tropical luxuriance, thanks to the mildness of the climate, the abundant winter rains and the system of irrigation which carries water from the hills to the fields and gardens along the coast through countless canals (*levadas*) and underground tunnels (*furados*). The trees which grow here include not only pines and European deciduous species but also a great range of evergreen trees and shrubs of subtropical and tropical origin: palms, araucarias, hickory, cork-oaks, camphor trees, fig-trees, yuccas, medlars, mimosa, eucalyptus, bamboos, papyrus, tree ferns, agaves, etc. There are also small numbers of dragon trees, wild laurels and Oreodaphne foetens (Portuguese tíl), a handsome tree of the laurel family which is found only on Madeira. These relics of the primeval forest which once covered the island and gave it its name are now found only in the gorges on the north coast and are protected by law.

The gardens of Funchal, usually surrounded by high walls, are filled in winter and particularly spring with a glorious profusion of flowers of every hue: roses, camellias, rhododendrons, azaleas, pelargoniums, begonias, bignonias (including jacaranda cuspidifolia), daturas, bougainvillea, wisteria and many more.

Population

The population, originally purely Portuguese and still exclusively Portuguese-speaking, has in the course of the centuries received an admixture of Moorish, Jewish, Italian and African blood, particularly on the south coast. The high population density (320 to the sq.km, or 829 to the sq.mile) and the predominance of large landholdings have long been reflected in a high emigration rate, particularly to South America (Brazil).

History

According to legend Madeira was part of the lost kingdom of Atlantis. The islands were known to the Phoenicians, and in the time of King Juba II of Mauretania (1st c. B.C.) they were called the Insulae Purpuriae, after the purple dye produced there. When they were rediscovered by the Portu-

*Funchal: the coast . . .*          *. . . and Reid's Hotel*

guese navigator João Gonçalves Zarco in 1419 they were uninhabited and covered with dense forest, hence the name Ilha da Madeira – island of timber.

After the Portuguese colonisation Madeira prospered by the growing of sugar-cane and later also by the production of wine. Together with mainland Portugal and the Azores it was under Spanish rule from 1580 to 1640. Between 1807 and 1814 it was occupied by Britain. The influx of tourists (at first mainly British) began in the middle of the 19th c. and has grown steadily since then.

The Madeira Separatist movement, FLAMA (Frente de Libertação da Madeira), was particularly active in the 1970s in pursuing freedom for Madeira from Portugal, but since the loss of Communist influence on the Lisbon Government the radical anti-communist independence movement has declined in importance.

Only about a third of the island's area can be cultivated. Soon after Madeira's rediscovery in the 16th c. deforestation by burning was begun, leading to the almost total destruction of the natural forest. Thereafter centuries of effort went into building up thousands of terraces (*poios*) on the hillsides which now constitute the major part of the cultivable land and give the island its characteristic appearance from the sea.

Economy

Since 1452 sugar-cane, grown on the north coast and, to an even greater extent, along the south coast, has been one of Madeira's most important products. Other crops include bananas, sweet potatoes, grain and early vegetables of all kinds. Much fruit is also grown, including, in addition to melons and grapefruit, such less usual species as the sugar apple or sweet-sop (anona), passion fruit (maracuja) and loquat. Wine production was introduced to Madeira soon after the discovery of the island and developed on a flourishing scale from the 17th c. onwards, only to suffer subsequent setbacks as a result of a grape disease (*oïdium tuckeri*, from 1852) and phylloxera (1878–88) and also from competition from the port

*Funchal (Madeira), the main tourist centre of the island*

produced on the mainland. The main wine-producing area lies west of Funchal, around Câmara de Lobos, Estreito and Campanário.

The intensive use of even the smallest cultivable area is only possible because of the irrigation system that has been in place for centuries whereby countless canals (*levadas*) carry the water from the north of the island, where rain is plentiful, to the south which is drier but where the farming is more intense.

Further contributions to the economy are made by cattle-farming, and the dairy produce associated with it, and, along the coasts, fishing for tuna, mackerel, etc.

Needlework has been an additional source of income since the mid 19th c. when the craft was introduced by an Englishwoman named Miss Phelps. Nowadays Madeira's internationally famous embroidery employs some 30,000 women, most of them working at home.

Tourism

Tourism nowadays is another more substantial factor in the economy. The first prosperous English visitors came to Madeira in the mid 19th c., and they still come in large numbers today, but the island is also a popular winter destination for Scandinavians and Germans. Madeira has around 12,000 hotel bedspaces altogether, many of them in the deluxe category. About 300,000 holidaymakers overnight here in a year, plus a further 60,000 or so cruise passengers.

The attraction for most visitors to Madeira is the pleasant climate and the luxuriant vegetation, but many also come for the unique opportunities for walking that exist on the island because of the narrow paths installed for the repair of the levadas. These paths now function as a network of walks, many of them easy to use and lined with flowers, others only a foot's width and difficult for even the most experienced walker.

## Funchal

Funchal (from *funcho*, i.e. fennel), capital of the archipelago and the see of a bishop, is picturesquely situated amid rich subtopical vegetation on the south coast of Madeira. It has a population of about 100,000 and as the only port of any size on the island, though often exposed to heavy surf, it is an important port of call for cruise ships. The town's steep streets, like most streets in the hilly parts of the island, are paved with smooth round basalt cobbles which make stout footwear very desirable. The *carros de cesta*, which now serve more as a tourist attraction than a means of transport, are toboggans with a basketwork frame that depend for their motive power on the force of gravity and are controlled by ropes held by two men running alongside. The ox-drawn *carros de bois*, the other sleds that used to transport goods and people around Funchal, have become museum pieces.

Situation and Importance

There is plenty to do of an evening in the island capital, with theatres, cinemas, casino and nightclubs, and folk-dancing displays almost every night in one or other of the large hotels. A traditional firework display greets the New Year. The most popular souvenirs are wickerwork, embroidery and, of course, Madeira wine.

Funchal is ranged amphitheatre-like on hillslopes climbing up to 1200m/3936ft, with some of its outskirts as high as 550m/1804ft above sea

★★Townscape

239

1 Quinta Vigia
  (Quinta Angustias)
2 Theatre

3 Palácio de São Lourenço
4 Antiga Alfândega
  (Old Customs House)

5 Vicentes Photographic
  Museum
6 Museum of Sacred Art

7 Convent church of Santa
  Clara
8 Quinta das Cruzes

level, making it a spectacular sight, particularly seen from the sea. Hotels
have come increasingly to dominate the townscape; almost all Madeira's
12,000 hotel beds are in Funchal, and not all of these establishments share
the venerable appearance of Reid's Hotel which dates from 1891. However,
around nearly every hotel, and private villa as well, there are superb parks
and gardens – Funchal has trees and flowers wherever you look.

## Sights in Funchal

West town centre

Near the seafront promenade, the Avenida das Comunidades Madeirenses, is the Palácio de São Lourenço (16th c.; much altered in later
periods), the first fort built on Madeira and now the Governor's Palace (not
open to the public). In front of the Governor's Palace, reaching out into the
sea, is the Cais (landing stage) and alongside it the new marina.

Over from the Governor's Palace, to the north-west, is the start of the
Jardim de São Francisco, a park luxuriantly planted with palms and other
tropical species. On the south side of the park is the theatre, the teatro, built
at the turn of the century.

Just east of the park, and worth a visit, is Vicente's photography
museum, containing the original photographer's studio founded in 1865,
and hence Portugal's first, by Vicente Gomes da Silva, where many historical pictures of Madeira are also on display.

Back on the Avenida do Dr Manuel de Arriaga, this runs westward into
the Praça do Infante, and above this square, to the south-west, is the little
chapel of Santa Catarina (15th c.), one of the oldest churches on the island,
with beyond it the Parque de Santa Catarina, on the site of an old cemetery,
the Cemitério das Augustas. The pink building on the west side of the park
is the Quinta Vigia, also known as Quinta das Angústias, where Madeira's
government is based. The original Quinta Vigia, once home to the Austrian
Empress Elisabeth (Sissi), had to give way to the Casino Hotel. Next to it is
the round casino building, with a fine view of the town from its terrace.

From the west end of the Avenida das Comunidades Madeirenses the
Rua da Pontinha continues south-west along the seafront, passing below

the Parque de Santa Catarina to the old Molhe da Pontinha, a breakwater begun in the 18th c. and several times extended, below the Fort of Nossa Senhora da Conceição. From the end of the breakwater there is a fine general view of the town.

The harbour promenade east of the new marina has been given a recent facelift, and the floating cafés include the "Beatles Boat" which actually belonged to the Beatles at one time.
    The old Customs House, the Antiga Alfândega, is on the other side of the Avenida das Comunidades Madeirenses. Little is left of the 16th c. original, and there was considerable rebuilding in the 18th c.
    Just north of the Customs House a relatively new pedestrian precinct leads to the cathedral, the Sé, which is Manueline and was built between 1485 and 1514 – the first Portuguese cathedral overseas. The interior has an interesting ceiling of juniper-wood with ivory inlay.
    To the east of the cathedral is the market, the Mercado, with fine tiling decorating the main entrance. It is at its busiest on Fridays and Saturdays when farmers bring in their produce from the surrounding villages. Beyond the Campo Dom Carlos I, the former drill ground, to the east of the beach is the Forte de São Tiago, built in 1614 and named after St James the Less, patron saint of Funchal. Close by is the church of Nossa Senhora do Socorro (or Santa Maria Maior), where a great procession is held on May 1st every year commemorating the plague of 1538.

East town centre

The Câmara Municipal (town hall), begun in 1758, is on the east side of the Praça do Municipio, which is flanked on the north-west by the 17th c. collegiate church of São João Evangelista. On the south side of the square (entrance at 21 Rue do Bispo) is the former Bishop's Palace containing a Museum of Sacred Art, with an important collection of Flemish paintings (expected to close soon for renovations).
    A stroll westward from the Praça do Municipio passes through the Rua C. Pestana and then on up to the church of São Pedro, its interior clad entirely with tiles, and the Municipal Museum of Natural History opposite, which has its own library and small aquarium. The steep Calçada de Santa Clara leads up to the former convent church of the same name, containing the tomb of the navigator João Gonçalves Zarco, who rediscovered Madeira in 1419. North-west of the church is the Quinta das Cruzes, set in beautiful gardens and said to have been where the Zarcos lived. Although some parts of the house do actually date back to when Madeira was first settled it is unlikely that Zarco did live here, remote as it would have been at that time. Since 1953 the property has served as a museum; the park contains carvings in stone ranging from the 15th to the 19th c. and the house is used for exhibitions. Continuing north-west up the Calçada do Pico and turning left along Rua do Castelo we come to the Forte de São João do Pico (1632), famed for its view.

North town centre

About 4km/2½ miles north-east of Funchal centre, on the old estate of Quinta do Bom Sucesso, is the very fine Botanic Garden (Jardim Botânico), with a rich and varied collection of plants and flowers. From the terraces there are delightful views (open: daily 9am–6pm).

★★Botanic Garden

## Excursions on Madeira

Madeira's roads are good, albeit often narrow and winding. Some byroads are paved rather than asphalted, making it advisable to keep average speeds down to about 20 m.p.h.

## To Faial via Monte (about 35km/22 miles)

From Funchal a good road winds its way up between handsome villas and beautiful gardens to the little town of Monte (alt. 550m/1804ft; pop. 8000),

★Monte

Archipélago da Madeira

20km

Lat. 33° N

O c e a n o

Ilha do
Porto Santo

507 m
Porto
Santo

33°

Santa Maria
Madalena ○ Porto Moniz
Ribeira ○
da Janela ○ Seixal
Ponta
do Pargo ▲ 1165 m
Prazeres
Calheta

Ponta
Delgada ○ São Jorge
Santana
São Vicente Faial
Paúl da Serra 1861 m Porto
Curral 1412 m da Cruz
1419 m da Freiras ○ ○ ○ Portela
Serra de 1115 m Poiso
Água ▲ Terreiro Santo ○ Caniçal
da Luta ○ da Serra ○ Machico
Ponta Monte ○ ○ Santa Cruz
do Sol Ribeira ○ Camacha
Brava Câmara ○ Caniço
de Lobos **Funchal**

Ilha da
Madeira

A t l â n t i c o

Ilhéu Chão

Deserta
Grande

Ilhas
Desertas
Ilhéu
do Bugio

© Baedeker

Long. 17° W

8km/5 miles north. Set amid magnificent plane and oak-forests, this was once a popular health resort.

On a spur of hill near the old cableway station is the pilgrimage church of Nossa Senhora do Monte (founded 1470, completely rebuilt in the 18th c.), with the tomb of Karl of Habsburg, the last Austrian Emperor, who died in the nearby Quinta do Monte in 1922. From the terrace in front of the church (68 steps) there is a superb view of Funchal and the sea, extending south-west as far as Cabo Girão. At the foot of the flight of steps is the Neo-Baroque chapel of Nossa Senhora da Conceição (1906).

From here it is possible either to return direct to Funchal – perhaps in one of the local wickerwork toboggans – or to walk down by a longer route (3 hours) on beautiful footpaths.

**Terreiro da Luta**

An attractive alternative is to continue 3km/2 miles north (either by road or on footpaths) to Terreiro da Luta (876m/2874ft), with a statue of Nossa Senhora da Paz (Our Lady of Peace, 1918, commemorating the end of the First World War) and even more extensive views than from the church at Monte.

**Pico Poiso**

From Terreira da Luta the road continues up through the hills and reaches in another 6km/4 miles the pass on Pico Poiso (1412m/4633ft).

From here a good road (7km/4¼ miles) goes off left to viewpoints on the Pico de Juncal (1800m/5941ft) and Pico do Arieiro (1810m/5940ft), the second highest summit on the island. From both of these viewpoints there are magnificent panoramas of Madeira's central mountain range.

*The "Eagle Rock", near Faial* ▶

Faial        From the Poiso pass it is another 20km/12½ miles through wild mountain scenery to the little town of Faial.

## Funchal to Curral das Freiras (14km/9 miles)

Pico dos Barcelos    The road runs north-west from Funchal, at first through hilly country, well wooded and bright with flowers. After 6km/4 miles it reaches Pico dos Barcelos (355m/1165ft). From the viewpoint terrace, with its profusion of flowers, there is a magnificent prospect of the south coast of Madeira.

Pico Serrado    The road continues uphill, with many bends, through a forest of eucalyptus trees and passing a number of superb viewpoints, to Eira do Serrado (1026m/3366ft), the "Serrado saddle" on the north-east edge of the Pico Serrado. From the saddle itself, and particularly from the nearby summit of the Pico Serrado (literally, sawn-off peak, 1115m/3658ft), there is perhaps the very best view of Madeira's central mountain range, extending from the Pico Ruivo (1861m/6106ft) and Pico Arieiro (1810m/5939ft) in the east to the Pico Grande (1607m/5273ft) and Pico do Jorge (1692m/5515ft) in the west.

★Curral das Freiras    From the saddle it is possible either to drive down on the modern road or to walk down the old bridle-path, endlessly twisting and turning, into the Curral das Freiras (nuns' valley) or Gran Curral, the crater of an extinct volcano, enclosed within high rock walls.

Far below, above the rock-strewn bed of the Ribeira dos Socorridos, can be seen the village of Curral das Freiras (690m/2265ft), an oasis in a waste of stone. The village was founded in the middle of the 16th c. by nuns from the convent of Santa Clara in Funchal who sought safety from pirate raids in the seclusion of the mountains and in later centuries pastured their cattle here. From Curral das Freiras a very attractive footpath descends through the valley of the Ribeira dos Socorridos to the north coast of the island.

## Funchal to São Vicente via Câmara de Lobos (55km/34 miles)

Pico da Ponta da Cruz    The road runs west from Funchal on the Estrada Monumental (magnificent views), at some distance from the sea, and then circles the south side of the Pico da Ponta da Cruz (263m/863ft; view), an old volcanic crater near the headland of the same name.

After 6km/4 miles a road forks right via São Martinho (alt. 250m/820ft) to Pico dos Barcelos.

Câmara de Lobos/★Cabo Girão    3km/2 miles further on is the little fishing port of Câmara de Lobos (wolves' gorge), picturesquely situated under the east side of Cabo Girão (589m/1933ft), a rugged headland falling almost vertically down to the sea and said to be the highest cliff of its kind in Europe. The village has long been a favourite with painters, among them Sir Winston Churchill. The village owes its name to the wolf-fish which were once found here in large numbers. The grapes grown on the terraces around the village provide some of the finest wine on the island.

Beyond Câmara de Lobos the road climbs away from the coast, with numerous turns, to make its way around the north side of Cabo Girão.

Estreito de Câmara de Lobos    Next comes Estreito de Câmara de Lobos (alt. 500m/1640ft), a village renowned for its wine.

From here a minor road runs 4km/2½ miles north to the Jardim da Serra (750m/2460ft), from which there are beautiful views. About 4km/2½ miles beyond Estreito de Câmara de Lobos a road forks left to the viewpoint over Cabo Girão.

Campanário    Campanário (alt. 300m/985ft) is a village perched attractively on the hill-side, with a 17th c. church.

Ribeira Brava    It is a further 6km/4 miles from Campanário to Ribeira Brava (pop. 7500), a little fishing town beautifully situated at the mouth of the stream of the

*A church in Monte*

*Câmara de Lobos*

same name, which is beginning to be modernised. In the main square, which is paved with pebble mosaic, is a charming 16th c. church. Standing above the stream is a small 17th c. fort. The picturesque Festas de São Pedro, with a procession and various folk events, take place here at the end of June every year.

The São Vicente road running north from Ribeira Brava climbs inland, mostly on the west side of the river, through magnificent scenery.

12km/7½ miles further on the road passes the Pousada dos Vinháticos (alt. 660m/2165ft), a good climbing base (Pico Grande, Pico do Jorge, Pico Ruivo, etc.) in a beautiful setting.

Pousada dos Vinháticos

2km/1¼ miles beyond this the road reaches the pass, the Boca da Encumeada (1007m/3304ft), with superb views of the Serra de Água (1405m/4610ft) to the left and the Pico Grande to the right.

Boca da Encumeada

From the pass a path runs west to the Paúl da Serra plateau and the Rabaçal mountain hut.

Once through the pass, the road descends via Rosário to the coast and São Vicente (pop. 5000). This is a straggling settlement in wild mountain scenery on the north coast of the island. It was partly buried by a landslide in 1928. São Vicente is a good base for climbing the Pico dos Tanquinhos (1524m/5000ft) and the Pico Ruivo do Paúl (1642m/5387ft), both offering magnificent views of mountain scenery, as well as opportunities for exploring the beautiful Paúl da Serra area.

São Vicente

## From Ribeira Brava to São Vicente via Calheta (92km/57 miles)

Ponta do Sol (pop. 6000) is on the coast road north-west out of Ribeira Brava. It is a picturesque little place built on both sides of the river of the

Ponta do Sol

245

*Ponta do Sol, on the south coast of Madeira*

same name. The church of Nossa Senhora da Luz (15th c.) has a painted wooden ceiling and some fine examples of silversmith's work.

About 2km/1¼ miles north-east of Ponta do Sol, surrounded by banana plantations, is the Capela do Santo Espírito, rebuilt in the 18th c. but founded in the 16th by João Esmeraldo, one of Columbus's companions, who owned big sugar-cane plantations in this area.

**Paúl da Serra**

About 5km/3 miles beyond Ponta do Sol a road forks right to the plateau 12km/7½ miles north of Paúl da Serra (1419m/4656ft). Often shrouded in mist, this is sheep country, and a good starting point for treks in the mountains.

**Nossa Senhora de Loreto**

5km/3 miles further on is the chapel of Nossa Senhora de Loreto, in Mozarabic and Manueline style.

**Calheta**

Calheta (pop. 4000) is a little port below the coast road set amid banana plantations and vineyards. The choir of the parish church (1639) has a carved wooden ceiling in Mudéjar style.

From Calheta a minor road runs 10km/6 miles north to the Rabaçal hut (1143m/3750ft). From the "Balcão" (balcony), a short distance north-east, there are superb views of the Risco Falls and the green gorge known as Vinte e Cinco Fontes (twenty-five springs).

**Estreito da Calheta**

Beyond the Calheta turning the coast road continues to climb, with many bends, to Estreito da Calheta, off to the left (339m/1112ft). The 16th c. Capela dos Reis Magos (chapel of the Magi) has fine painted woodwork, a carved wooden ceiling and a triptych depicting the Three Kings.

From here a side road runs down to Jardim do Mar, in a beautiful setting.

**Prazeres**

Prazeres (621m/2038ft), further along the main road, is finely situated on a wooded plateau, and also has magnificent views.

6km/4 miles farther on a road forks left to the village of Fajã da Ovelha, which lies in a forest setting at the foot of a massive crag, and to the little fishing settlement of Paúl do Mar (canning factory).

Ponta do Pargo (473m/1552ft), near the western tip of the island (lighthouse), is a little country town in an area that has preserved many old traditions and customs. The beautiful old local costumes are still worn on highdays and holidays.
Ponta do Pargo

From the village a footpath leads down to the Praia do Pesqueiro (fisherman's beach), enclosed by cliffs.

Santa Maria Madalena (500m/1640ft; pop. 800), with an unusual church, is reached via Achadas da Cruz (673m/2208ft).
Santa Maria Madalena

The road now drops down to the coast, with lots of hairpin bends, to Porto Moniz (pop. 2500), a little fishing town at the north-west corner of the island. Protected by a rocky headland and the offshore islet of Ilhéu More with its fishermen's houses, this is the most sheltered harbour and the principal port on the north coast of Madeira. There are many natural swimming pools on the rugged coast about 2km/1¼ miles south-east of the village.
Porto Moniz

Ribeira da Janela lies at the mouth of the river of the same name. Just off the rivermouth are three rock-stacks, one of which, the Ilhéu da Ribeira da Janela, has the natural rock window (janela = window) from which the village gets its name.
Ribeira da Janela

The coast road next passes Seixal (pop. 900) which is beautifully situated amid vineyards on the slopes of a projecting spur of hill.
Seixal

Beyond Seixal begins the most impressive section of the road along the north coast and one of the finest stretches of scenery in the whole of Madeira.

The magnificently engineered road, hewn out of the almost vertical cliffs, with numerous tunnels and projecting sections, runs high above the thundering sea and under the shadow of mighty rockfaces, as if suspended between sea and sky.

About 2km/1¼ miles beyond Seixal is a viewpoint with a famous view of the gorge at the mouth of the Ribeira do Inferno. The road then continues through tunnels and under waterfalls to São Vicente.
Ribeira do Inferno

## From São Vicente to Funchal via Machico (90km/56 miles)

The coast road continues east from São Vicente along the steep rockface. The next place is Ponta Delgada (pop. 2000), delightfully perched on a promontory amid orange-groves and sugar-cane plantations, with a simple little white church and a sea-water swimming pool.
Ponta Delgada

Ponta Delgada has a "Romaria" festival on the first Sunday in September.

The road now leaves the coast and describes a wide bend inland before returning to the coast. After 2km/1¼ mile it reaches Boaventura (pop. 3000), set in fruit orchards and willow plantations (raw material for the local wickerwork), and popular with tourists as a starting point for walks, especially for the Curral das Freiras.
Boaventura

Beyond Arco de São Jorge is a viewpoint with a famous prospect of the north coast.
Arco de São Jorge

São Jorge (pop. 3000) has a 17th c. Baroque church (fine altarpieces). From the nearby Ponta de São Jorge there are extensive views of the north coast, extending to Porto Moniz in the west and Porto da Cruz in the east.
São Jorge

## Madeira/Archipélago da Madeira

| | |
|---|---|
| ★Santana | Santana (420m/1380ft; pop. 4500) is chief town of the Comarca de Santana, the most fertile district on Madeira, and one of the most picturesque places on the island, with its thatched houses set amid a profusion of flowers. |

From Santana it is a pleasant excursion to the mountain hut of Casa das Queimadas (883m/2896ft), continuing south on foot to the Parque das Queimadas on the slopes of the Pico Ruivo (1861m/6102ft), which can be climbed from here. From the summit, on clear days (which are rare), there is a magnificent panoramic view of the mountains of Madeira.

| | |
|---|---|
| Faial | 7km/4½ miles beyond Santana, the road, now running close to the sea again and affording constantly changing views, reaches Faial (150m/490ft; pop. 1500), a modest little village surrounded by terraced vineyards, sugar-cane plantations and vegetable patches. There is a good view from the church terrace. |
| Penha de Aguia | Towering over the landscape is the mighty crag of the "Eagle Rock", the Penha de Aguia. |
| Porto da Cruz | The little port of Porto da Cruz (pop. 4000) at the foot of massive rockfaces, has a little volcanic beach. |
| Portela Pass | Beyond Porto da Cruz the road turns away from the sea southward and climbs up into the mountains, reaching 662m/2172ft at the Portela pass, with a view of Porto da Cruz and Machico Bay. |
| Shortcut to Funchal via Santo da Serra | It is 30km/19 miles from the pass on the EN 102 straight back to Funchal, passing through beautiful forest scenery, via the health resort of Santo (António) da Serra (671m/2200ft; pop. 2000; golf-course), on a plateau of grazing land and with the Quinta Jardim da Serra, which is worth seeing, and Camacha (715m/2345ft; pop. 6500), a little town notable for its folklore and its thriving wickerwork industry. |
| Quinta do Palheiro Ferreiro | About 8km/5 miles before Funchal, to the left of the road, is the Quinta do Palheiro Ferreiro, a beautiful private park to which the public are admitted and which harmoniously combines French and English gardening skills. |
| Machico | Beyond the Portela pass the main road descends the Machico valley to the coast and Machico itself (pop. 13,000), an important fishing port (boatyard) at the mouth of the Rio Machico, with a government school for Madeira embroidery. This was the landing place of the first settlers. |

The town is said to be named after an Englishman called Machin who was shipwrecked here about 1344 while eloping with his bride and who has been claimed as the discoverer of Madeira. The Capela dos Milagres (1420; rebuilt in the 19th c.) is said to have been erected over the graves of the two lovers. The late 15th c. parish church (originally Manueline but later much altered) has a painted wooden ceiling. In the Capela de São Roque there are fine azulejo paintings. Above the northern entrance to the bay stands a small 17th c. fort. The feast of the Senhor dos Milagres is celebrated every year on the evenings of October 8th and 9th by the lighting of bonfires on the surrounding hills.

| | |
|---|---|
| Detour to the peninsula of Ponta de São Lourenço | From Machico the EN 101-3 runs east via the little whaling station of Caniçal (8km/5 miles) to the bathing beach of Prainha, on the south side of the narrow peninsula of Ponta de São Lourenço, the most easterly tip of Madeira, and a place where many fossils have been found. |
| Miradouro Francisco Álvares Nóbrega | The coast road continues south-east from Machico, running close to the sea. About 1km/¾ mile beyond Machico a road off to the right leads to the Miradouro Francisco Álvares Nóbrega (another 1km/¾ mile), with a beautiful view of Machico Bay and the São Lourenço peninsula. |

Beyond the turning the main road continues along the coast, passing the Água de Pena tourist village and the Santa Catarina airport.

Below the coast road is Santa Cruz, with a 16th c. church and town hall. Around the village are extensive banana and sugar-cane plantations and terraced vineyards, and the locals also catch ornamental fish.

Santa Cruz

Caniço, at the mouth of the river of the same name, has an 18th c. parish church and the Manueline chapel of the Madre de Deus (16th c.). There is a pleasant walk from here to Cabo Garajau.

Caniço

There is a last, lovely view from the Miradouro do Pináculo before the final 5km/2½ miles to Funchal.

Miradouro do Pináculo

## Other islands in the Madeira archipelago

### Porto Santo

Some 23 nautical miles north-east of Madeira (by boat, several times weekly, 3 hours; by air, several times daily, 20 minutes) is the table-shaped island of Porto Santo (pop. 3000; highest point Pico do Facho, 517m/ 1696ft), surrounded by five small rocky islets. Porto Santo, 12km/7½ miles long by 6km/4 miles wide, covering 42 sq.km/16 sq.miles, is very different in character from the main island of Madeira. Its sandy uplands and aridity make farming very difficult for its inhabitants. Tourists seem little interested in the barren island, and there are only a few holiday bungalows and flats.

Location and General

In the little port of Porto Santo, or Vila Baleira, on the south-east coast, the chief settlement on the island, is the house where Columbus, whose father-in-law was the first governor, lived in about 1479.

Sights

Porto Santo has the only long beach of fine sand in the whole of the Madeira archipelago. It extends right along the south coast, but the tourist facilities are still limited.

★Beach

*Porto Santo and its seemingly endless sands*

249

# Ilhas Desertas

Location and
General

About 11 miles south-east of Madeira are the Ilhas Desertas, the "deserted" islands, three waterless and uninhabited rocky islets: Deserta Grande (491m/1611ft), Ilhéu do Bugio (411m/1348ft) and the flat Ilhéu Chão (104m/341ft). Landing is possible only when the sea is calm. The islands have many features of geological interest. They are also the home of the great wolf spider (*geolycosa ingens*), one of Europe's biggest spiders; seals live in the caves of Deserta Grande.

## Mafra                                                                    A6

Historical province: Estremadura. District: Lisbon
Altitude: 237m/778ft. Population: 7000

Situation and
Importance

The modest little town of Mafra, about 50km/30 miles north-west of Lisbon, is widely famed for its enormous monastery-palace, the largest complex of the kind in the Iberian peninsula.

It is where King João V founded the "Mafra school", a major school for instruction in the art of sculpture by teachers that included such leading artists as José Almeida and Joaquim Machado de Castro.

Townscape

Mafra is an unassuming little town, its centre dominated by the enormous monastery-palace. The carefully restored 13th/14th c. Gothic church of Santo André, containing the tombs of Dom Diogo de Sousa and his wife, is also worth a visit.

## ★★Palácio Nacional de Mafra (Plan page 252)

History

The Palácio Nacional de Mafra was founded in 1717 by João V and his queen, Maria Ana of Austria, in fulfilment of a vow made in 1711 and in thanksgiving for the birth of an heir (later José I). It was built by a force of as many as 50,000 workmen under the direction of the Italian-trained German architect Johann Friedrich Ludwig and his son Johann Peter Ludwig and consecrated in 1730, although it was 1750 before the whole complex was finally complete.

The monastery buildings were originally occupied by Franciscans but in the late 18th c. were transferred to the Augustinians. When the monastery was closed following the dissolution of all religious orders in 1834 parts of it were allocated to the army.

The former royal apartments were hardly ever occupied. King João V and his Queen spent only a few days here, and it wasn't until the early 19th c. that the palace enjoyed its brief heyday when João VI resided here in 1806–07. With the approach of French troops the royal family made a hurried departure from the palace, en route for Lisbon and subsequently Brazil, taking most of the valuable furnishings and works of art with them. Nor did later Portuguese rulers spend much time in Mafra, usually only stopping here in order to hunt nearby.

Layout

The huge building consists of the monastery church, the monastery accommodation containing the cells and the communal rooms used by the monks, and a further section to serve the royal family as their accommodation. Built on an almost square plan and designed with the strictest regard for symmetry, the building as a whole is 251m/825ft long by 221m/725ft wide and covers a total area of 40,000 sq.m/48,000 sq.yd. It has 900 rooms, 2500 windows and 5200 doors. It bears comparison with the Escorial, Philip II's monastery-palace near Madrid, but was intended by its founder to surpass even the Escorial in size and splendour. It is the supreme exemplification in Portugal of cool Baroque magnificence, lavish extravagance and absolute royal power. The church is open to the public, as are the former

*Mafra: the gigantic Palace-Monastery*

royal apartments (guided tours), but parts of the monastery cannot be visited since they are occupied by a military academy, etc.

The basilica is in the middle of the main front, which is precisely articulated and almost without decoration. It is flanked by twin towers 68m/223ft high. The carillon of 114 bells was made by an Antwerp bell-founder named Lavache. In the vestibule of the church are 14 large marble statues of saints by the Italian sculptor Alessandro Giusti. The aisleless interior is faced with white marble and has a coffered barrel-vaulted ceiling. Above the crossing is a mighty dome 70m/230ft high.

Basilica

Guided tours of the palace also take in the pharmacy, the infirmary, with the original 18th c. fittings, the kitchen, faced with blue azulejos, the oval chapterhouse, some of the communal rooms and the monks' cells.

Other monastery buildings

The former royal apartments are in the east section of the palace, with those of the King in the south and the Queen in the north.
Although much of the valuable furnishings was removed in the early 19th c. what remains is still considerable. All the rooms are furnished with 18th and 19th c. furniture and objets d'art. The throne-room is most impressive, with its early 19th c. murals.

Royal apartments

Of particular interest is the Library, 88m/290ft long, with 30,000 volumes, including many incunabula and manuscripts, first editions of Camões' "Lusiads", and the plays of Gil Vicente, a trilingual Bible of 1514 and the earliest edition of Homer in Greek.

Library

In the left-hand corner pavilion on the main front is the Museum of Comparative Sculpture (Museu de Escultura Comparada), with casts of famous works by Portuguese, Italian and French sculptors of the 12th to 16th c.

Museu de Escultura Comparada

To the rear of the palace extends the Tapada de Mafra, the royal deer-park enclosed by a wall 20km/12½ miles long, in which the royal family still hunted at the beginning of the 20th c.

Tapada de Mafra

251

## Palácio Nacional de Mafra

1 Entrance
2 Tower
3 Vestibule (statues of saints)
4 Tower
5 Dome
6 Cloister
7 Cloister
8 Chapterhouse
9 Sacristy
10 Campo Santo Chapel
11 Refectory
12 Cloister garth (gardens)
13 Library (upper floor)
14 Museum of Sculpture

---

## Marvão                                                    C5

Historical province: Alto Alentejo. District: Portalegre
Altitude: 862m/2828ft. Population: 1000

Situation and Importance

The little market town of Marvão, the Roman Herminio Minor, lies near the Spanish frontier on a steep-sided hill in the Serra de São Mamede. Its great attractions are its unspoiled medieval atmosphere and its castle, with a commanding view from above the town.

This strategically situated little town was strongly fortified by King Dinis in the 13th c. In 1833, during the Miguelist wars, it played an important part as stronghold of the Liberals.

★★Townscape

The town is still completely surrounded by its medieval walls. The steep and narrow streets are paved with stone slabs, spanned by flying buttresses and lined with flower-decked houses, many of them with fine 17th c. wrought-iron window grille, including one that has been turned into a pousada. It is advisable to leave cars outside the walls and to walk up through the maze of alleyways to the castle.

## Sights

Castelo

Above the town stands the castle (Castelo), built in the 13th c. and enlarged in the 15th and 17th c.

From the keep, enclosed within several rings of walls, there are panoramic views, extending northward to Castelo Branco and the Serra da Estrela, southward and westward to the Serra de São Mamede and eastward to Spain.

Convento de Nossa Senhora da Estrela

Outside the town is the former Convento de Nossa Senhora da Estrela (originally 15th c.), now a hospital. The church has a fine Gothic doorway.

*Marvão is dominated by its castle*

## Surroundings of Marvão

A visit to Marvão can easily be combined with one to the equally interesting Castelo de Vide (see entry), 12km/7½ miles north-west, and Portalegre (see entry), 12km/7½ miles south-west.

*Castelo de Vide, Portalegre*

## Matosinhos

B3

Historical province: Douro Litoral. District: Porto
Altitude: sea level. Population: 25,000

Just 9km/5½ miles north of Oporto, the industrial town and port of Matosinhos at the mouth of the little Rio Leça, has large fish-canning factories. Because of its excellent beach it is also a popular resort with the Portuguese, who are not put off by an industrial background.

*Situation and Importance*

At the mouth of the river is the modern port of Leixões, which serves as Oporto's outer harbour. The harbour, which dates from 1884 and has since been much extended to make this one of the biggest commercial ports on the Iberian peninsula, is protected by two breakwaters reaching out pincer-like into the sea, 1597m/1750yd and 1145m/1250yd long respectively.

*Porto de Leixões*

The church of Bom Jesús de Bouças, originally built in the 16th c. and enlarged in the 18th c., has several features of art-historical interest. The interior has carved and gilded decoration in the choir, a fine coffered ceiling and a very ancient and much revered crucifix (Whitsun pilgrimages).
   There is a fine municipal park, the Quinta da Conceição, on the site of a convent now represented only by the 18th c. chapel of São Francisco and the 15th c. cloister.

*Sights*

## Surroundings of Matosinhos

| | |
|---|---|
| Leça da Palmeira | Opposite Matosinhos on the right bank of the Leça (bascule bridge) is the little fishing town of Leça da Palmeira, nowadays dominated by oil refineries.<br><br>Anyone not deterred by these can go swimming from Boa Nova beach, about ¾ mile to the north, under a cliff on the top of which stands the pilgrimage chapel of São João. |
| Santa Cruz de Bispo | A drive from here up the Leça valley brings you to Santa Cruz de Bispo with two Roman bridges, the Ponte de Guifões and the Ponte do Carro. |

## Mértola                                                                    C7

| | |
|---|---|
| | Historical province: Baixo Alentejo. District: Beja<br>Altitude: 85m/280ft. Population: 7000 |
| Situation and Importance | Mértola is picturesquely set on the slopes above the left bank of the Guadana, joined here by its tributary the Oreias, about 70km/43 miles north-west of the coastal border town of Vila Real de Santo António.<br><br>In Roman times the site was occupied by the town of Mirtilis, mentioned by the Alexandrian geographer Ptolemy (2nd c. A.D.), which later had to give way to a Moorish stronghold. |
| ★Townscape | With its narrow and twisting alleys Mértola is still rather Moorish in appearance. From the main square its narrow streets, lined with little white houses, lead uphill to the parish church and then on up to the castle. |

## Sights in Mértola

| | |
|---|---|
| Igreja Matriz | The fortified Romanesque parish church, Igreja Matriz, with crenellated walls and a handsome Renaissance doorway, was converted in the 16th c. |

*Mértola: Igreja Matriz*

from an earlier mosque – an origin revealed by the square ground-plan, the arrangement of the clustered columns, the mihrab, or Islamic prayer niche, behind the high altar, and the horseshoe arch above the sacristy door.

It is a short distance from the parish church up to the old Moorish castle, the Castelo dos Mouros, which was considerably enlarged in the late 13th c. From the keep there is a magnificent view of the town and the River Guadiana, which is navigable below this point.

*Castelo dos Mouros*

Mértola's privately initiated archaeological museum is still taking shape. Most of the exhibits come from excavations close to the castle where in 1980 a dig started exposing Roman foundations and mosaic, and unearthing Islamic ceramics. The oldest pieces date from the 10th c. and are from Andalusia. It already appears that the museum will contain one of the most important collections of Islamic ceramics on the Iberian peninsula.

*Archaeological Museum*

# Minho

Historical province: Minho. Districts: Braga and Viana do Castelo
Area: 4928 sq.km/1902 sq.miles
Population: 966,000. Chief town: Braga

The ancient province of Minho in the extreme north-west of Portugal – formerly known, more accurately, as Entre Douro e Minho, the land between the Douro and Minho rivers – lies to the south of the river of the same name. It is bounded on the south by the province of Douro Litoral and on the east by Spain and the province of Trás-os-Montes; on the west it lies open to the Atlantic on the Costa Verde (see entry), an almost northern-seeming stretch of coast.
    Formerly part of Castile the Minho region has, ethnically and culturally, a unity with Galicia, an affinity which is reflected also in certain linguistic features which the two provinces have in common.

*Location and General*

The Minho region is occupied by an ancient mountain massif of granites, gneisses, argillaceous schists and quartzes which increases in height towards the east, reaching almost 2000m/6560ft in the Serra do Gerês, and is traversed from north-east to south-west by the three wide parallel valleys of the Minho, the Lima and the Cávado. These valleys allow moisture-bearing winds from the Atlantic to penetrate far inland, making this the rainiest part of the whole Iberian peninsula (1000–3000mm/40–120 in. a year). Numerous recent fault lines allow the water to sink deep underground, where it is heated and re-emerges in many places as thermal springs.
    The Minho landscape is more reminiscent of northern Europe than of the south. The easy availability of granite has resulted in a very individualistic form of architecture in stone, giving a grey appearance to the towns and villages.

*Topography*

The people of Minho, the Minhotes, are particularly attached to tradition and to the Catholic faith, and the many church festivals and romarias are celebrated enthusiastically with music and dancing.
    Its very fertile soil has meant that the Minho region has always been densely populated. However, the very limited area of the smallholdings which form the farms, and the consequently unviable working that this entails, has meant there has never been adequate subsistence for its population so that many of the Minhotes, particularly the ablebodied younger men, have had to find jobs as seasonal workers in South America (particularly Brazil) or, in recent years, as migrant workers in Germany and other European countries.

*Population*

Minho's economy is predominantly based on agriculture. The fertile, well-watered basins and valleys yield two harvests a year, wheat followed by

*Economy*

*"Espigueiros", typical storehouses of Minho*

maize, providing food for human consumption and feed for the flourishing livestock sector. Another major source of revenue is the production of wine. The vines, trained in the ancient Roman fashion on young trees (mainly eucalyptus) or on trellises, produce the much esteemed vinho verde (or vinho não murado), a wine that because of the early autumn has an early vintage, and is characterised by youthful freshness, a slightly sharp taste and a natural effervescence (see Practical Information, Wine). The uplands, deforested in ancient times, now provide pasturage for sheep.

In addition to agriculture the region has old-established small-scale industries: textiles (originally linen-weaving, now also cotton), the manufacture of cutting instruments and blades, leather-working, pottery and crafts such as embroidery and lace-making. There is no heavy industry. In recent years hydro-electric power stations have been established on the rivers in the mountains.

Espigueiros

Throughout the countryside can be seen what amounts to the symbol of the region, the little grainstores that the Portuguese call *espigueiros*. Their walls are made of tablets of stone with slits in them that are designed, with an aperture of only 5mm, to let the wind in but keep the birds and larger insects out. The espigueiros have stone supports to render them damp-proof by raising them off the ground, and the flat stone discs at the top of these supports serve to stop mice getting in, since they can't negotiate the smooth undersurface. Nowadays the grain they used to hold has largely been replaced by maize cobs.

# Miranda do Douro                                                      D3

Historical province: Trás-os-Montes. District: Bragança
Altitude: 690m/2264ft. Population: 6000

The old episcopal city of Miranda do Douro in the north-east of Portugal lies on a rocky hill above the deep valley of the Douro (Spanish Duero and dammed at this point), which here marks the frontier with Spain (no frontier crossing). The remoteness of the region, one of the most thinly populated parts of Portugal, has acted as a brake on its cultural and linguistic development, so that it has preserved not only many old customs and traditions but also a local dialect close to Vulgar Latin, the *lingua charra* or *mirandês*.

Situation and Importance

Traditional crafts such as weaving and pottery are still widely practised. Every year on the third Sunday in August (the feast of St Barbara) the dance of the *pauliteiros* (wooden staves) takes place, a folk dance for men that harks back to the Roman sword-dances.

Rather a sombre little town, around its marketplace Miranda do Douro has a number of handsome old burghers' houses with coats of arms and Manueline ornamentation.

Townscape

## Sights in Miranda do Douro

The 12th c. castle which once dominated the town was destroyed by an explosion in 1760, leaving only a watch-tower.

Castelo

On a projecting spur of rock above the Douro stands the Cathedral (Sé), a 16th c. building with a wide west front flanked by towers. The spacious interior gets its effect from the massive piers. The high altar depicts scenes from the life of the Virgin and the Crucifixion. A quaint feature is the "Infant Jesus in a Tophat", a naïve ex-voto of the mid 19th c.

Sé

From the terrace in front of the Cathedral there is an impressive view of the grey rocky valley of the Douro.

Near the Cathedral is the Baroque arcaded courtyard which is all that remains of the Archbishop's Palace, burned down in 1706.

Archbishop's Palace

## Surroundings of Miranda do Douro

About 3km/2 miles east of Miranda do Douro is the Barragem de Miranda do Douro, the first of a series of five dams on the Douro built and operated jointly by Spain and Portugal. Some 25km/15 miles downstream the Barragem do Picote is followed by the Barragem da Bemposta, the Barragem de Aldeiadávila and the Barragem de Saucelle.

Dams on the Douro

About 17km/11 miles north-west of the town, at the village of Caçarelhos, are large marble and alabaster quarries and beautiful stalactitic caves.

Caçarelhos

The village of Vimioso, 10km/6 miles farther west, has the ruins of a castle of King Dinis which was destroyed in the 18th c.

Vimioso

## Mirandela
C3

Historical province: Trás-os-Montes. District: Bragança
Altitude: 250m/820ft. Population: 6000

The attractive little town of Mirandela lies on the left bank of the Rio Tua about 70km/44 miles south-west of Bragança in one of the most isolated areas of the Portuguese mainland.

Situation

## Sights

On an eminence in the heart of the town stands the 18th c. Paço dos Távoras, with a granite Baroque façade, now the Town Hall.

Paço dos Távoras

Bridges — There was a crossing of the Rio Tua here in Roman times, and the position of the Roman bridge is now occupied by a medieval bridge of 18 arches, 232m/254yd long. Beside it is a modern bridge.

## Surroundings of Mirandela

★Murça — Murça, 33km/20 miles south-west of Mirandela, was granted a municipal charter by King Sancho II in 1224. It is famous for the granite figure of a wild boar (on the main street), the subject of many legends, and originally thought to be Iron Age but now considered more likely to be 7th c.

Other features of interest are the 17th c. church of the Misericórdia, the parish church (Igreja Matriz) with a Classical granite façade in the pretty market square, and a Manueline pelourinho (pillory column), the symbol of municipal authority.

Vila Flor — About 28km/17 miles south of Mirandela is the little country town of Vila Flor (alt. 565m/1855ft; pop. 2000), with a handsome 18th c. palace, a Gothic town hall, an azulejo-clad parish church and remains of the town walls.

## Monção                                                                         B2

Historical province: Minho. District: Viana do Castelo
Altitude: 98m/322ft. Population: 2500

Situation and Importance — The old fortified frontier town of Monção, situated on the left bank of the River Minho (Spanish Miño) opposite the Spanish town of Salvatierra de Miño, is now a spa, with hot springs used for the treatment of rheumatism, skin and bronchial ailments.

The local delicacies are salmon trout and *lampretes* (lampreys).

Townscape — The centrepoint of the town, still surrounded by its 17th c. walls, is the flower-bedecked Praça Deu-la-Deu. The square is named after the local hero, Deu-la-Deu Martins, who distinguished himself in 1368 in the battle against the Castilians and whose monument graces the square. Around the square and the adjoining Largo do Loreto there are many attractive balconied houses. The northern end of the Largo do Loreta has a broad view over the river landscape of the Rio Minho.

Above the town are the ruins of a medieval castle.

## Sights

Igreja Matriz — The original Romanesque parish church of Santa Maria dos Anjos (Holy Mary of the Angels), remodelled in the 16th c., has a fine Manueline main doorway. Inside is the tomb of Deu-la-Deu Martins among others, as well as rich talha dourada decoration, and azulejos in the choir. A Manueline side-chapel dating from 1521 is also worth seeing.

## Surroundings of Monção

Palácio de Brejoeira — About 3km/2 miles south of the little town, on the road from Braga, is the imposing early 19th c. Brejoeira Palace (not open to the public), set in beautiful gardens.

Peso de Melgaço — About 24km/15 miles east of Monção is the health resort of Peso de Melgaço (alt. 180m/590ft), with mineral springs used in treating digestive and metabolic ailments.

The neighbouring village of Melgaço has a 12th c. Romanesque parish church, and, above the village, a 12th c. castle.

Monção: view of the Minho . . .

. . . and Praça Deu-la-Deu

See entry

Valença do Minho

## Montemor-o-Velho

B4

Historical province: Beira Litoral. District: Coimbra
Altitude: 51m/167ft. Population: 3000

The little town of Montemor-o-Velho, about halfway between Figueira da Foz and Coimbra, on a hill above the right bank of the Mondego, was of importance during the Middle Ages as an outpost defending the approach to Coimbra against the Moors advancing from Estremadura. The local economy is mainly given over to agriculture, with rice the main crop.

Montemor-o-Velho is the birthplace of the navigator Cavaleiro Diogo de Azambuja (1432–1518), the writer and world traveller Fernão Mendes Pinto (c. 1510–83), and the poet Jorge de Montemor (1520–61).

Situation and Importance

## Sights

Above the town are the forbidding ruins of its massive castle (Castelo), at one time amongst Portugal's strategically most important fortresses. Nothing remains of the original castle, first mentioned in 716 when occupied by the Moors. The existing ruins date from the 11th and 12th c. and are enclosed within a double circuit of walls, oval in plan, with imposing towers and battlements. From the top of the towers, some of which can be climbed, there is a superb view over the surrounding countryside. Within the walls is the Manueline church of Santa Maria de Alcáçova (16th c.) by the famous architect Boytaca, with a beautiful wooden ceiling, azulejo decoration in 16th c. Moorish style and a double font.

★Castelo

259

Nossa Senhora
dos Anjos

In the romantic little town itself is the noteworthy Manueline church of
Nossa Senhora dos Anjos (Our Lady of the Angels), originally a monastic
church. The real treasure lies in the spacious interior which holds Renaissance sculpture of the Coimbra school, including the magnificent sarcophagus of Diogo de Azambuja, carved during his lifetime by Diogo
Pires-o-Moço.

## Surroundings of Montemor-o-Velho

Tentúgal

About 10km/6 miles north-east is the little town of Tentúgal, with the church
of Nossa Senhora do Mourão, belonging to the former Carmelite convent
(15th c.), the church of the Misericórdia (16th c.) and a number of handsome
patrician houses. Some 3km/2 miles farther north-east the church of the
Hieronymite convent of São Marcos (burned down in 1860) was a depen-
dency of the convent at Belém (see Lisbon); it was founded in 1452 by Dona
Brites de Meneses, later Afonso V's wife, and subsequently became the
burialplace of the Silva Meneses family. The decoration of the church, with
its clearly articulated structure, betrays the hand of the architect of the
convents of Belém and of Santa Cruz in Coimbra.

Coimbra

From Tentúgal it is a further 15km/9 miles to Coimbra (see entry), famous
for its university and rich in tradition.

Figueira da Foz

Figueira da Foz (see entry), the seaside resort 16km/10 miles west of
Montemor-o-Velho, is a popular destination in the summer months.

## Moura                        C6

Historical province: Baixo Alentejo. District: Beja
Altitude: 180m/1062ft. Population: 8500

Situation and
Importance

The little spa of Moura, some 60km/37 miles north-east of Beja on the left
bank of the Guadiana, has alkiline mineral springs in its park that are
particularly called upon in the treatment of rheumatism. Known by the
Romans as Nova Civitas Arruccitana, the town owes its present name
(Moura = Moorish girl), and its coat-of-arms – a dead girl below the castle-
walls – to a young Moorish maiden called Salúquia. She was the daughter
of the town's leading citizen and is supposed to have plunged from the
castle battlements after her betrothed and his followers had been
ambushed and slain by the Christians on the eve of the wedding. The
Christians had then donned the clothing of their ambushed enemies to trick
their way past the guards to capture the castle.

## Sights

Praça de Sacadura
Cabral

The Praça de Sacadura Cabral is the town's central square on which stands
the Church of John the Baptist, the Gothic-Manueline Igreja de São João
Baptista. In the right-hand side chapel are azulejo versions of the Cardinal
Virtues.
    The town hall on the opposite side of the square also contains the tourist
information centre plus a small regional museum with displays of archaeological finds.
    In front of it is the Três Bicas fountain (with three jets). The Arabic
inscription recalls Almotadide, Emir of Seville, who wrote much of his
poetry in Moura.
    Also on the square is the entrance to Moura's little spa park, full of
flowers and with an inviting café and a view from the terrace at the end of
the gardens.

Convento de
Nossa Senhora do
Carmo

The Convento de Nossa Senhora do Carmo in Moura is the oldest Carmelite convent in Portugal, founded about 1250. Its elegant cloister dates from
the 16th/17th c., and the convent church has an interesting choir fresco.

*Moura: Igreja de São João Baptista*

The old quarter of Mouraria, near the main square, betrays Moura's Moorish past. Many of its low white houses are embellished with azulejos and the characteristic chimneys, and one of them, on the Largo da Mouraria, has been reconstructed in the Eastern style, complete with courtyard.

Mouraria

Above the town centre are the ruins of the Castle, originally Moorish but rebuilt by King Dinis at the end of the 13th c. Within the walls stands the church of Nossa Senhora da Assunção with the Capela dos Rolins, the last resting place of the conquerors Álvaro and Pedro Rodrigues.

Castelo

## Surroundings of Moura

About 3km/2 miles south-east are the mineral springs of Pisões-Moura, the source of "Aguas de Castelo", a popular Portuguese mineral water.

Pisões-Moura

## Nazaré

A5

Historical province: Estremadura. District: Leiria
Altitude: 0–110m/0–360ft. Population: 10,000

The particularly picturesque little fishing town of Nazaré has drawn increasing numbers of visitors in recent years because of its good beaches and the still genuinely colourful life and activity of its fisherfolk. It is now one of the most popular seaside towns on this part of Portugal's Atlantic coast, or the Costa de Prata as it is known.

Situation and Importance

Nazaré is believed to have been founded by the Phoenicians. It is on what used to be a bay, but which is now silted up, sheltered on the north by Monte Sítio. The harbour has been reconstructed relatively recently, doing away with the need to push the brightly painted local boats, with their high pointed prows, into the water from the beach by hand, and then, on their return, using oxen to haul them up on shore again to be unloaded by the waiting women and the fishermen. Another fishing method was *arte xávega*, whereby nets were laid offshore then hauled in from the beach. Since this no longer pays its way, tourists have to content themselves with the traditional fish auctions that take place daily on the return of the fishermen.

**Costume**

For special occasions and for the folk-dance displays laid on by the tourist information centre the people of Nazaré still wear their characteristic traditional costumes. The fishermen have check shirts, trousers in a different check, and black stocking caps, used like a purse for money, etc. The women's costume is covered in lace and has wide bouffant skirts with up to seven petticoats.

**Townscape**

Nazaré has no historic buildings, and what makes a visit a lasting experience is solely the lively, colourful activity of its people and the singular sense of being in a little town imbued with tradition.

Although the building of the harbour has meant the fishing activity is more in the southern part of town, tourists still share the sizeable beach with fishermen drying their catch on wire racks.

It is quite crowded at the weekends when day-trippers flock here from Lisbon, Coimbra and Oporto.

**View**

In the Pederneira district in the lower part of the town the square in front of the 16th c. church of the Misericórdia has a fine view over the beach towards Monte Sítio.

## Sítio

**★View**

A much better view is to be had from the district of Sítio (110m/360ft) on the small promontory of Monte Sítio, reached by car, by funicular, or by walking up the steps of the Ladeira de Sítio.

The extensive view over Nazaré and the Atlantic coast may be somewhat marred by the activity of the many stallholders usually to be found there.

**Capela da Memória**

According to legend the Capela da Memória was founded by a local dignitary named Dom Fuas Roupinho who was out hunting here in 1182 when the stag he was chasing leapt off the cliff at this point. His horse was about to follow when the Virgin heard the Dom's fast and fervent prayer and, dazzling the beast with her appearance, halted the horse on the brink of the precipice. In thanksgiving for this miraculous aid Dom Fuas Roupinho forthwith had the Capela da Memória built at this point.

*Nazaré*

Near the chapel there is a pillar with an inscription which commemorates Vasco da Gama's visit here, after his voyage to India, to give thanks for his safe return.

Opposite the Capela da Memória is the 17th c. pilgrimage chapel of Nossa Senhora de Nazaré, containing an image of the Virgin which is revered as miraculous.
The annual pilgrimages here on August 15th and in the second week of September attract visitors from near and far.

Nossa Senhora de Nazaré

Some 500m/550yd west is the old Fort of São Miguel, now a lighthouse.

São Miguel

## Surroundings of Nazaré

About 12km/7½ miles south of Nazaré, on the north-east side of a narrow sheltered bay, rather like a lake and known as "concha" (conch shell), because of its unusual shape, is the little seaside resort of São Martinho do Porto, much favoured by families with small children.

São Martinho do Porto

See entry

Costa de Prata

See entry

Alcobaça

## Óbidos

A5

Historical province: Estremadura. District: Leiria
Altitude: 70m/230ft. Population: 5000

Óbidos is probably included in every tour of western central Portugal. Because of its prettiness and general attractiveness the whole town has

Situation and Importance

been declared a national monument. This also means that in order to preserve the original townscape there are no big hotels in Óbidos, although there are several small, de luxe establishments inside the old walls. The number of beds is therefore extremely limited, and it is almost impossible to get a room here in the summer months without early reservation.

In earlier centuries the Lagoa de Óbidos, a big lagoon with a narrow opening into the sea and now more than 10km/6 miles north-west of Óbidos, reached almost to the little town. This Atlantic dimension made Óbidos strategically important and it was therefore strongly fortified in Moorish times. Already a place of great attraction in the Middle Ages, Óbidos was frequently chosen as the queen's dowry, and it was a favourite residence of St Isabel and other queens and kings of Portugal. Queen Leonor lived here for several years, mourning her only son who had been killed in a riding accident.

★★Townscape

The old town centre is surrounded by walls 13m/45ft high, battlemented and reinforced by towers, and laid out on the lines of an acute-angled triangle. Within the walls is the picturesque old town full of interesting corners and alleys with handsome patrician Renaissance and Baroque houses, most of them covered in flowers. Nowadays Óbidos is obviously a place for tourists and artists, so that there is a correspondingly large number of antique shops and selling points for arts and crafts, including locally woven carpets, together with commercial art galleries.

## Sights

Pelourinho

The main street, the Rua Direita, leads from the town gate, the Porta da Vila (decorated inside with 18th c. azulejos), to the main square, the Praça de Santa Maria, which has a beautiful fountain and a 15th c. pelourinho bearing the emblem of Queen Leonor, a fisherman's net. The Queen chose

*Óbidos: two picturesque streets*

this emblem when her dying son was brought to her by fishermen who had wrapped his body in a net from the Tagus.

The town museum is in the old town hall on the Praça de Santa Maria. Exhibits range from archaeological finds to 15th–17th c. sculpture and paintings.

Museu de Óbidos

Also on the Praça de Santa Maria is the parish church of Santa Maria (originally Gothic but later remodelled in Renaissance style), its interior entirely faced with 17th c. azulejos. The church also contains the tomb of João de Noronha, the castle governor who died in 1575, by Jean de Rouen, and the painting the "Mystic Marriage of St Catherine" by Josefa de Ayala Figueira (17th c.).

Igreja de Santa Maria

Close by the parish church is the Igreja da Misericórdia with a fine Baroque doorway.

Igreja da Misericórdia

There was a castle on the town's highest point in Moorish times. This was rebuilt and reinforced by Afonso I Henriques after the capture of Óbidos in 1148. The former palace within the castle walls has been converted into a pousada. From the keep there are fine views of the town and surrounding area.

Castelo

Outside the town walls, on the road to Caldas da Rainha, is the church of Senhor Jesus da Pedra, a Baroque church built on a hexagonal plan between 1740 and 1747. The cross on its altar is probably 2nd or 3rd c.

Senhor Jesus da Pedra

## Surroundings of Óbidos

To the south of the town is the Amoreira aqueduct, built at the behest of Catherine of Austria in 1575.

Aqueduct

About 7km/4½ miles west of Óbidos is Serra d'El Rei (141m/463ft) where there is a magnificent view of Peniche (see entry). The place's only other interesting feature is the ruined 14th c. castle built by King Pedro I.

Serra d'El Rei

See entry

Caldas da Rainha

See entry

Peniche

## Olhão

C7

Historical province: Algarve. District: Faro
Altitude: sea level. Population: 17,000

Gradually affected by tourism, Olhão is the second largest town on the Algarve, a few miles east of its chief town, Faro. The town's main industry is its sardine and tuna fisheries, the catches being processed straightaway in the local cannery. The port has the second largest turnover in the Faro district (after Portimão).

Situation and Importance

Olhão has a very Moorish air about it (although modern buildings are creeping in), with its square white flat-roofed houses, two or three storeys high, topped with terraces (açoteias), openwork chimneys and look-outs. This style of building has not in fact been inherited from the Moors, but was adopted here and in the surrounding villages as being particularly suited for the predominantly hot dry climate when large numbers of fisherfolk from Aveiro (see entry) settled here in the late 18th c.
Olhão has no particularly outstanding sights, but the harbour has plenty of atmosphere, and an eyecatching covered fishmarket. There is an interesting parish church, too, Nossa Senhora do Rosário, on the Praça da

Townscape

Restauração, built between 1681 and 1698 by the local fishermen. From the tower there is a fine view of the town. The chapel of Nossa Senhora dos Afiltos opposite is where the wives of Olhão pray for the safe return of their husbands from the sea.

Beaches

Boats ply regularly from Olhão harbour to the sandy offshore islands of Culatra and Armona. Both have excellent beaches, Culatra being less developed than Armona.

Surroundings

Places particularly worth visiting around Olhão include Faro and Tavira (see entries), while those farther afield can be found under the entry for Algarve.

## Oporto/Porto                                                                    B3

Historical province: Douro Litoral. District: Porto
Altitude: 0–140m/0–460ft. Population: 350,000

Situation and
Importance

The lively port, industrial and commercial city of Oporto (known in Portugal as Porto: the traditional English name preserves the older form, from "o porto" – the harbour), a university town and the see of a bishop, is Portugal's second largest town but also its least typical, with a matter-of-fact and businesslike approach to life which perhaps owes something to its British connections. Its enchanting location alone makes it one of the most beautiful towns in the Iberian peninsula.

Here, barely 6km/4 miles above its mouth, the River Douro cuts a narrow passage through granite rocks, with Oporto on the north side and the suburb of Vila Nova de Gaia on the south side. Farther west the banks of the river become lower, finally ending at the cliffs of São João da Foz.

Oporto is the economic hub of the best cultivated and most thickly populated northern part of Portugal. Trade in and out is mainly handled by its port and by the outer harbour at Leixões (see Matosinhos), while international air travel passes through Pedras Rubras, Oporto's airport 13km/8 miles to the north.

The city is internationally famed for its port, made from the wine of the upper Douro valley (see entry) by a process which is practised here and nowhere else (see Practical Information, Wine). The wine is stored in the wine lodges of the southern suburb of Vila Nova, and no visit to Oporto would be complete without a visit to one of these establishments.

History

In the Hellenistic period there was a trading post here, in Roman times the settlement of Portus Cale. Later the Suevi had a stronghold on this site, followed by the Visigoths. The town became the see of a bishop, but was taken by the Arabs in 716 and destroyed in 825. After the Christian reconquest in the 10th c. the territory between the rivers Minho and Douro, with the rebuilt town of Oporto as its capital, became the County of Portucalia, the nucleus of the later kingdom of Portugal.

Oporto was and still is a traditionally cosmopolitan and liberal city. It is the birthplace of Henry the Navigator, who opened up the way to Portugal's conquest of the world. Over the centuries the people of Oporto repeatedly opposed arbitrary and dictatorial rule in bloody uprisings, as in 1628, 1661, 1757 and 1927. Here in 1808 French troops under Junot suffered their first defeat. The Liberals' fight against absolutism also began in Oporto, and as a result the town was besieged and partly destroyed by Dom Miguel's forces in 1832/33.

★★Cityscape

The houses are packed close together against the steep rockfaces, forming highly picturesque terraces. Oporto is like Lisbon in having the old town on a hill to the east and the newer districts on another hill to the west. Large-scale replanning in recent years has given the heart of the city attractive new streets and squares, with parks and gardens mingling northern and southern flora.

1 Praça de Lisboa
2 Jardim de
   João Chagas
3 Hospital de
   Santo António
4 Igreja do Carmo
   Igreja das Carmelitas

5 Museu Nacional
   de Soares
   dos Reis
6 Museu Romântico/
   Solar do Vinho
   do Porto
7 Igreja da Misericórdia

8 Igreja de São Bento
   da Vitória
9 Museu de Etnografia
10 Mercado de
   Ferreira Borges
11 Praça do Infante
   Dom Henrique

12 Palácio da Bolsa
13 Igreja de São Francisco
14 Igreja dos Grilos
15 Museu Guerra Junqueiro
16 Igreja de Santo
   Ildefonso
17 Igreja da Trindade

Oporto's main shopping street is the Rua de Santa Catarina, which, like its side-streets, is full of shops, cafés and restaurants. The nearby Mercado do Bolhão is the best place to buy fruit and vegetables. The city's main sights can easily be seen on a day's walkabout, starting from the busy traffic intersection of the Praça da Liberdade.

## Sights

The spacious Praça da Liberdade is graced by a statue, on horseback, of King Pedro IV (d. 1834), who was also Emperor Pedro I of Brazil from 1822 to 1831. Off the north side of the square opens the Avenida dos Aliados, a broad avenue laid out in 1923–29 after the demolition of an old residential quarter and now lined by banks and imposing office blocks, leading up to the City Hall. With its high central tower this early 20th c. granite building is reminiscent of its Dutch and Belgian counterparts, and can be visited on weekdays.

★Praça da
Liberdade

## Oporto/Porto

*Oporto: View over the town*

**Igreja dos Clérigos**

From the south-west corner of the Praça da Liberdade the busy Rua dos Clérigos runs up to the Igreja dos Clérigos, built by the Italian architect Nicoló Nasoni in 1732–48, a Baroque church with an oval interior.

**★Torre dos Clérigos**

Linked to the church is the Torre dos Clérigos, 75m/245ft high and built in 1755–63 at the expense of the Oporto clergy. It has come to be the symbol of Oporto and there is a panoramic view from the top (open every day except Wed.) over the city and the Douro Valley to the Atlantic coast.

**Campo dos Mártires da Pátria**

North and west of the Clérigos church is the broad Campo dos Mártires da Pátria. A part of it is taken up by the Praça de Lisboa, with its market stalls, while another part holds the beautiful Jardim de João Chagas (Jardim da Cordoaria). On the south side stands the old prison (18th c.), and at the north-west corner the Hospital de Santo António (begun 1769). On the north side of the Campo is the University (founded in 1911; previously a technical college), which also has a small Natural History Museum.

To the north-west, opposite the University, on the Praça de Gomes Teixeira, are two adjoining churches. To the right is the Igreja do Carmo (1756), its east end covered with 19th c. blue azulejos, and to the left the Igreja das Carmelitas (1619–28), both of them containing richly gilded altars.

**★Museu Nacional de Soares dos Reis**

Some 500m/550yd north-west of the Campo dos Mártires, in Rua de Dom Manuel II, the Palácio dos Carrancas, built in 1795 as a royal palace, now houses the Soares dos Reis National Museum (Museu Nacional de Soares dos Reis, closed Mon. and public holidays). The museum's collections are of prehistoric and Roman antiquities, medieval and modern sculpture, pictures, pottery and porcelain, goldsmith's work, furniture and textiles.

The art collection deserves special mention, including as it does work by the Oporto sculptor Soares dos Reis (1847–99; "O Desterrado", "Inglesa", "Flor Agreste"), and by Teixeira Lopes ("Infância de Caim") and Diogo de

*The Town Hall, seen from the Avenida dos Aliados*

Macedo. In the field of painting the 16th c. Portuguese school is represented by Vasco Fernandes and Frei Carlos, the 19th and 20th c. by Henrique Pousão (collection of his principal works), Columbano Bordalo Pinheiro, António Carneiro, António Carvalho da Silva Porto, Marques de Oliveira, Aurélia de Sousa ("Self-portrait"), Eduardo Viana and Dordio Gomes ("Casas de Malakoff"). Works by non-Portuguese artists include pictures by Frenchmen Jean Clouet and Jean-Baptiste Pillement.

A little way south-west of the Soares dos Reis Museum is the flower-filled Jardim do Palácio de Cristal, the setting for the Pavilhão dos Desportos, the sports arena, with seating for 10,000 spectators and also a venue for concerts, exhibitions, etc., which in 1952 replaced the former "Crystal Palace".
From the south side of the park, where a chapel commemorating King Charles Albert of Sardinia was built in 1851 (see Museu Romântico), there is a superb view over the city, the river and the sea.

Jardim do Palácio de Cristal

Hidden away to the west of the Jardim do Palácio de Cristal is the Romantic Museum (Museu Romântico, closed Mon. and Sun.), fully furnished as a Portuguese house of the 19th c., with also on view the room in which King Charles Albert of Sardinia (b. 1798) died in 1849.
Next to the museum is the Solar do Vinho do Porto, the port wine institute where there are tastings of over 150 varieties of port from various producers every day except Sunday.

Museu Romântico/ Solar do Vinho do Porto

North of the Jardim do Palácio de Cristal, outside the actual city centre – and therefore probably not for inclusion on a first trip round Oporto – is the Praça de Mousinho de Albuquerque (or Rotunda da Boavista), in the middle of which stands a massive monument (erected 1923–29) commemorating the war with France of 1808/09.

Praça de Mousinho de Albuquerque

*Sports pavilion in the Jardim do Palácio de Cristal*

Just east of the square is the little Romanesque church of São Martinho de Cedofeita (12th c.), the city's oldest church whose name – cedo feita = soon finished – indicates the speed with which it was built.

**Museu Nacional de Arte Moderna**

A visit to the Museum of Modern Art (Museu Nacional de Arte Moderna; closed Mon.), on the western edge of the city, is also best left out of a first day's exploration of Oporto. The museum is in the impressive Casa de Serralves, situated in its own large park, and puts on temporary exhibitions from various sectors of the arts.

**Igreja de São Bento da Vitória**

Continuing with the tour of the city, the route goes back from the Jardim do Palácio de Cristal to the Jardim de João Chagas and then takes a turn to the right through one of the alleys to the twin-towered church of São Bento da Vitória. Its simple and rather shabby exterior, dating from the early 17th c., belies the magnificent furnishings and gilt carving of the interior.

**Rua das Flores**

From the terrace in front of the church steps lead down east to the Largo de São Domingos, on the north side of which is the end of the Rua das Flores. This former street of goldsmiths and cloth-merchants still has many jewellers' shops in it today.

The Igreja da Misericórdia, in the Rua das Flores, is a church built in the first half of the 18th c. by Nasoni, who was also responsible for the Clérigos church.

**Museu de Etnografia**

The route continues by turning right from Largo de São Domingos, down Rua de Belomonte, to arrive at the Ethnographic Museum (Museu de Etnografia, Largo S. João Novo; closed Sun. and Mon.) which is in an 18th c. building, also the work of Nasoni. The exhibits include furniture, musical instruments, costumes and sacred objects, plus imitation wine vaults.

**Praça do Infante Dom Henrique**

From the Largo de São Domingos Rue Ferreira Borges runs southward into the Praça do Infante Dom Henrique, with a monument to Henry the Navigator. The Mercado de Ferreira Borges on the north side of the square provides an exhibition venue in the covered market built in 1883.

On the west side of the square is Portugal's most important authority for the supervision of its wine trade, the Instituto do Vinho de Portugal.

Also on the west side of the Praça do Infante Dom Henrique, occupying the site of a Franciscan convent which was destroyed by fire, is the Stock Exchange, the Palácio da Bolsa, built in 1842 and headquarters of Oporto's Chamber of Commerce. A modern glass building also stands where the convent cloisters once stood. The interior of the building can be visited on weekdays (guide compulsory), and the Moorish Hall, used for official receptions, is particularly worth seeing.

Palácio da Bolsa

South of the Palácio da Bolsa is the former church of the Franciscan convent, the Igreja de São Francisco (closed Sun. and Mon.). Originally Gothic but remodelled in Baroque style, it has a large rose window. The interior has sumptuous talha dourada decoration (17th/18th c.); also of interest is the elegant Renaissance tomb of the merchant Francisco Brandão Pereira (d. 1528) decorated with gilded vines, birds and angels.

Igreja de São Francisco

It is very doubtful whether the Casa do Infante, or its predecessor (in the Rua Alfândega Velha, below the Praça do Infante Dom Henrique) actually is the site of the house where Henry the Navigator was born. The current building was put up in 1677 on the site of the old customs house, serving as both customs house and, at times, the mint into the 19th c. Some of the rooms are nowadays used for temporary exhibitions (closed Sat. and Sun.).

Caso do Infante

The Rua de São João continues down to the banks of the Douro. Although the only boats that moor in the former harbour quarter of Ribeira are those taking people for trips on the river, this part of Oporto still retains much of its former charm. Life centres on the Praça da Ribeira. Here and in the alleys around about, the "travessas", there is a maze of colourful houses which are a picturesque attraction for the tourists, albeit less attractive for the people who live here as the quarter is in urgent need of investment. There is a market selling fish, flowers and handicrafts. Walking east, passing by innumerable stalls, shops and simple restaurants, the visitor arrives at the lower tier of the Dom Luis I Bridge.

★★Ribeira

From here it is possible either to walk over the bridge, enjoying the view of Oporto's sea of houses, and ending up by looking around one of the port wine lodges in Vila Nova de Gaia (see entry), or carrying on with the tour to the north and the Cathedral.

The twin-towered Cathedral (Sé) was originally a Romanesque church built in the 12th c. but later altered in Gothic style and almost completely rebuilt in the 17th and 18th c. while retaining much of its fortified character. The rosette over the portal on the west façade is still Romanesque, and the loggia on the north façade was by Nasoni in 1736. The interior is predominantly Romanesque and there are several richly decorated altars, including the carved and gilded wooden main altar below the choir from the early 18th c., and, even more magnificent, the silver Altar of the Sacrament to the left of the high altar, in the Capela-mór, and the work of several Portuguese artists between 1632 and 1732. In the left-hand aisle can be seen the statue of Nossa Senhora de Vendoma, patron saint of Oporto. In the south aisle is an entrance, through the sacristy, into the Gothic cloister (1385); the azulejos date from the early 18th c. Adjoining this are the remains of the Romanesque cloister.

★Sé

The terraces on the north and west sides of the cathedral afford views far out over Oporto's maze of streets and houses. The Manueline pelourinho on the Cathedral's west façade dates from the late 19th c.

To the south of the cathedral is the former Bishop's Palace (begun 1771), an imposing building with an elegant staircase and now occupied by civic offices.

**Oporto/Porto**

Loggia

Chapel of Sacrament

Terreiro da Sé

High altar

©Baedeker

**Gothic cloister**

**Cathedral Sé**

Sacristy

| | |
|---|---|
| Igreja dos Grilos | The terrace on the west façade of the Cathedral faces the Igreja dos Grilos which was built in 1614 by Baltazar Alvarés as a Jesuit seminary church. |
| Museu Guerra Junqueiro | Near the Igreja dos Grilos is an 18th c. Baroque building, at 32 Rua D. Hugo, which is also ascribed to Nasoni and houses the Guerra Junqueiro Museum (closed Sun. and Mon.). It brings together the furniture, tapestry, ceramics, silverware and many other objets d'art collected by Abílio Manuel de Guerra Junqueiro (1850–1923), the poet and political activist whose verses vehemently championed the Republican cause. |
| Igreja de Santa Clara | To the east, on the other side of the road onto the Ponte de D. Luis I, is the church of Santa Clara, originally Gothic but much altered at the time of the Renaissance and with an interior full of talha dourada (closed Sun.). |

*Street scene in Oporto*

The Rua Augusto Rosa leads north-east from the Santa Clara church to the traffic-thronged Praça da Batalha. Here the most impressive buildings are the Igreja de Santo Ildefonso, with blue and white azulejos on its Baroque façade, and the Teatro de São João (1920).

Oporto's main shopping street, the Rua de Santa Catarina, runs from the north end of the square to the Praça do Marquês de Pombal, where the church of the Immaculate Conception, the Igreja da Imaculada Conceição, built between 1939 and 1947, is a good example of more modern Portuguese church architecture.

For another magnificent view, take the Rua de Alexandre Herculano from the southern end of the Praça da Batalha to the Alameda das Fontainhas, a lovely promenade high above the Douro.

To return to the start of the city-walk go west from the Praça da Batalha along Rua 31 de Janeiro to the main railway station, Estação de São Bento.

This station was built in the early 20th c., and the walls of its concourse are covered in azulejos depicting historical themes and the story of various means of transport.

Opposite the station stands the Igreja dos Congregados, built around 1700 and flanked by shops and flats, with azulejos over much of its façade.

It's just a few hundred yards from here to the Praça da Liberdade, thus completing this walk round the city.

## Vila Nova de Gaia

The port-wine trade, and its lodges, to which Oporto owes much of its fame, is concentrated in the suburb of Vila Nova de Gaia on the south bank of the Douro. "Gaia" is a version of the Latin "cale", i.e. lovely, as in "Portus Cale" (i.e. Portugal).

There are three bridges linking Vila Nova de Gaia with Oporto:

Ponte de Dona Maria Pia, east of the centre, is a railway bridge, operational since 1877 and designed by Alexandre Gustave Eiffel. Its iron structure is 344m/1128ft long and about 60m/197ft above the river.

The bridge further west, outside the centre, is the Ponte da Arrábida which was opened in 1963 and carries the motorway.

The bridge of Louis I, the Ponte de Dom Luis I, leads directly from the centre of Oporto to Vila Nova de Gaia. An iron bridge, it was built between 1881 and 1885 by the Belgian Willebroeck Company and spans the Douro in a single arch 172m/565ft wide. There are two roads, the lower one 10m/33ft, the upper one 68m/223ft above the water. From the upper road, which is also open to pedestrians, and from the south end in particular, there are magnificent views of the city and the river within its steeply sloping banks.

On a hill east of the Ponte de Dom Luis is the former Augustinian monastery of Serra do Pilar (17th c.). Adjoining the round church with its splendid dome is a cloister, also circular, its barrel-vaulting borne on 36 Ionic columns.

From the terrace there is what is probably the very best view over Oporto and the Douro Valley with its bridges.

West of the Ponte de Dom Luis are the long, low *armázens*, or lodges, often sunk deep in the granite, of Oporto's wine merchants, many of them British in origin.

Almost all the port producers offer tours daily of their lodges. These include tastings and an opportunity to buy. (The section Wine, in Practical Information, includes some of the vocabulary used for port wine.)

Porto (Ponte da Arrábida)  Porto

**Vila Nova de Gaia**

Ponte de
Dom Luis I

Castelo

~ Douro

Serra
do
Pilar

Corpus
Christi

Junta Nacional
dos Vinhos

© Baedeker

(Armázens/Lodges)

| | | | |
|---|---|---|---|
| 1 | Calem | 16 | Mac-kenzie |
| 2 | Sandeman | 17 | Bur-mester |
| 3 | Borges | 18 | Dow |
| 4 | Noval | 19 | Barros |
| 5 | Croft | 20 | Cockburn |
| 6 | Rainha Santa | 21 | Martinez Gassiot |
| 7 | Ramos Pinto | 22 | Nie Poort |
| 8 | Taylor | 23 | Delaforce |
| 9 | Offley Forrester | 24 | Companhia Velha |
| 10 | Warre | 25 | Ferreira |
| 11 | Gonzalez Byass | 26 | Diez Hermanos |
| 12 | Wiese & Krohn | 27 | Graham |
| 13 | Kopke | 28 | Fonseca |
| 14 | Rozés | | |
| 15 | Hunt Roope | | |

In the old days the wine was carried down to Vila Nova de Gaia from the upper reaches of the Douro on the *barcos rabelos*, shallow skiffs that nowadays tend to be moored alongside the port lodges on the south bank of the Douro for advertising purposes only.

## Surroundings of Oporto

Foz do Douro

About 5km/3 miles downstream from Oporto, on a road which runs immediately above the steep bank of the Douro, with fine views back over the

*Vila Nova de Gaia: "Barcos Rabelos", now used for advertising*

city, lies São João da Foz (or Foz do Douro), a suburb of Oporto, and a very popular bathing resort, beautifully situated at the mouth (foz, from Latin *fauces*) of the Douro. The Douro Litoral beach is fringed by palms, and from the breakwater with the harbour light there is an impressive view of the coast and the mouth of the river, commanded by the Castelo da Foz (1570).

Further north-west, on the road to Matosinhos, is the 17th c. Castelo do Queijo, built to protect the coast against pirates from North Africa.

Leça do Bailio, a few miles north of Oporto, has a fortified Romanesque/ Gothic church (1336) from what was a monastery of the Hospitallers of John of Jerusalem. It contains richly sculpted capitals, 16th c. tombs and a fine 16th c. Manueline font. The Manueline calvary next to the church dates from 1514.

*Leça do Bailio*

See entry

*Matosinhos*

About 14km/9 miles south of Oporto is the village of Grijó, with a monastery founded in the 12th c. and comprehensively remodelled in the 16th c. The cloister has beautiful azulejo decoration and contains the tomb of Rodrigo Sancho (d. 1245), son of Sancho I. The church has a fine altar with talha dourada decoration.

*Grijó*

35km/22 miles east of Oporto on the hill between the valleys of Rio Sousa and Rio Tâmega is the long straggling little town of Penafiel (alt. 500m/1640ft; pop. 6000) which was known until the late 18th c. as Arrifana de Sousa. It has a 14th c. castle and the Renaissance-style church of the Misericórdia (16th c.), originally the church of a Franciscan convent.

*Penafiel*

Some 10km/6 miles south-west of Penafiel is the important Romanesque monastic church of Paço de Sousa (12th c.). Comprehensively restored after a fire in 1927, the church belonged at one time to a Benedictine monastery, and a part of its cloister has been retained.

The church has also maintained its Romanesque strength in the interior; the column bases are hewn from millstones. At the far end of the church is the sarcophagus (12th c.) of Egaz Moniz (1050–1140), tutor and confidant of Afonso Henriques, who played a major part in the history of his time. He is particularly remembered for an occasion in 1130 when, after Afonso Henriques I had broken his word to Afonso VII of León, he made his way to the Spanish king's court with a rope around his neck, accompanied by his wife and children, in order to do penance on behalf of his master. Impressed by his honesty and nobility, the Spaniard forgave the offence and allowed Moniz to return to Portugal. The very affecting reliefs on the sarcophagus, supported by lions, show scenes from the life of the dead man.

*Paço de Sousa*

# Palmela

B6

Historical province: Estremadura. District: Setúbal
Altitude: 238m/781ft. Population: 6000

The little hill town of Palmela, in the Serra de São Luís, an eastern outlier of the Serra da Arrábida, is famous for the local wine, and the vintage in September and October is accompanied by several festivals.

The town owes its name to the Roman praetor of Lusitania province, Aulio Cornelio Palma.

*Situation and Importance*

Palmela is a simple hill-town with no particular sights other than its castle. However, a walk round the town should take in the 18th c. church of São Pedro on the Largo do Município, below the castle, with fine azulejo pictures of scenes from the life of St Peter. The hall in the 17th c. town hall diagonally opposite is adorned with portraits of Portuguese kings.

*Townscape*

*Palmela*

## ★Castelo

| | |
|---|---|
| History | During the Moorish period Palmela had the most formidable fortress in southern Portugal. This was captured by King Afonso Henriques first in 1147 and then finally, after the Moors had retaken it, in 1166 when he had it further enlarged and gave it to the knightly Order of Santiago, who made it their headquarters in the 15th c. In the 18th c. the castle was again strengthened to protection it against attack from artillery as well. |
| Torre de Menagem | From the late 14th c. keep, the Torre de Menagem, there is a good view over the whole castle complex and on a clear day you can see as far as Lisbon and the Tagus estuary. In 1484 the bishop of Évora, Garcia de Meneses, was incarcerated in the cistern of the keep, with other prisoners, for his involvement in a conspiracy, and presumed to have been poisoned there. |
| Igreja de Santa Maria do Castelo | Within the castle precincts are the ruins of the Igreja de Santa Maria do Castelo, a Renaissance church built on the site of an earlier Moorish mosque and which collapsed in the 1755 earthquake. |
| São Tiago | The western end of the castle precinct is occupied by the former Convent of Santiago, built in the 15th c. but subsequently much altered. Nowadays part of it is a pousada. The convent church, in a style transitional between Romanesque and Gothic, has beautiful azulejo decoration (17th and 18th c.) in the interior, and contains the tomb of Jorge de Lencastre (1481–1550), a natural son of King João II. |

## Surroundings of Palmela

| | |
|---|---|
| Quinta do Anjo | At Quinta do Anjo, 3km/2 miles west of Palmela, there are tombs which were carved out of the rock about 5000 years ago, and which served as burial chambers until the Middle Ages. These are reached by turning left in |

the centre of Quinta do Anjo, coming from Palmela, and turning left again at the end of the houses into a track across the fields.

See entry

Setúbal

See Costa de Lisboa

Serra da Arrábida

## Peneda-Gerês National Park/Parque Nacional da Peneda-Gerês B/C 2/3

Historical provinces: Minho and Trás-os-Montes
Districts: Viana do Castelo, Braga and Vila Real
Area: 50,000 hectares/193 sq.miles. Altitude: up to 1545m/5070ft

The Peneda-Gerês National Park, Portugal's first national park, extends along the Spanish frontier from the Castro Laboreiro plateau by way of the Peneda, Soajo, Amarela and Gerês mountains to the Mourela plateau in the south. Large areas within the park boundaries, which were officially defined in 1971, are protected nature reserves. The park can be explored by car, and also has several good walks.

The park includes expanses of completely unspoilt country with magnificent forest and mountain scenery and beautiful artificial lakes (reservoirs: Barragens de Vilarinho, de Caniçada, da Salamonde, de Paradela). The highest peaks are in the Serra do Gerês, which rises within Portuguese territory to 1545m/5069ft in the Nevosa and 1538m/5046ft in the Altar de Cabroês.

★★Topography

The very varied pattern of relief gives rise to widely different microclimates, and in consequence the plant life of the park shows unusual variety. Moreover, the remoteness of this region has protected many endemic species from destruction by man, so that plants are found here which have disappeared from the rest of Europe. In addition to great tracts of coniferous forest there are stands of centuries-old oaks (particularly at Pincães and São Lourenço), cork-oaks (at Ermida), eucalyptus, and expanses of rocky country covered with heather.

Vegetation

The wildlife includes deer, wild boar, hares, partridges, wild horses, lizards, snakes and even wolves and golden eagles.

Fauna

The many archaeological sites show that the Peneda-Gerês National Park area was one of ancient human settlement. The dolmens (megalithic chamber tombs) of Mezio, Paradela, Cambezes, Pitões and Tourém date from the 3rd millennium B.C. Pre-Roman, presumably Celtic, castros (camps) have been excavated at Pitões, Tourém and Cidadelhe, and there are believed to be still more prehistoric settlements as yet undiscovered.

Human settlement

## Touring by car

The names in the margin refer to the park entrances.

Although not all the park roads are surfaced with tarmac most of them are quite good to drive on. The signing is minimal, and it's not unusual to find that what seems at first a reliable way ahead suddenly comes to a dead end. Since all the roads are full of bends it is wise to allow plenty of time for the tours.

It should be borne in mind that the Spanish frontier crossing-points are only open in the summer. Further information can be had from the tourist information centre in Braga (see Practical Information, Information).

The Lamas de Mouro entrance is at the north end of the park, about 10km/ 6 miles south-east of Melgaço. Castro Laboreiro is about 8km/5 miles

Lamas de Mouro

south-east of the entrance. Its nearby castle was probably originally a Roman fortress, and was then rebuilt by Afonso Henriques and extended by King Dinis. It was, however, almost completely destroyed by an explosion when the powder tower was struck by lightning. Since the road ends soon after Castro Laboreiro, go back to Lamas de Mouro and then south to the pilgrimage church of Nossa Senhora da Peneda (pilgrimages in first week in September).

Mezio

The Mezio entrance is 18km/11 miles north-east of Arcos de Valdevez. Five km/3 miles south-east on a tarmacked road is the mountain eyrie of Soajo,

*In the Peneda-Gerês National Park* ▶

its houses built of undressed granite blocks without the use of mortar. Its 10th c. pelourinho is the oldest stone column in Portugal. On the roadside there are a number of espigueiros, the small stone grainstores that are characteristic of this region (see Minho). A road runs south from here through the valley of the Rio Lima, past electric power-stations, to Cidadelhe, where the route described in the next paragraph can be joined.

**Entre-Ambos-os-Rios**

The Entre-Ambos-os-Rios entrance, 13km/8 miles north-east of Ponte da Barca, is also often used for through traffic to Spain. The route runs east along what used to be the very scenic valley of the Rio Lima. The road passes the rather gloomy-looking mountain villages of Britelo and Cidadelhe, with their sombre granite houses, ascending to Lindoso (alt. 468m/1536ft; pop. 1000), just before the Spanish frontier. Looming over it is a castle built under King Dinis in 1287, and here you can see more of Minho's typical espigueiros (see Minho). Lindoso is the jumping-off point for a number of good walks – to the artificial lake of Viarinho das Furnas; to the Miradouro Leira do Canto, with a beautiful view of the Lima valley; to the pass of Portela do Homem (822m/2697ft) on the Spanish frontier, affording a magnificent prospect of the rocky valley of the Rio Homem; and south to the Cabril Forest.

**São João do Campo**

From the São João do Campo entrance, 17km/10 miles north-east of Terras do Bouro, you can either drive south-east along the narrow, winding little road to Caldas do Gerês, or take the old Roman road. This was built between 79 and 353 A.D., and runs along the south-east side of the Vilarinho reservoir up to the Portela do Homem on the Spanish frontier. It has the largest number of original Roman milestones on the Iberian peninsula.

**Senhor da Saúde**

Probably the most frequented road in the National Park runs from the Senhor da Saúde entrance, 32km/20 miles north-east of Braga, near the Barragem de Caniçada. It is also the main road to the little spa of Caldas do Gerês (alt. 400m/1312ft), scenically located in a narrow valley. Also known simply as Gerês, the spa specialises in complaints connected with the gall-bladder and the liver, and is a good base for walking and clmbing in the Serra do Gerês. From here a good road runs north to Portela do Homem, on the frontier. The route then takes you east, on foot in places, to Carris at the foot of the Altar de Cabrões, which has a fine lookout point.

**Paradela/Covelães**

The easternmost section of the park has two entrances, Paradela (65km/40 miles north-east of Braga, on the Barragem de Paradela reservoir), and Covelães (75km/47 miles north-east of Braga, 13km/8 miles north-west of Montalegre), providing access to narrow, little-used tracks leading to the prehistoric sites of Pitões and Tourém.

# Peniche                                                                                      A5

Historical province: Estremadura. District: Leiria
Altitude: 0–15m/0–50ft. Population: 15,500

**Situation and Importance**

The busy little fishing town of Peniche is one of Portugal's most important places for crayfish, sardine and tuna fisheries (cannery). It lies on a rocky peninsula on the Portuguese Atlantic coast, almost 3km/2 miles long and just over 2km/1¼ miles wide, edged by rugged cliffs and linked to the mainland by a narrow sandspit. Peniche's tourism has remained within reasonable bounds. There are few hotels of any size in the town itself, and seaside pursuits tend to be enjoyed on the long sandy beaches on both sides of the isthmus (istmo).

Peniche has a State school of pillow-lace making, which is a traditional local craft.

**Townscape**

Fortifying walls and a moat, securing the town to landward, run from the fortress in the south of the town to the northernmost point of the peninsula.

**Peniche**

500 m

PAPOA

Oceano Atlântico

Forte da Luz

N. S. da Ajuda

E. N. 114

Calvário

Campo de Futebol

E. N. 114

Santuário dos Remédios

Ponte Velha

ISTMO

Óbidos

† Cruz dos Remédios

Sant' Ana

Misericórdia

N. S. da Conceição

São Pedro

Porto de Pesca

NAU DOS CORVOS

Farol

Santa Cruz

Fortaleza

E. M. 581

CABO CARVOEIRO

Oceano Atlântico

The harbour, protected by two breakwaters, is the scene of lively activity. In the summer a regular boat service runs from here to the Berlenga Islands (see entry), and there is also the spectacle of the arrival of the fishing boats to be speedily unloaded so that their perishable cargoes can be appraised and prepared for processing.

## Sights

The town, and indeed the whole peninsula, is dominated by the well-preserved fort (fortaleza) near the harbour, built by Filippo Terzi in the 16th c. and considerably enlarged in the 17th c., with Vauban-style fortifications. It achieved notoriety under Salazar's dictatorship when he used it to incarcerate political prisoners. Part of the former prison – cells, visitors' room and other communal facilities – is open to the public, and there are also displays designed to give an idea of the repression and the resistance during the Salazar regime. Also in the fortress is the regional museum, with exhibits particularly related to the fishing industry.

★Fortaleza

In the centre of the town, near the ramparts, is the Baroque church of the Misericórdia, with scenes from the New Testament on its wooden ceiling. A few yards further south is another Baroque church, the 17th c. church of São Pedro, with 18th c. talha dourada in the choir, while right in the north of the town, near the football field, is the Igreja Ajuda, with rich azulejo decoration and ceiling paintings in the choir.

Other sights

## Surroundings of Peniche

Several roads lead to Cabo Carvoeiro, and its lighthouse (farol), 2km/1¼ miles west of the town, on a rocky headland which has been eroded into bizarrely shaped pinnacles and sea-caves and has excellent fishing and

★Cabo Carvoeiro

281

crayfish grounds. There are views of the Nau dos Corvos ("raven's ship") rock offshore, and beyond to the Berlenga Islands (see entry). There are also fine views from the fish restaurant that has been opened on this exposed spot.

| | |
|---|---|
| Santuário dos Remédios | Several hundred yards north of the cape stands the chapel dos Remédios, a place of pilgrimage entirely clad with azulejos. |
| Óbidos | The picturesque town of Óbidos (see entry) is 25km/15½ miles east of Peniche. |

## Ponte da Barca
B3

Historical province: Minho. District: Viana do Castelo
Altitude: 178m/584ft. Population: 1500

| | |
|---|---|
| Situation and Importance | Ponte de Barca is a quiet little market town 30km/19 miles north of Braga on the left bank of the Rio Lima. It is also a popular base for excursions around the Peneda-Gerês National Park (see entry). |
| Townscape | There is a fine view of the town from the old 15th/16th c. bridge over the Rio Lima.<br>The main building in the town centre is the handsome 15th c. parish church, which has a beautiful coffered ceiling and a silver crucifix presented by King Manuel I.<br>The pelourinho in the market place in the lower part of town dates from the 16th c. |

## Surroundings of Ponte da Barca

| | |
|---|---|
| ★Bravães | About 5km/3 miles west of Ponte da Barca, on the outskirts of Bravães, is the 12th c. little Romanesque church of São Salvador which owes its fame to its elaborately sculpted portals, where animal and plant motifs vie with geometric patterns and human faces. The interior also has rich relief decoration and carved friezes, as well as what is left of 14th c. frescoes, the best of these being on display in the Soares dos Reis Museum in Oporto (see Oporto). |
| Ponte de Lima | The old-world little town of Ponte de Lima lies a further 15km/9 miles west of Bravães, where the river Lima is spanned by a medieval bridge of 24 arches. The town also has several impressive 16th c. town-houses, an interesting Manueline portal on the former convent church Santo António dos Frades, and, in the Torre de São Paulo, a remnant of the medieval ramparts. |
| Arcos de Valdevez | Five km/3 miles north of Ponte da Barca, straddling the Rio Vez, is the little market town of Arcos de Valdevez (pop. 3000), with a 14th c. parish church (remodelled in the 17th c.). In front of the church is a remarkably fine Manueline pelourinho; behind it, in the Praça do Terreiro, stands the 16th c. Casa do Terreiro. Also worth looking at are the Baroque façade of the church of Nossa Senhora da Lapa and a monolithic column in front of the Espírito Santo church in the upper town, commemorating the town's support of Afonso Henriques in his conflict with the Spaniards. |

## Portalegre
C5

Historical province: Alto Alentejo. District: Portalegre
Altitude: 477m/1565ft. Population: 16,000

*Ponta da Barca: an old bridge over the Rio Lima*

The district capital of Portalegre (happy gate), the Roman Amoea, lies near the Spanish frontier at the foot of the Serra de Portalegre, a westerly outlier of the Serra de São Mamede. With its white houses reaching up the steep slopes of the hill and its numerous handsome old palaces it is the great showcase of Portuguese Baroque architecture. The old episcopal city rose to prosperity in the 16th c. through its woollen industry, in particular the production of tapestries, but its real heyday came in the late 17th c. with the rise of the silk-weaving industry. Today Portalegre is still important for its woollens, but also for woodworking and cork-processing.

Situation and Importance

Since its nearby industry makes Portalegre a rather noisy and hectic place tourists usually only pause briefly on their way through to the two pleasant resorts further north, Castelo de Vide and Marvão (see entries).

The old town centre of Portalegre is surrounded by medieval walls, with the ruins of the massive medieval castle (1290) at the highest point. The town's most notable buildings, many of them no longer at their best, are grouped around the Praça do Município. North of it is Portalegre's modern centre, the traffic swirling round the Rossio, in its splendid garden setting. Around the busy square are handsome mansions, government buildings, the Misericórdia hospital, with an 18th c. façade and a beautiful patio, and the tourist information centre.

Townscape

## Sights

The Cathedral, or Sé, forms the west side of the Praça do Município. Built in the 16th c. it was considerably altered in the 18th c. when the main façade, flanked by two towers, was also added. The three-aisled Renaissance interior has been preserved in its 16th c. form. In the second chapel on the right can be seen an altarpiece with scenes from the life of the Virgin, while the sacristy has an azulejo version of the Flight into Egypt. The cloister is 18th c.

Sé

*Portalegre: The Rossio*

| | |
|---|---|
| Museu Municipal | Opposite the Cathedral, to the north-east, is the Municipal Museum, which has an outstanding collection of ceramics and tiles from Portugal (17th/18th c.), Spain (Moorish), Italy, Flanders and Holland (particularly 18th c. Delftware), together with archaeological material, arms and armour and religious art. |
| Câmara Municipal | The 18th c. town hall, the Câmara Municipal, on the same square is also of interest. |
| Palácio Amarelo | Take the alley between the Cathedral and the Museum, then keep right to reach the Palácio Amarelo (yellow palace, after its colour), or Palácio dos Albrançalhas, to give it its proper name. Nowadays used as a house, and not in the best state of repair, the 17th c. ironwork on its balconies and windows is among the finest in Portugal. |
| Convento de Santa Clara | South-east of the Praça do Município in the Rua Santa Clara is the 14th c. Convent of Poor Clares, with a noteworthy cloister. |
| Praça da República | From the Praça do Município the Rua do 19 de Junho, lined by fine 17th and 18th c. patrician houses, leads south-east to the Praça da República. Here too there are handsome mansions, some of them faced with azulejos, including the Palácio dos Condes de Avilés (now occupied by the Civil Governor) and the Palácio dos Fonseca Acciolo (now a school). Also on the Praça da República is a former Franciscan convent, founded in the 13th c. and largely rebuilt in the 18th c. |
| Casa de José Régio | Lovers of religious sculpture would be well advised to visit the Casa de José Régio Museum, once the home of the poet José Régio (1901–1969), in the Rua de José Régio, just south of the Praça da República. Its contents include the Portuguese poet's unusual private collection of figures of Christ and other religious statuettes. |

The Manufactura de Tapeçarias, north-east of the old town by the Parque do M. Bombarda, can be traced back to silk-weaving and tapestry workshops founded by Marquês de Pombal in 1772. It is based in a former 17th c. Jesuit convent, and can be visited, with tours taking place at 10am and 4pm.

Manufactura de Tapeçarias

The former convent of São Bernardo is a short distance north of the Parque do M. Bombarda. Now a barracks, it can be visited on request. It was founded in 1518 and later remodelled in Baroque style. It contains the splendid marble tomb of the bishop of Guarda, Dom Jorge de Melo, founder of the convent, which is ascribed to the 16th c. French sculptor Nicolas de Chanterène. The convent also has two fine cloisters, one Manueline and the other Renaissance; in the larger of the two can be seen a beautiful marble fountain. The chapterhouse has fine groined vaulting.

Convento de São Bernardo

## Surroundings of Portalegre

The scenery around Portalegre is exceptionally attractive. There are superb views from Penha de São Tomé, a rocky outcrop 2km/1¼ miles north-west of the town, and from Pico São Mamede (1025m/3363ft), 13km/8 miles to the east and the highest point in the Serra de São Mamede.

Viewpoints

See entry

Castelo de Vide

See entry

Marvão

About 12km/7½ miles north of Portalegre, near the village of Aramenha, are the remains of the Roman settlement of Medóbriga. Discoveries from the site can be seen in the National Museum of Archaeology and Ethnology in Belém (see Lisbon).

Medóbriga

Crato is about 20km/12 miles west of Portalegre and was the headquarters of the Maltese Order. Little is left of the great convent complex which was destroyed by Spanish troops in 1662.

Crato

The former Maltese convent in Flor da Rosa, 2km/1¼ mile north of Crato, is much better preserved, and parts of the complex, which was built around 1350 and extended in the 16th c., now contain a pousada. The convent church is impressive, and the Late Gothic cloister boasts sleek marble columns.

Flor da Rosa

Alter do Chão, 30km/19 miles south-west of Portalegre, is famous for having the National Stud which dates back to 1748 when the "Coudelaria Real", or royal stud, was founded. In addition to some 18th c. mansions the interesting little town has a 14th c. castle, complete with battlements, a lovely Renaissance fountain (1556), and the Vasconcelos family castle (1732).

Alter do Chão

## Portimão

**B7**

Historical province: Algarve. District: Faro
Altitude: 0–35m/0–115ft. Population: 26,000

The busy industrial town and port (cannery, shipyard) of Portimão, which is believed to occupy the site of a Carthaginian settlement known to the Romans as Portus Hannibalis, or Portus Magnus, is in the Algarve on the west side of the wide estuary of the Rio Arade.

The 337m/370yd long bridge across the Rio Arade at Portimão can often prove a bottleneck for traffic in the rush-hours.

Situation and Importance

Townscape

Portimão has no major tourist sights, but visitors are increasingly attracted by the busy life and activity of its harbour and waterside cafés, the popular beaches within easy reach of the town and the good opportunities for shopping it offers. The sardine landings on the quayside are quite a spectacle as well.

The originally Gothic parish church, the Igreja Matriz, is on a low hill. It was rebuilt in the 18th c. after the 1775 earthquake, and the portal is all that is left of the Gothic original. The beautiful azulejo decoration dates from the 17th and 18th c.

## Surroundings of Portimão

Praia da Rocha

The popular tourist resort of Praia da Rocha (see entry), with its magnificent beaches, lies 3km/2 miles south of the harbour.

Ferragudo

The village of Ferragudo, which has a good bathing beach and a 16th c. castle, is opposite Portimão, on the east side of the Rio Arade.

Silves

Silves (see entry), about 15km/9 miles north-east of Portimão, still has an old-world air about it.

Algarve

Other destinations worth visiting around Portimão are described in the entry on the Algarve.

## Póvoa de Varzim                                                    B3

Historical province: Douro Litoral. District: Porto
Altitude: sea level. Population: 24,000

Situation and
Importance

The little fishing town of Póvoa de Varzim straggles along the Atlantic coast 20km/12 miles north of Oporto, almost merging with neighbouring Vila do Conde (see entry). Because of its 2km/1¼ miles long, broad beach it is a popular seaside resort, particularly with the Portuguese themselves.

Póvoa de Varzim is the birthplace of the great Portuguese novelist Eça de Queirós (1845–1900), who is commemorated by a monument outside the Town Hall.

The local speciality is a fish stew – caldeirada à Póvoa.

Townscape

Póvoa de Varzim's skyline is dominated by innumerable imposing apartment buildings, and the businesses that have sprung up around the centre have also made Póvoa de Varzim look less like a seaside resort.

The Municipal Museum, the Museu Municipal de Etnografia e História, contains interesting material on local history and folk traditions.

Beaches

The village of Aguçadoura, as yet untouched by tourism, is about 4km/2½ miles north of the town. This too has a long, wide sandy beach, although polluted in places. Larger hotels are a few miles further north in Ofir and Esposende (see Barcelos).

## Praia da Rocha                                                    B7

Historical province: Algarve. District: Faro
Altitude: 20m/65ft. Population: 2000

Situation and
Importance

The popular seaside resort of Praia da Rocha, or "rocky beach", boasts an unusually mild climate and beautiful golden-yellow sandy beaches edged by rugged cliffs. Administratively part of the town of Portimão (see entry) 3km/2 miles to the north, it is in one of the most beautiful parts of the

Algarve. Originally a favourite residential area with well-to-do citizens of Portimão, who built their elegant villas here, around the turn of the 19th c. Praia da Rocha started becoming increasingly attractive to visitors from other parts of Portugal and abroad, especially Britain.

Along the clifftop above the chief beach, almost 2km/1¼ miles long and 100m/110yd wide, runs the Avenida Tomás, the town's promenade and main thoroughfare, lined with hotels, restaurants, cafés, shops and boutiques. At its eastern end the 16th c. Fortaleza de Santa Catarina, nowadays a restaurant with a view, overlooks the mouth of the Rio Arade.

Townscape

The Miradouro at the western end of the Avenue provides a particularly good view of Praia da Rocha's rocky scenery.

Praia da Rocha's main beach is very picturesque, and consequently very popular. To the west extends a series of idyllic sandy bays separated from one another by projecting crags and reefs, although since a number of large holiday colonies are located around here, particularly near Alvor (see Algarve), it is not easy to find a secluded little spot. Recent developments have led to increasing numbers of highrise blocks, giving rise to overcrowding and commercialisation. There is an extremely pleasant boat trip from Praia da Rocha past rugged seacliffs, with their bizarre rock formations, to Praia dos Três Irmãos, the "beach of the three brothers".

★Beaches

## Queluz

A6

Historical province: Estremadura. District: Lisboa
Altitude: 125m/410ft. Population 48,000

This town, 15km/9 miles north-west of Lisbon, owes its importance and its fame to the charming Rococo palace of Queluz ("what light!"), once a summer residence of the Bragança kings, and still used today for official government receptions.

Situation and Importance

Apart from the palace Queluz has no sights to recommend it, but since it is on a direct commuting line to Lisbon it now has additional housing for about 30,000 people.

Townscape

### ★Palácio Nacional de Queluz

The palace and gardens are normally open Mon., Wed.–Sun. 10am–1pm and 2–5pm, but since they are used for official receptions it pays to check

287

*The Palace of Queluz, surrounded by beautiful gardens*

with the tourist information centre in Lisbon whether the palace complex will be open.

**History of the building**

The palace was built between 1747 and 1794 for Pedro III and his wife, later Queen Maria I, originally to the design of the Portuguese architect Mateus Vicente de Oliveira (1706–85), a pupil of the German architect Johann Friedrich Ludwig who built the Convent-Palace of Mafra (see entry). The central block was complete by 1758, then in 1760 the west wing of the palace was built by the French architect, Jean-Baptiste Robillon, who also designed the gardens and many of the rooms.

**Castle square**

In front of the palace is the spacious Largo do Palácio, with a statue of Queen Maria I. The Palace Chapel, in the purest Rococo style and containing the military music school and accommodation for the royal guard, is separated from the rest of the palace buildings by a road.

**Palace of Queluz**

The Palácio Nacional de Queluz – consisting of a central block and two wings – gives the impression of a warm and friendly building and is therefore sometimes compared, not unreasonably, with Frederick the Great's palace of Sanssouci near Berlin. The rich interior decoration is notable for the high quality of the craftsmanship and the sure taste with which the details are contrived and related to one another. Outstanding among the many rooms in the palace are the Throne Room, the Queen's Wardrobe (beautiful azulejo pictures) and the Hunting Room (ceiling paintings of hunting scenes). The Kitchens, also decorated with azulejos, are now occupied by a luxury restaurant, the Cozinha Velha.

**Gardens**

Behind the palace are Jean-Baptiste Robillon's Rococo gardens, with fountains, grottoes and sculpture, some of them in lead cast in England. In the lower part of the gardens is the 115m/126yd long Ribeira de Jamor basin, beautifully faced with azulejos.

# Ribatejo

Historical province: Ribatejo. District: Santarém
Area: 6600 sq.km/250 sq. miles
Population: 460,000. Chief town: Santarém

Taken in the narrowest sense, the Ribatejo ("bank of the Tagus") region, roughly corresponding to the present district of Santarém, comprises only the alluvial basin of the lower Tagus valley, in the east of the province of Estremadura. This is a highly fertile area of some 600 sq.km/230 sq.miles which is still sinking as a result of tectonic movements.

Location and Topography

The historical province of Ribatejo, however, with its capital at Santarém, also includes the fertile upland regions to the north and south and the plateau to the east – all relics of the Tertiary and Quaternary tableland through which the Tagus has carved its course.

The drier upland region to the north is densely populated and intensively farmed, mainly by smallholdings practising mixed farming (wheat, olives, wine, citrus fruits, figs). The area to the south, on the other hand, is sparsely populated. Here the large estates and the increasing custom of single-crop farming (wheat, olives, cork-oaks) show the same agricultural structure as in the Alentejo region (see Alentejo) to the south.

Population and Agriculture

The water meadows, which form a strip some 50km/30 miles wide along the Tagus and which are flooded every spring (January–April), provide ideal conditions for growing grain and rice.

Here, too, is the grazing land, often rather acidic, for the traditional horse and cattle rearing. Most of Portugal's fighting bulls come fron Ribatejo, especially from around Vila Franca de Xira (see Alenquer).

*The fertile Tagus valley near Santarém*

## Sagres                                                                B8

Historical province: Algarve. District: Faro
Altitude: 35m/115ft. Population: 2000

Situation and
Importance

The modest little houses of the port of Sagres lie widely dispersed on the rocky plateau, swept bare by the wind, in the extreme south-west corner of Portugal, and indeed of Europe. As a holiday destination this part of the Algarve is only for those hardy people who revel in a bracing climate, or who are keen on scuba-diving or fishing.

Despite the somewhat inhospitable weather Sagres is attracting growing numbers of tourists and an international airport is being built nearby, as well as a campsite catering for 2500 visitors.

## ★Fortaleza

History

The ruins of the Fortaleza are south of the actual centre of Sagres, on the Ponta de Sagres, a narrow promontory reaching out into the sea, and called the Promontorium Sacrum, or sacred promontory, by the Romans who thought this remote area had been the home of the gods.

Here at the end of the world Henry the Navigator (1394–1460; see Famous People) spent the last 40 years of his life and devoted himself, in the company of his country's greatest geographers, cartographers and astronomers, to developing new seafaring techniques, such as the caravels which were then built in his shipyards, and were far superior in manoeuvrability and seaworthiness to the traditional types of sailing ships. All these new techniques were passed on to the young men trained in the school of seamanship founded in 1421 alongside the fortress.

Little remains of the original fort built in Henry the Navigator's time. This was largely destroyed in an attack by Sir Francis Drake and the 1755

*Fortaleza at Sagres*

earthquake, but the fortifications were rebuilt in the 18th c., hence the date of 1793 over the entrance.

Once inside the fort the visitor immediately encounters the tourist information centre and the youth hostel. These are where the School of Seamanship and supposedly also Henry the Navigator's residence once stood, although it is possible that this could have been outside the fort itself where the Pousada do Infante stands today, or even on Cabo de São Vicente (see Algarve).

The little chapel on the right (not open) still survives from the 15th c. The commemorative column was erected in 1960 for the 500th anniversary of Henry's death.

A prominent feature of the parade ground within the Fortaleza is the windrose that probably dates from Henry the Navigator's time and was used for training the seamen. The stone circle, which was discovered in 1928, has a diameter of 43m/141ft.

A film about the history of Sagres and the Portuguese voyages of discovery is shown several times a day in summer, in different languages (details in tourist information centre). | Film shows

## Surroundings of Sagres

For destinations around Sagres see Algarve. | Algarve

## Santarém | B5

Historical province: Ribatejo. District: Santarém
Altitude: 108m/354ft. Population: 20,000

Santarém, capital of the old province of Ribatejo, is a town of low whitewashed houses built on a hill above the right bank of the Tagus, occupying a position of great strategic importance. | Situation and Importance

The town is worth visiting for its interesting churches and the splendid views from here over the Tagus.

In Roman times, as Iulianum Scalabitanum, the town ranked with Braga and Beja as one of the main trading posts in Lusitania. During the Moorish period (8th–12th c.) it was fortified by a castle. After its recapture by Afonso Henriques in 1147 Santarém became the residence of several kings. Here in 1319 King Dinis received the papal bull recognising the order of the Knights of Christ which he had founded. | History

## Sights

The Jardim da República, the fine park in the north of the town, is a good starting point for a walk round Santarém. | Jardim da República

On the east side of the park is the Convento de São Francisco, founded as a Franciscan convent in the mid-13th c., now a barracks but still with its original cloister.

North of the Jardim da República is the 18th c. town hall, while the covered market on the west has a façade with azulejo pictures of the local sights and rural motifs.

North-east of the Jardim da República, just outside the old town, stands the Gothic church of Santa Clara (13th c.), belonging to a convent founded by Queen Leonor. Her simple tomb is in the church. | Igreja de Santa Clara

The Gothic fountain, the Fonte das Figueiras, is just south of the Igreja de Santa Clara, while the São Bento viewpoint is about 500yd to the east.

The main sights of Santarém are south of the Jardim da República. The Praça de Sá da Bandeira was the scene of the gruesome execution in 1357 | ★Igreja do Seminário

291

Torres Novas     São Bento

Câmara Municipal

Jardim da República  Convento de São Francisco

Santa Clara

200m

Mercado

N. S. da Piedade

Fonte das Figueiras

Igreja do Seminário

Praça Sá da Bandeira

E.N. 114

Bus station

Largo do Barão

Torre das Cabaças

Museu Arqueológico

Igreja de Marvila

Largo Cândido dos Reis

Largo Pedro A. Cabral

Igreja da Graça

Portas do Sol

Cartaxo

Rio Tejo

Almeirim

© Baedeker

Praça de Touros     Caneiras

of Álvaro Gonçales and Pedro Coelho, the murderers of Inês de Castro. The Igreja do Seminário, the seminary church of the former Jesuit convent, is on the west side of the square. It has a Baroque façade (1676) by Baltasar Álvares, and, inside, an impressive high altar, painted wooden ceiling and 17th c. azulejo pictures.

**Capela de Nossa Senhora da Piedade**

The Capela de Nossa Senhora da Piedade is opposite the Igreja do Seminário. It was founded by Afonso VI in 1665 in thanksgiving for his victory over Juan de Austria, commander of the Spanish army.

**Igreja de Marvila**

From the Praça de Sá da Bandeira the Rua Serpa Pinto runs south-east to the Marvila church which has a fine Manueline doorway (16th c.) and polychrome azulejo decoration (17th c.).

**★Igreja da Graça**

The Igreja da Graça lies to the south-east. This late Gothic convent church was built towards the end of the 14th c. possibly by the architects of Batalha Abbey (see entry). The chief feature of the façade is the rose window, one of the largest in Portugal, made from a single block of stone. The church was the burial-place of the Meneses family. The founders of the family, João Afonso Teles de Meneses and his wife Dona Guimar de Vila Lobos, lie under grave-slabs in the choir which bear their coats of arms , their daughter's tomb adjoining. To the right of the choir is the tomb of Pedro Álvares Cabral (1467/68–1526), discoverer of Brazil, and his wife.

**Museu Arqueológico de São João de Alporão**

The walk continues back to the Igreja de Marvila and then right to the Archaeological Museum, housed in the Romanesque and Gothic church of São João de Alporão. Apart from the fine stellar vaulting in the choir, and the many sculptures, ceramics and azulejos, it is worth looking at the

*Santarém: Igreja do Seminário* ▶

Gothic cenotaph of Duarte, son of Pedro I, who fell in the battle of Alcácer-Kibir (Morocco) in 1458. One of his teeth was all that was brought back to Portugal!

Torre das Cabaças    The Torre das Cabaças, Santarém's great landmark, is opposite the archaeological museum. Probably originally a minaret, the tower has soundboxes around the bell to heighten the resonance.

★Portas do Sol    Several hundred yards farther south-east is the Portas do Sol, where a park and a terrace have been laid out on the site of a Moorish castle, affording magnificent views over the Tagus valley, spanned at this point by the Ponte Dom Luís, built between 1876 and 1881 and 1200m/1312yd long.

## Surroundings of Santarém

Almeirim    Almeirim, where the Infante Afonso, son of João II and Queen Leonor, was killed while out riding in 1491, lies about 6km/4 miles south-east of Santarém.

Alpiarça    Alpiarça, 7km/4¼ miles north-east of Almeirim, has a museum well worth a visit in the Casa dos Patudos, the country house that belonged to the Portuguese statesman and art lover José Relvas (1858–1929). The collection contains notable works by many European painters, tapestries (17th–19th c.), porcelain and faience.

Golegã    Golegã is 25km/15½ miles further on. The highpoint of its year is the horse show in the second week of November. The parish church, built about 1500, has a Manueline portal, ascribed to Diogo Boytaca.

Almoster    Almoster, 10km/6 miles west of Santarém, has a church from a late 13th c. convent containing 17th c. azulejos.

## Santiago do Cacém                                                                    B6

Historical province: Estremadura. District: Setúbal
Altitude: 210–254m/689–833ft. Population: 7000

Situation and    The little country town of Santiago do Cacém occupies a commanding spot
Importance    on a hill crowned by a castle in the southern part of the Serra de Grândola, 20km/12½ miles north-west of the port of Sines.

## Sights

Castelo    The town is dominated by its Castelo, the old Templar castle, which can be reached by road. There is a pleasant walk round the outside of the walls, with views as far afield as Cabo de Sines. The parish church cemetery is within the walls, shaded by lovely cypresses.

Igreja Matriz    The parish church, the Igreja Matriz, alongside the castle, is originally 13th c. with later alterations including the façade, which is 18th c. while the side portal is still Romanesque-Gothic. The church contains a 14th c. relief of St Tiago, who was killed during a Moorish attack on the town.

Museu Municipal    The municipal museum contains local archaeological discoveries and an interesting collection of old coins.

## Surroundings of Santiago do Cacém

Miróbriga    The remains of the Roman settlement of Miróbriga, with temple ruins and a stretch of Roman road, are rather more than 1km/¾ miles east of the town, near the road to Beja.

*View of Santiago do Cacém*                *Santo Tirso: Convento de São Bento*

See Alcácer do Sal

Grândola

A pleasant excursion is to the seaside lagoon of Lagoa de Santo André,    Lagoa de S. André
passing through the dunes (waterbirds) to the quiet beaches on this section
of the Atlantic coast, known here as the Costa Dourada (see entry).

## Santo Tirso                                                                B3

Historical province: Douro Litoral. District: Porto
Altitude: 75m/245ft. Population: 12,000

The little town of Santo Tirso, situated in pleasant wooded country on the     Situation and
left bank of the Rio Ave about 25km/15½ miles north-east of Oporto, attracts   Importance
many visitors who come to explore the surrounding area. The town's main
source of income is the textile industry, supplemented by various handicrafts, including pottery.

The town's most important building is the Convent of São Bento (photo-     Convento de São
graph above), now containing an agricultural college. The Benedictines     Bento
founded a convent here in the 10th c. The present building, with its impressive Baroque façade, dates from the 14th to 18th c. The church is richly
decorated with talha dourada and sculpture. There is also a beautiful
two-storey cloister (14th–17th c.), with fine capitals.
   The adjoining little Abade Pedrosa museum has prehistoric and
medieval archaeological displays.
   A reddish granite calvary stands in front of the church.

## Surroundings of Santo Tirso

In Roriz, about 10km/6 miles east of the little town, is the interesting 12th c.    Roriz
Romanesque church of the former Benedictine convent, its main portal
embellished by an early Gothic rose window.

295

**São Pedro do Sul**

| | |
|---|---|
| Paços de Ferreira | The village of Paços de Ferreira lies 14km/9 miles east. It has an unusual Romanesque church with a separate tower. |
| Vila Nova de Famalicão | About 10km/6 miles north of Santo Tirso, Vila Nova de Famalicão is a centre for Portuguese watchmaking. The place is dominated by the former convent church of São Tiago de Antas (13th c.). The choir was decorated with azulejos in the 17th c. |
| Oporto | See entry |

# São Pedro do Sul                                                          B4

Historical province: Beira Alta. District: Viseu
Altitude: 168m/551ft. Population: 3500

| | |
|---|---|
| Situation and Importance | The attractive little town of São Pedro do Sul in the northern foothills of the Serra do Caramulo at the junction of the Rio Vouga and the Rio Sul, is a popular base for exploring the beautiful wooded hills in the immediate surroundings; particularly the Serra da Gralheira and the Serra do Caramulo (see Viseu). |

## Surroundings of São Pedro do Sul

| | |
|---|---|
| Termas de São Pedro do Sul | The little spa of Termas de São Pedro do Sul 3km/2 miles south has hot sulphur and sodium springs (68°C/154°F) which were already being frequented in Roman times (remains of Roman baths) and are still used.<br>    King Afonso Henriques spent some time here receiving treatment for a broken leg after the battle of Badajoz in 1169. |
| Vouzela | Another 3km/2 miles south-west is the ancient little town of Vouzela (pop. 1500), dominated by a 12th c. Romanesque and Gothic parish church which is decorated with remarkable sculpture. It has an unusual belfry which is basically just a narrow wall fronting one of the façades.<br>    The 18th c. Rococo chapel of São Gil in the market square is also worth seeing.<br>    The do Castelo church, on a hill with a view 3km/2 miles south of Vouzela, receives pilgrimages on the Sunday after August 5th. |
| Cambra | The village of Cambra is 6km/4 miles south-west of Vouzela and is overshadowed by castle ruins. Nearby to the south is the Celtiberian site of Cova de Lobishomem, or "cave of the werewolf". |

# Serra da Estrela                                                          C4

Historical province: Beira Alta
Districts: Viseu, Guarda, Coimbra and Castelo Branco

| | |
|---|---|
| Location | Famous for its scenery as the "star mountains", the Serra da Estrela is a mighty granite ridge which extends for some 100km/60 miles, with a breadth of 30km/20 miles, from Guarda to south of Coimbra. It is Portugal's main watershed range, formerly the southern frontier of the country and historically the dividing line between its north and south. |
| ★★Topography | With its bizarrely shaped crags and gorges, mountain streams and lakes, beautiful forests and magnificent views, the Serra da Estrela ranks among Portugal's outstanding scenic attractions. The range contains the country's highest peak, the Torre or Malhão da Estrela (1991m/6532ft).<br>    The bare hills provide grazing for sheep and goats, and the valleys have a centuries old woollen industry. |

# Tour

The following route covering about 140km/87 miles takes in the scenic highlights and main places of interest in the Serra da Estrela, starting at Covilhã (see entry) and finishing at Belmonte (see entry).

To extend the tour, instead of first going to Penhas de Saúde leave Covilhã on the N 230 travelling south to Unhais da Serra, beautifully situated in the Rio Alfora valley, and possessing sulphur springs. The route then winds its way uphill, with fine views, and leaves the N 230 20km/12 miles beyond Unhais da Serra turning north on the N 231 to Loriga (740m/2430ft). Beyond Loriga the road climbs steeply then descends in hairpin bends to Valezim, crossing the Rio Alva with lovely views from the Ponte da Jugais, to reach São Romão (590m/1935ft). From here there is a road running 12km/7½ miles south-east to the Senhora do Desterro hermitage (790m/2590ft), built in 1650, although the nearby power station detracts somewhat from the scenic effect.

The tour described below can be joined at Seia, 4km/2½ miles north.

*Extension*

Leave Covilhã on the N 339 going north-west – the road, which is not well signposted, goes uphill to the right out of the centre of Covilhã by the town hall. Passing through dense woods it gradually climbs up to the mountain and winter sports resort of Penhas da Saúde (10km/6 miles; 1453m/4767ft). With February temperatures of as low as −10°C/14°F the conditions here are very good for winter sports.

*Penhas da Saúde*

Past a reservoir, 10km/6 miles beyond Penhas da Saúde, is the Torre or Malhão da Estrela (1991m/6532ft), Portugal's highest peak, topped by a granite monument.

*Torre*

Seia (532m/1745ft) farther north-west, and a total of 52km/32 miles from Covilhã, has a parish church on a hill with a view, overlooking the township.

*Seia*

*In Serra da Estrela*

About 2km/1¼ miles beyond Seia the route joins the N 17 which comes in from the left from Coimbra, and carries on north-east to the right along this main road.

Gouveia

After 13km/8 miles turn right off the main road on the N 232 for 5km/3 miles to Gouveia (alt. 650m/2135ft), a little town on the Rio Mondego and a popular base for exploring the Serra da Estrela. The façade of the parish church is covered in blue and white azulejos, as is the Misericórdia church, which is part of what was an 18th c. Jesuit abbey.

Penhas Douradas

Beyond Gouveia the road winds its way up the rocky hillside, with ever more extensive views of the beautiful mountain scenery. After about 20km/12 miles there is a sign to Penhas Douradas (formerly Poio Negro, 1496m/4908ft), a group of houses and holiday villas (viewpoint), a good walking and climbing base for the mighty rock faces, such as the "golden rocks" from which the place takes its name.

Manteigas

Beyond Penhas Douradas the road descends through the forest to the Pousada de São Lourenço (1450m/4755ft), with a superb view of Manteigas and the Zêzere valley, which the road eventually reaches via many a hairpin bend. Since earnings from textiles have dwindled to next to nothing Manteigas (720m/2360ft, pop. 4000) has fallen back increasingly on tourism.

The spa of Caldas de Manteigas, with hot carbonic acid and sulphur springs (43°C/109°F), is in the upper Zêzere valley about 2km/1¼ miles south.

Poço do Inferno

The Poço do Inferno, the springs of Hell, where a waterfall hurtles down into a cavern, lies 3km/2 miles farther up the valley.

From Manteigas the route descends the Zêzere valley, past wooded slopes and cultivated fields and gardens, crossing the river on a narrow bridge just beyond Valhelhas. 23km/114 miles from Manteigas it joins the N 18 from Covilhã, turning left for 3km/2 miles before the appearance of the houses of Belmonte (see entry).

# Serra da Lousã                                                    B4

Historical province: Beira Litoral
Districts: Coimbra, Leiria, Castelo Branco and Santarém

Location and
General

The Serra de Lousã, a quartz and schist massif eroded into picturesque rock formations, extends south-west of the mighty granite ridge of the Serra da Estrela south-east of Coimbra. Reaching a height of 1204m/3950ft in the Alto do Trevim, it falls sharply down to the Lousã basin in the north and is bounded on the south by the Zêzere valley. The main crop is the maize grown on terraces in the often narrow river valleys, and there is also grazing of sheep and goats.

## Sights

Lousã

The best base from which to explore the Serra de Lousã is the little town of Lousã (alt. 172m/564ft, pop. 7500), at the northern foot of the range, which has some handsome 18th c. patrician houses and the Igreja da Misericórdia, which is worth seeing – built around 1550 with a beautiful Renaissance door.

High above the town (3km/2 miles south on the road to Castanheira de Pêra) is the Miradouro de Nossa Senhora da Piedade, from which there are panoramic views. A nearby castle has a massive 14th c. keep.

A pleasant walk from Lousã is along the narrow valley of the Rio Aronce, past many little white chapels, up to the Penhasco dos Eremitas, where there is a fine view.

Figueiró dos Vinhos (pop. 5000), about 2km/1¼ miles north-east of Lousã, is famous for its pretty pottery. It has a church with 18th c. azulejos lining the choir.

Figueiró dos Vinhos

## Serra de Monchique                                                    B7

Historical province: Algarve. District: Faro

The Serra de Monchique extends from east to west along the north side of the coastal plateau of the western Algarve, forming a protective barrier against cold air from the Atlantic and thus helping to give this area its almost North African climate. Geologically the range is a much broken-up mass of volcanic rock overlying the basement schists of the region, divided up into a western and an eastern half by the Ribeira de Odelouca. Because of the impermeability of the ground the abundant rainfall is channelled into innumerable rivers and streams (some of them dammed to form lakes), running down to the coastal plain, thus rendering it well watered and suitable even for rice. The volcanic nature of the region is also reflected in the presence of a number of hot springs.

Location and Geology

The pleasant upland landscape of the Serra de Monchique reaches its highest point in the peaks of Fóia and Picota, 902m/2959ft and 774m/2538ft respectively. The fertile volcanic soil and plentiful water supply have clothed the slopes and valleys with dense subtropical woodland in an unusually wide range of species, with mostly spruce, arbutus, eucalyptus and mimosa at the lower levels, and holm oaks and pines higher up.

★★Topography

Agriculture is the main occupation (cotton and sugar-cane, sometimes terraced), and the favourable climate means there can be two to three crops a year.

Economy

## Sights

The chief place in the Serra de Monchique is the little hill town of Monchique (458m/1503ft, pop. 7000) where the main source of income is the sale of local handicrafts and products, such as basketwork, pottery and arbutus brandy, or "medronho" – with or without "mel", i.e. honey. The best time to browse is at the large market on the third Friday of every month.

Monchique

Features of interest in the town are the parish church, with a Manueline doorway – unexpected in this remote rural area – and the highly picturesque flower-bedecked ruins of the convent of Nossa Senhora do Desterro.

From Monchique a little road winds its way for 6km/4 miles up past the beautiful Estalagem Abrigo da Montanha (view from terrace) to the bare summit of Fóia (902m/2959ft), the highest point in the range, where on a clear day there are superb panoramic views.

Fóia

4km/7 miles below Monchique, in a cool wooded valley, lies the old-established little spa of Caldas de Monchique (250m/820ft), visited for the treatment of rheumatism and skin ailments, and with an idyllic village square shaded by plane trees inviting the visitor to linger awhile.

Caldas de Monchique

## Sesimbra                                                              A6

Historical province: Estremadura. District: Setúbal
Altitude: 0–249m/0–817ft. Population: 8000

*Sesimbra: a picturesque fishing village on the Costa de Lisboa*

The pleasant little fishing town of Sesimbra, below rugged red cliffs on the southern slopes of the Serra da Arrábida, is also a popular seaside resort.

Situation and Importance

The promenade along the shore is lined with simple white houses and a few smaller hotels, with the larger hotel complexes outside the centre. Fishing still dominates the scene, however, together with tourism. Visitors can watch the fishermen mending their nets on the beach, or see them unloading their catch in the harbour at the western end of the town. The spectacle is particularly lively when the fish are auctioned, and the freshly landed fish and other seafood can be sampled in the relaxed atmosphere of one of the town's restaurants.

In the town centre, right on the beach, stands the Fortaleza de Santiago, a little 17th c. fort, at times a prison, with a lighthouse. The town museum, containing archaeological finds, a collection of coins and sacred objects, is a few hundred yards north.

Townscape

High above the town stands the Castelo, the castle originally built during the 12th and 13th c. but almost totally rebuilt early in the 17th c. by Cosmander, the Flemish Jesuit architect, for King João IV.

Castelo

Sesimbra is a good base for exploring the Costa de Lisboa (see entry) and the Serra da Arrábida (see Costa de Lisboa).

Surroundings of Sesimbra

## Setúbal

B6

Historical province: Estremadura. District: Setúbal
Altitude: sea level. Population: 98,000

◀ *The attractive landscape of the Serra de Monchique*

## Setúbal

**Situation and Importance**

The industrial city and district capital of Setúbal, situated on the wide estuary of the Rio Sado, is Portugal's fourth largest city and third largest port, with important fish canneries, a car assembly plant, shipyards and salt-pans. The Roman town which occupied this site was founded in the 5th c. to replace the Celtic settlement of Cetobriga on the Tróia peninsula to the south-east, which was destroyed by a tidal wave.

A royal residence for a time in the 15th c., Setúbal is also the birthplace of the poet and satirical writer Manuel Maria de Barbosa du Bocage (1765–1805; small museum in the house where he was born in the Rua do São Domingo).

**Townscape**

Setúbal is quite attractive for an industrial city. On the Rio Sado waterfront are the docks, the marina and the fishing harbour, where brisk auctions take place every morning when the fishermen have unloaded the day's catch. North of the waterfront runs one of the city's main throughfares, the Avenida de Luisa Todi, named after the celebrated opera-singer (1754–1833), who was born in Setúbal. The crowded and picturesque old town, centred around the Praça do Bocage with its statue of the poet, is on the other side of this avenue, and contains the few sights of the city spared by the 1755 earthquake.

## Sights

**Igreja de Jesús**

The Igreja de Jesús is in the west of the old town. It was Portugal's first Manueline church, begun in 1490/91 under the direction of Diogo de Boytaca, who went on to be architect of the convents at Batalha (see entry) and Belém (see Lisbon). Inside the relatively unadorned exterior can be seen impressive stellar vaulting in the choir and azulejo scenes from the life of the Virgin.

*Setúbal Harbour*

The adjoining monastic buildings and 17th c. Arrábida marble cloister of the Convento de Jesús now house the city's museum, with pictures by Portuguese, Flemish and Catalan artists and local archaeological discoveries.

Museu de Setúbal

The church of Saõ Julião just south-east of the Praça do Bocage is worth seeing. Originally 16th c., hence the two Manueline portals, it was almost completely rebuilt after the 1755 earthquake.

Igreja de São Julião

The church of Santa Maria da Graça at the east end of the old town dates back to a 13th c. building which was almost completely reconstructed in the 16th c. Its carved and gilded altars date from the 16th and 17th c., and the azulejos are 18th c.

Igreja de Santa Maria da Graça

The Museum of Oceanography and Fisheries on the Avenida de Luisa Todi has a significant collection of rare sponges and other sea creatures.

Museu Oceanográfico

The Archaeology and Folklore Museum next door has displays of tools and implements used in farming and fishing around Setúbal, and also model ships.

Museu de Arqueologia e Etnologia

Above the city, to the west, is the Castelo de São Filipe, built in the late 16th c. by the Italian military engineer Filippo Terzi. Part of it is now a pousada and there is a good view from here over the city and its surroundings.

Castelo de São Filipe

## Surroundings of Setúbal

Some 15km/9 miles west of Setúbal is the village of Vila Fresca de Azeitão, with the church of São Simão, with 17th c. azulejo decoration, and the Quinta das Torres, now a hotel surrounded by lovely gardens.

Vila Fresca de Azeitão

The nearby Palácio da Bacalhoa (privately owned), on the road to Setúbal, is a late 15th c. three-part building with Moorish domed towers, which was substantially altered in the 16th c. In the middle of its magnificent park stands the Casa de Prazer, a pleasure seat with an early tile version of Susanna and the Elders (mid 16th c.).

Vila Nogueira de Azeitão

Vila Nogueira de Azeitão, 2km/1¼ miles west of Vila Fresca de Azeitão, is famous for its wine cellars, which can be visited. It also has the palace of the Dukes of Aveiro, built by Jorge de Lencastre between 1520 and 1523.

Costa de Lisboa

There are very worthwhile trips from Setúbal into the Serra da Arrábida and to the Tróia peninsula, which can be reached by ferry from Setúbal (see Costa de Lisboa for both).

Palmela

The castle in the little mountain town of Palmela (see entry) makes it another place worth visiting.

## Silves                                                                B7

Historical province: Algarve. District: Faro
Altitude: 85m/280ft. Population: 10,000

Situation and Importance

The little country town of Silves, situated on the Rio Arade (Rio de Silves) 11 miles north-east of Portimão and surrounded by forests of cork-oak, was once the Moorish city of Xelb, capital of the Al-Gharb (see Algarve), and as such, with its 30,000 population at that time, was an intellectual and cultural centre that rivalled Granada in splendour and influence.

History

The town is believed to have been founded by the Phoenicians, and was ruled by the Moors from the first half of the 8th c. until its recapture from the Moors by Afonso III in 1242. It became the see of a bishop, but after the transfer of the see in 1580 to the new capital, Faro, and the destruction caused by the 1755 earthquake it sank into obscurity and insignificance.

Townscape

Silves is still an attractive old-world little town, presenting a charming picture with some venerable and handsome burghers' houses.

## Sights

★Castelo dos Mouros

Above the town rears the massive Moorish castle, the Castelo dos Mouros, with its imposing battlemented walls of red sandstone, restored in 1940, and the ventilation systems and cisterns, up to 60m/197ft deep, put in by the Moors. A walk along the top of the walls provides views far out over the surrounding countryside, and in the summer there are son et lumière performances in the castle courtyard, full of ancient trees. (Open daily: 8am–6pm.)

Sé

Near the castle stands the Gothic Cathedral, or Sé, built over a mosque in the 13th c. and subsequently much altered, containing the tombs of a number of crusaders.
The Igreja da Misericórdia opposite the cathedral has fine Manueline windows. (Open daily: 9am–7pm.)

Cruz de Portugal

The 16th c. Cruz de Portugal at the eastern exit from the town is an example of Manueline stone-masonry, rare in this region. It is a white limestone wayside cross, 3m/10ft high, with Christ on the Cross on the front, and a Piéta on the back.

## Surroundings of Silves

Serra de Monchique

Silves is a good base for some interesting excursions into the Serra de Monchique (see entry).

*View of Silves*

The busy little city of Portimão (see entry) is about 15km/9 miles south-west of Silves.

Portimão

Other sights around Silves can be found under the entry on the Algarve.

Algarve

## Sines

B7

Historical province: Baixo Alentejo. District: Setúbal
Altitude: sea level. Population: 12,000

Once an unassuming little fishing town in a rocky bay on a dune-fringed stretch of Portugal's southern coast, Sines has grown since the early 1970s to become one of the country's biggest ports and industrial centres (industry park, with oil refinery), although it has only been possible to achieve part of the ambitious plans for the town.

Situation and Importance

Sines is the birthplace of Vasco da Gama (1469–1524), discoverer of the sea-route to India in 1497/98.

The house where Vasco da Gama was born has been reconstructed as a museum.

Above the port is the fishermen's chapel of Nossa Senhora das Salas. The original chapel, built in 1335, was completely renovated by Vasco da Gama after his discovery of the passage to India. It has a magnificent Manueline doorway, with a terrace with a view in front of it.

There is another fine view from the recently restored 13th c. castle, which contains a small museum.

In the parish church (Igreja Matriz) are the relics of St Torpes, said to have been found on an abandoned ship which ran aground here in A.D. 45.

*Statue of Vasco da Gama*

The Cabo de Sines, a 56m/184ft high headland, with a lighthouse, extends into the Atlantic west of the town.

Cabo de Sines

Surroundings

Santiago do Cacém (see entry), perched on its hilltop, is about 17km/10½ miles north-east of Sines.

## Sintra

A6

Historical province: Estremadura. District: Leiria
Altitude: 225m/740ft. Population: 21,000

Situation and
Importance

The small city of Sintra (perhaps better known in English in the older spelling of Cintra) lies between Lisbon and the Atlantic on a promontory of land between two gorges on the north side of the well-wooded Serra de Sintra. With its beautiful setting and equable climate it was an early choice as the summer seat of the Portuguese royal family. The beauty of the scenery, combined with the magnificent subtropical vegetation and the nearness of the sea, is almost beyond compare, making Sintra one of the loveliest spots in the Iberian peninsula, wholly justifying Lord Byron's description of it as "glorious Eden".

Cityscape

Sintra is centred on the Largo Raínha D. Amélia with the imposing Palácio Nacional de Sintra on its northern side. In front of the Palácio stands a Late Gothic pelourinho which has been made into a fountain.

In the Praça da República, on the south-west corner of the Largo Raínha D. Amélia, are the Igreja de São Martinho, originally a 12th c. church and subsequently much altered, and the Museu Municipal, the municipal museum, which holds the tourist information centre as well. There is also a toy museum a few hundred yards further west.

Past Parque Liberdade, or Liberty Park, the Igreja de Santa Maria (another much altered 12th c. church) and the Convento da Trindade, lies the São Pedro part of town, with the parish church, and the location of a big market which is held every second and fourth Sunday in the month.

Immediately above the town, on its steep rocky mount, stands the Moorish castle which Afonso Henriques captured from the Arabs in 1147, and then, higher up, the Pena topped by its palace.

Sintra festivals

During June and July there is a very popular series of piano recitals of works by the Romantic composers in the palaces in and around Sintra.

Horse-drawn
carriages

A good way of covering the relatively long distance between the centre of Sintra and the Palácio da Pena is to take one of the horse-drawn carriages. These can be found plying for trade in front of the Palácio Nacional de Sintra.

## Sights

★★Palácio
Nacional de Sintra

The Palácio Nacional de Sintra, or Paço Real (closed Wed.), is the ancestral seat of the House of Avis. It appears that there was definitely a Moorish castle on this site in the 10th c., and its walls served as the foundations for the summer palace built there by King João I (1385 to 1433). This was extended and altered during the reign of Manuel I (1495–1521). Its most characteristic, and prominent, features are the two tall conical chimneys added in the 18th c. Completely restored and refurnished under Maria II, the palace was then chosen by Luís I as his favourite residence, and it became the dower house of his widow Maria Pia.

The Palace is not a single, uniform building, but consists of different, linked individual components. Through its history it has brought together Moorish, Gothic and Manueline architectural elements, together with Renaissance features. The palace frontage on the Largo Rainha D. Amélia, with its gently sloped flight of steps and the five Joanine double windows, was part of the first phase of the building and Manuel I then added the many Manueline-style windows and doorways.

The interior of the former royal palace offers an overview of Portuguese art and architecture of many different periods, with its shady patios and their refreshing fountains, its carpeted halls, its coffered ceilings and its many rooms faced with 15th and 16th c. azulejos.

The tour of the building usually begins in the Guardroom, then passes through the enormous kitchen into the Hall of the Arabs, furnished like an old Moorish palace. Next comes the Hall of the Stags, or Armorial Hall, which has an octagonal wooden domed ceiling embellished with the coats of arms and heraldic devices of 72 Portuguese noble families; that of King

*Sintra: Palácio Nacional*

Manuel, who had the room built, is in the centre of the dome, and those of his eight children are grouped around it. The walls of the room are covered with azulejo murals of hunting scenes.

The Hall of the Magpies owes its name to the 136 magpies painted on the ceiling, each one holding in its beak the motto of King João I, "por bem", i.e. for the best. The story goes that João I's Queen caught him kissing a lady in waiting, and his cool response was "Foi por bem", i.e. "I did it for the best". Since the ladies in waiting delighted in repeating this ever afterwards on every possible occasion, their chatter goaded João I into commissioning the ceiling. The 16th c. Carrara marble fireplace is by Nicolas Chanterène.

## Palácio Nacional de Sintra

1 Entrance
2 Guard-Room
3 Hall of Swans
4 Hall of Magpies
5 Hall of Sirens
6 Hall of Lions
7 Hall of Arabs
8 Hall of Chinese
9 Afonso VI's Room
10 Hall of Stags (Armorial Hall)
11 Chapel
12 Kitchen
13 Central Court
14 Court of the Lion
15 Court of Diana
16 Lindaraya Garden
17 Garden of the Negress

**Former Royal Palace**

© *Baedeker*

*Palácio Nacional de Sintra: the kitchen*

Through a courtyard is the Hall of Swans, the largest room in the palace, its doors and windows embellished in the 16th c. in a sumptuous Moorish-Manueline style. This former banqueting hall is still used today on festive occasions.

Another of the palace rooms was where Afonso VI was imprisoned for nine years until his death in 1683, following his exclusion from affairs of state by his brother, Pedro II, who had him declared insane.

On the Praça da República, several hundred yards south-west of the Palácio Nacional de Sintra, is the municipal museum, the Museu Municipal, with archaeological and local history exhibits, as well as sacred art, together with a collection of pictures connected with Sintra.

Museu Municipal

From the south side of the town a road forks right and snakes uphill, with many hairpin bends, first through magnificent gardens and then park-like woodland. After about 3km/2 miles a side-road branches off to the left to the Moorish castle, the Castelo dos Mouros (alt. 429m/1408ft). Ramparts and towers are still standing from the castle, which was originally built in the 8th or 9th c., recaptured in 1147 by Afonso Henriques and subsequently much altered. There is a splendid view of Sintra from the Torre Real. The inner courtyard has trees planted in the mid-19th c. for Ferdinand von Coburg-Koháry, consort of Queen Maria II.

Castelo dos Mouros

Following the road uphill from the Castelo dos Mouros, after about 1km/ ¾ mile we reach the entrance into the park of the Palácio Nacional da Pena, or Castelo da Pena, perched on its rocky crag (alt. 528m/1732ft; closed Mondays).

★★Palácio da Pena

This palace was also a royal summer residence and was built, as a medieval-style castle, for Ferdinand von Coburg-Koháry, Queen Maria II's consort (Fernando II), by Colonel von Eschwege 1840–50, who was instructed to incorporate elements of a 16th c. convent, and otherwise mix various building styles. He drew his inspiration from Bavaria's fairytale castles, but also incorporated Portuguese examples, such as modelling the principal tower on the Tower of Belém (see Lisbon). Probably the finest views of the Serra de Sintra are to be had from the walk along the top of the walls, the Galeria, and from the dome (external staircase).

The rooms of the "fairytale castle", which likewise lack any stylistic uniformity, are packed full of furniture, china, weapons, etc. The palace has also retained parts of the old 16th c. convent, namely, the two-storey Manueline cloister, with azulejo-lined walls, and the chapel, which has a Renaissance altar (1532) by Nicolas Chanterène and 19th c. German stained-glass windows.

★Parque da Pena

Ferdinand von Coburg-Koháry was also responsible for the extensive Parque da Pena around the castle. (The park is closed at night; cars are admitted for a fee, but there is no charge for admission to the castle car park.) The estate, which covers about 200ha/494 acres, contains over 400 species of trees and shrubs, including tree ferns; it is especially beautiful in spring when the camellias, rhododendrons and azaleas are in bloom.

Cars can be driven up to the Cruz Alta (540m/1771ft), a stone cross (1522) on the highest point in the Serra de Sintra, where there is a good view of the Palácio da Pena and of the whole mountain range and plain as far away as Lisbon.

## Surroundings of Sintra

Palácio de Seteais

The Palácio de Seteais, or Palace of the Seven Sighs, is on the N 375 westward to Colares, just outside Sintra. It gets its name from the fact that the Treaty of Sintra – the surrender declaration of the French forces – was signed here in 1808. The palace was built in the last quarter of the 18th c. and extended early in the 19th. The triumphal arch (1802) commemorates a visit by João VI. The magnificent building is now a luxury hotel, with a gourmet restaurant.

★Quinta de
Monserrate

A few miles past the Palácio de Seteais, on the same road, is the entrance to the Quinta de Monserrate, a Moorish-looking villa built in the 19th c. Originally owned by an Englishman, Sir Francis Cook, it is now the property of the State. It is worth a visit if only to look round its lovely hilly park, where there is an abundance of tall tree ferns along with many other species of subtropical plants.

Colares

Further along the road is Colares, famous for its wine, where a growing number of prosperous Lisbon citizens have their holiday homes.

About 1km/¾ mile beyond Colares the coast road that runs along the Costa do Sol (see entry) goes off to the left, but the right hand fork brings the visitor, after 3 and 4km/2 and 2½ miles respectively, to the little resorts of Praia das Maçãs and Azenhas do Mar, where the pounding of the waves has eaten deep into the rugged coastline.

Convento dos
Capuchos

The Convento dos Capuchos is 10km/6 miles along the road to the Palácio da Pena south-west out of Sintra. The Capuchin monastery, in its woodland setting, was founded in 1560. Its monks' cells, hewn out of rock, are both spartan and minute, some of them lined with cork.

Monte Peninha

A little road goes from here to Monte Peninha (489m/1604ft), with good views over the Serra de Sintra and the sea. The small chapel perched up here was built in 1711 and is decorated with azulejos.

Other nearby
destinations

A few miles south of Sintra are the popular coastal resorts of Cascais and Estoril (see entries), while Mafra (see entry), with its enormous convent-palace, is 20km/12 miles to the north.

*Palácio da Pena, a fairytale castle near Sintra* ▶

*Quinta de Monserrate, near Sintra*

The trip to Lisbon (see entry), the Portuguese capital, can be broken at Queluz (see entry) to see its palace and fine parks and gardens.

## Tavira

C7

Historical province: Algarve. District: Faro
Altitude: sea level. Population: 8000

Situation and Importance

The little town of Tavira, straddling the mouth of the Rio Gilão, or Rio Séqua, in the "sandy Algarve" part of the Algarve (see entry), has a Moorish look about it. Compared with other places on the Algarve it still has a certain restfulness, with tourism kept within reasonable bounds.

Tavira is the centre of the Algarve's tuna-fisheries, and has extensive salt-pans in the river estuary.

★Townscape

Tavira aquired its present appearance in the latter part of the 18th c., when it was almost completely rebuilt after the devastating 1755 earthquake, although in the narrow and picturesque little alleyways of the old town it has managed to retain something of its Moorish air. There is no intrusion by big hotels into the simple white houses on both sides of the Rio Gilão. These are interspersed instead by the many churches, most of them undistinguished, which set the seal on Tavira's townscape.

The Rua da Liberdade and the adjoining Praça da República to the north form the centre of Tavira. This is also the location for the town hall and the tourist information centre.

## Sights

Igreja da Misericórdia

The Igreja da Misericórdia is west of the tourist information centre on the Rua Galeria. Built in 1541 and restored again after the 1755 earthquake, it has a lovely Renaissance portal, and, inside, 18th c. azulejos (only open for concerts).

The Castro dos Mouros lies uphill from the Igreja da Misericórdia. The ruins of this old Moorish castle, in a garden setting, are privately-owned but can usually be visited. There is an exceptional view of Tavira from the tower in the ramparts.

Castro dos Mouros

Close by the castle ruins, the Santa Maria do Castelo church is originally Gothic, having been converted from a mosque. It too had to be completely rebuilt after the earthquake. The church choir holds the tombs of seven knights killed by the Moors in 1242 although a ceasefire had been agreed.

Igreja Santa Maria do Castelo

The Palácio da Galeria, a few hundred yards north of the church, puts on temporary art exhibitions.

Palácio da Galeria

The bridge over the Rio Gilão, near the Praça da República, is a 19th c. reconstruction based on its predecessors, although parts of the round arches are said to be of Roman origin.
   It is well worth crossing the bridge to enjoy from the other side the best view of Tavira.

Ponte

The Igreja do Carmo, on that side of the river in the northern part of town, dates from the 18th c. and has splendid choir-stalls, and fine talha dourada.

Igreja do Carmo

*Evening in Tavira*

## Surroundings of Tavira

★Ilha de Tavira  The 11km/7 mile long Ilha de Tavira lies offshore from Tavira, and boats sail there regularly in summer from the landing stage 2km/1¼ miles south-east of the town. There are campsites and restaurants on the island which has a broad sandy beach with good swimming.

Algarve  See entry

## Tomar  B5

Historical province: Ribatejo. District: Santarém
Altitude: 122m/400ft. Population: 15,000

Situation and Importance  Tomar is charmingly situated just north of the lower Tagus on its tributary, the Nabão, in the fertile Ribatejo landscape of central Portugal, and is very popular with tourists on account of its mighty Convent-Castle of the Knights of Christ.

Townscape  The little Rio Nabão divides this attractive small town into a west end and an east end, with the old centre around the Praça da República west of the river and a lovely park on a sandbank in the river.
A winding road leads past the chapel of Nossa Senhora da Conceição up to the castle of the Knights of Christ, above the west of the town.

## ★★Convento da Ordem de Cristo de Tomar

History of the Order  The Order of the Knights of Christ (Ordem de cavalharia de Nosso Senhor Jesús Cristo) was founded by King Dinis in 1317 for the purpose of "defend-

Convent of Knights of Christ

Convento da Ordem de Cristo de Tomar

1 Manueline doorway
2 Main choir
3 Chapterhouse
4 Manueline window

20 m

Claustro da Micha
Claustro da Hospedaria
Claustro dos Corvos
Claustro de Santa Bárbara
Claustro dos Felipes
Convent church
Sacristy
Templar church (Rotunda)
Claustro do Cemitério
Claustro da Lavagem
Entrance
Terrace
new Chapterhouse

© Baedeker

ing the faith, fighting the Moors and enlarging the Portuguese monarchy", following the dissolution in 1314 of the order of Knights Templar which had been established at Tomar since 1159. The new order flourished, particularly under its famous Grand Master Henry the Navigator (see Famous People).

The Order financed voyages of discovery to the west coast of Africa and thus began the process of colonial acquisition by the European nations. In the reign of King Manuel I (Grand Master from 1484) its possessions in Africa and the East Indies made it the wealthiest order in Christendom. The knightly order became a monastic order in 1523, was secularised in 1789 and dissolved in 1910.

In the 12th c., in order to defend the line of the Tagus, the Knights Templar built a castle high above the right bank of the Nabão, and some of this castle's walls, its keep and the round Templar church are still part of the complex.

The Order of the Knights of Christ was first based in Castro Marim (see Vila Real de Santo António), when it was founded in 1317, then moved to Tomar in 1356. As Grand Master, Henry the Navigator was responsible for the building around the Templar castle in the early 15th c. of the Claustro da Lavagem and Claustro do Cemitério. The Order's next flowering was under Manuel I, who around 1500 had the Church of the Knights of Christ added on to the Templar church, and had the Claustro de Santa Bárbara and the new Chapterhouse built. Although the Order waned in political significance in the 16th and 17th c. there was further building during this period in the convent precincts, and four more cloisters were added, the Claustro dos Felipes, Claustro dos Corvos, Claustro da Micha and Claustro da Hospedaria. The buildings were restored by the Counts of Tomar in the mid-19th c., and the green setting for the convent-castle was first landscaped in the 1930s.

History of the building

315

**Tomar**

Tour of the
complex

The entrance to the great complex of 12th to 17th c. buildings that go to make up the convent-castle of the Knights of Christ, high above Tomar, is through two gates of the old Templar castle. Passing through gardens to reach the terrace of the Templar Church, access to the interior of the convent is through the southern door of the Church of the Knights of Christ on the western end of the Templar building.

Templar Church

The crenellated Templar Church, or Rotunda, was begun in 1162 and modelled on the Church of the Holy Sepulchre in Jerusalem as a 16-sided polygon. This is supported by massive wall-pillars, one of which was later converted into a belfry, around a central octagon, or Charola, which was to hold the high altar. With the construction of the church of the Knights of Christ in the 16th c. the Charola became the choir of the new church.

All the extravagant embellishment of the interior – talha dourada, frescoes and statues – dates from the 16th c.

Knights of Christ
Church

The church of the Knights of Christ on the west end of the Templar church is one of Portugal's finest Manueline monuments. The work of João do Castilho, it was begun in 1515. Its exterior is sumptuously decorated. Statues of the prophets surround the portal on the southern façade, with the Virgin and Child under a baldachin in the centre. The west front is no less impressive, where the splendour of the ornate window of the Old Chapterhouse shows the Manueline style at its most accomplished (best view from the terrace of the Claustro de Santa Bárbara, see below).

Almost three-quarters of the church interior is taken up by the Coro Alto (the choirstalls are 19th c.), once reserved for the monks at prayer. The rest was originally intended to be the vestry but later became the chapterhouse, while the Templar Church served as the choir for the Knights of Christ Church.

Claustro do
Cemitério

The Gothic Claustro do Cemitério, or cemetery cloister, on the north-east of the Templar church, is the oldest of the convent cloisters, and has Mudejar azulejos. This is the resting place of Vasco da Gama's brother, Diogo da Gama, as well as other important members of the Order.

Claustro da
Lavagem

East of the Claustro do Cemitério is the two-storey Claustro da Lavagem, the "ablutions" cloister, which, like its neighbour, dates from the time of Henry the Navigator.

Claustro dos
Felipes

From the church of the Knights of Christ a richly ornamented doorway leads into the upper gallery of the Claustro dos Felipes, or Claustro de João III, a beautiful Late Renaissance building (1557–62). The terrace on the top of the cloister's two storeys affords a view over the whole of the convent. While the ground level gallery has Tuscan columns, the upper storey has Ionic pillars. The well-proportioned fountain in the courtyard dates from the 17th c.

A doorway on the east side of the Claustro dos Felipes leads into the so-called "New" Chapterhouse which remained unfinished and was destroyed by the collapse of the vaulting.

Claustro de Santa
Bárbara

The little early Renaissance cloister of Santa Bárbara is next to the Claustro dos Felipes and from it can be seen the detail of the magnificent Manueline window on the west façade of the Knights of Christ Church. The window is set between two convoluted masts around which twine coral, ropes, seaweed, anchor chains, cables and other stonework motifs associated with the sea. It is crowned with the Portuguese coat of arms and, above it all, the cross of the Order of Christ.

Other convent
buildings

To the north and west are three other cloisters. One of these, the Claustro da Hospedaria, or hostelry cloister, was, as its name suggests, for lodging

*Tomar: Castle of the Knights of Christ – the Templar Church* ▶

*Claustro dos Felipes . . .*                    *. . . and a Manueline window*

noble guests visiting the convent. The Claustro da Micha, or bread cloister
– where bread was handed out to the poor – contains a mission seminary
and military hospital, and is not normally open to the public. The same
applies to the Claustro dos Corvos, the cloister of the ravens, which used to
hold the convent kitchen, storerooms and monks' cells.

**Aqueduto dos Pegões**  The convent originally drew its water from springs and cisterns but from
the late 16th c., with the building of an aqueduct, the Aqueduto dos Pegões,
it was brought here from outlying springs in the north-east.

## Other sights in Tomar

**Igreja de São João Baptista**  The church of St John the Baptist stands in the centre of Tomar on the Praça
da República, where there is a statue of Gualdim Pais, the Templar Grand
Master who founded Tomar in 1162. The church, which was built about
1490, has an elegant Manueline doorway and contains six pictures from the
16th c. Portuguese school.

**Synagogue**  The 15th c. synagogue a few hundred yards south of the Praça da Repúblic
contains a small Jewish museum.

**Capela de Santa Iria**  Eastward across the old bridge, the Ponte Velha, on the other side of the Rio
Nabão, is the Capela de Santa Iria, with a fine Renaissance doorway (1536).

**Igreja de Santa Maria do Olival**  The Rue de Santa Iria leads south from here to the Igreja de Santa Maria do
Olival on the edge of town. This was long the seat of the Grand Chapter of
the Templars and later the Knights of Christ, the mother church of all the
Order's churches in the colonies. All that is left of the first church building
(c. 1160) is the porch and doorway. The interior of the former Templar
church is overwhelmingly Renaissance, and contains the tombs of many of
the Order's Knights and Masters.

In the north-east part of town, near the path up to the Knights of Christ Castle, is the 16th c. chapel of Nossa Senhora da Conceição, a lovely Renaissance building with delicately carved Corinthian capitals.

The pilgrimage chapel of Nossa Senhora da Piedade is farther north, on a hill above the town. It can be reached on foot up a flight of 286 steps, flanked by gardens. Built in 1613, it has azuelejo decoration in the interior. On the way up we pass São Gregório, an octagonal chapel with a shingle-roofed gallery all round it. Originally Manueline, it was later remodelled as Baroque.

## Surroundings of Tomar

Castelo de Bode (see Abrantes) stands in attractive surroundings 13km/ 8 miles south-east of Tomar.

Torres Novas is an industrial town 25km/15½ miles south-west of Tomar. The ruins of its 14th c. castle, and its Misericórdia church, with a fine Renaissance doorway, are worth seeing.

# Torre de Moncorvo      C3

Historical province: Trás-os-Montes. District: Bragança
Altitude: 390m/1279ft. Population: 3000

The ancient little town of Torre de Moncorvo, or Moncorvo for short, is situated in a vast dry landscape dotted with fruit groves and vegetable plots in the north of the Serra do Roboredo (800m/2625ft; iron-mining), roughly halfway between Bragança and Guarda. Its "cobertas", or sugared almonds, are a local delicacy.

The town has a number of handsome old houses bearing coats of arms. The 19th c. town hall stands on the site of one of King Dinis's castles.

## Sights

The parish church is a 16th c. three-aisled Renaissance building.
Inside there are beautiful talha dourada and a fine Gothic triptych of carved wood with scenes from the life of the Virgin's parents, St Anne and St Joachim. The choir has a coffered ceiling.

Also worth seeing is the Igreja da Misericódia, near the Largo do Castelo, which has an exceptionally fine Gothic granite pulpit.

## Surroundings of Torre de Moncorvo

The village of Vila Nova de Foz Côa (alt. 439m/1440ft; pop. 2500) is about 16km/10 miles south-west of Torre de Moncorvo and has a Manueline church (remodelled in the 18th c.) and a fine pelourinho.

About 18km/11 miles farther west there is a Romanesque church and some interesting castle ruins in the village of Freixo de Numão.

# Torres Vedras      A5

Historical province: Estremadura. District: Lisboa
Altitude: 66m/217ft. Population: 11,000

**Trás-os-Montes**

Situation and Importance
The ancient town of Torres Vedras, on the left bank of the Rio Sizandro, is about 60km/37 miles north of Lisbon, in a region famous for its wine.

It has a place in British military history as the base for Wellington's Torres Vedras Lines, fortified to defend Lisbon during the Peninsular War. Otherwise its rather unassuming townscape means that most tourists only pause briefly on their way through.

Sights
Features of interest in the town are the 16th c. churches of São Pedro and São Gonçalvo, a conventual church. Above the town are the ruins of an old Moorish castle, the Castelo dos Mouros, from which there is a good view. King Manuel added a handsome battlemented gateway after the reconquest of the town.

Termas dos Cucos
The little spa of Termas dos Cucos, which specialises in rheumatic ailments, is about 2km/1¼ miles east of the town.

## Trás-os-Montes                                                C/D 3

Historical province: Trás-os-Montes
Districts: Bragança, Vila Real, Viseu and Guarda
Area: 11,000 sq.km/4246 sq.miles
Population: 500,000. Chief town: Bragança

Location and General
The rugged mountain province of Trás-os-Montes, or "beyond the mountains", lies in the extreme north-east corner of Portugal, bounded on the north and east by Spain, on the west and south-west by Minho and Douro Litoral, and on the south by Beira Alta.

Because of its remoteness Trás-os-Montes has kept many of the old customs and traditions. The famous "romarias", which take place at many locations and which are very popular with visitors, are accompanied by processions in colourful national costume.

Geology
Geologically the province is part of the Spanish Meseta, which here reaches heights of between 1300m/4250ft and 1500m/4900ft (Serra do Mogadouro), and is fissured by broad tectonic collapse zones.

Climate
Its relative distance from the Atlantic reduces the moderating oceanic influence on the climate. This is a region of raw winds and widely fluctuating temperatures, marked by precipitation (often as snow in winter) that decreases towards the east.

Population and Economy
The host of archaeological evidence shows that Trás-os-Montes, like Minho province, is an area of prehistoric settlement. Now as in the past population is clustered in the fertile valleys (especially the upper Douro valley, see entry), where the soil is good for growing grapes and fruit. The bare, dry arid plateaux provide grazing for sheep and goats. In addition to agriculture the region has a long tradition of handicrafts such as weaving, lace and pottery, as well as yielding small amounts of gold and wolfram.

## Valença do Minho                                                B2

Historical province: Minho. District: Viana do Castelo
Altitude: 72m/236ft. Population: 2500

Situation and Importance
The ancient little town of Valença do Minho lies on commanding heights above the left bank of the River Minho, Miño in Spanish, which here forms the frontier between Spain and Portugal (frontier crossing). Nowadays there is hardly any sense of the past rivalry between the two states and

Valença do Minho

Rio Minho

**Valença do Minho**

**Fortaleza**

© Baedeker

1 Capela de São Sebastião
2 Baluarte do Faro (bastion)
3 Igreja Matriz (main church)
4 Church of Santa Maria dos Anjos (St Mary of the Angels)
5 Pousada (hotel)

there is a lively cross-border traffic between Valença do Minho and Tui on the other side of the river. The Spaniards come to Valença do Minho chiefly to purchase cloth goods, especially terry towelling.

The old core of Valença do Minho is enclosed by the ramparts of its massive walls. Although the town was always strongly fortified, the present Fortaleza, or fort, is 17th c., in the Vauban style. From various points on the walls there are superb views over the "new" town, some way below, the Minho valley and the mountains of Galicia.

★Townscape

Narrow alleys between whitewashed house criss-cross the old town, and this is where the textile shops can be found. Buildings worth seeing are the Capela de São Sebastião, the late-13th c. Igreja de Santa Maria dos Anjos, and the Igreja Matriz, which was founded as a collegiate church by João I in about 1400.

The railway station, or estação, in the lower-lying new part of town, is the terminus for the "19th c. train", an old steam locomotive with carriages from various European countries dating between 1875 and 1891, which runs regularly along the Minho line between Valença do Minho and Oporto.

Estação

## Surroundings of Valença do Minho

The Monte do Faro (566m/1857ft; chapel) is about 7km/4½ miles south-east of the town, on the left bank of the Minho. From the top there are views far into the Minho valley, as well as eastward to the Peneda-Gerês National Park (see entry) and westward to the Atlantic.

Monte do Faro

See entry

Monção

See entry

Caminha

## Viano do Castelo

B3

Historical province: Minho. District: Viana do Castelo
Altitude: 20m/65ft. Population: 15,000

The district capital of Viana do Castelo, charmingly situated at the mouth of the Rio Lima below Monte de Santa Luzia, is an important harbour on this part of the Portuguese Atlantic coast, here called the Costa Verde. Although it has some industry – textiles, timber, fish-processing and shipbuilding – its attractive townscape and good beaches also make it popular with tourists.

Situation and Importance

**Viano do Castelo**

*Valença do Minho: the stout surrounding walls (see page 321)*

History

Originally a Greek trading post, and still a modest little port in the Middle Ages, Viana achieved prosperity and importance at the time of the great voyages of discovery in the reign of Manuel I, especially on account of the then very profitable cod fisheries off the coast of Newfoundland.

In the 19th c., during the conflict between the Liberals and the monarchy, it sided with the Royalists and thus earned its charter from Queen Maria II and was henceforth known as Viana do Castelo, having previously been called Viana da Foz do Lima.

★Townscape

Its many handsome Manueline and Renaissance mansions and palaces, with their ornate granite façades, recall the splendours of the town's past.

Largo 5 de Outubro (car parking), on the Rio Lima, makes a good starting point for a walk round Viana do Castelo. Walk a short way upstream, then turn north, along the Rua S. Cabral, to the cathedral.

## Sights

Sé

The cathedral was built in the first half of the 15th c. and substantially altered in the 19th c. The two crenellated towers flanking the façade are Romanesque. The interior has fine polychrome wood carving, mainly 17th c. The Casa dos Velhos, north of the cathedral, is a 15th c. building with a distinct Galician look. Opposite the cathedral stands the Casa de João Jácome de Luna, mid-16th c. and with sculpture probably from a previous building on the south façade.

★Praça da República

Just north of here is the Praça da República, one of Portugal's most picturesque squares, with the broad basins of its Renaissance fountain dating from 1559 in the centre.

The old town hall, the Antigos Paços do Concelho on the east side of the square, is an early 16th c. granite building, now used for exhibitions, where bread used to be sold in its arcades at street level.

1 Casa de João
  Jácome de Luna
2 Casa dos Velhos
3 Antigos Paços
  do Concelho
4 Igreja da
  Misericórdia

The Igreja da Misericórdia, rebuilt in the 18th c., is on the north side of the square and has fine talha dourada and 17th c. ajulejos in the interior. Adjoining the church is the Misericord Hospice, a Flemish Renaissance-style building begun in 1589.

North along the Rua C. dos Reis is the present town hall, the Câmara Municipal, a mansion begun in the 16th c. and completely remodelled in the 18th c. Next comes the Convento de Santa Ana, now the Hospital da Caridade, a former Benedictine convent dating, with its Manueline tower, from the 16th c. Its church has rich talha dourada decoration.

Convento de
Santa Ana

The walk round the town continues westward through the Avenida da Carreira and the Rua S. Tiago to Nossa Senhora da Agonia, the chapel of Our Lady in Sorrow, a place of pilgrimage approached by a Baroque flight of steps. Begun in the mid-18th c., the chapel did not have a belfry until the late 19th c.

Nossa Senhora da
Agonia

In the south corner of the broad Campo do Castelo, south of the chapel, is the Castelo de São Tiago da Barra, built in the 16th c. to defend the harbour. The two towers were added in the 18th c.

Castelo de São
Tiago da Barra

Back at the square below Nossa Senhora da Agonia and then past the well-shaded Praça do Gen. Barbosa the walk continues to the Igreja de São Domingos which was built in Renaissance style between 1566 and 1575 as the church of a Dominican abbey. According to the local guidebook the talha dourada altar in the Nossa Senhora do Rósario side-chapel is the finest in Europe.

Igreja de São
Domingos

The municipal museum diagonally opposite is housed in the 18th c. mansion of the Barbarosa Macieis family, and has displays of furniture from Portuguese India (17th c.) and Moorish Spain, as well as an important collection of 18th c. Portuguese glazed earthenware.

Museu Municipal

The Rua de Altamira leading down to the river soon brings this walk round the town back to its starting point.

*Viana do Castelo: Old Town Hall*

## Surroundings of Viana do Castelo

Igreja de Santa Luzia

The Monte de Santa Luzia (250m/820ft) is about 5km/3 miles north-east of the town, topped by its 19th c. Neo-Byzantine church of Santa Luzia, a place of pilgrimage. It can be reached by car and by a funicular which leaves from near the station. It is worth making the trip if only for the magnificent view.

There are traces of a Celtic-Iberian settlement just north of the church which was inhabited until the 4th c. A.D.

Ponte de Lima

See Ponte da Barca

Costa Verde

For other places around Viana do Castelo see Costa Verde.

## Vila do Conde                                                                 B3

Historical province: Douro Litoral. District: Porto
Altitude: sea level. Population: 15,000

Situation and Importance

Vila do Conde, "town of the Counts", is about 20km/12 miles north of Oporto on the left bank of the mouth of the Rio Ave. Its people get their living from shipbuilding, cotton manufacture and, traditionally, pillow-lace making, while many other businesses have established themselves around the little town, which is also a seaside resort. Its old town centre makes it a favourite excursion for tourists from Póvoa de Varzim (see entry), a few miles to the north, which it now almost adjoins.

## Sights

Mosteiro de Santa Clara

The imposing bulk of the Monastery, or Mosteiro, of Santa Clara looms over the town. All that remains of the original monastery, founded in 1318, is the Gothic fortress church, still virtually unchanged. The monastery building, on the other hand, which looks more like a palace, dates from the end of the 18th c. and now houses a school.

The west face of the Gothic church has a beautiful rose window, while the interior, in the form of a single aisle, has the magnificent 16th c. Renaissance tombs of the founders of the monastery, Dom Afonso Sanches, illegitimate son of King Dinis I, and Dona Tareja Martins, and their children. The carved coffered ceiling and the choir screen are also worth looking at.

There is a good view from the square in front of the church over the town and the estuary.

The convent gets its water supply from an 18th c. aqueduct (7km/4½ miles long, with 999 arches) which runs from Póvoa de Varzim.

Aqueduto

The fortified parish church, the Igreja Matriz, is in the old part of town and was built in the 16th c. to a cruciform groundplan. It has a Manueline doorway and 17th c. belfry. Its gilded wood pulpit dating from the 17th and 18th c. is well worth seeing. The pelourinho in the little church square is 16th c., and the sword stands for justice.

Igreja Matriz

The 16th c. town hall, bearing Manuel I's coat of arms, is on the north of the square.

The Centro de Artesanato, the arts and crafts centre a few hundred yards east of the parish church, displays the products of Vila do Conde's traditional pillow-lace making.

Centro de Artesanato

The 17th c. Forte de São João Bapatista, with its five bastions, is outside the centre of town at the mouth of the Rio Ave.

Forte de São João Baptista

*Vila do Conde: the parish church . . .*     *. . . and pillory*

## Surroundings of Vila do Conde

Azurara — The little fishing port of Azurara is just 2km/1¼ miles south of Vila do Conde on the right bank of the river. It has an interesting 16th c. Manueline fortified church, which also has a pelourinho in its square.

Cividade de Bagunte — The remains of the Celtic settlement of Cividade de Bagunte, where there have been some beautiful stone and bronze finds, are about 6km/4 miles east of Vila do Conde, not far from where the Rio Este joins the Rio Ave.

Rio Mau — Rio Mau is barely 10km/6 miles north-east of Vila do Conde. Its Romanesque church of São Cristóvão, built for a convent founded in 1151, has interesting sculptural decoration.

Rates — Rates, 4km/2½ miles north-east of Rio Mau, is worth a detour for its important Romanesque church of São Pedro. It was built by French architects for Henry of Burgundy at the beginning of the 12th c., replacing an earlier church on the spot where St Pedro of Rates is believed to have been martyred by Roman soldiers in the 1st c. A.D. Subsequently altered in parts, the church still has rich 12th c. sculptural decoration.

# Vila Real                                                            C3

Historical province: Trás-os-Montes. District: Vila Real
Altitude: 422m/1385ft. Population: 14,000

Situation and Importance — Vila Real is an attractive old episcopal city and district capital, amid orchards and vineyards, 100km/62 miles east of Oporto and on the north side of the Serra de Marão, where the Rio Corgo joins with the Rio Cabril. It still has many fine 15th to 18th c. patrician houses. The black pottery from the locality, especially Biselhães, is famous.

Also produced nearby, and well-known throughout Europe, is the wine called Mateus rosé, in its characteristically shaped bottles.

Sights — The town's main shopping street and thoroughfare is the Avenida de Carvalho Aráujo, where Vila Real's main sights are also to be found. The birthplace of the navigator Diogo Cão, who discovered the mouth of the Congo, is at number 17, an Italian Renaissance building. The town hall is early 19th c.

The 14th c. Gothic Cathedral, or Sé, was originally the church of a Dominican convent, and still has Romanesque capitals from the first church on the site.

The 16th c. church of São Pedro is richly decorated with 17th c. polychrome azulejos and has a gilded coffered ceiling in the choir.

View — There are fine views from the hill above the town, once occupied by a castle, and from the Calvário (460m/1509ft), with the 16th c. church of Santo António.

## Surroundings of Vila Real

★Mateus — Mateus is a village about 4km/2½ miles east of Vila Real, and owes its fame to its rosé wine and the manor of the Counts of Vila Real, the Solar de Mateus, considered to be a perfect example of Portuguese Baroque. Although the Mangualde family still live there, parts of it are open to the public. Inside the palace there are magnificent wood ceilings as well as valuable furniture, carpets, paintings and silverware, and an interesting porcelain collection. The small private museum contains correspondence between members of the Mangualde family and royalty and other famous people, as well as engravings for Camões' Lusiades.

*Vila Real: Avenida de Carvalho Aráujo*

*Solar de Mateus in Vila Real . . .*          *. . . and Thuja Allee in palace garden*

327

However, the beauty of the gardens actually surpasses that of the Solar de Mateus, and the ancient tunnel formed by topiaried thuya is a minor work of art. The vineyards from which come the grapes to make the famous "Mateus" begin immediately behind the gardens.

Panóais

There are the remains of a Lusitanian/Roman temple of Serapis, with several rock inscriptions, at Panóais, 7km/4½ miles south-east of Vila Real.

Termas de Pedras Salgadas

Termas de Pedras Salgadas is a spa 35km/22 miles north of Vila Real on the Chaves road which is much visited for its radioactive springs and pleasant park.

Vila Marim

The village of Vila Marim about 4km/2¼ miles west of Vila Real has an interesting 14th c. granite tower, the Torre de Quintela.

Serra do Marão

There is a beautiful drive of 50km/30 miles westward from Vila Real through the wild and romantic Serra do Marão to Amarante (see entry).

Peso da Régua

Peso da Régua (see Lamego) is a wine-producing and trading centre about 25km/15½ miles south of Vila Real.

## Vila Real de Santo António    C7

Historical province: Algarve. District: Faro
Altitude: sea level. Population: 13,000

Situation and Importance

The little frontier town of Vila Real de Santo António lies on the right bank of the Guadiana which is navigable as far as Mértola. There are regular ferries to Ayamonte, the Spanish port on the other side, although a bridge over the Guadiana is scheduled to be built.

Vila Real de Santo António has become one of the largest fishing and commercial ports on the Algarve, exporting copper and tin, and processing the tuna caught between April and July.

Townscape

The town was founded in 1774 by the Marquês de Pombal on the site of Santo António da Avenilha which had been destroyed by a tidal wave at the beginning of the 17th c. He had it laid out like a chessboard, and settled it with fisherfolk from Aveiro (see entry).

The town centre is the Praça do Marquês de Pombal, paved with a black and white mosaic radiating from the obelisk that is a monument to José I, and lined with inviting street cafés.

## Surroundings of Vila Real de Santo António

Algarve

There are very enjoyable drives along the Algarve coast to Cape St Vincent (see Algarve).

Monte Gordo

See Algarve

★Castro Marim

Castro Marim, which overlooks the Guadiana plain about 4km/2½ miles north-west of Vila Real de Santo António, gets its name from the closeness of its castle to the sea. It was the seat of the Order of the Knights of Christ, founded in 1319, until this was transferred to Tomar (see entry) in 1334.

The castle ruins, which tower over the village to the north, date from this brief and glorious period in its history. The castle was originally late 13th c. and then extended by the Knights of Christ in 1319. From its towers and ramparts there is a lovely view of the village.

The Capela Nossa Senhora dos Martires near the castle is 18th c.

Alcoutim

Alcoutim, 40km/25 miles north of Vila Real de Santo António, is also on the Guadiana, where it has moorings for yachts as well as other vessels. Its small mid-13th c. castle is due for restoration in the near future.

*Vila Real de Santo António: Praça do Marquês de Pombal*

*Alcoutim by the Guadiana*

## Vila Viçosa                                                         C6

Historical province: Alto Alentejo. District: Évora
Altitude: 422m/1385ft. Population: 4000

Situation and
Importance

Vila Viçosa is about 55km/34 miles north-east of Évora, on the slopes of hills covered with orchards. It was at one time the seat of the Dukes of Bragança, and several kings from the same house, but with the abolition of the monarchy in 1910 it declined into provincial obscurity.

## Sights

★Paço Ducal

The main attraction, on the way into the town from Borba, is the Paço Ducal, the palace of the Dukes of Bragança. Built in the 16th and 17th c. on the remains of Moorish, possibly even Roman buildings, for centuries it hosted a brilliant court and was a hub of intellectual life. In 1640 João IV was the first of the Dukes of Bragança to ascend the Portuguese throne. Although Lisbon then became the seat of the monarchy João IV and his successors continued making frequent visits to Vila Viçosa. The marble façade, stretching over 100m/330ft, has the strict articulation of the Italian Renaissance.

There are guided tours round the palace, which is full of objets d'art from the 16th to the 19th c., although the most valuable were taken to the new quarters in Lisbon in the mid-17th. What remains is quite grand enough – painted ceilings and family portraits, 17th c. azulejos, tapestries, porcelain, a well-stocked armoury and a collection of coaches. The chapel, which has a 16th c. triptych, is particularly worth seeing. The inner courtyard appears to have been modelled on a cloister.

Terreiro do Paço

The spacious Terreiro do Paço, or palace square, in front of the palace has an equestrian statue of King João IV in the centre, and before the palace was built served at times as a bullring.

On the east side of the square, opposite the palace, is the church of the former Augustinian convent (17th/18th c.), with a richly decorated interior. It contains the tombs of the Dukes of Bragança; their spouses were interred in the Antigo Convento das Chagas, built in the 16th c. and restored in the 18th, which is on the south side of the square.

Porta dos Nós

The Porta dos Nós is the eyecatching "knot gate" north of the palace on the Borba road. It was part of the old 16th c. wall round the town and is the entrance to the 5,000-acre Tapada, once the royal deer-park, where the Portuguese royal family hunted until early this century.

Igreja de Santa
Cruz

Adjoining the 16th c. Igreja de Santa Cruz in the town centre is a small museum of sacred art.

Castelo

The massive battlemented castle, or Castelo, that looms over the town, was built by King Dinis in the 13th c. and reinforced with bastions in the 17th. Within the ramparts can be found the Renaissance da Conceição church and the archaeological section of the Bragança museum.

Pelourinho

There is a 16th c. pelourinho on the main road near the castle.

## Surroundings of Vila Viçosa

Alandroal

The village of Alandroal, with the ruins of one of King Dinis's 13th c. castles, is about 10km/6 miles south of Vila Viçosa.

Terena

Above Terena, 10km/6 miles farther south, are the ruins of another medieval castle, with panoramic views.

*Vila Viçosa: Paço Ducal*

| | |
|---|---|
| See entry | Borba |
| See entry | Estremoz |
| See Estremoz | Redondo |

## Viseu C4

Historical province: Beira Alta. District: Viseu
Altitude: 540m/1770ft. Population: 21,000

The old district capital of Viseu is on the left bank of the Rio Pavia, set in woodland in the famous wine-producing Dão region. It is an important centre for agriculture (grain, fruit, livestock) and crafts (lace, carpets, black pottery).

Situation and Importance

In the 16th c. Viseu had one of Portugal's most important schools of painting, foremost among them being the landscape painter Gaspar Vaz (d. about 1568) and Vasco Fernandes, known as Grão-Vasco (*c.* 1480–1543), who was born here.

Its handsome Renaissance and Baroque mansions and palaces, narrow alleys paved with granite sets, flights of steps and intriguing corners lend Viseu a particular charm.

★Townscape

## Sights

The Praça da República, in the centre with the town hall on its west side, is a good place to start a walk round the town.

Praça da República

The Baroque church of São Francisco, on the south side of the square, has rich azulejo and talha dourada decoration.

Igreja de São Francisco

The works of art, pictures, ceramics, porcelain, furniture, etc., collected by the connoisseur Almeida Moreira are on show in the Almeida Moreira museum north of the Praça da República.

Museu de Almeida Moreira

North from here, through the Porta do Soar, built in the town wall in the 15th c., is the old town, and at its heart, the Praça da Sé, where it is thought that in prehistoric times there was already a Celtic-Iberian fort.

Praça da Sé

A broad flight of steps leads up from the square to the church of the Misericórdia, a building of pure Baroque, its granite pilasters standing out against whitewashed walls.

Igreja da Misericórdia

# Viseu

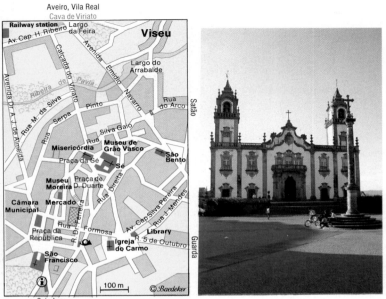

Viseu: Igreja da Misericórdia

★Sé

The Romanesque and Gothic Cathedral, or Sé, opposite the Misericord Church, was first built in the 12th c., remodelled in the 16th and extended in the 18th.

The interior was transformed into a hall church in the 16th c. by the reconstruction of the vaulting, which is Manueline but supported by Gothic pillars. Above the monumental Baroque high altar is a 14th c. figure of the Virgin. The chapterhouse contains a remarkable treasury of sacred art.

The ground floor of the cloister is Renaissance, the gallery in the upper storey having been added in the 17th c.

★Museu de Grão Vasco

The Grão Vasco, or "great Vasco" Museum is in the Paço dos Três Escalões, the Renaissance palace, remodelled in the 18th c., which adjoins the Cathedral. The museum has some 13th to 16th c. sculpture but primarily shows the work of the Viseu School of painting, including "St Peter" and "Crucifixion" by Vasco Fernandes, etc. There are also works by more modern Portuguese artists (19th and 20th c.), as well as by Spanish, French, Flemish and Dutch masters, together with ceramics (16th–18th c.), carpets and furniture (17th and 18th c.).

Rua Direita

From behind the Cathedral little streets lead down to Viseu's main street, now largely pedestrianised, the Rua Direita with particularly lovely 16th to 18th c. houses, some of them with wrought-iron grilles.

To get back to this little walk's starting point go south down the Rua Direita then right into the Rua Formosa, ending up back at the Praça da República.

Cava de Viriato

The Cava de Viriato, outside the town centre and in the northern part of Viseu, is a big pentagonal-shaped park where there was once a Lusitanian-Roman camp. There is a monument to the Lusitanian leader Viriathus who

*Viseu: the Cathedral*

was supposed to have made his heroic stand against the Romans here in the 2nd c. B.C.

## Surroundings of Viseu

A very attractive trip is the 40km/25 miles south-west through the scenic rugged hills of the Serra do Caramulo (up to 1071m/3514ft) to the charmingly situated hillside health resort of Caramulo (800m/2625ft). Its main attraction is the Museu do Caramulo, with exhibits ranging from medieval art, furniture, tapestries, porcelain and ceramics, to a remarkable collection of works by Portuguese and other European artists, particularly of the 19th and 20th c., including works by such famous painters as Picasso, Dalí, Miró, Chagall, Léger, Dufy and Vlaminck. The exhibition on the ground floor traces the development of the car since 1902 (about 50 veteran and vintage vehicles).

★Caramulo

The little town of Mangualde about 13km/8 miles south-east of Viseu has a 17th c. palace of the Counts of Anadia in the middle of a rather wild park. The pilgrimage church of Nossa Senhora do Castelo (628m/2060ft) stands on a hill with a view about 1.5km/1 mile to the north.

Mangualde

333

# Practical Information from A to Z

## Accommodation

See Camping, Hotels, Pousadas, Youth Hostels

## Airlines

Air Portugal (TAP)                                                    Lisbon
Praça Marquês de Pombal 3A; tel. 57 50 20
Lisbon airport: tel. 8 48 91 85

British Airways
Avenida da Liberdade 36; tel. 346 09 31

Air Portugal (TAP)                                                    Faro
Rua D. Francisco Gomes 8; tel. 80 32 49
Faro airport: tel. 2 42 01

British Airways, c/o TAP

Air Portugal (TAP)                                                    Oporto
Praça Mouzinho de Albuquerque 105; tel. 69 98 41
Oporto airport: tel. 9 48 19 38

Rua de Júlio Dinis 778/II; tel. 69 45 75                             British Airways

Air Portugal (TAP)                                                    Madeira
Avenida Dr António José de Almeida 17, Funchal; tel. 3 01 51
Funchal airport: tel. 5 23 62

Air Portugal (TAP)                                                    Azores
Rua Rio de Janeiro 25–27, Angra do Heroísmo, Terceira; tel. 2 44 89

Air Portugal (TAP)
Avenida Infante D. Henrique 55, Ponta Delgada, São Miguel; tel. 2 62 01/4

## Air Portugal (TAP) outside Portugal

1801 McGill College, Suite 1410                                       Canada
Montreal, P.Q.; tel. (514) 849 42 17

151 Bloor Street West, Suite 450
Toronto, Ontario; tel. (416) 964 07 83

19 Regent Street                                                      United Kingdom
London SW1Y 4LR; tel. (0171) 839 1031/2

Room 25, Level 7, International Airport
Manchester; tel. (0161) 499 21 61

521 Fifth Avenue                                                      United States
New York, N.Y. 10175; tel. (212) 661 00 35

◄ *Beach of Armação de Péra on the Algarve*

## Air Services

**Air routes** ——

### Railways

—— **Main lines**
—— **Branch lines**

© Baedeker

# Air Travel

Air Portugal (TAP) operates a number of Portuguese mainland domestic flights daily between Lisbon and Oporto and Lisbon and Faro.

   LAR, the regional airline, also operates scheduled flights serving Lisbon, Oporto, Chaves, Bragança, Vila Real, Viseu, Covilhã, Coimbra, Faro and Portimão; these can be booked through TAP.

*Portuguese Mainland*

There are several flights a day between Lisbon and Funchal (Madeira), and several a week between Oporto and Funchal. There is also a daily service from Funchal to the little island of Porto Santo.

*Mainland/Madeira*

TAP has several flights a day from Lisbon to Ponta Delgada (São Miguel), and a number of flights a week to Terceira and Horta (Faial). Weekly services also operate between Oporto and Ponta Delgada and Oporto and Horta.

   The local airline SATA operates light planes on inter-island flights in the Azores.

*Mainland/Azores*

There are a number of flights a week between Funchal and Ponta Delgada.

*Madeira/Azores*

# Beaches

The sign for a beach that is supervised is a green arrow and the words "Area Concessionada", while a red rectangular sign with a double arrow and the words "Praia Não Vigiada" means the beach is unsupervised. Coastal areas where swimming can be dangerous have a round red sign with a red arrow and the word "Danger".

   Supervised beaches use flags to show when it is safe to go swimming. A red flag means it is forbidden to enter the sea, even close to the coast for paddling; a yellow flag means no swimming, and a green flag indicates that paddling and swimming are safe. A blue/white chequered flag means the beach is temporarily unsupervised.

*Beach signs*

The following list gives the major beaches on the Portuguese mainland, numbered as on the map on page 338.

1 Moledo do Minho
  Fine sand, dunes (on this part of the coast the climate is rather raw); restaurant.

**Costa Verde**

2 Vila Praia de Ancora
  Fine sand, dunes; restaurant.

3 Viana do Castelo
  South of the Rio Lima beaches of fine sand – probably the best on the Costa Verde – shallow, dunes; restaurants.

4 Esposende
  Lagoon, sandbanks, the long sandy beach is often better for walks than for swimming and sunbathing because of the wind; swimming can be more sheltered in the Rio Cávado estuary.

5 Ofir
  Fine sand, shallow, woods; restaurant, growing tourist centre.

6 Póvoa de Varzim
  Sandy beach, dirty in parts; several restaurants; outlook industrial rather than scenic.

7 Vila do Conde
  Sandy beach, some cliffs, on the whole more attractive than Póvoa de Varzim beach; restaurants.

# Bathing Beaches in Portugal

(Mainland)

- ● Costa Verde
- ● Costa de Prata
- ○ Costa do Sol
- ○ Costa do Lisboa
- ○ Costa Dourada
- ○ Costa do Algarve

National Parks

© Baedeker

8 Miramar
Sandy beach, shallow, rather like the North Sea; several restaurants.

9 Espinho
Flat sandy beach, high surf sometimes; several restaurants.

10 Praia de São Jacinto
Fine sand, dunes, woods.

**Costa de Prata**

11 Palheiros de Mira
Sandy beach, dirty in parts.

12 Figueira da Foz
Flat sandy beach on the main road, very crowded in the high season, high surf sometimes – Figueira da Foz, with Nazaré, is the largest resort on this coast; several restaurants.

13 Pedrógão
Flat sandy beach, some rocks, good surf; fishing harbour.

14 Praia da Vieira
Fine sand, surf; several restaurants.

15 São Pedro de Muel
Fine sand, shallow, rocks, one of the most pleasant places for bathing on this coast; several restaurants.

16 Nazaré
Sandy beach, lying beside the main road; it is necessary to book a place early in the high season, water can be polluted; several restaurants.

17 São Martinho do Porto
Deep bay with calm water, dunes separate the bay from the open sea; scuba diving; several restaurants.

18 Peniche
Nearby sandy beach, shallow, rocks; scuba diving; several restaurants; fishing harbour.

19 Praia de Santa Cruz
Fine sand, good surf, dunes, cliffs and coves; restaurant.

20 Ericeira
Flat sandy beaches, rocks, cliffs, pleasant swimming and sunbathing but very crowded at weekends; several restaurants; fishing harbour.

21 Praia Grande
Flat sandy beach, cliffs; very busy at weekend; several restaurants.

22 Praia do Guincho
Fine sandy bay near road, pinewoods in background, but very over-crowded in high season; restaurants.

**Costa do Sol**

23 Cascais/Estoril
Small bays with flat beaches of fine sand extend out from these two resorts, which have merged to become one, rocks; very crowded in fine weather; water sports; pigeon shooting; restaurants.

24 Costa da Caparica
A long expanse of dunes stretches southward from here, with particu-larly fine beaches at the southern end; restaurants.

**Costa de Lisboa**

25 Sesimbra
Small sandy beach extending directly from the resort, very busy at weekends; scuba diving; fishing boats; several restaurants.

26 Portinho da Arrábida
Beaches in sheltered scenic coves, rocks, quiet beaches at the foot of Serra do Arróbida; several restaurants; fishing harbour.

**Beaches**

*Praia do Guincho on the Costa do Sol*

27 Tróia
Wooded peninsula, broad beaches of fine sand (the best are well apart from the hotels); scuba diving; several restaurants; ferry to Setúbal.

**Costa Dourada**

28 Porto Covo
Flat sandy beach, rocks, heavy surf; several restaurants; fishing harbour.

29 Vila Nova de Milfontes
Attractive long sandy beach, dunes; several restaurants.

Although there are no more big resorts on the rest of the Costa Dourada there are plenty of pretty little coves with a beach, such as Zambujeira do Mar and Praia de Odeceixe; some stretches of beach acquire impromptu bars in summer.

**Algarve**

30 Aljezur
Flat sandy beach, rocks, dunes, good surf; restaurant.

31 Sagres
Flat beaches of fine sand, as yet uncrowded, but quite windy; good scuba diving; restaurants; submarine caves.
There is good surfing at Beliche beach, 5km/3 miles north-west of Sagres, with a path leading down to a half-mile long stretch of beach; Praia do Martinhal, 2km/1¼ miles east of Sagres is another quite good beach: half a mile of white beach with dunes, protected by the harbour. It is also possible to swim at Zavial, further east, where there is a flat beach of fine sand with no rocks.

32 Salema/Burgau
Salema has a flat sandy beach about half a mile long where there are usually some fishing boats as well, cliffs; several restaurants; good surfing possible.

*Algarve: the beach at Tavira . . .*          *. . . and at Cabanas*

A mile or so further east there is a sandy beach at Burgau; fishing harbour; restaurants; surfing for beginners.

33 Praia da Luz
Broad sandy beach, rocks; scuba diving and various other water sports; several resaurants – beach also very good for children.

34 Lagos
Long sandy beach in Lagos, many others close by (e.g. Praia da Dona Ana, west of Lagos at the Hotel Golfinho), rocks; scuba diving; several restaurants; fishing harbour.
Meia Praia, east of Lagos, has one of the Algarve's longest beaches; good surfing.

35 Alvor
Flat sandy beach, rocks; tourist complex,; several restaurants; water sports also at Três Irmãos beach, just to the east (surfing suitable for beginners).

36 Praia da Rocha
Closely packed beach in the high season, picturesque rocks (road runs along top of cliff); scuba diving; several restaurants.

37 Carvoeiro
Sandy little cove, crowded in high season; a few fishing boats, rocks; several restaurants.

38 Armação de Pêra
Very long beach of fine sand, and relatively uncrowded compared with other Algarve resorts, dunes; scuba diving; restaurants.
Bathing is also possible farther west at Senhora da Rocha where there are also caves to be explored.

39 Albufeira
Beaches of fine sand, rocks, cliffs; scuba diving, several restaurants;

fishing harbour. The beach in Albufeira is very overcrowded in the high season but there is more chance of finding some space further east at, for instance, the Praia da Oura.

40 Olhos de Agua (Praia da Falesia)
   Flat beach of fine sand, rocks, cliffs; good surfing; restaurants.

41 Vilamoura
   Sandy beach, some cliffs; several restaurants, big tourist complex with many facilities for sports, excellent surfing conditions, ideal for children.

42 Quarteira
   Sandy beach, big tourist centre with various sports facilities; several restaurants; safe swimming for children.

43 Vale do Lobo
   Fine sand, flat in parts, rocks, cliffs; several restaurants; plenty of sports facilities, usually good surfing conditions.

44 Quinta do Lago
   Sandy beach, dunes, lagoon; good surfing conditions; speed boats.

45 Faro
   Long flat beach of fine sand, lagoon; several restaurants (access by road and by boat).

46 Olhão
   In the high season boats ply every hour and a half between Olhão and the offshore islands of Culatra and Armona which have fine long sandy beaches and dunes.

47 Tavira
   From Tavira you can go by boat to the wooded Tavira Island with a flat sandy beach and dunes. It is still relatively undisturbed here since there is no mass tourism facility in the vicinity; restaurants.

48 Cabanas/Cacela
   Still one of the Algarve's loveliest beaches: you cross by fishing boat to the little island with a flat beach of fine sand.

49 Monte Gordo
   Flat beach of fine sand, dunes; several restaurants.

Naturist beaches   There are specially designated beaches and holiday complexes where "naturism" can officially be practised, but nude sunbathing and swimming is also usually tolerated on more remote beaches. There is also plenty of topless sunbathing on the more popular beaches.

## Banks

See Opening Times and Currency

## Bullfighting

Bullfighting in Portugal (see Arts and Culture, Folklore) is far less gory than the Spanish variety, especially since the bull gets out of the arena alive, although it is tormented and later killed.

There is bullfighting between April and October, primarily in Lisbon and the Ribatejo, but in the summer many tourist centres, such as Lagos, Quarteira and Albufeira, also stage bullfights once a week, usually on Saturdays.

## Business Hours

See Opening Times

## Camping

As a general rule Portugal does not allow overnight camping at the roadside, in lay-bys, parks or open country.

Unofficial camping

In addition to a passport, some camp sites require a camping permit which must have been issued by an officially recognised national or international organisation.

Camping permit

Portugal currently has about 100 camp sites, most of them near the coast (see map on page 344):

Camp sites

| | | | |
|---|---|---|---|
| 1 | Vila Praia de Ancora | 2 | Caminha |
| 3 | Vilar de Mouros | 4 | Chaves |
| 5/6 | Viana do Castelo | 7 | Fão |
| 8 | Póvoa de Varzim | 9 | Braga |
| 10 | Caldas das Taipas | 11 | Guimarães |
| 12 | Amarante | 13 | Mondim de Basto |
| 14 | Vila Real | 15 | Matosinhos |
| 16 | Oporto | 17–19 | Vila Nova de Gaia |
| 20 | Lamego | 21 | Espinho |
| 22 | Esmoriz | 23 | Cortegaça |
| 24 | Oliveira de Azeméis (Lisbon) | 25 | Murtosa |
| 26 | Termas de São Pedro do Sul | 27 | São Pedro do Sul |
| 28 | Viseu | 29 | Guarda |
| 30 | Aveiro | 31 | Ilhavo |
| 32 | Vagos | 33 | Agueda |
| 34/35 | Mira | 36 | Figueira da Foz |
| 37 | Gala | 38 | Coimbra |
| 39 | Penacova | 40 | Oliveira do Hospital |
| 41 | Coja | 42 | Arganil |
| 43 | Fundão | 44 | Castelo Branco |
| 45 | Pedrógão Grande | 46 | Praia de Pedrógão |
| 47 | São Pedro de Muel | 48 | Nazaré |
| 49 | Valado | 50 | Alcobaça |
| 51 | Tomar | 52 | Castelo do Bode |
| 53 | Portalegre | 54/55 | São Martinho do Porto |
| 56 | Caldas da Rainha | 57 | Peniche |
| 58 | Praia de Areia Branca | 59 | Praia de Santa Cruz |
| 60 | Salvaterra de Magos | 61 | Mafra |
| 62 | Praia Grande | 63 | Sintra |
| 64 | Caneças | 65 | Cascais |
| 66 | Oeiras | 67 | Lisboa |
| 68–74 | Costa da Caparica | 75 | Setúbal Sul |
| 76/77 | Sesimbra | 78 | Tróia |
| 79 | Évora | 80 | Beja |
| 81 | Melides | 82 | Lagoa de Santo André |
| 83 | Sines | 84 | Vila Nova de Milfontes |
| 85 | Aljezur | 86 | Praia da Luz |
| 87–89 | Lagos and Espiche | 90 | Portimão |
| 91 | Ferragudo | 92/93 | Armação de Péra |
| 94 | Albufeira | 95 | Quarteira |
| 96 | Faro | 97 | Olhão |
| 98 | Vila Nova de Cacela | 99 | Monte Gordo |

343

## Camp Sites in Portugal
(Mainland)

© Baedeker

## Car Rental

To hire a car in Portugal you must be 23 or over and have held a driving licence for at least one year.

Avenida Praia da Vitória 12C; tel. 01/56 11 77          **Avis**
Avenida Liberdade 29; tel. 01/32 60 75                    Lisbon
Airport: tel. 01/89 48 36

Rua Igreja Nova 13; tel. 0 89/5 26 78                     Albufeira

Airport: tel. 0 89/2 45 38                                Faro

Lagos das Portas de Portugal 11; tel. 0 82/6 36 91        Lagos

In the Hotel Mare, Rua Mouzinho Albuquerque 8; tel. 0 62/5 17 50   Nazaré

Rua Guedes de Azevedo 125; tel. 02/31 59 47               Oporto
Airport: tel. 02/9 48 15 25

In the Hotel Algarve; tel. 0 82/2 20 29                   Praia da Rocha

Agents also in Arcos Valdevez, Aveiro, Braga, Coimbra, Estoril, Figueira da Foz, Guimarães, Leiria, Monte Gordo, Ofir, Póvoa de Varzim, Quarteira, Santarém, Setúbal, Viana do Castelo, Vilamoura and Viseu, as well as on Madeira and the Azores.

Avenida Fontes Pereira de Melo; tel. 01/53 77 17         **Budget**
Avenida de Roma 4b; tel. 01/88 61 57                      Lisbon
Airport: tel. 01/80 17 85

Cerro Grande; tel. 0 89/5 34 64                           Albufeira

Airport: tel. 0 89/2 48 88                                Faro

Rua Infante Dom Henrique 109; tel. 02/38 46 91           Oporto
Airport: tel. 02/9 48 57 14

Avenida Tomás Cabreira; tel. 0 82/2 23 70                 Praia da Rocha

Avenida Infante de Sagres; tel. 0 89/3 30 46             Quarteira

Agents also in Beja, Castelo Branco, Évora, Monte Gordo and Santarém.

Avenida António Augusto de Aguiar 24; tel. 01/53 51 15/9   **Europcar**
Airport: tel. 01/80 11 76                                  **(InterRent)**
                                                          Lisbon

Rua Dr Diogo Leote; tel. 0 89/5 24 44                     Albufeira

Avenida Marginal, Centro Comercial Cisne Negro; tel. 01/2 86 44 38   Cascais

Avenida República 2; tel. 0 89/2 37 78                    Faro
Airport: tel. 0 89/81 83 16

Rua de Santa Catarina 1158–1164; tel. 02/31 83 98        Oporto
Airport: tel. 02/9 48 24 52

Avenida Tomás Cabreira; tel. 0 82/2 44 65                 Praia da Rocha

Agents also in Aveiro, Beja, Castelo Branco, Lagos, Leiria, Monte Gordo, Nazaré, Portimão, Vila Nova de Gaia and Vilamoura.

## Casinos

| | |
|---|---|
| **Hertz**<br>Lisbon | Avenida 5 de Outubro 10; tel. 01/53 98 16 |
| Albufeira | In the Hotel Albufeira Jardim; tel. 0 89/5 36 51 |
| Faro | Rua 1 de Maio 9; tel. 0 89/2 48 77<br>Airport: tel. 0 89/2 40 48 |
| Figueira da Foz | Edificio do Grande, Avenida 25 de Abril; tel. 0 33/2 21 46 |
| Lagos | Internacional Viagens, Rua Victor Costa E. Silva 6; tel. 0 82/6 16 50 |
| Oporto | Rua de Santa Catarina 899; tel. 02/31 23 93<br>Airport: tel. 02/9 48 14 00 |
| Praia da Rocha | Avenida Tomás Cabreira; tel. 0 82/2 58 86 |
| Agents | In Alvor, Armação de Pêra, Cascais, Leiria, Portela, Troia and Vilamoura. |

## Casinos

French and American roulette, blackjack and baccarat are usually played in Portuguese casinos. There are also one-armed bandits, fruit machines, etc. Most of the casinos have their own restaurant where international shows are presented. You should take your passport if you are going to gamble. Casinos are usually open daily between 5pm and 4am.

| | |
|---|---|
| Algarve | Casino de Vilamoura, Vilamoura, near Quarteira |
| | Casino de Monte Gordo<br>Monte Gordo, near Vila Real de Santo António |

*Casino in Monte Gordo*

Casino Solverde, Rua 19, no. 85, Espinho

Casino de Póvoa de Varzim
Póvoa de Varzim, about 20km/12 miles north of Oporto

Casino da Figueira, Figueira da Foz

Casino do Estoril, Estoril, near Lisbon

Casino da Madeira, Funchal

## Chemists

Chemists (farmácias) sell both locally produced medicines and those imported from abroad. These are usually cheaper in Portugal than in their country of origin.

See Opening Times

## Currency

The Portuguese unit of currency is the escudo, pronounced "shkudoh", made up of 100 centavos, and its symbol – the dollar sign $ – is written between the escudos and the centavos. There are banknotes for 100, 200, 500, 1000, 5000 and 10,000 escudos, and coins in denominations of 1, 2½, 5, 10 20, 25, 50 and 100 escudos. 1000 escudos is now officially known as a conto.

*Portuguese coins and banknotes*

**Customs Regulations**

Rates of Exchange

The escudo is subject to considerable fluctuations and rates can be found in national newspapers, at banks and at tourist bureaux. As is usually the case with countries that have a weak currency it pays to change money before going to Portugal. When changing back Portuguese banknotes you usually lose from 11 to 30% on the deal.

Currency import and export

There is no limit on how much foreign currency can be taken into Portugal but to avoid problems on the way out it is advisable to declare large sums.

Export of Portuguese currency is limited to 10,000 escudos; up to 500,000 escudos in foreign currency may be taken out, or up to the amount declared on entry.

Eurocheques

Eurocheques can be issued up to an amount of 30,000 escudos.

If a Eurocheque card is lost it should be reported immediately by telephone to the relevant number in the country of issue, so that it is cancelled immediately.

Credit Cards

Banks, the larger hotels, top restaurants, car hire firms and many shops accept the major international credit cards. If credit card(s) are lost the relevant organisation in the country of issue should be notified immediately.

Banks, Changing Money

Foreign currency, eurocheques, travellers' cheques, etc. can be changed or cashed at banks, and money changing is exclusive to banks. These are open Monday to Friday from 8.30 to 11.45am and 1 to 2.45pm.

Outside these times money can be changed at Lisbon airport and central station (Santa Apolónia), at Oporto airport, and at the airport in Faro, but here only up until 8pm. On the Algarve you can change money at banks outside the regular business hours all year round. Some places also have money-changing cash dispensers which accept various foreign currencies.

## Customs Regulations

On entry from EU countries

From 1 January 1993 new regulations came into operation. In theory there are no limits to the amounts of goods imported from one EU country to another, *provided they have been purchased tax paid in an EU country, are for personal use and are not intended for resale.* However the customs authorities have issued a list of maximum amounts considered reasonable for persons over 17 years of age, of alcoholic drinks, tobacco goods, perfume, etc. These are: spirits or strong liqueurs over 22% volume – 10 litres; fortified wines (port, sherry, etc.) – 20 litres; table wine – 90 litres (of which not more than 60 litres may be sparkling wine); beer – 110 litres; cigarettes – 800 or cigarillos 400 or cigars 200 or pipe tobacco 1kg. Personal use includes gifts, but if a passenger is receiving any payment in return for buying alcohol and tobacco (such as help with travelling expenses) the transaction will be dutiable and the duty must be paid to the Customs authorities.

Video equipment must be declared to customs. Six hunting guns and 400 cartridges may be brought in for 60 days, but must be declared, and 1000 escudos deposit is required for each gun.

Caravanners must have an inventory (in Portuguese, English or French) of the contents of their caravan for presentation to the Portuguese customs officials. There are no special requirements for the temporary import of boats, provided the usual international papers are available.

"Citizens' band" radios may only be operated with an official Portuguese permit. Further information can be obtained from motoring organisations or the Portuguese tourist offices; applications should be sent to Direcção dos Serviços Rádio-Eléctricos, Rua do Conde de Redondo 70, P-1100 Lisbon.

For those coming direct from a country outside the EU or who have arrived from another EU country without having passed through customs control with all their baggage, the allowances for goods obtained anywhere outside the EU are: Spirits – 1 litre or fortified wine – 2 litres or table wine – 3 litres plus a further 2 litres of table wine. Perfume – 60cc; toilet water – 250cc, 200 cigarettes or 100 cigarillos or 50 cigars or 250g of tobacco. All other goods, including gifts, £36 worth. "Duty-free" goods are still available at major airports, on aircraft and ferries; amounts are virtually the same as those above and are controlled by the carriers concerned. The duty-free allowances are scheduled to be phased out by 1996.

Entry from non-EU countries

The usual EU concessions apply.

Re-entry to the United Kingdom

See Currency

Currency Regulations

## Diplomatic Representation

United Kingdom

Embassy/Consulate
Rua de Sao Domingos à Lapa 35–37
Lisbon 1200. Tel. 01 66 11 91, 01 66 11 47

Consulate (Hon)
Avenida Do Zarco 2, Funchal, Madeira. Tel. 091 22 12 21

Consulate
Avenida da Boa Vista 3072, Oporto. Tel. 02 68 47 89

Rua Dr Bruno Tavares
Carreiro 9500, Ponta Delgada, Azores. Tel. 2 52 15 6

Consulate
Rua Santa Isabel 21, (1st Floor), Portimao. Tel. 082 2 30 71

Embassy
Avenida das Forças Armadas, Lisbon. Tel. 01 72 66 60 0

United States of America

Consulate
Apartado 88, Rua de Júlio Dinis 826–30
Oporto. Tel. 02 6 30 94

Consulate
Avenida Dom Henrique, Ponta Delgada
Azores. Tel. 2 22 16

Embassy
Rua de Rosa Aráujo 2, 2nd Floor, Lisbon. Tel. 01 56 38 21

Canada

## Electricity

The usual voltage on the Portuguese mainland and on most of Madeira is AC 220 with continental two pin plugs. The Azores still have AC 110 volts. In the large hotels most standard European plugs can be used, but American flat pin plugs should be used with a transformer for 220 volts and an adaptor.

## Emergency

Police, Ambulance | The emergency number for police, fire, ambulance, etc. throughout Portugal is 115. The call is free of charge.

Breakdown service | See Motoring

## Events

Almost every place in Portugal has its own saints and its quite special ceremonies for honouring them at the "romarias". Although originally purely pilgrimages these romarias have become popular festivals that last for days, with praying and penance, but also singing, dancing, drinking and lovemaking. The following calendar of events lists the most impressive of these romarias, as well providing a selection of other events.

## January

Northern Portugal | Vila Nova de Gaia (Oporto): Festa de São Gonçalo e São Cristóvão.
Vila de Feira (Aveiro): Festa de São Sebastião with processions.

## February

Northern Portugal | Ovar (Aveiro): carnival.

Central Portugal | Nazaré: carnival.

Southern Portugal | Évora: Festa da Senhora das Candeias with fair and religious ceremonies in the São-Brás Chapel.
Loulé and Portimão (Algarve): carnival.
Carnival week, preceding Shrove Tuesday, takes place all over the country.

## March

Northern Portugal | Aveiro: Feira de Março, this region's biggest industrial and trade fair with various forms of entertainment (until April).
Braga, Póvoa de Varzim and Ovar: see April for ceremonies during Holy Week.
Ovar (Aveiro): Procissão dos Terceiros; procession.
Póvoa de Lanhoso (Braga): Festa de São José.

Central Portugal | Lisbon: Procissão do Senhor dos Passos da Graça; procession.

Southern Portugal | Loulé (Faro): Romaria da Senhora da Piedade; romaria.

## April

Northern Portugal | Braga, Póvoa de Varzim (Oporto) and Ovar (Aveiro): Festas da Semana Santa; Holy Week is celebrated in these places on a particularly grand scale with many processions. The streets of Braga are decorated with lights and flowers, and Ovar has a romaria and fireworks.
Fão and Esposende (Braga): Romaria do bom Jesús de Fão; romaria in honour of Lord Jesús de Fão, processions, fireworks.
Barcelos and Guimarães (sometimes in early May): Festas das Cruzes; big popular festival, processions, fair, fireworks.

Central Portugal | Idanha-a-Nova (Castelo Branco): Romaria à Senhora do Almurtão; the foremost romaria in Beira Baixa, with folk events and religious ceremonies.
Monsanto (Castelo Branco: sometimes in early May); Festa das Cruzes or Festa do Castelo; religious ceremonies, popular festival, folk events.

## May

Viana do Castelo: Festa da Senhora das Rosas; festival honouring the Madonna of the Roses, with processions and popular festivals.
Alvarães (Viana do Castelo): Festa da Santa Cruz or Festa dos Andores Floridos; procession with flower-bedecked statues of saints.
Barcelos: Festas das Cruzes; flower carpeted procession of sixteen crosses, culminating in dancing and fireworks.

Northern Portugal

Vila Franca de Xira: Agrinxira; industrial and agricultural show.
Leira: Feira de Maio; May Fair with exhibition of regional products, including handicrafts.
Fátima: Primeira Peregrinação Anual a Fátima; the season of pilgrimages to Fátima opens on the eve of May 13th (although there are pilgrimages on the eve of the 13th of each of the following months until October, the first and last of these pilgrimages attract the most pilgrims).

Central Portugal

Alte (Faro): Festa da Fonte Grande or Festa do Primeiro de Maio; popular festival, folk events, and lots of flowers.
Sesimbra (Setúbal): Festa do Senhor das Chagas; fishermen's festival, procession on May 4th.

Southern Portugal

Ponta Delgada (São Miguel): Festas do Senhor Santo Cristo dos Milagres; big festival on the island, when those who still live there and those who have left celebrate together; religious celebrations, sporting contests, lengthy festival programme.

Azores

## June

Amarante: Romaria de São Gonçalo; romaria, folk events, bullfights, fireworks.
Matosinhos (Oporto): Festas do Senhor de Matosinhos; folk dancing, bull-running, fireworks, fair.
Quintela (Viseu): Romaria da Senhora da Lapa; romaria, processions.
Vila Praia de Ancora (Viana do Castelo): folk festival.
Amares and Vila Verde (both near Braga): Festas de Santo António; processions, folk events, in Vila Verde, also regional produce and livestock show.
Penafiel (Oporto) and Monção: Festa do Corpo de Deus; Corpus Christi is celebrated in Penafiel by processions in traditional costume, with flowers and, in Monção, by traditional folk events.
Braga, Barcelinhos, Oporto, Vila do Conde: Festas de São João; the traditional festival is celebrated every year in the various places from June 23rd to June 25th with processions, fireworks, regional folk events and, in Barcelinhos, a pottery fair.
Viseu: Cavalhadas de Vil de Moínhos; cavalcade of horsemen and festival church service, medieval games, folk song and dance.
Póvoa de Varzim (Oporto): Festas de São Pedro; popular festival, with folk dances and processions.
São Torcato (Braga): Romaria de São Torcato; romaria, processions, folk events.

Northern Portugal

Santarém: Feira Nacional de Agricultura; National Agricultural Show.
Lisbon: Festas dos Santos Populares; popular festival, fairs, lengthy festival programme with the greatest displays on the 12th and 13th.
Figueira da Foz: Festas de São João; midnight procession in traditional costume, dancing in the casino, folk events.
Sintra: Feira Grande de São Pedro; big regional fair with agricultural produce, antiques, handicrafts, regional specialities.

Central Portugal

Reguengos de Monsaraz (Évora): Festas de Santo António; festival in honour of the town's patron saint, bullfights, Alentejo male-voice choirs.

Southern Portugal

**Events**

Évora: Feira de São João; one of the most important fairs in southern Portugal, exhibitions of handicrafts and folk displays.
Montijo (Setúbal): Festas de São Pedro; popular festival, bullfights, the fishermen hand out sardines to visitors.

Madeira      Ribeira Brava: Festas de São Pedro; religious ceremonies, processions, folk dancing.

Azores      Ribeira Grande (São Miguel): Cavalhadas de São Pedro; medieval horse-back contests.

## July

Northern Portugal    Maia (Oporto): Romaria da Senhora do Bom Despacho; romaria, pilgrim-age, folk events, fireworks.
Santo Tirso (Oporto): Festas de São Bento; pottery exhibition, folk festival.
Paredes (Oporto): Festas do Divino Salvador; procession, animal contests, fireworks.
São Torcato (Braga): Festival Internacional de Folclore de São Torcato; International Folk Festival, contest of the top Portuguese and foreign folk groups.
Vila do Conde (Oporto): Feira de Artesanato; handicraft fair, exhibition of work from all over Portugal.
Lousada (Oporto): Festas do Senhor dos Aflitos; processions, folk events.
Gulpilhares (Oporto): Festival Internacional de Folclore de Gulpilhares.

Central Portugal    Vale da Maceira (Coimbra): Romaria da Senhora das Preces; romaria, with popular festival and market.
Vila Franca de Xira: Festas do Colete Encarnado; contests, folk events, bullfights.
Estoril: Feira de Artesanato do Estoril; exhibition of handicrafts, folk events, specialities.
Ançã (Coimbra): Romaria de São Tomé e São Tiago; romaria of the patron saints, folk dances, etc., horseback games.
Sintra: Jornadas Musicais de Sintra; concerts in castles and palaces in and around Sintra (in the summer months)
Tomar: Festa dos Tabuleiros (even-numbered years only): festival with processions of girls bearing tabuleiros, or platters, on their heads, piled very high with loaves, etc.

Southern Portugal    Faro: Feira da Senhora do Carmo: fair of regional handicrafts, folk displays.
Setúbal: Feira de São Tiago; regional agricultural, industrial and crafts fair, folk displays, bullfights (usually until August).

## August

Northern Portugal    Meadela (Viana do Castelo): Festas da Meadela, em Honra de Santa Cris-tina; traditional costumes, folk events, processions.
Terras de Bouro (Braga): Festas de São Brás; processions, parades, bull-running.
Mirandela (Bragança): Festas da Senhora do Amparo e Feira de Santiago; religious ceremonies, popular festival, cultural and sporting events.
Viana do Castelo: Festas da Senhora da Agonia; one of Portugal's most distinctive festivals and pilgrimages, festival of regional dancing and singing and procession in regional costumes, bull-running, carnival parade, fireworks.
Neves (Viana do Castelo): Festa da Senhora das Neves; religious ceremo-nies, popular festival, fireworks, folk festival, handicrafts exhibition, and one particular custom, the "marriage market", where the girls stroll down one side of the street and the boys down the other, and through eye contact try to find the right partner.

Guimarães (Braga): Festas Gualterianas; popular festival, with many regional specialities and wines, fireworks, folk events.

Caminha (Viana do Castelo): Festas de Santa Rita de Cássia; processions in traditional costumes, water sports contests, fireworks.

Portuzelo (Viana do Castelo): Festas de Santa Marta de Portuzelo; fairs, folk festivals with Portuguese and foreign groups.

Baião (Oporto) and Ponte da Barca: Festas de São Bartolomeu; religious ceremonies, old dances and songs, traditional riding contests, bullfights, and, in Ponte da Barca, processions.

Monção: Festa da Virgem das Dores; processions, show of handicrafts, popular festival, fireworks.

Oporto: Festa de São Bartolomeu e Cortejo de Papel; religious ceremonies, popular festival, procession with paper figures satirising important people.

Viseu: Feira de São Mateus; agricultural, wine, livestock and handicraft fair, folk festival, bullfights.

Arga de São João (Viana do Castelo): Romaria de São João de Arga; romaria, magnificent processions, old dances and songs.

Ria Caldo (Braga): Romaria de São Bento da Porta Aberta; romaria.

Torno (Oporto): Romaria à Senhora Aparecida; romaria, processions.

Castelões (Aveiro): Romaria da Senhora da Saúde da Serra; pilgrimage, romaria, mainly religious.

Póvoa de Varzim (Oporto): Festas da Senhora da Assunção; traditional fisher-festival, procession of decorated boats on the sea, bullfights, folk festival, fireworks.

Esposende (Braga): Festa da Senhora da Saúde e Soledade; traditional fisher-festival, water sport contests on the Rio Cávado, folk events, processions.

Vila Boas (Bragança): Romaria à Senhora da Assunção; romaria, large festival programme.

Caldas de Vizela (Braga): Festas de Vizela; varied festival programme, processions, traditional costumes, folk festival.

Miranda do Douro: Festas de Santa Bárbara; popular festival with male traditional dances.

Mar (Braga): Romaria de São Bartolomeu do Mar; religious celebrations, popular festival.

Peniche: Festas da Senhora da Boa Viagem; traditional fisher-festival in honour of their patron saints, seaborne procession, folk events, fireworks, popular festival. — Central Portugal

Batalha: Festas da Senhora da Vitória; popular festival, folk events.

Coruche (Santarém): Festas da Senhora do Castelo; folk events, bullfights and bull-running.

Alcobaça (Leiria): Feira de São Bernardo; industrial and agricultural show, with folk events and handicrafts.

Gouveia (Guarda): Festas do Senhor de Calvário; procession, sheep fair and sheepdog competition, folk song and dance festival.

Beja: Feira de Agosto or Feira de São Lourenço e Santa Maria; big fair with handicrafts show, festival programme, bullfights. — Southern Portugal

Alcochete (Setúbal): Festas do Barrete Verde e das Salinas; very local festival, with blessing of the saltpans, bullfights, popular festival.

Ponta Delgada (São Miguel): Festas do Divino Espírito Santo; island festivities with tradition. — Azores

Monte: Festa da Senhora do Monte; processions, traditional costumes, dances and songs. — Madeira

## September

Guimarães: Peregrinação à Senhora da Penha; pilgrimage. — Northern Portugal

Monte Farinha (Vila Real): Romaria da Senhora da Graça; romaria.

**Events**

Gavieira (Viana do Castelo): Romaria da Sehora da Peneda; romaria, traditional costumes.

Lamego: Romaria da Senhora dos Remédios; pilgrimage, folk festival, processions, sporting events.

Vila Praia de Ancora (Viana do Castelo): Festas da Senhora da Bonança; fisher-festival in honour of their patron saints, processions and blessing of the boats, popular festival, folk events, fireworks.

Praia da Torreira (Aveiro): Romaria de São Paio da Torreira; traditional "holy bathe", waterborne processions, blessing of the boats, popular festival, fireworks.

Póvoa (Bragança): Romaria à Senhora do Nazo; pilgrimage, big fair.

Póvoa de Varzim (Oporto): Festas da Senhora das Dores; religious ceremonies, festival events.

Ponte de Lima: Feiras Novas e Festas da Senhora das Dores; fairs, processions, folk festival, procession in traditional costumes, fireworks on the Rio Lima.

Cabeceiras de Basto (Braga): Feira e Festas de São Miguel; popular festival, religious ceremonies, ancient contests.

Buçaco (Aveiro): Festa da Senhora da Vitórem em Comemoração da Batalha do Buçaco; festival commemorating the battle of Buçaco, processions in uniforms of the period, popular festival.

Vila Nova de Famalição (Braga): Feira Grande de São Miguel; agricultural show, handicrafts, folk events.

Arouca (Aveiro): Feira das Colheitas; fair for regional handicrafts, folk events.

Central Portugal

Rio Maior (Santarém): Frimor; annual industrial and agricultural show, regional handicrafts, folk events, bull-running.

Arganil (Coimbra): Feira de Montalto; fair, with lengthy festival programme.

Nazaré: Romaria da Senhora de Nazaré; romaria, with impressive processions, traditional costumes, folk events, fair, fireworks, bullfights.

Castelejo (Castelo Branco): Romaria de Santa Luzia e Santa Eufémia; romaria with folk events.

Elvas: Festas do Senhor Jesus da Piedade e Feira de São Mateus; among the most typical of Alentejo's festivals, processions, popular festival, bullfights.

Reguengo de Fétal (Leira): Festas da Senhora do Fétal or Festas dos Caracóis; popular festival, processions.

Southern Portugal

Palmela (Setúbal): Festa das Vindimas; popular festival, bullfights, fireworks.

Many places in the Algarve: Festival de Folclore do Algarve; folk festival, with groups from the mainland and the islands, processions in traditional costume and fireworks.

Moita (Setúbal): Festas da Senhora da Boa Viagem; impressive procession, with blessing of the boats, popular festival, funfairs, bullfights, big firework displays.

Viana do Alentejo (Évora): Romaria da Senhora de Aires; romaria, bullfights

# October

Northern Portugal

Vieira do Minho (Braga): Feira da Ladra; festival fair, with regional agricultural and livestock show, lengthy festival programme.

Gondomar (Oporto): Romaria da Senhora do Rosário e Feira das Nozes; festival procession, funfair and folk dance evening, Walnut Fair.

Chaves: Feira dos Santos; fair.

Central Portugal

Vila Franca de Xira: Feira de Outubro; October fair.

Fátima: last of the big pilgrimages to Fátima on the eve of October 13th.

Moura (Beja): Festa da Senhora do Monte do Carmo; processions, regional folk events.

Faro: Feira de Santa Iria; a wide variety of entertainments take place at the same time as the industrial fair.

Castro Verde (Beja): Feira de Outubro; October Fair.

Algarve: Algarve Car Rally (sometimes early in November).

## November

Cerdal (Viana do Castelo): Feira dos Santos; traditional fair.

Penafiel (Oporto): Feira de São Martinho; fair, regional specialities.

Cartaxo (Santarém): Feira dos Santos; fair with bullfights.

Golegã (Santarém): Feira de São Martinho – Feira Nacional do Cavalo; national horse fair, riding competitions, bullfights, lengthy programme (sometimes the last week in October).

Ribatejo (Santarém): National Gastronomic Fair; samples of regional food and wine.

## December

Freamunde (Oporto): Romaria de Santa Luzia e Feira dos Capões; romaria and fair.

Festas de São Silvestre or Festas do Fim do Ano; internationally famous New Year's Eve celebration, with magnificent fireworks.

## Fado

The Portuguese fado (see Art and Culture, Folklore), with its sad, soulful songs, usually about the forces of destiny, is based on Lisbon. Students in Coimbra also have their own special version, and the odd fado venue can be found in Oporto as well. The kind of fado put on in the Algarve is not really to be recommended since this is solely for tourists.

Although as a rule there is no admission charge to listen to fado customers are expected to buy something to eat or drink. Plenty of time is needed as the best fado singers mostly do not appear until midnight or later.

It is advisable to book a table at the following fado venues.

Senhor Vinho
Rua do Meio à Lapa 18. Tel. 01/397 74 56
Open: Mon.–Sat. 8.30pm–3.30am.

Adega Machado
Rua do Norte 91. Tel. 01/346 00 95

Fado Menor
Rua das Praças 18. Tel. 01/67 18 56
Open: daily 8.30pm–3.30am.

Arcadas do Faia
Rua da Barroca 56. Tel. 01/342 67 42

Forte Dom Rodrigo
Estrada de Birre. Tel. 01/2 85 13 73. Closed Mon.

A Ponte Restaurante
Bairro S. José
Fado performances Fridays and Saturdays.

## Food and Drink

## Eating habits

Meals

Breakfast in Portugal, as in other southern countries, is a rather frugal affair, and only the larger tourist hotels, particularly in the Algarve, serve meat, cheese and eggs as well as bread, butter, jam and coffee.

Midday and evening meals are, however, taken very seriously. Meetings of any kind are always associated with a meal, and the Portuguese normally have two hot meals a day, even when there is no special excuse. There are often three courses at both the midday and the evening meal, with a light soup frequently served as the starter, although in the north of Portugal soup is traditionally not dished up until after the main course. Generally speaking the main course is accompanied by rice or potatoes, and only rarely by vegetables, although in the summer months an appetising salad is offered. Bread is always on the table.

Mealtimes

Lunch is earlier than in other southern countries. It can be as early as noon, and is seldom later than 1 o'clock. The evening meal is generally after 8 o'clock but seldom later than 9.

Cuisine

Portuguese cooking is solid and nourishing, its mainstays being olive oil and such herbs as thyme, bay, rosemary, etc. Expectations should not be too high so far as typical Portuguese cuisine is concerned since even in the best restaurants the choice and quality of the dishes is simple. This should come as no surprise given the fact that in the past Portugal was a relatively poor country and that in the south at least there were severe limitations on what local agriculture could produce. Like other examples of peasant cuisine this one does, however, have the advantage of being genuine, because pains are taken to make the most of the local produce. It therefore pays to try the simple fish and meat dishes, which are usually freshly prepared, and to avoid sauces, etc. with fancy names.

Vocabulary

See Language

## Dishes

Soup

The Portuguese national dish is "cozido à portuguesa", a tasty thick stew of vegetables with various kinds of meat. "Caldo verde" is a finely shredded kale soup found in the Minho. A favourite of southern Portugal is "gaspacho", a cold, spicy vegetable soup. "Caldeirada", a nourishing fish soup, is found everywhere along the coastline.

Fish

Naturally Portugal has a particularly wide variety of fish dishes, but other sorts of seafood, shrimp and crayfish, crab and lobster, are almost always available relatively cheaply and fresh; they can actually be seen crawling around in many restaurant windows!

One of Portugal's national dishes is "bacalhau" (dried, salted cod). Anyone who can not afford bacalhau for a special occasion has to be very poor indeed. There are very many different ways of preparing it – "bacalhau com todos" is dried cod with a selection of vegetables, "bacalhau à brás" is with onions, potatoes and olives, and "bacalhau dourada" is with tomatoes, parsley, garlic and wine.

Throughout Portugal people can be seen at midday and in the evenings grilling their "sardinas assadas" (grilled sardines) in front of their houses.

Anyone who orders "arroz de lampreia" will get the Minho speciality of lampreys on rice. "Bife de atum", tuna steaks, and "amêijoas na cataplana", clams and sausage spiced with herbs steamed in a copper pan, often appear on menus in the Algarve. Visitors to Peniche should sample "lagosta suada" (casseroled crayfish).

One of the really famous creations of Portuguese cuisine is "carne de porco à alentejana", the Alentejo dish of pork garnished with clams. Sucking pig, or "leitão assado", is another excellent Portuguese speciality.

Not to everyone's taste, but typical of Oporto, "tripas à moda do Porto", tripe with haricot beans, is a dish that has quite a history. When Henry the Navigator, who was born in Oporto, sent a vessel to conquer Ceuta the people of Oporto slaughtered all their livestock to provision the crew. They just kept the intestines, and hence have been popularly known as "tripeiros", or tripe-eaters, ever since.

Oporto is also the source of "linguiças", smoked tongue sausages. "Presunto", smoked ham, is generally excellent, especially if it comes from Chaves. "Espeta da Madeira", meat roasted on a spit, is a speciality from Madeira, and "alcatra dos Açores", a form of beef roast, comes from the Azores.

Beans are a favourite vegetable in Portuguese cooking. "Feijão guisado" are haricot beans braised with bacon and served with a tomato sauce, while "feijão verde à poviciana" are French beans braised with onions, garlic and small sausages, served up with a poached egg. "Grão com tomates" consists of chick-peas in a purée of garlic, olive oil and tomatoes.

Portugal has some good cheeses. "Queijo da serra" is a sheep's cheese from the Serra da Estrela, "Cabreiro", which is widely available, is a salty goat's cheese, and "Rabaçal", which is a speciality from around Pombal, is another goat's cheese. "Queijo da ilha" is a strong-flavoured hard cheese produced in the Azores but also obtainable on the mainland. "Queijinhos" are small white cheeses that are a speciality from the Tomar area.

The Portuguese are fond of very sweet confections, not only after meals but also between them, so there are plenty of cake shops selling delicious little pastries.

"Doces de ovos" is a sweet egg speciality of central Portugal. The Algarve has excellent marzipan cakes, "bolo de ovos e amêndoa", and on Madeira you get "bolo de mel" which are honey cakes. Popular desserts found on most menus are "arroz doce", which is rice pudding sprinkled with cinnamon, and "pudim flan", a kind of individual egg custard à la creme caramel.

See entry

## Drink

Agua Mineral, mineral water, can be obtained still or carbonated (com/sem gás), and even the carbonated variety is only mildly fizzy. Portugal has long been proud of its mineral waters. The Romans were familiar with their therapeutic qualities, and in the 19th c. Portugal had the most elegant spas in Europe (see Spas), with luxury hotels, casinos, bathing establishments and, of course, pump-rooms. This tradition continues, though only relatively few spas bottle their water – there are only ten firms bottling a total of fifteen brands of mineral water. At least 75% of the mineral water market is taken up by the still mineral water. The most popular brand is "Luso", which is still, and has a low mineral content. There are also "Vimeiro" and "Castelo de Vide", both either still or carbonated, and with a moderate mineral content, and "Pedras Salgadas", which has a high mineral content, and is naturally slightly fizzy.

In addition to the internationally marketed soft drinks there are local variants, and frequently fresh-pressed fruit juice can be obtained.

Lunch and dinner are often rounded off with strong black coffee (café or bica), although many Portuguese prefer their coffee with milk (galao).

Meat · Vegetables · Cheese · Desserts and cakes · Restaurants · Mineral water · Soft drinks, coffee

357

**Getting to Portugal**

Beer — Portugal's most popular form of beer (cerveza) is "Sagres", a kind of pale ale, while the same brewery, which is based at Vialonga, near Lisbon, also brews "Presta", which is more of a stout. There are also "Cristal" and "Cergal", which are both of the lager type. Beer consumption in Portugal has tripled since 1970, but wine continues to be the traditional drink with meals.

Wine — See entry

Spirits — Coffee after a meal is often accompanied by a marc (bagaço) or a brandy (aguardente or brandy). Fruit brandies include "medronho" from the arbutus berry, "cana" from sugar cane, and "ginjinha", which is a cherry brandy. Imported spirits – whisky is popular – are relatively expensive.

## Getting to Portugal

By air — There are scheduled services from London (Gatwick) to Lisbon and Oporto (British Airways); from London (Heathrow) to Lisbon, Oporto, Faro, Madeira and the Azores (TAP-Air Portugal); and London (Heathrow) to Lisbon (Varig). Seats are also available on many charter services.
There are direct services to Lisbon from the major cities in the United States and Canada.

By Road — There is a wide choice of cross-channel car ferry services between Britain and France. From the French Channel ports it is approximately 1200 miles to Lisbon, 1100 miles to Oporto and 1400 miles to Faro.

The most direct road route is to cross the frontier between France and Spain at Hendaye/Irún, then, via San Sebastián, cross from Spain to Portugal between Ciudad Rodrigo and Guarda. The longer way round, which allows you to see something of Spain en route, is to travel south through France down the Rhône valley, via Nîmes, Montpellier and Perpignan, to cross the Spanish frontier at Le Perthus/La Junquera, then follow the coast from Barcelona to Tarragona before turning inland and driving via Monreal to Madrid, when the route turns south-west, via Trujillo, to the Portuguese frontier at Badajoz.

There are regular coach services between London and Lisbon, Oporto, Coimbra, Lagos and Faro.

Frontier crossings — The frontier crossings at Elvas Caia, Valença do Minho and Vilar are open 24 hours a day. The crossing at Vila Real de Santo António is normally open from 7am to 11pm but at holiday times throughout the 24 hours. Other frontier posts are open from 7am to midnight, but close earlier in the winter.

Motorail — Anyone who wishes to take a car but does not want the long drive can avail themselves of the motorail service from Paris to Lisbon. Information from French Railways, 179 Piccadilly, London W1; tel. 071/409 3518.

By sea — An alternative route is by the car ferry from Plymouth to Santander in northern Spain. From Santander it is some 600 miles to Lisbon, 500 miles to Oporto and 800 miles to Faro. Information from Brittany Ferries, Millbay Docks, Plymouth PL1 3EW; tel. 0752/26 99 26.

Another, more infrequent, sea-route is the service run three or four times a year from Antwerp, Le Havre and Bordeaux to Lisbon by Compagnie Maritime Zairoise.

By rail — There is a daily service from London (Victoria) to Lisbon via Paris and Irún/Hendaye. The journey from Paris to Lisbon takes about 25 hours. For information contact British Rail Continental Section, Victoria Station, London SW1; tel. 071/834 2345, or your travel agent. For anyone with an

Interrail pass this is a particularly economical way to travel and can cost as little as a cheap charter flight.

See entry                                                                    Travel Documents

## Golf

Golf has been played in Portugal since 1890 when the founding of Europe's second golf course, the Oporto Golf Club took place. Portugal now has over 20 golf courses, varying very widely in their degree of difficulty, with new ones frequently being opened.

Miramar Golf Club                                                            Northern Portugal
Praia de Miramar, Valadares; tel. 02/7 62 20 67
9 holes

Oporto Golf Club
Pedreira, Espinho; tel. 02/72 20 08
18 holes

Vidago Golf Club
Vidago; tel. 076/9 71 06
9 holes

Vimeiro Golf Club                                                            Around Lisbon
Praia do Porto Novo, Vimeiro; tel. 061/9 81 57
9 holes
Small, well-kept course, on both sides of a little river

Estoril Golf Club
Avenida Republica, Estoril; tel. 01/2 68 01 76
18 + 9 holes
Comparatively short, but interesting course

Estoril-Sol Golf Club
Estrada da Lagoa Azul, Linhó; tel. 01/9 23 24 61
9 holes

Marinha Golf Club
Quinta da Marinha, Cascais; tel. 01/28 98 81
18 holes

Lisbon Sports Club
Casal da Carregueira, Belas; tel. 01/96 00 77
14 + 4 holes

Tróia Golf Club
Torralta Tróia, Setúbal; tel. 065/4 41 51
18 holes

Palmares Golf Club                                                           Algarve
Meia Praia, Lagos; tel. 082/76 29 53
18 holes

Parque da Floresta Golf Club
Vila do Bispo, 10 miles west of Lagos; tel. 082/6 53 33
18 holes

Penina Golf Club
Penina, Portimão; tel. 082/41 54 15
18 holes and another 18-hole short course
One of Portugal's most difficult courses

Carvoeiro Golf Club
Carvoeiro
27 holes

Quinta do Lago Golf Club
Almansil, Loulé; tel. 089/39 45 29
18 + 3 × 9 holes; other courses are being constructed
These are amongst Europe's finest golf courses

São Lourenco Golf Club
Quinta do Lago, Almansil; tel. 089/9 46 35
18 holes

Vale do Lobo Golf Club
Vale do Lobo, Loulé; tel. 089/39 44 44
18 + 9 holes
Hilly links, attractive course

Vilamoura I Golf Club
Vilamoura, Loulé; tel. 089/31 36 52
18 holes

Vilamoura II Golf Club
Vilamoura, Loulé; tel. 089/31 55 62
18 holes

Vilamoura III Golf Club
Vilamoura, Loulé; tel. 089/38 07 24
18 + 9 holes

Madeira

Santo Serra Golf Club
15½ miles north of Funchal; tel. 091/5 51 39
9 holes

Azores

There is an 18-hole golf course on Terceira and a 9-hole one on São Miguel.

## Hotels

Hotels, motels and aparthotels

Hotels in Portugal are classified according to the quality of the accommodation, ranging from five star de luxe to simple one star, and with a considerable quality range within the individual categories.
    For motels and aparthotels the categories, in terms of price and comfort, are approximately the same as for hotels.

Pousadas

Pousadas are state-owned hotels in important tourism sites, and are furnished to a high standard of comfort and convenience. Portugal's pousadas are listed, with a map, in their own separate section.

Estalagens

Estalagens (estalagem in the singular) are similar to pousadas but privately run. They are often in old restored buildings.

Stately homes

In this kind of accommodation the visitor stays in typical traditional stately homes, often with the owner still in residence.
    A list of these stately homes can be obtained from:

P.I.T. (Promoções e Ideias Turísticas, S.A.)
Alto da Pampilheira, Torre D-2
P-2750 Cascais. Tel. 01/2 86 79 58

Pensões, residencials, albergarias

Portugal has a great many pensions (pensões, singular pensão), or guesthouses. They fall into four categories (there are some, however, that are unclassified), and although in terms of comfort they often do not differ from the hotels in the categories given below, they do tend to be less expensive than hotels with the same number of stars. Proprietors are permitted to add up to 20% to the price of the room overnight if the guest does not have a main meal in-house. "Residencials" are comparable with pensions so far as price and comfort are concerned, while "albergarias" correspond to top category pensions.

Hotel rates vary considerably according to the season. The following table gives the rates for a double (hotel) room with bath. A single room costs 30% less than a double. A double room in the pensions on the following list will cost between 3000 and 10,000 escudos.

Prices

| category | double room | meals |
|---|---|---|
| ★★★★★ | 13,000–22,000 esc. | 2500–6000 esc. |
| ★★★★ | 8000–16,000 esc. | 1800–4000 esc. |
| ★★★ | 6000–12,000 esc. | 1000–3500 esc. |
| ★★ | 4000–8500 esc. | 800–3000 esc. |
| ★ | 2500–5000 esc. | 600–2500 esc. |

The hotels that follow are listed with their official category, address and number of rooms. SP stands for swimming pool and T for tennis courts. All the pensions listed have three or four official stars and are therefore comparable with the simpler hotels.

Since beds are in very short supply in many places such as Coimbra, Évora, Óbidos, etc., it is as well in the high season, at least, to telephone for a reservation well in advance.

★★★Hotel Turismo de Abrantes, L. de S. António; tel. 0 41/2 12 61, 40 r.   **Abrantes**
Pensão Tabuci, Avenida 25 de Abril 49; tel. 0 41/2 13 76, 8 r.

★★★★Hotel Boavista, Rua Samora Barros 6; tel. 0 89/58 91 75; 100 r., SP   **Albufeira**
★★★★Hotel Califórnia, Rua Cândido dos Reis 10–16; tel. 0 89/58 68 33; 54 r.
★★★★Hotel Montechoro, Montechoro; tel. 0 89/58 66 11; 410 r., SP, T
★★★★Estalagem do Cerro, Cerro da Piedade; tel. 0 89/58 61 91; 83 r., SP
★★★★Estalagem Mar à Vista, Cerro da Piedade; tel. 0 89/5 21 91/5; 30 r.
★★★Hotel Rocamar, Rua Jacinto d'Ayet; tel. 0 89/51 26 96; 95 r.
★★★Hotel Sol e Mar, Rua José Bernardino de Sousa; tel. 0 89/58 67 21; 74 r., SP
★★★Hotel Topázio, Areias de São João; tel. 0 89/51 21 21; 46 r.
★★★Hotel Tropical, Areias de São João; tel. 0 89/5 38 41; 75 apart., SP, T
★★Hotel Baltum, Avenida 25 de Abril; tel. 0 89/5 21 02; 75 r.
★★Aparthotel Afonso II., Praia da Oura; tel. 0 89/ 5 53 92; 200 apart.

★★★★Estalegem Herdade da Barrosinha, 2 miles south-east on the N 5;   **Alcácer do Sal**
tel. 0 65/6 23 63; 12 r.

★★Hotel Santa Maria, Rua Dr. Francisco Zagalo; tel. 0 62/4 32 95; 31 r.   **Alcobaça**
Pensão Mosteiro, Avenida João de Deus 1; tel. 0 62/4 21 83; 15 r.

★★★Hotel Navarras; tel. 0 55/42 40 36; 61 r., SP   **Amarante**
★★Hotel Amaranto; tel. 0 55/42 21 06 17; 36 r.

★★★★Hotel Garbe, Avenida Marginal; tel. 0 82/31 21 88; 109 r., SP   **Armação de**
★★★★Hotel Viking, Praia Senhora da Rocha; tel. 0 82/31 48 76; 184 r., SP   **Pêra/Algarve**

★★★★Hotel Afonso V, Rua Dr. Manuel das Neves 65; tel. 0 34/2 51 91; 82 r.   **Aveiro**
★★★Hotel Imperial, Rua Dr. Nascimento Leitão; tel. 0 34/2 21 41; 110 r.
★★Hotel João Padeiro, Rua da República 13; tel. 0 34/9 13 26; 27 r.
★★Hotel Arcada, Rua Viana do Castelo 4; tel. 0 34/2 30 01; 52 r.
Pensão Paloma Blanca, Rua de Carvalho 23; tel. 0 34/2 60 39; 50 r.

★★★★Hotel Avenida, Ponta Delgada (São Miguel); tel. 0 96/2 73 31; 80 r.   **Azores**
★★★★Hotel de São Pedro, Ponta Delgada (São Miguel); tel. 0 96/2 22 23; 30 r.
★★★★Hotel Fayal, Horta (Faial); tel. 0 92/2 21 81; 83 r., SP, T
★★★★Estalagem das Velas, Velas (São Jorge); tel. 0 95/4 26 42; 24 r.
★★★★Estalagem de Santa Cruz, Horta (Faial); tel. 0 92/2 30 21; 25 r.

**Hotels**

★★Hotel Canadiano, Ponta Delgada (São Miguel); tel. 0 96/2 74 21; 50 r.
★★★Hotel de Angra, Angra do Heroismo (Terceira); tel. 0 95/2 40 41; 42 r.
★★★Hotel Terra Nostra, Furnas (São Miguel); tel. 0 96/5 41 04; 37 r., SP, T
★★Hotel Do Infante, Ponte Delgada (São Miguel); tel. 0 96/2 33 31; 39 r.
Residencial Pico, Madalena (Pico); tel. 0 92/9 23 92; 21 r.
Residencial Santa Cruz, Santa Cruz (Graciosa); tel. 0 95/7 23 45; 10 r.

| | |
|---|---|
| **Barcelos** | ★★★Albergaria Conde de Barcelos, Avenida Alcaide de Faria; tel. 0 53/81 10 61; 30 r.<br>Pensão Dom Nuno, Avenida Dom N.A. Pereira; tel. 0 53/81 50 84; 27 r. |
| **Batalha** | ★★★Motel São Jorge on the N 1; tel. 0 44/9 61 81; 25 r., SP |
| **Beja** | Pensão Bejense, Rua Capitão João F. de Sousa 57; tel. 0 84/2 50 01; 28 r.<br>Pensão Cristina, Rua de Mértola 71; tel. 0 84/2 30 35; 31 r.<br>Pensão Santa Bárbara, Rua de Mértola 56; tel. 0 84/2 20 28; 26 r. |
| **Belmonte** | ★★Hotel Belsol, on the N 18; tel. 0 75/91 23 15; 39 r.<br>Pemsão Altitude, Rua Alvares Cabral 33; tel. 0 75/4 21 70; 10 r. |
| **Braga** | ★★★★Hotel do Elevador, Bom Jesús do Monte; tel. 0 53/67 66 11; 24 r.<br>★★★★Hotel do Parque, Bom Jesús do Monte; tel. 0 53/67 65 48; 50 r., T<br>★★★Hotel Turismo, Praceta João XXI.; tel. 0 53/61 22 00; 132 r., SP<br>★★★Hotel Carandá, Avenida da Liberdade 96; tel. 0 53/61 45 11; 100 r.<br>★★Hotel João XXI, Avenida João XXI 849; tel. 0 53/61 66 30; 28 r.<br>★Hotel Francfort, Avenida Central; tel. 0 53/2 26 48; 15 r.<br>Residencial São Marcos, Rua de São Marcos 80; tel. 0 53/7 71 77; 13 r. |
| **Bragança** | ★★★★Albergaria Santa Isabel, Rua A. Herculano 67; tel. 0 73/2 24 27; 14 r.<br>★★Hotel Bragança, Praça Prof. Cavaleiro Ferreira; tel. 0 73/2 25 79; 42 r.<br>Residencial Nordeste Shalon, Avenida Abade de Baçal; tel. 0 73/2 46 67; 30 r.<br>Pensão São Roque Estacada; tel. 0 73/2 34 81; 36 r. |
| **Buçaco National Park** | ★★★★★Palace Hotel do Buçaco, M. do Buçaco; tel. 0 31/93 01 01; 60 r., T, other hotels see Luso. |
| **Caldas da Rainha** | ★★★Hotel Malhoa, Rua António Sérgio 31; tel. 0 62/84 21 80; 111 r., SP<br>Residencial Europeia, Rua das Montras 64; tel. 0 62/3 47 92; 50 r.<br>Pensão Dom Carlos, Rua de Camões 39; tel. 0 62/83 25 51; 20 r. |
| **Caminha** | Pensão Galo de Ouro, Rua de Corredoura 15; tel. 0 58/9 21 60; 12 r.<br>Residencial São Pedro, Seixas do Minho; tel. 0 58/92 14 75; 34 r., SP |
| **Carvoeiro** | ★★★★Hotel Almansor, Vale Covo; tel. 0 82/5 05 12/2; 400r., SP, T |
| **Cascais** | ★★★★★Hotel Albatroz, Rua Frederico Arouca; tel. 01/4 83 28 21; 40 r., SP<br>★★★★★Hotel Estoril Sol, Parque Palmela; tel. 01/4 83 28 31; 347 r., SP<br>★★★★Hotel Cidadela, Avenida 25 de Abril; tel. 01/4 83 29 21; 129 r., SP<br>★★★★Estalagem Do Farol, Estrada da Boca do Inferno 7; tel. 01/4 83 01 73; 15 r., SP, T<br>★★★★Albergaria Valbom, Avenida Valbom 14; tel. 01/4 86 58 01; 40 r.<br>★★★Hotel Baia, Estrada Marginal; tel. 01/4 83 10 33; 87 r.<br>★★★Hotel Nau, Rua Dr. Iracy Doyle; tel. 01/4 83 28 61; 57 r.<br>★★★Aparthotel Equador, Alto da Pampilheira; tel. 01/2 84 05 24; 120 apart., SP |
| **Castelo Branco** | ★★★Motel da Represa, on the Retaxo road; tel. 0 72/5 23 46; 38 r., SP, T<br>Pensão Arraiana, Avenida 1 de Maio 18; tel. 0 72/2 16 34; 31 r.<br>Pensão Caravela, Rua do Sobreiro 24; tel. 9 72/2 39 39; 30 r. |

★★★★Albergaria Jardim, Rua Sequeira Sameiro 6; tel. 0 45/9 12 17; 40 r. **Castelo de Vide**
★★★Hotel Sol e Serra, Estrada de S. Vicente; tel. 0 45/9 13 01; 50 r., SP
Pensão Casa do Parque, Avenida do Aramanhã; tel. 0 45/9 12 50; 26 r.

★★★★Estalegem Santiago, Rua do Olival; tel. 0 76/2 25 45; 31 r. **Chaves**
★★Hotel Trajano, Travessa Cândido dos Reis; tel. 0 76/2 24 15; 39 r.
★Hotel de Chaves, Rua 25 de Abril; tel. 0 76/2 11 18; 32 r.

★★★Hotel Astória, Avenida Emídio Navarro 21; tel. 0 39/2 20 55; 64 r. **Coimbra**
★★★Hotel Bragança, Largo das Ameias; tel. 0 39/2 21 71; 83 r.
★★★Hotel Oslo, Av. Fernão de Magalhães 23–25; tel. 0 39/2 90 71; 40 r.
Pensão Almedina, Av. Fernão de Magalhães 203; tel. 0 39/2 91 61; 39 r.
Pensão Avis, Av. Fernão de Magalhães 64; tel. 0 39/2 37 18; 17 r.
Pensão Domus, Rua Adelino Veiga 62; tel. 0 39/2 85 84; 15 r.
Pensão Infante Dom Henrique, Rua Dr. Manuel Rodrigues 43;
   tel. 0 39/2 21 42; 20 r.
Pensão Moderna, Rua Adelino Veiga 49; tel. 0 39/2 54 13; 19 r.

★★Hotel Miramonte, Pinhal da Nazaré; tel. 01/9 29 12 30; 89 r., SP **Colares**

★★Hotel Praia do Sol, Rua dos Pescadores 12; tel. 01/2 90 00 12; 54 r. **Costa da Caparica**
Pensão Copacabana, Rua José Alves Martins 14; tel. 01/2 90 01 03; 10 r.
Pensão Real, Rua Mestre Manuel 18; tel. 01/2 90 17 01; 10 r.

★★★Hotel Solneve, Rua Visconde de Coriscada 126; tel. 0 75/2 30 01; 30 r. **Covilhã**
Residencial Santa Eufémia, on the N 18; tel. 0 75/31 33 08; 80 r.

★★★Hotel das Termas; tel. 0 31/51 21 85; 36 r., SP **Curia**
★★★Palace Hotel da Curia; tel. 0 31/51 57 20; 130 r., SP, T
★★Hotel do Parque; tel. 0 31/51 20 31; 23 r.
Pensão Lourenço; tel. 0 31/51 22 14; 42 r.

★★★★Estalegem D Sacho II, Pr. da República 20; tel. 0 68/62 26 86; 26 r. **Elvas**
★★★Hotel D. Luís, Avenida de Badajoz; tel. 0 68/62 27 56; 61 r.
Pensão Quinta das Aguias, Avenida de Badajoz; tel. 0 68/62 22 45; 6 r.

★★★★Estalegem Morais; tel. 0 61/86 42 00; 40 r., SP **Ericeira**
★★★★Estalegem Pedro o Pescador; tel. 0 61/86 40 32; 25 r.
★★★Hotel de Turismo da Ericeira; tel. 0 61/86 40 45; 150 r., SP

★★★★Hotel Praia Golfe, Rua 6; tel. 02/72 06 30; 145 r., SP, T **Espinho**
★★★★Aparthotel Solverde; tel. 02/72 28 19; 83 apart., SP, T
★★Hotel de Espinho; tel. 02/72 00 02; 32 r.
★★Hotel Mar Azul; tel. 02/72 08 24; 25 r.

★★★Hotel Nélia; tel. 0 53/96 13 94; 42 r. **Esposende**
★★★Hotel Suave-Mar; tel. 0 53/92 11 44; 68 r., SP, T

★★★★★Hotel Palácio, Parque do Estoril; tel. 01/4 68 04 00; 200 r., SP **Estoril**
★★★★Grande Hotel, Avenida Sabóia; tel. 01/4 68 02 70; 71 r., SP
★★★★Hotel Atlântico, Estrada Marginal; tel. 01/4 68 02 70; 175 r., SP
★★★★Hotel Estoril Anka, Estrada Marginal; tel. 01/4 68 18 11; 91 r., SP
★★★★Aparthotel Eden, Avenida Sabóia; tel. 01/4 67 05 98; 160 apart., SP, T
★★★★Estalegem Belvedere, Rua Dr. A. Martins 8; tel. 01/4 68 91 63; 24 r.
★★★★Estalegem do Fundador, Rua D. Afonso Henriques 11;
   tel. 01/4 68 23 46; 10 r.
★★★Hotel Lido, Rua do Alentejo; tel. 01/4 68 41 23; 62r.,
★★★Hotel Londres, Avenida F. Figueiredo; tel. 01/4 68 42 45; 90 r., SP
★★★Hotel Paris, Avenida F. Figueiredo; tel. 01/4 68 00 18; 100 r., SP
★★★Hotel Zenith, Avenida Belmonte; tel. 01/2 68 11 22; 48 r., SP
★★Hotel Inglaterra, Avenida de Portugal; tel. 01/4 68 44 61; 49 r., SP
★Albergaria Barra, Rua Trouville 6; tel. 01/4 68 76 51; 12 r.

## Hotels

**Estremoz**
Pensaõ Carvalho, Largo da República 27; tel. 0 68/2 27 12; 12 r.
Pensão Estremoz, Rossio Marquês de Pombal 15; tel. 0 68/2 28 43; 8 r.
Pensão Mateus, Rua Dr. Gomes Resende 26; tel. 0 68/2 22 26; 10 r.

**Évora**
★★★★Albergaria Vitória, Rua Diana de Lis; tel. 0 66/27 17 74; 48 r.
★★★Hotel Planície, Rua Miguel Bombarda 40; tel. 0 66/2 40 26; 33 r.
★★Hotel Santa Clara, Travessa da Milheira 19; tel. 0 66/2 41 41; 47 r.
Residencial Riviera, Rua 5 de Outubro 49; tel. 0 66/2 33 04; 22 r.
Estalgem Poker, on N 114; tel. 0 66/3 37 21.

**Faro**
★★★★Hotel Eva, Avenida da República; tel. 0 89/80 33 54; 150 r., SP
★★★Hotel de Faro, Praça D. Francisco Gomes 2; tel. 0 89/80 32 76; 52 r.
★★Hotel Albacor, Rua Brites de Almeida 23–25; tel. 0 89/80 35 93; 38 r.
★★Hotel Santa Maria, Rua de Portugal 17; tel. 0 89/82 40 64; 40 r.
Residencial Afonso III, Rua Miguel Bombarda 64; tel. 0 89/80 35 42; 25 r.
Pensão Algarve, Rua D. Francisco Gomes 4; tel. 0 89/82 33 46; 15 r.
Pensão Condado, Rua Gonçalo Barreto 14; tel. 0 89/82 20 81; 20 r.
Pensão Marim, Rua Gonçalo Barreto 1; tel. 0 89/82 40 63; 22 r.

**Fátima**
★★★Hotel Cruz Alta, Cova da Iria; tel. 0 49/53 14 81; 24 r.
★★★Hotel da Fátima, Rua Jacinta Marto; tel. 0 49/53 23 51; 121 r.
★★★Hotel Dom José, Av. D. José Correia da Silva; tel. 0 49/53 22 15; 63 r.
★★★Hotel Santa Maria, Rua de Santo António; tel. 0 49/53 10 15; 60 r.
★★★Hotel Três Pastorinhos, Rua João Paulo II; tel. 0 49/53 24 29; 92 r.
★★Hotel Católico, Rua de Santa Isabel; tel. 0 49/53 23 55; 45 r.
★★Hotel Cinquentenário, Rua F. Marto 101; tel. 0 49/53 21 41; 115 r.
Pensão Casa Beato Nuno, Avenida Beato Nuno 51; tel. 0 49, 53 21 99; 88 r.
Pensão Floresta, Estrada da Batalha; tel. 0 49/53 14 66; 31 r.

**Figueira da Foz**
★★★★Grande Hotel, Avenida 25 de Abril; tel. 0 33/2 21 46; 91 r.
★★★★Estalagem da Piscina, Rua de Santa Catarina 7; tel. 0 33/2 21 46; 20 r., SP
★★★Hotel Costa de Prata 2, Rua M. Bombarda 59; tel. 0 33/2 20 82; 120 r.
★★★Hotel Internacional, Rua da Liberdade 20; tel. 0 33/2 20 51; 55 r.
★★★Hotel Tamargueira, Buarcos; tel. 0 33/3 25 14; 69 r.
★★★Hotel Wellington, Rua Dr. Calado 23; tel. 0 33/2 67 67; 34 r.
★★Aparthotel Atlântico, Rua 25 de Abril; tel. 0 33/2 40 45; 70 apart.
★★★Aparthotel Sottomayor, Rua dos Lusíadas; tel. 0 33/2 75 55; 74 apart.
★★Hotel Hispania, Rua Dr. Francisco A. Dinis 61; tel. 0 33/2 21 64; 34 r.
★Hotel Universal, Rua Miguel Bombarda 50; tel. 0 33/2 62 28; 36 r.

**Figueira de Castelo Rodrigo**
Pensão Figueirense, Avenida 25 de Abril; tel. 0 71/3 21 07
Pensão Santos, Rua Osório de Vasconcelos; tel. 0 71/3 21 71; 18 r.

**Fundão**
★★★★Estalagem da Neve, Quinta de Sebastião; tel. 0 75/5 22 15; 6 r., SP
★★★Hotel Fundão, Rua Vasco da Gama; tel. 0 75/7 12 99; 50 r.

**Gerês**
★★Hotel das Termas, Av. M. Francisco da Costa; tel. 0 53/6 51 43; 32 r.

**Guarda**
★★★Hotel Turismo da Guarda, Avenida Coronel Orlando de Carvalho; tel. 0 71/21 22 05; 105 r., SP
Pensão Aliança, Rua Vasco da Gama 8; tel. 0 71/2 21 35; 30 r.
Pensão Filipe, Rua Vasco da Gama 9; tel. 0 71/21 26 58; 37 r.
Pensão Santos, Rua Tenente Valadim 14; tel. 0 71/2 29 31; 20 r.

**Guimarães**
★★★Hotel Fundador Dom Pedro, Avenida D. Afonso Henriques 760; tel. 0 53/51 37 81; 63 r.
★Hotel do Toural, Largo do Toural; tel. 0 53/41 12 50; 40 r.
Pensão São Mamede, Rua de São Gonçalo 1–4; tel. 0 53/41 10 92; 15 r.

**Lagos**
★★★★Hotel de Lagos, Rua Nova da Aldeia; tel. 0 82/76 99 67; 287 r., SP, T
★★★★Hotel Golfinho, Praia Dona Ana; tel. 0 82/76 99 00; 262 r., SP

★★★★Albergaria Cidade Velha, Rua Joaquim Tello 7; tel. 0 82/6 20 41; 17 r.
★★★Hotel São Cristóvão, Rossio de São João; tel. 0 82/6 30 51; 80 r.
★★★Hotel da Meia Praia, Meia Praia; tel. 0 82/76 20 01; 66 r., SP, T
★★Motel Marsol, on the N 125; tel. 0 82/6 20 31; 25 r.
Pensão Lagosmar, Rua Dr. Faria e Sousa 13; tel. 0 82/76 37 22; 45 r.
Pensão Mar Azul, Rua 25 de Abril 13; tel. 0 82/76 91 43; 18 r.
Pensão Rubi Mar, Rua das Barrocas 70; tel. 0 82/6 31 65; 10 r.

★★★★Albergaria do Cerrado, Lugar do Cerrado; tel. 0 54/6 31 64; **Lamego**
30 r.
★★Motel Turisserra, Estrada Florestal; tel. 0 54/6 20 82; 25 r.
★Hotel do Parque; tel. 0 54/6 21 05; 38 r.

★★★Hotel Dom João III, Avenida Heróis de Angola; tel. 0 44/81 25 00; **Leiria**
64 r.
★★★Hotel Eurosol and Eurosol Jardim, Rua Dr. José Alves Correia da
Silva; tel. 0 44/81 22 01; 92 r., SP, T
Residencial Fétal; Avenida Heróis de Angola 42; tel. 0 44/81 29 95; 11 r.
Pensão São Francisco, Rua de São Francisco 26; tel. 0 44/2 51 42; 18 r.

★★★★★Hotel Alfa, Avenida Columbano Bordalo Pinheiro; **Lisbon**
tel. 01/7 26 21 21; 375 r.
★★★★★Hotel Altis, Rua Castilho 11; tel. 01/52 24 96; 307 r.
★★★★★Hotel Meridien, Rua Castilho 149; tel. 01/69 09 00; 331 r.
★★★★★Hotel Tivoli, Av. da Liberdade 185; tel. 01/52 11 01; 344 r., SP, T
★★★★Hotel Continental, Rua Laura Alves 9–13; tel. 01/7 93 50 05; 220 r.
★★★★Hotel Diplomático, Rua Castilho 74; tel. 01/3 56 20 41; 90 r.
★★★★Hotel Fénix, Praça Marquês de Pombal 8; tel. 01/53 51 21; 107 r.
★★★★Hotel Lisboa Plaza, Travessa do Salitre; tel. 01/3 46 39 22; 93 r.
★★★★Hotel Mundial, Rua Dom Duarte 4, tel. 01/886 31 01; 147 r.
★★★★Hotel Penta, Av. dos Combatentes; tel. 01/7 26 40 54; 592 r., SP
★★★★Hotel Tivoli Jardim, Rua Júlio César Machado 7; tel. 01/53 99 71;
119 r., SP
★★★Hotel Berna, Avenida António Serpa 13; tel. 01/7 93 67 67; 154 r.
★★★Hotel Eduardo VII, Av. Fontes Pereira de Melo; tel. 01/53 01 41; 122 r.
★★★Hotel Flamingo, Rua Castilho 41; tel. 01/53 21 91; 39 r.
★★★Hotel Miraparque, Avenida Sidónio Pais 12; tel. 01/57 80 70; 100 r.
★★★Hotel Presidente, Rua Alexandre Herculano 13; tel. 01/53 95 01; 59 r.
★★★Hotel Roma, Avenida Roma 33; tel. 01/76 77 61; 263 r., SP
★★Hotel Borges, Rua Garrett 108; tel. 01/3 46 19 51; 101 r.
★★Hotel Lis, Avenida da Liberdade 180; tel. 01/53 77 71; 63 r.
★★Hotel Metrópole, Rossio 30; tel. 01/3 46 91 64; 48 r.
★★Hotel Vip, Rua Fernão Lopes 25; tel. 01/3 52 19 23; 54 r.
★Hotel Bragança, Rua Alecrim 12; tel. 01/32 70 61; 40 r.
Hotel Portugal, Rua João das Regras 4; tel. 01/86 31 35; 47 r.
Pensão Alicante, Avenida Duque de Loulé 20; tel. 01/53 05 14; 36 r.
Pensão Imperador, Avenida 5 de Outubro 55; tel. 01/3 52 48 84; 43 r.
Pensão Nazareth, Av. A.A. de Aguiar 25; tel. 01/54 20 16; 32 r.
Pensão Residencia York House, Rua das Janelas Verdes 47;
tel. 01/39 96 25 4; 48 r.

★★★Grande Hotel das Termas; tel. 0 31/93 04 50; 157 r., SP, T **Luso**
★★★Hotel Eden; tel. 0 31/93 91 71; 57 r.
Pensão Astória; tel. 0 31/9 31 82; 35 r.

★★★★★Casino Park Hotel, Funchal; tel. 0 91/23 33 11; 400 r., SP, T **Madeira**
★★★★★Hotel Madeira Palácio, Funchal; tel. 0 91/76 44 76; 260 r., SP, T
★★★★★Hotel Savoy, Funchal; tel. 0 91/2 20 31; 353 r., SP, T
★★★★★Reid's Hotel, Funchal; tel. 0 91/76 64 66; 163 r., SP, T
★★★★Hotel Alto Lido, Funchal; tel. 0 91/3 26 23; 118 r., SP
★★★★Hotel Vila Ramos, Funchal; tel. 0 91/76 41 55; 108 r., SP, T
★★★★Hotel Apartamento Duas Torres, Funchal; tel. 0 91/3 00 61;
137 apart.

## Hotels

★★★★Hotel Apartamento do Mar, Funchal; tel. 0 91/3 10 01; 141 apart., SP
★★★Hotel Estrelícia, Funchal; tel. 0 91/23 01 31; 148 r., SP, T
★★★Hotel Apartamento Casa Branca, Funchal; tel. 0 91/3 00 43; 45 apart., SP
★★★Hotel Apartamento Florasol, Funchal; tel. 0 91/3 31 21; 100 apart., SP
Hotel Apartamento Mimosa, Funchal; tel. 0 91/3 10 21; 100 apart., SP, T
Pensão Flamenga, Funchal; tel. 0 91/2 90 41; 35 r.
Pensão Greco, Funchal; tel. 0 91/3 00 81; 28 r.
Pensão Santa Clara, Funchal; tel. 0 91/2 41 94; 15 r., SP

**Mafra**

★★★★Albergaria Castelão, Avenida 25 de Abril; tel. 0 61/81 20 50; 27 r.

**Mirandela**

★★Hotel Mira Tua, Rua da República 85; tel. 0 78/2 24 03; 31 r.
Pensão Globo, Avenida N.S. do Amparo; tel. 0 78/2 27 11; 40 r.

**Monção**

★★★★Albergaria Atlántico, Rua Gen. de Castro 13; tel. 0 51/65 23 55; 24 r.
Pensão Chave d'Ouro, Largo da Estação; tel. 0 51/65 22 33; 8 r.
Pensão Mané, Rua General Pimenta de Castro 5; tel. 0 51/65 24 90; 8 r.

**Monchique**

★★★★Estalagem Abrigo da Montanha, Corte Pereira; tel. 0 82/9 21 31; 8 r.
★★★★Albergaria Bia-Boa, Estrada de Lisboa; tel. 0 82/9 22 71; 20 r., SP

**Monte Gordo**

★★★★Hotel Vasco da Gama, Avenida Infante Dom Henrique; tel. 0 81/4 43 21; 200 r., SP, T
★★★Eurotel Altura, Praia de Altura; tel. 0 81/9 54 50; 135 r., SP, T

**Moura**

★★Hotel de Moura; tel. 0 85/2 24 94; 40 r.

**Nazaré**

★★★Hotel da Nazaré, Largo Afonso Zuquete; tel. 0 62/56 13 11; 52 r.
★★★Hotel da Praia, Avenida Vieira Guimarães 39; tel. 0 62/56 14 23; 40 r.
★★★Hotel Maré, Rua Mouzinho de Albuquerque 8; tel. 0 62/56 11 22; 36 r.
★★Hotel Dom Fuas, Avenida Manuel Remígio; tel. 0 62/56 13 51; 35 r.
Pensão Beira Mar, Rua dos Lavradores; tel. 0 62/5 14 58; 15 r.
Pensão Central, Rua M. de Albuquerque 83; tel. 0 62/5 15 10; 20 r.
Pensão Cubata, Avenida da República 6/7; tel. 0 62/56 17 06; 21 r.
Pensão Madeira, Praça Sousa Oliveira 70; tel. 0 62/5 11 80; 35 r.

**Óbidos**

★★★★Estalagem do Convento; tel. 0 62/95 92 17; 23 r.
★★★★Albergaria Josefa d'Óbidos; tel. 0 62/95 92 28; 20 r.
★★★★Albergaria Santa Isabel; tel. 0 62/95 91 15; 20 r.
Pensão Martim de Freitas; tel. 0 62/95 91 85; 6 r.

**Ofir**

★★★★Hotel Ofir; tel. 0 53/96 13 83; 220 r., SP, T
★★★Hotel do Pinhal; tel. 0 53/96 14 73; 100 r., SP, T

**Olhão**

★★Hotel Ria-Sol, Rua Gen. H. Delgado 37; tel. 0 89/71 21 67; 52 r.
Pensão Bela Vista, Rua Teófilo Braga 65; tel. 0 89/7 26 00; 10 r.

**Oporto/Porto**

★★★★★Hotel Infante de Sagres, Praça D. Filipa de Lencastre 62; tel. 02/2 01 90 31; 84 r.
★★★★★Hotel Meridien, Avenida da Boavista 1466; tel. 02/6 00 19 13; 232 r.
★★★★★Hotel Tivoli Porto Atlântico, Rua Afonso Lopes Vieira 66; tel. 02/69 49 41; 58 r., SP, T
★★★★★Porto Sheraton, Av. da Boavista 1269; tel. 02/66 88 22; 253 r., SP
★★★★Grande Hotel da Batalha, Praça da Batalha; tel. 02/2 00 05 71; 142 r.
★★★★Hotel Castor, Rua das Doze Casas 17; tel. 02/57 00 14; 63 r.
★★★★Hotel Dom Henrique, Rua Guedes de Azevedo 179; tel. 02/2 00 57 55; 113 r.
★★★★Hotel Inca, Praça Coronel Pacheco 52; tel. 02/38 41 51; 62 r.
★★★★Hotel Ipanema, Rua do Campo Alegre 156; tel. 02/66 80 61; 150 r.
★★★★Hotel Porto Boega, Rua do Amial 605; tel 02/82 50 45; 126 r., SP

★★★Grande Hotel do Porto, Rua de S. Catarina 197; tel. 02/2 00 81 76; 100 r.
★★★Hotel Antas, Rua Padre M. da Nóbrega 111; tel. 02/48 50 00; 15 r.
★★★Hotel Corcel, Rua de Camões 135; tel. 02/38 02 58; 60 r.
★★★Hotel de São João, Rua do Bonjardim 120; tel. 02/2 00 16 62; 14 r.
★★Hotel Malaposta, Rua da Conceição 80; tel. 02/2 00 62 78; 37 r.
★★Hotel Nave, Avenida Fernão de Magalhães 247; tel. 02/57 61 31; 81 r.
★★Hotel Peninsular, Rua Sá da Bandeira 21; tel. 02/2 30 12; 48 r.
★★Hotel Tuela, Rua do Arq. Marques da Silva 200; tel. 02/66 71 61; 197 r.
Pensão Escondidinho, Rua Passos Manuel 135; tel. 02/2 00 40 79; 23 r.
Pensão Norte, Rua Fernandes Tomás 579; tel. 02/2 35 03; 25 r.
Pensão Portinari, Rua da Arroteia 68; tel. 02/49 84 10; 20 r.

★★★Hotel da Praia Norte; tel. 0 62/7 11 61; 92 r., SP          **Peniche**
Pensão Félita; tel. 0 62/7 21 90; 10 r.

Residencial do Cardal, Largo do Cardal; tel. 0 36/2 30 06; 27 r.          **Pombal**
Residencial Senhora de Belém, Urb. Senhora de Belém; tel. 0 36/2 31 85;
  27 r.

Residencial San Fernando, Maceiras; tel. 0 58/4 25 80; 24 r.          **Ponte da Barca**
Pensão Freitas; tel. 0 58/4 21 13; 15 r.

★★★Hotel Dom João III, Avenida da Liberdade; tel. 0 45/ 2 11 92; 60 r.          **Portalegre**
Pensão Platano, Rossio 40; tel. 0 45/2 21 60; 23 r.

★★★★Albergaria Miradoiro, Rua M. dos Santos 13; tel. 0 82/2 30 11; 26 r.          **Portimão**
★★★Hotel Globo, Rua 5 de Outubro 26; tel. 0 82/41 63 50; 71 r.
Pensão Afonso III, Rua Heróis do Ultramar 1; tel. 0 82/41 45 04; 30 r.
Pensão Nelinanda, Rua Vicente Vaz das Vacas 22; tel. 0 82/2 31 56; 32 r.
Pensão Pimenta, Rua Dr. Ernesto Cabrita 7; tel. 0 82/2 32 03; 35 r.

★★★★Hotel Vermar, Av. dos Banhos; tel. 0 52/61 55 66; 208 r., SP, T          **Póvoa de Varzim**
★★★Grande Hotel da Póvoa, Passeio Alegre; tel. 0 52/61 54 64; 100 r.
★★★Hotel Costa Verde, Avenida Vasco da Gama; tel. 0 52/61 55 31; 50 r.

★★★★★Hotel Algarve; tel. 0 82/41 50 01; 220 r., SP, T          **Praia da Rocha**
★★★★★Hotel Alvor Praia, Praia dos Três Irmãos; tel. 0 82/2 40 21; 220 r.,
  SP, T
★★★★★Hotel do Golfe da Penina, Montes de Alvor; tel. 0 82/2 20 51; 192 r.,
  SP, T
★★★★Hotel Delfim, Praia dos Três Irmãos; tel. 0 82/2 71 71; 325 r., SP, T
★★★★Hotel Júpiter, Av. Tomás Cabreira; tel. 0 82/41 50 41; 180 r., SP
★★★★Hotel Oriental, Av. Tomás Cabreira; tel. 0 82/41 30 00; 85 r., SP
★★★★Estalagem Mira-Sol, Rua Francisco Bivar; tel. 0 82/24 00 46; 36 r.
★★★Hotel Avenida Praia, Avenida Tomás Cabreira; tel. 0 82/8 58 72; 61 r.
★★★Hotel da Rocha, Avenida Tomás Cabreira; tel. 0 82/2 40 81; 80 r.

★★★★Hotel Quarteira sol; tel. 0 89/30 36 21; 90 r., SP          **Quarteira**
★★★Hotel Beira Mar; tel. 0 89/3 40 30; 51 r.
★★★Hotel Dom José; tel. 0 89/30 27 50; 140 r., SP
★★★Hotel Zodíaco; tel. 0 89/38 95 92; 60 r., SP, T
★★★Aparthotel Atis; tel. 0 89/38 97 71; 57 apart., SP

★★★★★Hotel Quinta do Lago; tel. 0 89/39 66 66; 150 r., SP, T          **Quinta do Lago**

Pensão Rio Maior, Rua Dr. Francisco Barbosa; tel. 0 43/9 20 87; 36 r.          **Rio Maior**

★★★Hotel Baleeira; tel. 0 82/6 42 12; 118 r., SP, T          **Sagres**
★★★Motel Gambozinos, Praia do Martinhal; tel. 0 82/6 43 18; 17 r.

★★Hotel Abidis, Rua Guilheme de Azevedo 4; tel. 0 43/2 20 17; 28 r.          **Santarém**
Pensão Jardim, Alto da Bexiga; tel. 0 43/2 71 04; 20 r.
Pensão Muralha, Rua Pedro Canavarro 12; tel. 0 43/2 23 99; 16 r.

**Hotels**

*Luxury accommodation: the "Palace of the seven Signs" in Sintra*

| | |
|---|---|
| **Santiago do Cacém** | ★★★★Albergaria D. Nuno; tel. 0 69/2 33 25; 75 r.<br>Pensão Esperança; tel. 0 69/2 21 93; 45 r.<br>Pensão Gabriel; tel. 0 69/2 22 45; 23 r. |
| **Santo Tirso** | Pensão Caroço; tel. 0 52/5 28 23; 14 r. |
| **São Pedro do Sul** | ★★Hotel Vouga; tel. 0 32/7 12 63; 20 r.<br>Pensão David; tel. 0 32/7 32 05; 17 r.<br>Pensão Lafões; tel. 0 32/7 26 16; 24 r. |
| **Sesimbra** | ★★★★Hotel do Mar, Rua Combatantes de Ultramar 10; tel. 01/2 23 33 26;<br>119 r., SP, T<br>★★Hotel Espadarte, Avenida 25 de Abril; tel. 01/2 23 31 89; 80 r.<br>Pensão Náutico, Bairro Infante D. Henrique 3; tel. 01/2 23 32 33; 10 r. |
| **Setúbal** | ★★★Hotel Esperança, Avenida Luísa Todi 220; tel. 0 65/52 51 51; 76 r.<br>Pensão Bocage, Rua de São Cristóvão 14; tel. 0 65/2 15 98; 38 r.<br>Pensão Mar e Sol, Avenida Luísa Todi 606; tel. 0 65/3 30 16; 32 r.<br>Pensão Naval Setubalense, Avenida Luisa Todi 300; tel. 0 65/2 36 74; 20 r. |
| **Sines** | ★★★Aparthotel Sinerama, Rua Marquês de Pombal 167; tel. 0 69/63 38 45;<br>105 apart.<br>Pensão Búzio, Avenida 25 de Abril 14; tel. 0 69/63 21 14; 38 r. |
| **Sintra** | ★★★★★Hotel Palácio dos Seteais, on the Colares road; tel. 01/9 23 32 00;<br>18 r., SP, T<br>★★★★Hotel Tivoli Sintra, Praça da República; tel. 01/9 23 35 05; 75 r.<br>Pensão Sintra, São Pedro de Sintra; tel. 01/9 23 07 38; 12 r. |

★★★Eurotel Tavira, Quinta das Oliveiras; tel. 0 81/32 43 24; 80 r., SP, T **Tavira**
★★Aparthotel Cabanas Golden Club, Cabanas; tel. 0 81/2 04 80; 150 apart., SP, T

★★★Hotel dos Templários, Largo Cândido dos Reis; tel. 0 49/32 17 30; **Tomar**
84 r., SP, T
Pensão Luanda, Avenida Marquês de Tomar; tel.0 49/3 29 29; 15 r.
Pensão Trovador, Rua Dr. Joaquim Ribeiro; tel. 0 49/32 25 67; 33 r.
Pensão União, Rua Serpa Pinto 94; tel. 0 49/3 28 31; 25 r.

Pensão Brasilia, on the N 220; tel. 0 94/2 24 94; 10 r. **Torre de Moncorvo**

Pensão Moderna, Avenida Tenente Valadim, tel. 0 61/2 31 46; 28 r. **Torres Vedras**

★★★★★Hotel Dona Filipa; tel. 0 89/39 41 41; 135 r., SP, T **Vale do Lobo**

★★★Hotel Lara, Rua São Sebastião; tel. 0 51/2 23 48; 54 r. **Valença do Minho**
★★★Hotel Valença do Minho, on the N 13; tel. 0 51/2 22 11; 36 r., Sp

★★★★Hotel Afonso III, Av. D. Afonso III 494; tel. 0 58/2 41 23; 89 r., SP **Viana do Castelo**
★★★★Hotel Santa Luzia, Monte de Santa Luzia; tel. 0 58/82 88 89; 47 r., SP
★★★★Hotel do Parque, Parque da Galiza; tel. 0 58/82 86 05; 123 r., SP
★★★Motel Abrigo do Postilhão, Darque; tel. 0 58/32 18 21; 23 r., SP
★★★Viana Sol Hotel, Largo Vasco da Gama; tel. 0 58/82 89 95; 65 r., SP
★Hotel Aliança, Avenida dos Combatentes da Grande Guerra;
tel. 0 58/2 30 01; 29 r.
Residencial Jardim, Largo 5 de Outubro 68; tel. 0 58/82 89 15; 20 r.
Pensão Alambique, Rua Manuel Espregueira 86; tel. 0 58/2 38 94; 24 r.

★★★Motel de Sant'Ana, Lugar de Sant'Ana; tel. 0 52/62 17 17; 34 r., SP **Vila do Conde**

★★★★★Marinotel; tel. 0 89/38 99 88; 389 r., SP, T **Vilamoura**
★★★★Hotel Atlantis; tel. 0 89/38 99 77; 333 r., SP, T
★★★★Hotel Dom Pedro Golf; tel. 0 89/38 96 50; 261 r., SP, T
★★★Golf-Motel Vilamoura; tel. 0 89/3 29 77; 52 r., SP

★★★★Albergaria Cabanelas, Rua D.P. de Castro; tel. 0 59/2 31 53; 24 r. **Vila Real**
★★★Hotel Mira Corgo, Avenida 1 de Maio; tel. 0 59/2 50 01; 76 r., SP

★★Hotel Apolo, Avenida dos Bombeiros Portugueses; tel. 0 81/4 44 48; **Vila Real de Santo**
42 r. **António**

★★★Hotel das Termas do Vimeiro, Maceira; tel. 0 61/9 81 03; 100 r., SP, T **Vimeiro**
Pensão Rainha Santa, Quinta da Piedade; tel. 0 61/98 42 34; 20 r.

★★★★Hotel Grão Vasco, Rua Gaspar Barreiros; tel. 0 32/42 35 11; 86 r., SP **Viseu**
★★★Hotel Maná, on the N 16; tel. 0 32/47 92 43; 47 r.
★★★Hotel Moinho de Vento, Rua Paulo Emilio 13; tel. 0 32/42 41 16; 30 r.
★★Hotel Avenida, Avenida 28 de Maio 1; tel. 0 32/42 34 32; 40 r.

## Information

## Portuguese National Tourist Offices outside Portugal

22–25A Sackville Street
London W1X 1DE. Tel. (0171) 494 1441

United Kingdom

919 North Michigan Avenue, Suite 3001
Chicago, IL 60611. Tel. (312) 236 6603

U.S.A.
Chicago

3440 Wilshire Boulevard, Suite 1616
Los Angeles, CA 90010. Tel. (213) 380 6459

Los Angeles

## Information

| | |
|---|---|
| New York | 590 Fifth Avenue<br>New York, NY 10036. Tel. (212) 354 4403 |
| Canada<br>Toronto | 60 Bloor Street, West Suite 1005<br>Toronto, Ontario M4W 3B8. Tel. (416) 921 7376 |
| Montreal | Suite 1150, 1801 McGill College Avenue<br>Montreal, Quebec H3A 2N4. Tel. (514) 282 1264 |

## Tourist Information Centres in Portugal

| | |
|---|---|
| By telephone | The Portuguese National Tourist Office maintains a 24 hour information line in various languages, including English: tel. 01/70 63 41. |
| **Abrantes** | Largo da Feira; tel. 0 41/2 25 55 |
| **Agueda** | Largo Dr. João Elisio Sucena; tel. 0 34/6 14 12 |
| **Albufeira** | Rua 5 de Outubro; tel. 0 89/5 21 44 |
| **Alcobaça** | Praça 25 de Abril; tel. 0 62/4 23 77 |
| **Algarve** | See individual places |
| **Amarante** | Rua Cândido dos Reis; tel. 0 55/42 42 59 |
| **Armação de Pêra** | Avenida Marginal; tel. 0 82/31 21 45 |
| **Arraiolos** | Praça Lima e Brito; tel. 0 66/4 23 21 |
| **Aveiro** | Praça da República; tel. 0 34/2 44 85 |
| **Azores** | See Ponta Delgada |
| **Barcelos** | Largo da Porta Nova; tel. 0 53/81 18 82 |
| **Batalha** | Largo Paulo VI; tel. 0 44/9 61 80 |
| **Beira** | See Castelo Branco, Coimbra and Guarda |
| **Beja** | Rua Capitão João Francisco de Sousa 25; tel. 0 84/2 36 93 |
| **Braga** | Avenida da Liberdade 1; tel. 0 53/2 25 50 |
| **Bragança** | Avenida Ciudade de Zamora; tel. 0 73/2 22 73 |
| **Buçaco National Park** | Rua Emídio Navarro, Luso; tel. 0 31/9 31 33 |
| **Caldas da Rainha** | Praça da Republica; tel. 0 62/3 45 11 |
| **Caminha** | Rua Ricardo Joaquim de Sousa; tel. 0 58/92 19 52 |
| **Cascais** | Alameda Combatentes da Grande Guerra 25; tel. 01/4 86 82 04 |
| **Castelo Branco** | Alameda da Liberdade; tel. 0 72/2 10 02 |
| **Castelo de Vide** | Rua Bartolomeu Alvares da Santa 81; tel. 0 45/9 13 61 |
| **Chaves** | Rua de Santo António 213; tel. 0 76/2 10 29 |
| **Coimbra** | Largo da Portagem; tel. 0 39/2 29 35 and 2 37 99 |
| **Costa de Lisboa** | See Lisbon, Sesimbra and Setúbal |

| | |
|---|---|
| See Aveiro, Ericeira, Espinho, Figueira da Foz, Nazaré, Oporto, Peniche and Torres Vedras | **Costa de Prata** |
| See Cascais and Estoril | **Costa do Sol** |
| See Setúbal | **Costa Dourada** |
| See Barcelos, Caminha, Oporto, Póvoa de Varzim, Viana do Castelo and Vila do Conde | **Costa Verde** |
| Praça do Municipio; tel. 0 75/2 21 70 | **Covilhã** |
| Largo da Rotunda; tel. 0 31/5 22 48 | **Curia** |
| Praça da República; tel. 0 68/62 22 36 | **Elvas** |
| Rua Mendes Leal; tel. 0 61/6 31 22 | **Ericeira** |
| Angulo da Ruas 6; tel. 02/72 09 11 | **Espinho** |
| Rua 1 de Dezembro; tel. 0 53/96 13 54 | **Esposende** |
| Arcadas do Parque; tel. 01/4 68 01 13 | **Estoril** |
| See Lisbon | **Estremadura** |
| Largo da República 26; tel. 0 68/2 25 38 | **Estremoz** |
| Praça do Giraldo; tel. 0 66/2 26 71<br>Avenida de São Sebastião; tel. 0 66/3 12 96 | **Évora** |
| Rua Ataíde de Oliveira; tel. 0 89/80 36 67<br>Rua da Misericórdia 8–12; tel. 0 89/80 36 04 | **Faro** |
| Avenida D. José Alves Correira da Silva; tel. 0 49/53 11 39 | **Fátima** |
| Avenida 25 de Abril; tel. 0 33/2 76 83 | **Figueira da Foz** |
| Avenida Arriaga 18; tel. 0 91/2 90 57 and 2 56 58 | **Funchal** |
| Avenida Manuel Ferreira da Costa; tel. 0 53/6 51 33 | **Gerês** |
| Praça de Luís de Camões, Edificio da Câmara Municipal; tel. 0 71/21 22 51 | **Guarda** |
| Avenida da Resistência ao Fascismo 83; tel. 0 53/41 24 50 | **Guimarães** |
| Largo Marquês de Pombal; tel. 0 82/76 30 31 | **Lagos** |
| Avenida Visconde Guedes Teixeira; tel. 0 54/6 20 05 | **Lamego** |
| Praça de Goa; tel. 0 44/3 27 48 | **Leiria** |
| Central Tourist Bureau, Av. A. A. de Aquior; tel. 01/57 50 91<br>Praça dos Restauradores (Palácio Foz); tel. 01/3 46 63 07<br>Airport; tel. 01/89 42 48 | **Lisbon** |
| See Funchal | **Madeira** |
| Avenida do 25 de Abril; tel. 0 61/5 20 23 | **Mafra** |
| Rua do Dr. Matos Magalhães; tel. 0 45/9 32 26 | **Marvão** |
| Rua França Júnior 1; tel. 02/93 44 14 | **Matosinhos** |

**Information**

| | |
|---|---|
| Minho | See Braga |
| Monção | Largo do Loreto; tel. 0 51/5 27 57 |
| Monte Gordo | Avenida Marginal; tel. 0 81/4 44 95 |
| Moura | Praça de Sacadura Cabral; tel. 0 85/2 25 89 |
| Nazaré | Avenida da República; tel. 0 62/56 11 94 |
| Óbidos | Rua Direita; tel. 0 62/9 52 31 |
| Olhão | Largo da Lagoa; tel. 0 89/71 39 36 |
| Oporto | Praça Dom João I 43; tel. 02/31 39 57<br>Rua do Clube dos Fenianos 25; tel. 02/31 27 40<br>Largo do Chafariz; tel. 01/2 35 00 89 |
| Peneda-Gerês<br>National Park | See Gerês |
| Peniche | Rua de Alexandre Herculano; tel. 0 62/7 95 71 |
| Pombal | Largo do Cardal; tel. 0 36/2 32 30 |
| Ponta Delgada | Avenido do Infante Dom Henrique; tel. 0 96/2 57 43 |
| Portalegre | Estrada de Santana 25; tel. 0 45/2 18 15 |
| Portimão | Largo 1 de Dezembro; tel. 0 82/2 36 95 |
| Póvoa de Varzim | Avenida Mouzinho de Albuquerque 166; tel. 0 52/62 46 09 |
| Praia da Rocha | Avenida Tomás Cabreira; tel. 0 82/2 22 90 |
| Quarteira | Avenida Infante Sagres; tel. 0 89/31 22 17 |
| Ribatejo | See Santarém |
| Sagres | Promontório de Sagres (Fortaleza); tel. 0 82/6 41 25 |
| Santarém | Rua Capelo Ivens 63; tel. 0 43/2 31 40 |
| Santo Tirso | Praça do Município; tel. 0 52/5 10 91 |
| São Pedro do Sul | On the N 16; tel. 0 32/7 13 20 |
| Serpa | Largo D. Jorge de Melo 2/3; tel 0 84/9 03 35 |
| Serra da Estrela | See Covilhã |
| Serra da Lousã | See Coimbra |
| Sesimbra | Largo de Marinha; tel. 01/2 23 57 43 |
| Setúbal | Rua do Corpo Santo; tel. 0 65/2 95 07 |
| Silves | Rua do 25 de Abril; tel. 0 82/44 22 55 |
| Sines | Avenida do General Humberto Delgado; tel. 0 69/63 44 72 |
| Sintra | Praça da República; tel. 01/9 23 11 57 |
| Tavira | Praça da República; tel. 0 81/2 25 11 |

| | |
|---|---|
| Avenida Dr Cândido Madureira; tel. 0 49/31 32 37 | **Tomar** |
| Edifício da Câmara; tel. 0 94/2 22 88/9 | **Torre de Moncorvo** |
| Rua do 9 de Abril; tel. 0 61/2 30 94 | **Torres Vedras** |
| See Bragança | **Trás-os-Montes** |
| On the N 13; tel. 0 51/2 21 82 | **Valença do Minho** |
| Rua do Hospital Velho; tel. 0 58/2 26 20 | **Viana do Castelo** |
| Avenida do 25 de Abril; tel. 0 52/63 14 72 | **Vila do Conde** |
| See Quarteira | **Vilamoura** |
| Jardim do Morro; tel. 02/30 92 78 | **Vila Nova de Gaia** |
| Avenida Carvalho Araújo; tel. 0 59/2 28 19 | **Vila Real** |
| Praça Marqués de Pombal; tel. 0 81/4 44 95<br>Avenida Infante Dom Henrique; tel. 0 81/4 44 95 | **Vila Real de Santo António** |
| Praça da República; tel. 0 68/4 23 05 | **Vila Viçosa** |
| Avenida de Calouste Gulbenkian; tel. 0 32/42 20 14 | **Viseu** |

## Insurance

Visitors are strongly advised to ensure that they have adequate holiday insurance including loss or damage to luggage, loss of currency and jewellery.

*General*

British citizens, like nationals of other European Union countries, are entitled to obtain medical care under the Portuguese health services on the same basis as Portuguese people. This means that they must pay the cost of treatment and medicine but are reimbursed 70–80% of the cost through the local sickness insurance office. The level and nature of the payments depend on the Portuguese rules and regulations, but it is necessary to have obtained an E111 form from the local DSS office before leaving home, which certifies entitlement to insurance cover. In the event of treatment being necessary (apart from casualty-type emergencies) a set of vouchers for medical treatment must be obtained from the relevant regional health authority, the Administração Regionais de Saúde; a list of these can be obtained from health insurance agencies.

*Health*

It is nevertheless advisable, even for EU nationals, to take out some form of short-term health insurance providing complete cover and possibly avoiding delays. Nationals of non-EU countries should certainly have insurance cover.

*Additional Private Insurance*

Visitors travelling by car should ensure that their insurance is comprehensive and covers use of the vehicle in Europe.

*Vehicles*

See also Travel Documents.

## Language

The foreign languages most commonly spoken in Portugal are Spanish, English and French, and there are now also numbers of returned "guest

*Knowledge of foreign languages*

workers" who have learnt some German while working in Germany. In any event, however, it is well worth having at least a smattering of Portuguese.

**Portuguese**

On first hearing Portuguese spoken a visitor may not quite know what to make of it because it can sound rather like a Slav language (e.g. Polish). The written form of the language, however, can at once be recognised as a Romance language, and some knowledge of Latin or Spanish will be a great help in understanding it.

Grammar

Portuguese grammer is notable for the rich tense system of the verbs, in particular for the preservation of the Latin pluperfect (e.g. fora, "I had been"). A further peculiarity is the inflected personal infinitive: "entramos na loja para comprarmos pão" = "we go into the shop to buy bread".

The plural is formed by the addition of "s", in some cases with the modification of the preceding vowel or consonant:

| Singular | Plural |
|----------|--------|
| o animal | os animais |
| o hotel | os hotéis |
| a região | as regiões |

The definite article is "o" (masculine) or "a" (feminine) in the singular, "os" or "as" in the plural. The declension of nouns and adjectives is simple. The nominative and accusative are the same; the genitive is indicated by "de" (of), the dative by "a" (to). The prepositions "de" and "a" combine with the definite article as follows:

| de + o = do | de + a = da |
|-------------|-------------|
| de + os = dos | de + as = das |

| a + o = ao | a + os = aos |
|------------|--------------|
| a + a = à | a + as = às |

The Portuguese spoken in Portugal seems lacking in resonance, but is soft and melodious, without the hard accumulations of consonants and the rough gutturals of Castilian Spanish. It is notable for its frequent sibilants and for the nasalisation of vowels, diphthongs and triphthongs. Unstressed vowels and intervocalic consonants are much attenuated or disappear altogether. The stressed syllable of a word so dominates the rest that the vowels of the other syllables are radically altered in tone quality and not infrequently are reduced to a mere whisper. In the spoken language the boundaries between words are so blurred (in the phenomenon know as "sandhi") that the individual word within a group largely loses its independence: thus the phrase "os outros amigos" ("the other friends") is run together into a single phonetic unit and pronounced something like "usótrushamígush".

The nine vocalic phonemes used in Portuguese are represented by the five vowels a, e, i, o and u together with three diacritic signs or accents ( í ì î ) also indicate the stress. Nasalisation is indicated by the tilde (Portuguese "o til": ĩ ) or by the consonant "m" or "n".

The stress is normally on the penultimate syllable of a word ending in a vowel or in "m" or "s" and on the last syllable of a word ending in a consonant other than "m" or "s". Exceptions to this rule are marked by the use of an accent. It should be noted that "ia", "io" and "iu" are not treated as diphthongs as in Spanish but as combinations of separate vowels. Thus the word "agrário", for example, with the stress on the second "a", requires an accent to indicate this in Portuguese but not in Spanish where it is "agrario" without an accent.

Some peculiarities
of Portuguese
pronunciation

| | |
|---|---|
| a | unstressed, like a whispered e |
| à | long "ah" |
| c | k before a, o and u; s before e and i |

| | |
|---|---|
| ç | s |
| ch | sh |
| e | unstressed, like a whispered i; in initial position before s, practically disappears ("escudo" pronounced "shkúdo"; Estoril pronounced "Shturíl") |
| ê | closed e |
| é | open e |
| g | hard g (as in "go") before a, o and u; zh (like s in "pleasure") before e and i |
| gu | hard g |
| h | mute |
| i | nasalised after u ("muito" pronounced "muínto") |
| j | zh |
| l | in final position as in English or, in Brazil, like a weak u ("animal" pronounced "animáu") |
| lh ly | (with consonantal y): cf. Spanish ll |
| m,n | in final position nasalise the preceding vowel |
| nh ny | (with consonantal y): cf. Spanish ñ |
| o | unstressed, like u |
| ô | closed o |
| ó | open o |
| qu | k |
| r | trilled |
| rr | strongly rolled |
| s | s before vowels; z between vowels; sh before hard consonants and in final position; zh before soft consonants |
| v | v |
| x | sh |
| z | in final position sh; otherwise z |

The Brazilian pronunciation of Portuguese is markedly different from the Portuguese mainland. In particular final "s" and "z" are pronounced "s" and not "sh", and initial "r" sounds almost like "h".

## Numbers

| | | |
|---|---|---|
| 0 | zero | Cardinals |
| 1 | um, uma | |
| 2 | dois, duas | |
| 3 | três | |
| 4 | quatro | |
| 5 | cinco | |
| 6 | seis | |
| 7 | sete | |
| 8 | oito | |
| 9 | nove | |
| 10 | dez | |
| 11 | onze | |
| 12 | doze | |
| 13 | treze | |
| 14 | catorze | |
| 15 | quinze | |
| 16 | Dezasseis | |
| 17 | dezassete | |
| 18 | dezoito | |
| 19 | dezanove | |
| 20 | vinte | |
| 21 | vinte-e-um | |
| 22 | vinte-e-dois (duas) | |
| 30 | trinta | |
| 31 | trinta-e-em (uma) | |

| | | |
|---|---|---|
| | 40 | quarenta |
| | 50 | cinquenta |
| | 60 | sessenta |
| | 70 | setenta |
| | 80 | oitenta |
| | 90 | noventa |
| | 100 | cem, cento |
| | 101 | cento-e-um (uma) |
| | 200 | duzentos, -as |
| | 300 | trezentos, -as |
| | 400 | quatrocentos, -as |
| | 500 | quinhentos, -as |
| | 600 | seiscentos, -as |
| | 700 | setecentos, -as |
| | 800 | oitocentos, -as |
| | 900 | novecentos, -as |
| | 1000 | mil |
| | 2000 | dois (duas) mil |
| | 1 million | um milhão de |
| Ordinals | 1st | primeiro, -a |
| | 2nd | segundo, -a |
| | 3rd | terceiro, -a |
| | 4th | quarto, -a |
| | 5th | quinto, -a |
| | 6th | sexto, -a |
| | 7th | sétimo, -a |
| | 8th | oitavo, -a |
| | 9th | nono, -a |
| | 10th | décimo, -a |
| | 11th | undécimo, -a; décimo primeiro |
| | 12th | duodécimo, -a; décimo segundo |
| | 13th | décimo terceiro |
| | 20th | vigésimo, -a |
| | 21st | vigésimo primeiro, -a |
| | 30th | trigésimo, -a |
| | 40th | quadragésimo, -a |
| | 50th | quinquagésimo, -a |
| | 60th | sexuagésimo, -a |
| | 100th | centésimo, -a |

Fractions ½ meio, meia
⅓ um terço, uma terça parte
¼ um quarto
¾ três quartos, três quartas partes

## Idioms and Vocabulary

Forms of address — Men are usually addressed as "Senhor", women as "minha Senhora". If you know a man's name you should address him by his name with the prefix "Senhor"; ladies are addressed by "Senhora Dona" and their Christian name, if this is known. "You" in direct address is "o Senhor", "a Senhora" or "Você", in the plural "os Senhores", "as Senhoras" or "Vocês".

In Portuguese names, which are frequently very long, the maternal surname usually comes first.

| Idioms | | |
|---|---|---|
| | Good morning, good day | Bom dia |
| | Good afternoon | Boa tarde |
| | Good evening, good night | Boa noite |
| | Goodbye | Adeus, Até à vista |

| | |
|---|---|
| Yes, no (Sir) | Sim, não (Senhor) |
| Excuse me (apologising) | Desculpe, Perdão |
| Excuse me (e.g. when passing in front of someone) | Com licença |
| After you (e.g. offering something) | A vontade! |
| Please (asking for something) | Faz favor |
| Thank you (very much) | (Muito) obrigado |
| Not at all (You're welcome) | De nada, Não tem de què |
| Do you speak English? | O senhor fala inglês? |
| A little, not much | Um pouco, não muito |
| I do not understand | Não compreendo (nada) |
| What is the Portuguese for . . .? | Como se diz em português . . .? |
| What is the name of this church? | Como chama-se esta igreja? |
| Have you any rooms? | Tem um quarto livre? |
| I should like . . . | Queria . . . |
| A room with private bath | Um quarto com banho |
| With full board | Com pensão completa |
| What does it cost? | Quanto custa? |
| Everything included | Tudo incluído |
| That is very dear | É muito caro |
| Bill, please! | Faz favor, a conta! |
| Where is . . . Street? | Onde fica a rua . . .? |
| the road to? | a estrada para . . .? |
| a doctor? | um médico? |
| a dentist? | um dentista? |
| Right, left | À direita, esquerda |
| Straight ahead | Sempre a direito |
| Above, below | Em cima, em baixo |
| When is it open? | A que horas está aberto? |
| How far? | Que distância? |
| Wake me at six | Chamé-me às seis |

| | | |
|---|---|---|
| Alfândega | Customs | Road signs |
| Alto! | Stop | |
| Atenção! | Caution | |
| Auto-estrada | Highway | |
| Bifurcação | Road fork | |
| Cuidado! | Caution | |
| Curva perigosa | Dangerous curve | |
| Dê passagem! | Give way/yield | |
| Desvio | Diversion | |
| Devagar! | Slow | |
| Direcção única; Sentido único | One-way street | |
| Estacionamento proibido | Parking prohibited | |
| Ir a passo! | Dead slow | |
| Ir pela direita, esquerda | Keep right, left | |
| Nevoeiro | Mist, fog | |
| Obras na estrada | Road works | |
| Parque de estacionamento | Car park, parking place | |
| Passagem proibida | No entry | |
| Peões | Pedestrians | |
| Perigo! | Danger! | |
| Portagem | Toll | |
| Praia | Beach | |
| Proibido ultrapassar | No overtaking | |
| Rebanhos | Beware of livestock | |
| Serviço de reboque | Towing service | |

| | | |
|---|---|---|
| accelerator | o acelerador | Vehicle terms |
| automobile | o auto, o carro | |
| axle | o eixo | |
| battery | a bateria | |

377

| | |
|---|---|
| bearing | a chumaceira |
| bolt | o parafuso |
| bonnet/hood | o capot |
| brake | o travão |
| breakdown | a avaria |
| bulb | a lâmpada eléctrica |
| bumper | o pára-choque |
| bus | a camioneta (de passageiros) |
| car | o auto, o carro |
| carburettor/carburetor | o carburador |
| change (oil, tyre/tire, etc.) | mudar |
| charge (battery) | carregar |
| check | verificar |
| clutch | a embraiagem |
| contact | o contacto |
| cylinder | o cilindro |
| damaged | avariado, avariada |
| diesel engine | o motor Diesel |
| direction indicator | o indicador de direcção |
| distributor | o distribuidor |
| driver | o motorista, o condutor |
| driving licence | a carta de condutor |
| dynamo | o dínamo |
| engine | o motor |
| exhaust | o escape |
| fan belt | a correia da ventoinha |
| fault | a avaria |
| float | o flutuador |
| fuse | o fusível |
| garage | a garage, a garagem |
| gas/petrol | a gasolina |
| gas/petrol pump | a bomba de gasolina |
| gas/petrol station | o posto de gasolina |
| gas/petrol tank | o depósito de gasolina |
| gasket | o empanque |
| gear | a velocidade, a mudança |
| gearbox | o câmbio de velocidades |
| grease (verb) | lubrificar |
| headlamp | o farol |
| hood/bonnet | o capot |
| horn | a buzina |
| ignition | a ignição |
| inflate | dar à bomba |
| inner tube | a câmara-de-ar |
| jack | o macaco |
| jet | o gicleur |
| lorry/truck | o camião |
| magneto | o magneto |
| make (of car) | a marca |
| map | o mapa das estradas |
| maximum speed | a velocidade máxima |
| mixture | a mistura |
| motorcycle | a motocicleta |
| number-plate | a placa, a matrícula |
| nut | a porca |
| oil | o óleo |
| oil-pump | a bomba de óleo |
| park (verb) | estacionar |
| parking place, car park | o estacionamento |
| petrol/gas | a gasolina |
| petrol/gas pump | a bomba de gasolina |
| petrol/gas station | o posto de gasolina |

| | |
|---|---|
| petrol/gas tank | o depósito de gasolina |
| piston | o postão |
| piston ring | o segmento de pistão |
| pump | a bomba |
| radiator | o radiador |
| rear light | a luz traseira |
| repair | reparar |
| repair garage | a oficina de reparação |
| road map | o mapa das estradas |
| scooter | o scooter |
| shock absorber | o amortecedor |
| snow chain | a cadeia antideslizante |
| spanner | a chave inglesa |
| spare part | a peça de sobresselente |
| sparking plug | a vela |
| speedometer | o velocimetro |
| spring | a mola |
| starter | o arranque |
| steering | a direcção |
| steering wheel | o volante |
| tow away | levar a reboque |
| transmission | a condução |
| truck/lorry | o camião |
| two-stroke engine | o motor do dois tempos |
| tyre/tire | o pneu |
| tyre/tire pressure | a pressão dos pneus |
| valve | a válvula |
| wash | lavar |
| water-pump | a bomba de água |
| wheel | a roda |
| windscreen/windshield | o párabrisas |
| windscreen/windshield wiper | o limpa-pára-brisas |
| wing | o guarda-lama |

| | | |
|---|---|---|
| aircraft | aeroplano, avião | Travelling |
| airport | aeroporto | |
| all aboard! | partida! | |
| all change! | mudar! | |
| arrival | chegada | |
| baggage | bagagem | |
| baggage check | guia, senha | |
| bus | autocarro, camioneta | |
| conductor (ticket-collector) | revisor | |
| couchette car | furgoneta | |
| departure | partida | |
| fare | preço | |
| flight | vôo | |
| information | informação | |
| line (railway) | via férrea | |
| luggage | bagagem | |
| luggage ticket | guia, senha | |
| no smoking (carriage) | não fumadores | |
| platform | plataforma, gare | |
| porter | moço de fretes | |
| restaurant car | carruagem restaurante | |
| railway station | estação | |
| sleeping car | carruagem-cama | |
| smoking (carriage) | fumadores | |
| steward | comissário de bordo | |
| stewardess | hospedeira (do ar) | |
| stop | paragem | |
| ticket | bilhete | |

## Language

|  |  |  |
|---|---|---|
|  | ticket-collector (conductor) | revisor |
|  | ticket office | bilheteria, guichet |
|  | timetable | horário |
|  | toilet | lavatório |
|  | train | combóio |
|  | waiting room | sala de espera |
| Months | January | janeiro |
|  | February | fevereiro |
|  | March | março |
|  | April | abril |
|  | May | maio |
|  | June | junho |
|  | July | julho |
|  | August | agosto |
|  | September | setembro |
|  | October | outubro |
|  | November | novembro |
|  | December | dezembro |
|  | month | mês |
|  | year | ano |
| Days of the week | Monday | segunda-feira |
|  | Tuesday | terça-feira |
|  | Wednesday | quarta-feira |
|  | Thursday | quinta-feira |
|  | Friday | sexta-feira |
|  | Saturday | sábado |
|  | Sunday | domingo |
|  | day | dia |
|  | holiday, feast-day | dia de festa, dia feriado |
| Holidays and Religious Festivals | New Year's Day | Ano-Novo |
|  | Easter | Páscoa |
|  | Ascension | Ascensão |
|  | Whitsun | Espírito Santo, Pentecostes |
|  | Corpus Christi | Festa do Corpo de Deus |
|  | All Saints | Todos os Santos |
|  | Christmas | Natal |
|  | New Year's Eve | Véspera do Ano-Novo, Noite de São Silvestre |
| At the post office | address | endereço |
|  | air mail | correio aéreo |
|  | by airmail | por avião |
|  | express letter | carta urgente |
|  | letter | carta |
|  | letter-box, post-box | marco postal |
|  | packet | embrulho |
|  | parcel | pacote |
|  | postage | porte |
|  | postcard | bilhete postal |
|  | poste restante | poste-restante |
|  | postman | carteiro |
|  | post office | correio |
|  | registered letter | carta registrada |
|  | stamp | selo, estampilha |
|  | telegram | telegrama |
|  | telephone | telephone |
|  | telex | telex |
| Glossary | abadia | abbey |
|  | água | water |

| | |
|---|---|
| aldeia | small village, hamlet |
| altura | hill, eminence |
| ancoradouro | anchorage |
| anfiteatro | amphitheatre |
| aqueduto | aqueduct |
| arquipélago | archipelago |
| avenida | avenue |
| azulejos | glazed tiles |
| baía | bay |
| bairro | district of town |
| balneário | bath(s) |
| barco | boat |
| barragem | dam, reservoir |
| bolsa | purse |
| cabo | cape |
| caldas | hot springs, spa |
| calvário | calvary |
| câmara municipal | town hall |
| caminho | path, track road |
| caminho de ferro | railway |
| campo | field, countryside |
| capela | chapel |
| capela-mór | main chapel with high altar |
| casa | house |
| casal | farm, hamlet |
| cascata | waterfall |
| castelo | castle |
| cemitério | cemetery, churchyard |
| cidade | town, city |
| ciências naturais | natural history |
| circulação | round trip |
| citânia | prehistoric fortified settlement |
| claustro | cloister |
| colina | hill |
| convento | convent (in the general sense of religious house) |
| coro | choir |
| costa | coast |
| cova | cave, pit |
| cumeada | mountain ridge |
| cúpula | dome |
| desfiladeiro | pass, defile |
| doca | dock |
| encruzamento de ruas | street intersection |
| ermida | pilgrimage chapel, hermitage |
| estabelecimento balnear | spa establishment |
| estrada | road |
| estreito | straight |
| farol | lighthouse |
| floresta | forest |
| fonte | spring, fountain |
| fortaleza | fortress, castle |
| foz | mouth of river |
| fronteira | frontier |
| funicular | funicular |
| garganta | gorge |
| hospital | hospital |
| hotel | hotel |
| igreja | church |
| ilha | island |
| janela | window |
| jardim | garden |

## Language

| | |
|---|---|
| lago | lake |
| lagoa | small lake, lagoon |
| landa | heath, moor |
| leste | east |
| mar | sea |
| mirador | viewpoint |
| montanha | mountain (range) |
| monte | hill |
| muralha | (town) wall |
| museu | museum |
| norte | north |
| oeste | west |
| paço | palace |
| paço de concelho | town hall |
| padrão | monument |
| palácio | palace |
| pântano | marsh, bog |
| parque | park |
| parque nacional | national park |
| pátio | courtyard |
| pelhourinho | pillory column |
| península | peninsula |
| pensão | pension; guest-house |
| pico | peak |
| pintura | painting |
| planalto | plateau |
| planície | plain |
| poço | well, spring |
| ponte | bridge |
| portão | gateway |
| porto | harbour, port |
| pousada | (State-run) hotel, inn |
| povoação | village |
| praça | square |
| praça de touros | bullring |
| praia | beach |
| quinta | country house |
| retábulo | retable, reredos |
| rio | river |
| roca, rocha | rock, crag |
| rua | street |
| sala | hall, room |
| sé | cathedral |
| serra | mountain range, range of hills |
| sul | south |
| tapeçaria | tapestry |
| termas | hot springs, spa |
| tesouro | treasure |
| torre | tower |
| vale | valley |

| Portuguese menu | | |
|---|---|---|
| | a conta | the bill |
| | açorda | garlic and bread soup |
| | água | water |
| | água mineral | mineral water |
| | aguardente, brandy | brandy |
| | alho | garlic |
| | almoço | lunch |
| | amêndoa | almond |
| | antepastos | starter, hors d'oeuvre |
| | arroz | rice |
| | assado | grilled |

| | |
|---|---|
| aves | poultry |
| azeite | olive oil |
| azeitonas | olives |
| batatas | potatoes |
| batatas fritas | fried potatoes |
| bebidas | drinks |
| bife | steak |
| bolo | cake |
| cabrito | kid (goat) |
| caça | game |
| café | coffee |
| café com leite | coffee with milk |
| carne | meat |
| carneiro | mutton |
| carta (or lista, ementa) | menu |
| cebolas | onions |
| ceia | late-night snack, supper |
| cerveja | beer |
| chá | tea |
| chávena | cup |
| chocolate | chocolate |
| coelho | rabbit |
| colher | spoon |
| colher de chá | teaspoon |
| copo | glass |
| corço | venison |
| cordeiro | lamb |
| couve | cabbage |
| couve-flor | cauliflower |
| cozido | cooked |
| doces | sweets |
| ervilhas | peas |
| espargos | asparagus |
| espinafre | spinach |
| faca | knife |
| feijões | beans |
| frango | chicken |
| fruta | fruit |
| garfo | fork |
| gelado | ice cream |
| guardanapo | napkin |
| jantar | dinner, evening meal |
| javalí | boar |
| laranja | orange |
| lebre | hare |
| leitão | sucking pig |
| leite | milk |
| legumes (hortaliça) | vegetables |
| maçã | apple |
| manteiga | butter |
| massa(s) | pasta |
| molho | sauce |
| mostarda | mustard |
| óleo | oil |
| ovo (ovos estrelados) | egg (fried) |
| pão | bread |
| pãozinho | roll |
| pato | duck |
| peixe | fish |
| pepinos | cucumber |
| pequeno almoço | breakfast |
| pera | pear |

**Language courses**

| perdiz | partridge |
| perua | turkey |
| pimenta | pepper |
| pimento | paprika, green pepper |
| porco | pork |
| prato | plate |
| prato do dia | dish of the day |
| presunto | ham |
| queijo | cheese |
| repolho | white cabbage |
| sal | salt |
| salada | salad |
| salame | salami |
| sobremesas | dessert |
| sopa | soup |
| sumo de fruta | fruit juice |
| talher | cutlery |
| tomates | tomatoes |
| uva | grapes |
| vaca | beef |
| vinagre | vinegar |
| vinho | wine |
| vitela | veal |

## Language courses

Various institutes in Lisbon, Oporto, Coimbra and the Algarve provide courses in the Portuguese language, both at advanced level and for beginners, usually lasting from two to four weeks. A number of courses include "learn while on holiday" programmes, whilst others are aimed at the business community. Some tour operators also offer special language-learning holidays.

**Language schools in Lisbon**

Berlitz
Avenida Cd Valbom 6; tel. 01/3 52 01 23

Cambridge School
Avenida Guerra Junqueiro 8; tel. 01/89 96 01, 88 45 44

CIAL – Centro de Línguas
Avenida da República 14; tel. 01/73 02 31

Faculdade de Letras da Universidade de Lisboa
Cidade Universitária; tel. 01/73 33 56

**Oporto**

Cambridge School
Rua Duque da Terceira 381; tel. 02/56 11 30, 56 03 80

Faculdade de Letras da Universidade do Porto
Rua do Campo Alegre 1055

**Coimbra**

Cambridge School
Praça da República 15; tel. 0 39/3 49 69

Faculdade de Letras da Universidade de Coimbra
Praça Porta Férrea; tel. 0 39/3 46 13

**Algarve**

Instituto Línguas de Faro
Avenida 5 de Outubro, Faro; tel. 0 89/2 45 56

Interlíngua
Rua Santa Isabel 12, Portimão; tel. 0 82/2 76 90

A full list of all the language schools in Portugal that offer courses in Portuguese as a foreign language is available from the Portuguese National Tourist Offices (see Information).

## Markets

Portugal's major towns and cities have covered markets which are open in the mornings from Monday to Saturday, selling a great variety of produce.

Covered markets

Almost every smaller place has a weekly market, as well as some stalls selling fruit and vegetables during the rest of the week.

Weekly markets

Mercado da Ribeira Nova, Avenida 24 de Julho
Big covered market

Markets in Lisbon

Rua de São Pedro in the Alfama
Fish market

Feira da Lada, Campo de Santa Clara
(near the church of São Vicente de Fora)
Tuesdays and Saturdays, 9am–6pm.
   This famous flea-market is where all kinds of curios, antiques, junk and jumble change hands.

Almost every part of Lisbon also has its own fruit and vegetable market.

*Market in Coimbra . . .*          *. . . in Estremoz*

## Medical Assistance

Medical Care

Adequate medical care is available in Portugal, with rural areas the only places where it may prove difficult to consult a specialist. There are also many English-speaking doctors in Portugal and a British Hospital at 49 Rue Saraiva de Carvalho, Lisbon; tel. 60 20 20.

In a real emergency you should contact the casualty department (urgência) of the nearest hospital. UK visitors requiring emergency treatment can, on production of their British passport, receive free hospital treatment (outpatient only) under the medical/social agreement between the UK and Portugal.

Medical Insurance

See Insurance

Emergency Services

See Emergency

## National Holidays

See Public Holidays

## Motoring

Automobile Service and Assistance

The Portuguese Automobile Club (ACP) represents all the motoring organisations which belong to FIA and AIT.

Automobile Club Head Office

Automóvel Club de Portugal (ACP)
Sede 62, Avenida Republica, P-1200 Lisbon. Tel. 01/7 93 61 91

Northern Area

Rua Gonçalo Cristóvão, 2–6, P-4000 Oporto. Tel. 02/31 67 32

ACP has other branches in Aveiro, Braga, Caia, Castelo Branco, Coimbra, Faro, Valença do Minho and Vilar Formoso.

Breakdown service

The ACP's breakdown service can be reached on the following numbers:

North Portugal: tel. 02/8 30 11 27
South Portugal: tel. 01/9 42 50 95

Emergency phones

Motorways have emergency phones on the hard shoulder.

Emergency services

See Emergency

Insurance

See entry

Traffic Regulations

As in the rest of continental Europe, the rule of the road in Portugal is drive on the right, with overtaking on the left. As a general rule, hoot when overtaking. Road signs and markings conform with the international standards.

Priority

Traffic on the main road – which is indicated by a yellow rectangular sign edged with black and white – has priority, but at junctions or intersections of roads of equal importance traffic coming from the right has priority. However, motorised vehicles always have priority over non-motorised traffic.

For cars and motorcycles the speed limits are 60km.p.h/37 m.p.h. in built-up areas, and 90km.p.h/56 m.p.h. on roads outside built-up areas other than motorways where the speed limit is 120km.p.h/74 m.p.h.

Speed Limits

For lorries, coaches and cars with trailers speed limits are lower at 50km.p.h./31 m.p.h in built-up areas, 70km.p.h./43 m.p.h. outside built-up areas, and 80km.p.h./50 m.p.h. on motorways. Infringements can be punished with on the spot fines.

Drivers who have not yet held a licence for a full year may not drive over 90km.p.h./56 m.p.h., and have to carry a sticker to that effect. This can be obtained from the Portuguese Automobile Club (see above).

Seat-belts must be worn outside built-up areas. Children under 12 must travel on the back seat of the car unless the front seat is fitted with a child restraint.

Seat-belts

The legal alcohol limit for drivers is 0.5 grammes per litre.

Alcohol limit

Portugal has quite a good network of filling stations on the main roads. The only time when it can prove difficult to fill up is at night.

Fuel and Filling Stations

Petrol and diesel prices are considerably higher than in other parts of Europe.

Fuel prices

Lead-free petrol (gasolina sem chumbo) is available from most filling stations throughout the country, and there is a map of them which is obtainable from the Portuguese Tourist Office (see Information).

Leadfree Petrol

Portugal has developed a good road network but there are still many little villages in the more remote parts of the country that can only be reached by unadopted roads.

Roads

The motorway system is being extended and currently there are some 300km/186 miles of "auto-estrada". Apart from the motorway between Lisbon and Oporto there are short stretches from Lisbon across the Tagus to Setúbal and towards Cascais. From Oporto a motorway is under construction north to Braga and Matosinhos.

The national highways between the larger towns and cities are well surfaced and provided with stopping places. Emergency lanes and laybys are, however, few and far between. In the thinly populated south of the country a good speed can be maintained on the trunk roads, but in the more mountainous northern regions a maximum speed of only about 40km.p.h./25 miles an hour is possible. The roads have many bends and there are few places for overtaking.

Secondary roads to important tourist points are often being improved but are pleasant alternatives to main roads, even though road markings are sometimes missing. If using side roads to explore the country it is advisable to have a good road map since road signs in the smaller places can be totally inadequate; the Portuguese Automobile Club (see above) publishes a revised map every two years.

In the north of the country and around Lisbon in particular the main roads can get very congested, with travel reduced to a snail's pace in the rush-hours. In the Algarve also there are traffic jams to contend with in the summer.

Traffic congestion

The standard of driving is not particularly high and motorists should beware of drivers overtaking, etc., dangerously.

Warning

## Newspapers and Periodicals

In major Portuguese towns and cities and in holiday areas British and American newspapers and magazines are usually obtainable on the day of publication.

## Opening Times

Shops
Most shops are open Mon.–Fri. from 9am to 1pm, and from 3 to 7pm, and Sat. 9am to 1pm. In the winter months, in particular, many open on Saturday afternoons as well. Tobacconists and food stores are often open until late in the evening, some of them also on Sundays.

Shopping Centres
The large shopping centres of Lisbon are open from 10am until midnight, even at the weekends.

Chemists
Chemists (farmácias) are open Mon.–Fri. 9am to 1pm and 3 to 7pm, Saturdays 9am to 1pm. They display notices showing which chemists are open outside these hours. Lists can also be found in local newspapers.

Banks
Banks are open Mon.–Fri. 8.30–2.45pm. They stay open longer at airports and some tourist centres in the Algarve (see Currency).

Post Offices
Post Offices are generally open Mon.–Fri. 8.30am–12.30pm and 2.30–6pm, although there can be regional variations.

Filling Stations
Filling stations providing a 24-hour service can be found in tourist centres and the larger towns and cities.

Museums
Museums are generally open Tues.–Sun. from 10am to 5pm, though most close for one or two hours at midday.

Restaurants
Restaurants are usually open in the middle of the day from noon, and in the evening from 7pm.

*A Portuguese letter-box . . .*                    *. . . and a telephone box*

## Post

Stamps (selos) are sold in post offices (correios) and in shops displaying the sign "CTT Selos". Post to the United Kingdom normally takes between 3 and 7 days.

Postal Services

Portuguese letterboxes are red.

Letterboxes

See Opening Times

Post Offices

Poste Restante items should be sent to the appropriate post office marked "Posta restante". A passport or other form of personal identification is necessary when collecting mail.

Poste Restante

Telegrams can be handed in at post offices and hotel reception desks or sent by telephone (dial 10).

Telegrams

## Pousadas

Pousadas – the Portuguese means something like "place of rest" – are state-run inns located in castles, palaces, and monasteries as well as modern buildings, and they are predominantly near places of interest or in areas of exceptional scenic beauty. Even the modern buildings are in the local traditional style, with furnishings of a very high standard, often including antiques. Meals in the pousadas are usually very good with an outstanding range of wines available.
 Generally speaking the maximum stay is five days.

General

Pousadas fall into four categories – CH, C1, C and B, with B standing for the simplest, and CH always for pousadas in historic buildings.

Categories

Overnight rates for pousadas are somewhat higher than for other hotels in a comparable category. In the high season, from July to September, a double room with breakfast in the CH category is around £60 to £75, in the C category about £45 to £60 and in the B category £32 to £45. Single rooms cost about 15% less than doubles.

Prices

Since pousadas normally have a very limited number of rooms it is advisable to make a reservation well in advance. This can be done with the pousada direct, through a local travel agent or via the Portuguese national tourism agency, Enatura:

Reservation

  ENATUR (Empresa Nacional de Turismo E.P.)
  Avenida Santa Joana Princesa 10A
  P-1700 Lisboa (Lisbon); tel. 01/8 48 90 78

The following list gives the category of the pousada and the number of rooms; SP = swimming pool; T = tennis courts.

Pousadas on mainland Portugal

1 Pousada de São Teotónio (C1; 15 r.)
  P-4930 Valença do Minho, tel. 0 51/82 40 20

2 Pousada de Dom Dinis (CH; 26 r.)
  P-4920 Vila Nova de Cerveira; tel. 0 51/79 56 02

3 Pousada de São Bartolomeu (B; 16 r.)
  P-5300 Bragança; tel. 0 73/2 24 93

4 Pousada de São Bento (C1; 18 r., SP, T)
  P-4850 Vieira do Minho (Caniçada); tel. 0 53/5 71 90/1

5 Pousada de Santa Catarina (C; 12 r.)
  P-5210 Miranda do Douro; tel. 0 73/4 22 55

6 Pousada de Santa Maria da Oliveira (C1; 13 r.)
  P-4800 Guimarães; tel. 0 53/51 41 57

## Pousadas in Portugal

(Mainland)

© Baedeker

7 Pousada de Santa Marinha da Costa (CH; 55 r.)
  P-4800 Guimarães; tel. 0 53/51 44 53

8 Pousada de Barão de Forrester (B; 11 r., SP, T)
  P-5070 Alijó; tel. 0 59/9 54 67

9 Pousada de São Gonçalo (B; 15 r.)
  P-6400 Amarante (Serra de Marão); tel. 0 55/46 11 13

10 Pousada da Ria (C; 16 r., SP, T)
  P-3870 Murtosa (Torreira); tel. 0 34/4 83 32

11 Pousada da Senhora das Neves (C; 21 r.)
  P-6350 Almeida; tel. 0 71/5 42 83/90

12 Pousada de Santo António (C; 12 r., SP, T)
  P-3750 Agueda (Serém); tel. 0 34/52 12 30

13 Pousada de São Jerónimo (C; 6 r., SP)
  P-3475 Caramulo; tel. 0 32/86 12 91

14 Pousada de Santa Bárbara (C; 16 r., T)
  P-3400 Oliveira do Hospital (Póvoa das Quartas); tel. 0 38/5 22 52

15 Pousada de São Lourenço (C; 21 r.)
  P-6260 Manteigas (Serra da Estrela); tel. 0 75/9 81 50

16 Pousada do Mestre Afonso Domingues (C; 20 r.)
  P-2440 Batalha; tel. 0 44/9 62 60

17 Pousada de São Pedro (C; 15 r.)
  P-2300 Tomar (Castelo do Bode); tel. 0 49/38 11 59

18 Pousada de Santa Maria (C1; 13 r.)
  P-7330 Marvão; tel. 0 45/9 32 01/2

19 Pousada do Castelo (CH; 9 r.)
  P-2510 Obidos; tel. 0 62/95 91 05

20 Pousada de Santa Luzia (C1; 15 r.)
  P-7350 Elvas; tel. 0 68/62 21 94

21 Pousada da Rainha Santa Isabel (CH; 23 r.)
  P-7100 Estremoz; tel. 0 68/2 26 18 94

22 Pousada de Palmela (CH; 27 r., SP)
  P-2950 Palmela; tel. 01/2 35 12 26

23 Pousada de São Filipe (CH; 13 r.)
  P-2900 Setúbal; tel. 0 65/52 38 44

24 Pousada dos Lóios (CH; 32 r., SP)
  P-7000 Évora; tel. 0 66/2 40 51/2

25 Pousada do Vale de Gaio (B; 7 r.)
  P-7580 Alcácer do Sal (Torrão); tel. 0 65/6 61 00

26 Pousada de São Tiago (B; 8 r., SP)
  P-7540 Santiago do Cacém; tel. 0 69/2 24 59

27 Pousada de São Gens (C; 16 r., SP)
  P-7830 Serpa; tel. 0 84/9 03 27

28 Pousada de Santa Clara (B; 6 r., SP)
  P-7665 Santa Clara-a-Velha; tel. 0 83/9 82 50

29 Pousada de São Brás (C; 23 r., SP)
  P-8150 São Brás de Alportel; tel. 0 89/84 23 05/06

30 Pousada do Infante (C1; 21 r., SP, T)
  P-8650 Sagres; tel. 0 82/6 42 22/3

31 Pousada dos Vinháticos (B; 12 r.)
  P-9350 Ribeira Brava; tel. 0 91/95 21 48

32 Pousada do Pico do Arieiro (C; 18 r.)
  P-9000 Funchal; tel. 0 91/23 01 10

## Public Holidays

| | |
|---|---|
| January 1st | New Year's Day |
| February | Shrove Tuesday (often including the week before) |
| March/April | Good Friday |
| April 25th | Liberation Day (anniversary of the Carnation Revolution on April 25th 1974) |
| May 1st | Labour Day |
| May/June | Feast of Corpus Christi |
| June 10th | Camões Day (anniversary of the poet's death on 10th June 1580) |
| August 15th | Feast of the Assumption |
| October 5th | Republic Day (fall of the monarchy on October 5th 1910) |
| November 1st | All Saints Day |
| December 1st | Independence Day (anniversary of the restoration of the independent kingdom of Portugal on December 1st 1640 after expulsion of the Spaniards) |
| December 8th | Feast of the Immaculate Conception |
| December 25th | Christmas Day |

## Radio and Television

Portuguese Radio

In the summer Radiodifusão Portuguesa, the Portuguese radio service, RDF, broadcasts daily bulletins of news and information for visitors (in English at 8.15am, French at 8.30 and German at 8.45) on 1034 and 782 kHz (medium wave) and 94.3 MHz (VHF).

Broadcast messages for visitors

In cases of extreme emergency the Portuguese radio service will transmit messages for visitors to Portugal; details of this service can be obtained from the police and motoring organisations.

Television

Portuguese television transmits many English-language films in the original version with Portuguese sub-titles. Many of the larger hotels also have satellite TV.

## Railways

Portuguese railways are run by a semi-State owned company, Companhia dos Caminhos de Ferro Portugueses, or CP. There are "comboios tranvias", local trains, "comboios regionais", regional trains, "comboios directos", intercity trains, and "comboios rápidos", express trains. Most trains have first and second class, and some of the coaches have old-style interiors. The frequency and punctuality of trains is very much on a par with the rest of Europe, although it has greatly improved recently; many services are very crowded on Friday and Sunday nights.

Apart from around Lisbon and Oporto the rail network is rather sparse (see map of Air Services and Railways on page 336). However, the routes run through some truly wonderful scenery, as on the Douro line for example.

Rail fares in Portugal are relatively low. At smaller stations the ticket office often only opens an hour before the train leaves. For local trains the journey has to be within two hours of having bought the ticket. One-way tickets are only valid for the date of purchase. Tickets can only be bought in advance at the stations in Lisbon and Oporto.

Children under four travel free and children between four and twelve travel half-price.

Tourist tickets, which are non-transferable, are available and permit the holder to travel anywhere in the country for one, two or three weeks. There are also reduced rates for families, groups, senior citizens, etc. Further details can be had from the Portuguese Tourist Office (see Information) or from Portuguese Railways.

See Getting to Portugal

Portuguese Railways occasionally operate historic steam trains on two lines. One runs on the Tâmega line between Livração and Arco de Baúlhe (German 1905 steam locomotive, German and Belgian dining cars, Portuguese passenger coaches, French luggage van), and a 19th c. train (English 1875 steam locomotive, Portuguese and French dining cars, French and Swiss passenger coaches, and a French luggage van) runs on the Minho line between Valença do Minho and Oporto.

## Restaurants

Many restaurants, especially the good-class ones, are closed on Sundays and public holidays. At these establishments it is usually advisable to book in advance. The food in simple local eating places is often as good as in restaurants with a more elaborate decor.

O Pelicano, Rua Nossa Senhora da Conceição 1; tel. 0 41/2 23 17

**Abrantes**

Michael's, opposite the Hotel Montechoro; tel. 0 89/5 59 97 (music, singing and dancing)
O Montinho; tel. 0 89/5 39 59 (French cuisine; terrace)
Rendez-vous, on the Montechoro road; tel. 0 89/5 28 17 (Portuguese and French cuisine)

**Albufeira**

Casa do Zé de Calçada; tel. 0 55/42 20 23 (lovely terrace by the river)
Navarras, Rua António Carneiro; tel. 0 55/42 40 36

**Amarante**

Clipper, Avenida Beira-Mar; tel. 0 82/3 23 27 (aimed solely at the tourist trade, menu limited but good)

**Armação de Pêra**

A Cozinha do Rei, Rua Dr. Manuel das Neves 65; tel. 0 34/2 68 02

**Aveiro**

Turismo, Rua Duques de Bragança; tel. 0 53/81 14 79 (terrace)

**Barcelos**

Conde Dom Henrique, Rua do Forno; tel 0 53/2 34 08
Inácio, Campo das Hortas; tel. 0 53/61 32 25 (plenty of local colour)
Ragú, Avenida João XXI; tel. 0 53/2 37 61

**Braga**

Paraíso da Montanha; tel. 0 82/9 21 50 (specialities: air-dried ham, chicken with piri-piri; excellent view)

**Caldas de Monchique**

Galo d'Ouro, Rua da Corredoura 15; tel. 0 58/92 11 60

**Caminha**

## Restaurants

**Cascais**

Adega do Morgado, Avenida Marechal Carmona 1; tel. 01/2 86 71 98 (unostentatious place; speciality: kid)
Beira Mar, Rua das Flores 6; tel. 01/4 83 01 52 (rustic setting)
Dom Leitão, Avenida Vasco da Gama 36; tel. 01/4 86 54 87
Faroleiro, on Praia do Guincho; tel. 01/2 85 02 25 (popular simple place)
O Batel, Travessa das Flores 4; tel. 01/4 83 02 15 (very well-known restaurant, intimate atmosphere; speciality: fish dishes)
Pimentão, Rua das Flores 16; tel. 01/2 84 09 94 (speciality: shellfish)
Reijos, Rua Frederico Arouca 35; tel. 01/28 03 11

**Coimbra**

Dom Pedro, Av. Emídio Navarro 58; tel. 0 39/2 91 08 (attractive decor, food and service could be better)
Piscinas, Rua Dom Manuel; tel. 0 39/71 70 13

**Elvas**

Alentejo, Rua da Cadeia; tel. 0 68/62 21 13
Dom Quixote, Pedras Negras; tel. 0 68/62 20 14

**Ericeira**

Cesar, on the N 247; tel. 0 61/6 29 26 (speciality: fish dishes)
Poço, Calçada da Baleia 10; tel. 0 61/6 36 69
Toca do Caboz; tel. 0 61/6 22 48

**Espinho**

A Cabana, Rotunda da Praia da Seca; tel. 02/72 19 66 (terrace, also snack-bar)
Aquário, Esplanada Dr. Oliveira Salazar; tel. 02/72 03 77

**Estoril**

A Choupana, in the São João do Estoril district, Estrada Bolina, Rua de Olivença 3; tel. 01/42 68 30 99 (simple place, delicious fish dishes)
Dom Pepe, in the Parede district, Avenida Marginal; tel. 01/2 47 06 36 (beautiful view over Estoril/Cascais bay)
English Bar, Estrada Marginal; tel. 01/4 68 04 13 (international and Portuguese cuisine; rustic English decor)
Marginal; tel 01/4 68 30 99 (international cuisine; dance music)

**Estremoz**

Aguias d'Ouro, Rossio; tel. 0 68/2 21 96

**Évora**

Cozinha de Santo Humberto, Rua da Moeda 39; tel. 0 66/2 42 51 (restaurant in a beautifully converted vaulted cellar; particularly delicious: pork with clams)
Lampião, Rua dos Mercadores 72; tel. 0 66/2 64 95
Tipico Guião, Rua da República 81; tel. 0 66/2 30 71

**Faro**

Cidade Velha, Rua Domingos Guieiro, largo de Sé 19; tel. 0 89/2 71 45 (in an 18th c. building)
Dois Irmãos, Largo do Terreiro do Bispo (opened in 1925; Portuguese cuisine); tel. 89/2 33 37
Kappra, Rua Brites de Almeida 45; tel. 0 89/2 00 33 66
Monte do Casal, in Estoi; tel. 0 89/9 15 03 (pleasant atmosphere, lovely terrace)

**Figueira da Foz**

Santa Catarina, Rua Joaquim Sotto Maior; tel. 0 33/2 21 78
Teimoso, in Buarcos, Estrada do Cabo Mondego; tel. 0 33/2 27 85

**Guarda**

O Telheiro, on the N 16; tel. 0 71/21 13 56

**Guimarães**

Vira Bar, Largo Condessa do Juncal; tel. 0 53/41 41 16

**Lagos**

A Lagosteira, Rua 1 de Maio 20; tel. 0 82/76 24 86
Alpendre, Rua António Barbosa Viana 17; tel. 0 82/76 27 05
Dom Sebastião, Rua 25 de Abril 20; tel. 0 82/76 27 95

**Leiria**

Aquário, Rua Capitão Mouzinho Albuquerque 17; tel. 0 44/2 48 34
O Casarão, on the N 1 (Cruzamanto de Azóia); tel. 0 44/87 10 80

★ Casa da Comida, Travessa das Amoreiras 1; tel. 01/68 53 76 (attractive garden courtyard)

★ Tágide, Largo da Academia das Belas Artes 18; tel. 01/32 07 20 (elegant interior with antique tile pictures)

★ Tavares, Rua da Misericórdia 37; tel. 01/3 42 11 12 (luxurious and prestigious restaurant)

Aviz, Rua Serpa Pinto 12B; tel. 01/3 42 83 91 (international cuisine)

Cervejaria da Trindade, Rua Nova da Trindade 20; tel. 01/3 42 35 06 (in an old cloister, excellent fish dishes)

Clara, Campo dos Mártires da Patria 49; tel. 01/3 53 76 41 (one of Lisbon's top restaurants)

Comida de Santo, Calçada Engenheiro Miguel Pais 39; tel. 01/3 96 33 39 (Brazilian cuisine)

Faz Figura, Rua do Paraíso 15; tel. 01/88 68 98 1 (terrace with a view on the Tagus)

Gambrinus, Rua das Portas de Santo Antão 23; tel. 01/32 14 66 (speciality: seafood)

Lanterna Verde, Rua São João da Praça 45 (in the Alfama); tel. 01/86 99 06 (unappealing decor, but very good typical Portuguese cuisine)

Michel, Largo de Santa Cruz do Castelo 5 (in the Castelo de São Jorge); tel. 01/86 43 38 (French cuisine)

Mister Cook, Avenida Guerra Junqueiro 1; tel. 01/80 72 37 (restaurant and snack-bar, live music in the evenings)

O Polícia, Rua Marquês Sá da Bandeira 112; tel 01/76 35 05 (simple restaurant with good fish specialities)

Rive Gauche, Rua da Rosa 253; tel. 01/36 36 22 (French cuisine)

Sua Excelencia, Rua do Conde 40; tel. 01/60 36 14 (exclusive atmosphere, interesting clientele, high prices, one of Lisbon's most attractive restaurants)

Vicentino, Rua da Voz do Operário 1; tel. 01/86 46 95 (fin de siècle decor, Portuguese country cooking)

Xêlê Bananas, Praça das Flores 29; tel. 01/3 95 25 15 ("tropical" decor; new Portuguese cuisine)

Girassol, Caniço; tel. 0 91/93 22 29

Jardim do Sol, Caniço (on the Funchal road); tel. 0 91/93 21 23

Caravela, Funchal; tel. 0 91/22 84 64

Golfinho, Funchal; tel. 0 91/22 67 74

Romana, Funchal; tel. 0 91/2 89 56

Cachalote, Porto Moniz; tel. 0 91/85 21 80

Calamar, São Vicente; tel. 0 91/84 22 18

Quebra-Mar, São Vicente; tel. 0 91/84 23 38

Arre Burro, Barras; tel. 0 61/9 61 45

Esplanada Marisqueira, Rua Roberto Ivens 638; tel. 02/93 06 60 (speciality: fish and seafood)

Garrafão, in Leça da Palmeira; tel. 02/9 95 16 60 (among the best restaurants in this region)

Beira Mar, Avenida da República 40; tel. 0 62/55 14 58

Maresia, Avenida Manuel Remigio; tel. 0 62/5 12 01

Porto d'Abrigo, Rua Mouzinho de Albuquerque 58; tel. 0 62/5 12 24

Alcaide, Rua Direita; tel. 0 62/95 92 20

Dom João V, on the Caldas da Rainha road; tel. 0 62/9 51 34

★ Portucale, Rua da Alegria 598; tel. 02/ 57 07 17 (panoramic view over Oporto's rooftops)

Chinês, Avenida Vimara Peres 38; tel. 02/2 00 89 15 (Chinese cuisine)

Degrau-Chá, Rua Alfonso Lopes Vieira 180; tel. 02/69 87 64 (art nouveau decor, some incidental music)

Escondidinho, Rua Passos Manuel 144; tel. 02/2 00 10 79

## Restaurants

Foco, Rua Afonso Lopes Vieira 86; tel. 02/66 72 48 (international cuisine)
Girassol, Rua Sá da Bandeira 131; tel. 02/2 73 93 (unostentatious place, regional cuisine)
King Long, Largo Dr. Tito Fontes 115; tel. 02/31 39 88 (Chinese cuisine)
Mal Cozinhado, Rua do Outeirinho 13; tel. 02/38 13 19 (some fado)
Mille Cose, Rua da Cerca 440; tel. 02/68 74 92 (Italian cuisine)
Montenegro, Rua do Campinho 30; tel. 02/2 33 51 (speciality: "bacalhau")
Orfeu, Rua de Júlio Dinis 928; tel. 02/6 06 43 22 (typical local dishes, fish specialities; aimed at the tourist trade)
Ribeiro, Rua Santo Ildefonso 128; tel. 02/2 86 37 (local regional specialities)
Tasca VIP, Rua da Madeira 12; tel. 02/38 14 03 (grilled specialities)
Taverna Bébodos, Cais da Ribeira 24; tel. 02/31 35 65 (small typical place on the edge of the Douro)
Tripeiro, Rua Passos Manuel 195; tel. 02/2 00 58 86 (typical, unostentatious place)

**Portalegre**
Alpendre, Rua 31 de Janeiro 19; tel. 0 45/2 16 11
O Tarro, Avenida do Movimento das Forças Armadas; tel. 0 45/2 43 45

**Portimão**
A Casa de Jantar, Rua de Santa Isabel 14; tel. 0 82/2 20 72 (international cuisine)
A Lanterna, in Parchal; tel. 0 82/2 39 48
Alfredo's, Rua Pé da Cruz 10; tel. 0 82/2 29 54
O Pescador, Rua Dr. José Joaquim Nunes 6
Por-do-Sol, on the Alvor road; tel. 0 82/2 05 05
Sete Mares, Rua Júdice Biker 10

**Póvoa de Varzim**
Casa dos Frangos, on the Viana do Castelo road; tel. 0 52/68 15 22 (seafood and chicken specialities; terrace)
Euracini, Avenida Mouzinho de Albuquerque 29; tel. 0 52/62 71 36 (French cuisine)
Leonardo, Rua Tenente Valadim 75; tel. 0 52/62 23 49
O Marinheiro, on the N 13; tel. 0 52/68 21 51 (specialities: fish and seafood)

**Praia da Rocha**
A Cabaça, Avenida Tomás Cabreira
A Falésia, Avenida Tomás Cabreira; tel. 0 82/2 35 24
O Búzio, on the Praia dos Três Irmãos road; tel. 0 82/2 95 61
Safari, Rua António Feu 8; tel. 0 82/2 35 40 (speciality: seafood and African dishes)
Titanic, Rua Engenheiro Francisco Bivar; tel. 0 82/2 23 71

**Quarteira**
Alphonso's, Centro Comercial Abertura Mar; tel. 0 89/31 46 14
Romeu, Rua Conçalo Velho 40; tel. 0 89/3 39 90 (fish specialities)

**Queluz**
★Cozinha Velha, Largo do Palácio; tel. 01/4 35 02 32 (the restaurant is in what was the palace kitchen)

**Sagres**
Fortaleza do Beliche, on the Cabo de São Vicente road; tel. 0 82/6 41 24

**Santarém**
Portas do Sol, near the park of the same name; tel. 0 43/2 96 20
Solar, Largo Emilio Infante da Câmara 9; tel. 0 43/2 22 39

**Santo Tirso**
São Rosendo, Praça do Municipio 6; tel. 0 52/5 30 54

**Sesimbra**
Angelus, in Santana; tel. 01/2 23 13 40 (speciality: fondues)
O Pirata, Rua Heliodoro Salgado 3; tel. 01/2 23 04 01
Ribamar, Avenida dos Naufragos; tel. 01/2 23 43 17 (big selection of fish and seafood)

**Setúbal**
O Capote, Largo do Carmo 6; tel. 0 65/2 02 98
Roda, Travessa Postigo do Cais; tel. 0 65/2 92 64 (traditional Portuguese cuisine)

O Retiro do Augusto, Rua da Pendoa 11; tel. 01/9 23 01 65 (traditional Portuguese cuisine)
Refúgio do Roca, in Azóia, Colares; tel. 01/9 29 08 98
Solar de São Pedro, Praça D. Fernando II 12; tel. 01/9 23 18 60

**Sintra**

Imperial, Rua José Padinha (the chicken "à la maison" is particularly delicious)
Ponto de Encontro, Praça Dr. António Padinha 39; tel. 0 81/2 37 30 (simple place with easygoing atmosphere; fish specialities)

**Tavira**

Bela Vista, Fonte do Choupo 6; tel. 0 49/31 28 70

**Tomar**

Barrete Preto, Rua Paiva de Andrade 7B; tel. 0 61/2 20 63

**Torres Vedras**

Bistro da Praça; tel. 0 89/39 44 44
O Favo; tel. 0 89/39 46 53 (excellent wines)

**Vale do Lobo**

Lido, on the N 13 in Tuido-Gandra; tel. 0 51/2 26 31

**Valença do Minho**

Alambique, Rua Manuel Espregueira 86; tel. 0 58/2 38 94
Beira Mar, Campo do Castelo; tel. 0 58/2 36 06
Minho, Rua Gago Coutinho 103; tel. 0 58/2 32 61
Oceano, Rua Cândido dos Reis 1; tel. 0 58/2 26 22

**Viana do Castelo**

Regata, Júlio Graca; tel. 0 52/63 17 81

**Vila do Conde**

Espadeiro, Avenida Almeida Lucena; tel. 0 59/32 23 02

**Vila Real**

Copacabana, Avenida Infante Dom Henrique; tel. 0 81/4 15 36
Panorama, Avenida Infante Dom Henrique; tel. 0 81/4 30 51

**Vila Real de Santo António**

O Cortiço, Rua Augusto Hilário 43; tel. 0 32/42 38 53 (small quiet place)
Trave Negra, Rua dos Loureiros 40; tel. 0 32/2 61 38 (imaginative preparation of dishes; intimate atmosphere)

**Viseu**

## Shopping and Souvenirs

In Portugal many folk-art products are still items of everyday use. This is particularly true of pottery and ceramics which vary in form and style according to where they are made, and which range from the blackish ware for everyday use to brightly painted ornaments. The famous multi-hued clay Barcelos cockerel has come to be a symbol for Portugal as a whole.

Ceramics

Azulejos, the glazed, decorative, often blue-coloured tiles, are a form of ceramics dating back to Moorish times. Nowadays, however, the tendency is very much for those on sale to have been mass-produced.

Azulejos

The town of Arraiolos specialises in colourful embroidered woollen carpets. These are for sale and on display in Arraiolos town hall, but can also be bought throughout Alentejo, especially in Évora.

Arraiolos carpets

Beautiful lace is made all along the coast, while inland hand-woven blankets, cloth, etc. are produced. Filigree work in gold and silver wire, sometimes forming part of the traditional costume, is another popular souvenir.
Fine carvings, basket-work and wrought-iron objects are also on offer.

Other handicrafts

Port is undoubtedly a favourite souvenir from Portugal. Although the best known makes are not much cheaper than they are in the UK, the range of different kinds and qualities of port is much greater. A tour of the port-wine lodges in Vila Nova de Gaia (see Wine) usually includes port-tasting.

Port

Fado tapes and records are certainly a good souvenir of Portugal, and Amália Rodrigues has for years undoubtedly been the best-known exponent of this art.

Fado tapes and records

*Ceramic articles are on sale everywhere*

## Spas

Towards the end of the 19th c. Portugal's spas were the most elegant in Europe, with stylish pump-rooms and casinos, and exclusive hotels and restaurants.

It has continued to uphold this tradition and the Portuguese mainland and the Azores together have over 40 spas. In the summer, in particular, more than 150,000 people go to a spa for a one or two-week cure. Most of the spas have, however, become somewhat less grand than they were at the turn of the century.

Selection

A selection of these spas is listed below:

Caldas da Felgueira
Skin, respiratory passages, rheumatism.

Caldas da Rainha
Rheumatism, respiratory passages, gynaecological conditions

Caldas de Chaves
Stomach and intestines, liver, rheumatism, metabolic disorders

Caldas de Manteigas
Rheumatism

Caldas de Monchique
Stomach and intestines, liver, rheumatism, respiratory passages

Caldas de São Jorge
Rheumatism, skin, respiratory passages

Caldas de Vizela
Rheumatism, skin, respiratory passages, gynaecological disorders

Caldas do Gerês
Liver, diabetes

Caldelas
Stomach and intestines, skin

Curia
Kidneys and urinary tract, rheumatism, hypertension

Fonte Santa de Monfortinho
Liver, kidneys and urinary tract, skin

Luso
Kidneys and urinary tract, rheumatism, skin, circulation, hypertension

Melgaço
Diabetes

Monção
Rheumatism, respiratory passages, bronchitis

Pedras Salgadas
Stomach and intestines, liver, diabetes

Piedade
Stomach and intestines, liver, skin

Termas de Monte Real
Stomach and intestines, liver

Termas de São Pedro do Sul
Rheumatism, skin, respiratory passages, gynaecological disorders

Termas de São Vicente
Respiratory passages, rheumatism, hypertension

Vidago
Stomach and intestines, liver, metabolic disorders

Vimeiro
Stomach and intestines, liver, skin

## Sport

Portugal is a land of opportunity for anglers. There is still very good fishing near the coast and inland, in the lakes and river, while deep sea fishing is to be had at Sagres, in the Algarve (including the chance to fish for shark), and off Madeira and the Azores.

Angling, Sea fishing

The best bathing beaches are in and around those places listed in the entry for Beaches. Nearly all the big hotels also have their own swimming pools.

Swimming, Bathing

See entry

Golf

Portugal is ideal both for riding holidays and for those who just want to spend a few hours on horseback. Most riding stables also give tuition. The following list is a selection of riding schools and stables in the Algarve, but there are also opportunities for riding around Lisbon, on the Costa Verde and in Ofir or Viana do Castelo.

Horse riding

**Sport**

Riding Centre
Quinta dos Almarjões, Burgau; tel. 0 82/6 51 52

Telha Riding Centre
Aljezur; tel. 0 82/7 21 74

Casa Pegasus
Carvoeiro; tel. 0 82/5 72 62

Solear Riding School
Porches (on the Pêra road); tel. 0 82/5 24 44

Quinta dos Amigos
Almansil; tel. 0 89/39 56 36

Centro Hipico
Vilamoura; tel. 0 89/6 62 71

Pinetrees Riding Centre
Quinta do Lago; tel. 0 89/39 43 69

Shooting
Portugal has over 20 clubs for clay pigeon or target shooting. Most are in the Algarve (Albufeira, Faro, Portimão, Praia da Falésia, Vale do Lobo and Vilamoura) or on the Costa Verde at Espinho, Ofir, Póvoa de Varzim and Viana do Castelo, as well as Estoril.
The Azores has three shooting clubs.

Sailing
Many places have sailing clubs which hire out boats and offer courses both for beginners and more advanced sailors. Besides Vilamoura in the Algarve, probably the finest marina of them all, with the best facilities for boats and crew, there are lots of smaller harbours and anchorages all along the Portuguese coast. The best places to stay on a Portuguese sailing holiday are in the Algarve, at Albufeira, Armação de Pêra, Alvor, Lagos, Monte Gordo, Portimão, Praia da Falésia, Praia da Oura, Praia da Rocha, Quinta do Lago, Tavira, Vale do Lobo and, of course, Vilamoura, as well as Cascais and Estoril or Sesimbra, plus, on the Costa Verde, Póvoa de Varzim and Viana do Castelo.
There is also good sailing to be had around Madeira and the Azores.

Surfing
There are many places in the Algarve for learning how to surf and hiring surfboards. Surfing is becoming increasingly popular from the beaches on the Estoril coast; Carcavelos is ideal for beginners, while Guincho and Figueira da Foz are is a challenge to the more expert. There is surfing around Madeira as well.

Scuba diving
Scuba divers who take their own equipment with them will find scenic bays and still virtually untouched diving grounds in the south-west of the Algarve around Sagres, the Costa Verde and the Costa de Prata. To hire equipment and have one or two hours tuition the best place to go is the Algarve where there are new scuba diving centres in Albufeira, Alvor, Lagos, Monte Gordo, Praia da Falésia and Vilamoura. The most fascinating diving grounds are between 5 and 30m/16 and 98ft, so snorkellers can also share in the discovery of this wonderful undersea world.

Tennis
There are tennis courts at nearly all Portugal's big hotels, many of them with floodlighting (see the entries for Hotels and Pousadas). There are also public tennis courts as well as the special tennis centres run by professionals, the Roger Taylor Tennis Centre in Vale do Lobo in the Algarve (tel. 0 89/39 47 79) being one of the best. The area around Cascais and Estoril is also particularly well endowed with tennis facilities. On Madeira and the Azores it is possible to play on the hotel courts.

Rambling
The island of Madeira is a veritable rambler's paradise. However, rambling is becoming increasingly popular on the Portuguese mainland as well, and a few tour operators are already offering organised walking holidays in the

Algarve (Serra de Monchique). For solo travellers the Peneda-Gerês National Park is also a particularly attractive terrain.

There are water ski centres where equipment can be hired and tuition is given in the major tourist centres of the Algarve, Cascais, Estoril and Sesimbra, and on the Costa Verde, in Ofir, Vila do Conde and Póvoa de Varzim, as well as Madeira and the Azores.

Water Ski-ing

## Taxis

Taxis in Portugal, which in towns and cities are black with green roofs, tend to be considerably cheaper than in some other parts of Europe. They are fitted with meters and it is wise to check that these are at zero before starting a journey. Outside built-up areas the fare is calculated by the kilometre, and even on one-way journeys the passenger has to pay for the return trip.

Extra is charged for baggage over 30kg/67lb (up to 50%) and for journeys between 10pm and 6am (20%).

It is customary to give a tip of 10 to 15% of the fare.

## Telephone

It is possible to make international calls from public call boxes in Portugal, but these only take coins for 5, 10, 20 or 50 escudos. It is therefore necessary to have a good supply of these coins before making such calls. For longer calls it is more convenient to telephone from a post office or one of the public exchanges found in the major towns and tourist centres. Here it is possible to get enough change or to pay after making the call. There are also long-distance telephones which take phone-cards; the latter can be bought at post offices.

Hotels add large surcharges to the normal phone-call rates.

International calls usually require a certain amount of patience, since all the lines are often busy during the daytime. There is no cheap rate for international calls at night or weekends.

From the United Kingdom to Portugal 00 351
From the USA or Canada to Portugal 011 351

From Portugal to the United Kingdom 00 44
From Portugal to the USA or Canada 06 1

International codes

At the time of writing, Portugal's telephone system is being overhauled, with the changes not yet completed. A recorded message will give the new codes and numbers as they change.

## Time

Portugal is on Central European Time; one hour ahead of GMT (summer, 2 hours ahead of GMT – last Sunday in March to last Sunday in September).

Mainland and Madeira

The Azores is always one hour behind mainland Portugal.

Azores

## Tipping

Service is included in the bill for hotels and restaurants. Tipping is optional, but a tip ("gorjeta") of 5 to 10% of the total bill is always acceptable. An appropriate tip is expected for special services, tour guides, hairdressers,

## Traffic Regulations

**Distances on the Portuguese mainland** between important towns and frontier crossings (in km)

| | | | | | | | | | | | | | | | | | | | | | | | | | | |
|---|---|---|---|---|---|---|---|---|---|---|---|---|---|---|---|---|---|---|---|---|---|---|---|---|---|---|
| **AVEIRO** |
| 380 | **BEJA** |
| 120 | 500 | **BRAGA** |
| 320 | 560 | 230 | **BRAGANÇA** |
| 345 | 180 | 470 | 450 | **CAIA** |
| 216 | 254 | 330 | 310 | 150 | **CASTELO BRANCO** |
| 64 | 333 | 170 | 314 | 300 | 160 | **COIMBRA** |
| 306 | 78 | 425 | 484 | 100 | 175 | 255 | **ÉVORA** |
| 499 | 152 | 620 | 697 | 330 | 390 | 455 | 215 | **FARO** |
| 136 | 256 | 261 | 402 | 206 | 156 | 90 | 178 | 380 | **FÁTIMA** |
| 315 | 207 | 421 | 400 | 93 | 91 | 251 | 130 | 340 | 160 | **GALEGOS** |
| 180 | 360 | 260 | 203 | 255 | 106 | 169 | 282 | 495 | 259 | 199 | **GUARDA** |
| 121 | 265 | 238 | 380 | 231 | 170 | 67 | 190 | 390 | 23 | 183 | 236 | **LEIRIA** |
| 242 | 193 | 361 | 510 | 237 | 250 | 196 | 150 | 300 | 136 | 253 | 365 | 128 | **LISBOA** |
| 310 | 181 | 410 | 390 | 68 | 80 | 240 | 104 | 317 | 150 | 24 | 188 | 170 | 228 | **PORTALEGRE** |
| 68 | 450 | 53 | 255 | 415 | 277 | 118 | 270 | 575 | 208 | 366 | 220 | 185 | 314 | 360 | **PORTO** |
| 355 | 600 | 260 | 30 | 487 | 339 | 343 | 510 | 727 | 433 | 430 | 233 | 410 | 539 | 419 | 284 | **QUINTANILHA** |
| 185 | 195 | 310 | 450 | 204 | 169 | 138 | 118 | 300 | 61 | 160 | 281 | 70 | 79 | 145 | 254 | 479 | **SANTARÉM** |
| 285 | 315 | 388 | 370 | 207 | 59 | 218 | 234 | 450 | 215 | 150 | 165 | 226 | 304 | 136 | 335 | 396 | 225 | **SEGURA** |
| 290 | 139 | 417 | 560 | 190 | 270 | 246 | 108 | 250 | 240 | 218 | 372 | 180 | 50 | 192 | 362 | 590 | 121 | 324 | **SETÚBAL** |
| 194 | 580 | 91 | 323 | 538 | 407 | 250 | 502 | 702 | 338 | 497 | 348 | 314 | 443 | 484 | 123 | 350 | 384 | 467 | 492 | **VALENÇA DO MINHO** |
| 140 | 524 | 49 | 280 | 480 | 355 | 194 | 448 | 648 | 283 | 444 | 295 | 261 | 390 | 434 | 71 | 310 | 331 | 409 | 440 | 53 | **VIANA DO CASTELO** |
| 185 | 512 | 107 | 138 | 413 | 264 | 207 | 440 | 661 | 300 | 355 | 160 | 271 | 403 | 344 | 117 | 168 | 340 | 320 | 450 | 198 | 155 | **VILA REAL** |
| 506 | 125 | 625 | 685 | 306 | 378 | 451 | 203 | 52 | 381 | 330 | 485 | 387 | 317 | 306 | 580 | 714 | 318 | 436 | 267 | 707 | 650 | 640 | **V. REAL DE SANTO ANTÓNIO** |
| 440 | 65 | 563 | 600 | 237 | 292 | 394 | 140 | 202 | 318 | 245 | 399 | 326 | 254 | 220 | 512 | 680 | 256 | 350 | 203 | 640 | 587 | 580 | 153 | **VILA VERDE DE FICALHO** |
| 230 | 410 | 312 | 207 | 307 | 156 | 216 | 333 | 547 | 304 | 247 | 49 | 285 | 414 | 236 | 266 | 228 | 323 | 214 | 421 | 397 | 344 | 207 | 533 | 447 | **VILAR FORMOSO** |
| 95 | 450 | 187 | 238 | 340 | 190 | 96 | 370 | 580 | 187 | 283 | 85 | 164 | 293 | 270 | 131 | 267 | 233 | 250 | 343 | 263 | 210 | 111 | 570 | 483 | 135 | **VISEU** |

room maids, porters and taxi drivers, etc.; attendants at tourist sites and ushers at the theatre, cinema, bullfights, etc. also expect a tip.

## Traffic Regulations

See Motoring

## Transport

Urban Public Transport
There are bus services in the towns and cities. Lisbon and Oporto also have trams, and these provide an unusual but excellent way of exploring the Portuguese big cities. Lisbon has an Underground as well, the Metro, which runs from Sete Ríos to the Rossio and on north-east to the Alvalade. Another special feature of the Portuguese capital is the "elevadores", the lift-cum-funicular that carries people from one to the other of Lisbon's widely differing levels.

Coaches
The fact that rail services are rather limited means that coaches provide the main form of public transport. The intercity coaches, the "expressos", cover long distances in a relatively short time.

Shipping
Regular boat trips operate from the tourist centres along the Algarve.
Oporto has a "three-bridge" boat trip on the Douro and a tour along the port-wine route. Regular ferries ply from several landing stages in Lisbon to and from the south bank of the Tagus.